T0304135

Producer Cooperatives as a New Mode of Production

The notion that there is no alternative to capitalism emerged after the fall of the Berlin Wall and made rapid headway due to increasing economic globalisation. More recently, this belief that there is no viable alternative has held firm despite the financial crisis, high unemployment levels and an ever-increasing gap between rich and poor.

However, since the appearance of Benjamin Ward's seminal 1958 article, economic theorists have been developing a workable alternative: a system of self-managed firms. The core argument outlined in this book is that a well-organised system of producer cooperatives would give rise to a new mode of production and, ultimately, a genuinely socialist society.

This argument is developed through three key steps. First, following on from Jaroslav Vanek's definition, it is argued that a 'Labour-Managed Firm', a firm which strictly segregates capital incomes from labour incomes, would implement a new production mode because it would reverse the pre-existing relation between capital and labour. Second, given that a system of these 'Labour-Managed Firm' cooperatives would reverse the capital–labour relationship, it is suggested that this would constitute a form of market socialism. Third, it is argued that compared to capitalism a system of producer cooperatives offers a wealth of advantages, including the potential for efficiency gains, the eradication of unemployment and the end of exploitation. Ultimately, this book concludes that self-management could take the place of central planning in Marxist visions for the future.

Bruno Jossa is Full Professor of Political Economy at the 'Federico II' University, Naples, Italy.

Routledge frontiers of political economy

Producer Cooperatives as a New Mode of Production

Bruno Jossa

Routledge
Taylor & Francis Group

LONDON AND NEW YORK

First published 2014
by Routledge
2 Park Square, Milton Park, Abingdon, Oxon OX14 4RN

and by Routledge
711 Third Avenue, New York, NY 10017

Routledge is an imprint of the Taylor & Francis Group, an informa business

British Library Cataloguing in Publication Data
A catalogue record for this book is available from the British Library

Library of Congress Cataloging in Publication Data
Jossa, Bruno.
  Producer cooperatives as a new mode of production/Bruno Jossa.
  pages cm
  Includes bibliographical references and index.
  1. Producer cooperatives. I. Title.
  HD3121.J674 2014
  334'.6–dc23

                                                          2013031718

ISBN: 978-0-415-71988-9 (hbk)
ISBN: 978-1-315-86725-0 (ebk)

Typeset in Times New Roman
by Wearset Ltd, Boldon, Tyne and Wear

Contents

Introduction

1. The prospect of a feasible alternative to our present world that the Soviet Union had been holding out for nearly a century (the period of time that Hobsbawm described as 'the short twentieth century') has definitively collapsed. In the aftermath of the fall of the Berlin Wall, this idea made rapid headway and sparked off the idea of an unprecedented heyday of capitalism, despite the fact that capitalistic societies were actually bringing forth their worst: skyrocketing unemployment levels, iniquitous wealth and income distribution patterns and the creeping abandonment of all such values as ennoble man. The 'end of history' envisaged by Fukuyama in his 1992 book is 'the ultimate victory [of capitalism] as the only viable economic system' (1992: 110).

In point of fact, the permanency of the Fukuyama's idea has been called into question by numerous dissenting voices. The economist Frank Hahn (1993), for instance, contends that while we are unable to anticipate events that may slow down the present-day global triumph of capitalism, there are reasons to believe that this stage in history will be relatively short-lived and that capitalism might be nearing its end. The expert on cooperative firms Henry B. Hansmann (1996: 5) has argued:

> There is considerable enthusiasm today for promoting forms of ownership other than the conventional investor-owned corporation. Much of this interest centers on labor-managed enterprise and reflects an unusual convergence of economic thought from opposite ends of the political spectrum. On the left, recent years have brought the final collapse of state socialism as a persuasive economic ideal throughout the world. In the resulting ideological void, 'workplace democracy' has emerged as the principal institutional reform that commands widespread support among critics of capitalism.... Reformers on the right, in turn, have become increasingly discouraged with the efficiency of traditional forms of labor-management relations. As an alternative, many have turned to employee ownership, hoping that it will improve productivity and increase worker identification with the interests of capital.[1]

And in his review of an important book by Bowles and Gintis, Charles Efferson (2012: 253) suggests that the time for the actual establishment of a labour-managed system may be nearing, because 'the last two or three decades have brought a considerable body of research showing that people often exhibit strong forms of altruism, like cooperating in anonymous one-shot interactions with genetically unrelated individuals'.

The alternative solution to capitalism suggested in this book is, indeed, economic democracy, a system where corporate decisions are made in line with the democratic 'one head, one vote' principle in place of the 'one share, one vote' criterion adopted in business corporations. In this connection, Bourdet (1978a: 45) has argued that equality is both a fundamental human right and a potential springboard for a political movement demanding self-management.

Ideologically speaking, there is little doubt that economic democracy and political democracy are two facets of the same founding principle. According to Robert Dahl (1989: 331),

> if democracy is justified in governing the state, then it must also be justified in governing economic enterprises; and to say that it is not justified in governing economic enterprises is to imply that it is not justified in governing the state.[2]

Let us repeat that self-managed firms – specifically, producer cooperatives – can be categorised as fully democratic businesses, since they are managed in line with the 'one head, one vote' principle – i.e. a principle that makes workers free and is also expected to add to firm efficiency.[3]

When early cooperatives began to thrive and increase in number, several major economists, including J.S. Mill and Alfred Marshall, predicted that sooner or later they would supplant capitalistic firms altogether.

As soon as workers join to form a cooperative and become 'their own masters', Mill wrote, labour productivity tends to increase under the powerful stimulus given to productive energies by the inducement of the members of a cooperative to boost their incomes by working harder. And this material benefit, he added, 'is as nothing compared with the moral revolution in society that would accompany it', thanks to the fact that cooperation leads to

> the transformation of human life, from a conflict of classes struggling for opposite interests, to a friendly rivalry in the pursuit of a good common to all; the elevation of the dignity of labour; a new sense of security and independence in the labouring class; and the conversion of each human being's daily occupation into a school of the social sympathies and the practical intelligence.
>
> (Mill 1871: 716)

The most admired orthodox economist, Alfred Marshall, praised cooperation as a movement with 'a special charm for those in whose tempers the social element is stronger' (Marshall 1890: 292). The cooperative movement, he wrote, tends 'to develop the spontaneous energies of the individual while training him to collective action by the aid of collective resources, and for the attainment of collective ends' (Marshall 1889: 227). Significantly enough, 'the production of fine human beings' topped the list of the primary goals he assigned to this movement (Marshall 1889: 228).

In Marshall's view, an additional basic advantage of cooperation is its ability to make efficient use of a resource, capacity for work, which in capitalism is awfully wasted. Cooperation, he argued, makes workers feel as though they are their own masters within the factory, adds to their sense of responsibility and encourages them to become actively involved in their jobs and engage in production to the best of their abilities. The worker of a cooperative produces not for the benefit of another, but for his own benefit, and this mobilises huge potential for accurate and high-quality work that capitalism tends to stifle. 'In the world's history' – he wrote (1889: 229) – 'there has been one waste product, so much more important than all others that it has a right to be called THE Waste Product. It is the higher abilities of many of the working classes'.

In my estimation, the basic advantage of a democratic firm system is probably the above-mentioned substitution of the 'one head, one vote' principle for the 'one share, one vote' principle. The associated benefits are mainly reaped by the members of the firm, since sovereignty generates satisfaction and those exercising it feel free and released from the duty to obey other people's commands. First and foremost, however, the 'one head, one vote' principle offers the advantage of stripping power from capital and, consequently, affording great strides towards the full attainment of democracy. It is especially for this reason that a system of producer cooperatives is held to implement socialism.[4] Its primary advantage – let this be repeated – is to prevent large capitalists from imposing their wishes and interests on society (though large industrial concerns will obviously continue to exert a considerable influence on policy-making, even in a democratic firm system).[5]

In fact, the system that self-management theorists have been working out as a viable alternative to capitalism over the past fifty years would not only give rise to a genuine socialist order, but might be established without great difficulty by a parliamentary majority deciding to set to work with goodwill.

Let us clarify that the system suggested in this book is in no way associated with the short-lived 'workers' councils republic' that rose to power in Bavaria in 1919 and whose record of experience was the object of eager debate during the years of the Weimar Republic (on this subject, see, for instance, Villari 1978; Bolaffi 2002: ch. II). As we are convinced advocates of parliamentary democracy, it is a far reach to think of workers' councils as substitutes for parliamentary democracy. My main aim in this book – let this be spelt out again – is to endorse the transfer of corporate powers from capitalists to workers.

In Branco, we read (2012: 23):

> In mainstream economics there is only one best solution for each economic problem and thus the purpose of policy consists in finding out that solution and not in confronting collective preferences, in other words in engaging in political debate. In the realm of politics transformed into economics,

pluralism is, therefore, crowded out.... The conflict between economics and democracy does not result, therefore, from any moral weakness of economic actors but from an intrinsic incompatibility between the logic of economics and that of democracy; between the institutions of economics, such as the market, and the institutions of democracy.

In point of fact (as I will argue in greater detail further on), this widely shared opinion is far from convincing, because the antithetical terms are not democracy and markets, but democracy and capitalism. Notwithstanding the survival of markets, an employee-managed system can be categorised as fully democratic, thanks to its consistent adoption of the 'one head, one vote' principle.[6]

2. In the minds of orthodox Marxists, the most glaring contradiction of capitalism is the antithesis between socialised production and private appropriation – i.e. the contrast between the fact that hundreds and even thousands of jobholders work together in large-size industrial concerns and the fact that the means of production that they use are privately owned. And as capitalistic firms grow over time and increase their headcounts – they argue – the socialised nature of work becomes more and more pronounced, while appropriation invariably remains private.

From the perspective of other theorists, the crucial contradiction in our present world is the capital–labour conflict.

These differences of opinion have a major bearing on the way we define the essence of socialism. Economic theorists have identified three factors of production – capital, labour and land – but as a result of the lesser role of farming at a mature capitalistic stage, it is with capital and labour that they mainly concern themselves. Hence, it is possible to argue that capitalism arises when owners of capital (or their representatives) hire labour power, pay workers a fixed income (wages), make decisions within the enterprise in line with the 'one share, one vote' principle and appropriate the relevant profits. Conversely, if workers (or their representatives) borrow capital, pay capitalists a fixed income (interest), make every decision in line with the 'one head, one vote' principle and appropriate the residual, the firms that arise are run by workers and the resulting system is socialism. As I will clarify further on, this conclusion suggests that 'the antithesis between the institutions of a bourgeois democracy and those of a workers' democracy parallel the contrast between a bourgeois society split into classes and a socialist classless society' (Libertini and Panzieri 1958: 71).[7]

In the 1918 paper 'Our Program and the Political Situation', Rosa Luxemburg (1967: 615) wrote that 'today matters have reached a point at which mankind is faced with the dilemma: either collapse into anarchy, or safety through socialism' – a comment identical with Cortesi's remark that 'today, and even more so after the failure of the Soviet experience, the option is between socialism or annihilation' (Cortesi 2010: 287).

Accordingly, the ultimate aim of his book is defining the contours of a form of socialism that is feasible today and sketching a possible road to its practical implementation. My starting point is the idea that both Marx and Lenin thought of worker management as a new mode of production.

Several authors maintain that workers are not particularly keen on running firms themselves (see, for instance, Knight 1921; Devine 1988: 158ff.; Meade 1972; Kihlstrom and Laffont 1979; Albert and Hahnel 1991: 15ff.; Drèze 1989; and Campbell 2011: 329). All the same, it strikes us as surprising that the self-management proposal has never been extensively discussed in public or submitted to popular vote in a referendum. As argued by many, those workers who declare themselves prepared to take an active part in the management of their firms do not receive sufficient support from politicians or from those whom they consider to be their representatives.[8]

3. So far, our line of reasoning backs up the idea of two alternative forms of socialism – an idea that Durkheim forcefully endorsed when he distinguished between workers' socialism and state-socialism (see Durkheim 1928: 26).[9]

Lenin was one of the first theorists to draw a clear-cut distinction between socialism and communism and to contend that communism was to be built out of non-communistic bricks. Concerning the control issue, in *The Impending Catastrophe and How to Combat It* (Lenin 1917e) he claimed that control measures were far easier to put in place than was usually assumed and, specifically, that there was a 'very easy and quite practical method and way of control' that could be implemented by 'uniting the population according to profession, purpose of work, branch of labour, etc.' (1917f: 802). 'Bureaucracy must be abandoned for democracy', he wrote,

> the initiative of the workers and of other employees must be drawn on; they must be immediately summoned to conferences and congresses; a certain proportion of the profits must be assigned to them, provided they institute overall control and increase production.

In addition to this, he recommended suppressing commercial secrecy (1917f: 810–811).

Sometime before, these ideas had induced Lenin to describe socialism in Russia as a tiny island surrounded by an ocean of state capitalism. However, due to Bucharin's objection to his 'improper use of the word capitalism' (see Cohen 1973: 140), he further expatiated on his view of socialism in an article ('On Cooperation') where he argued that the 'immense' and 'quite exceptional' importance acquired by the cooperative movement in the post-revolutionary period necessitated the conclusion that cooperation 'nearly always coincides fully with socialism'. This idea of Lenin's will be forcefully endorsed in this book.

There is general agreement (see, *inter alia*, Miller 1989: 109) that a system of producer cooperatives is a 'pure market socialism model'. Ever since the appearance of the pioneer contributions of Benjamin Ward (1958), Jaroslav Vanek (1970) and James Meade (1972, 1979), this model has been studied in-depth by economic theorists, who have fleshed out its basic characteristics (see Bonin and Putterman 1987: 4).[10] As argued by Richard H. Tawney (1918: 103), managing firms in line with democratic principles is important, both because the right of individuals to join with others in forming autonomous firms is a prerequisite for the attainment of full freedom and because economic freedom can only be achieved if industry is governed by representative bodies.[11] In my estimation, the core idea behind self-management is neither outdated (as argued in Hart and Moore 1996) nor unrealistic (see Nuti 1992: 145).[12] It is a crucial issue of class struggle[13] and 'the primary goal of Marxism' (Garaudy n.d.: 187) and is therefore as topical as ever.[14] The awareness that democratic firm management is a pressing need in today's society is in synch with the recent call of Stefano Rodotà, a candidate in the latest presidential election in Italy, for expanding the range of human rights. Today, Rodotà writes, the revolutionary fight for the assertion of the principle of equality – the unfulfilled promise handed down to us by the 'short century' – acquires the connotations of a revolutionary fight for the assertion of dignity. In combination, these two revolutionary demands have resulted in a new anthropological approach centring on self-determination, the need to build individual and collective identities and the urgency of fleshing out different notions of social relationships and public responsibilities (Rodotà 2012: 14).

It is widely held that ownership of the instruments of production by the workers who use them brings with it the dangers of group individualism. The Webbs, for instance, saw a conflict of interest between the workers of a producer cooperative and the community at large (Webb and Webb 1921: 462ff.). However, this can neither justify the criticism that this idea is objectionable or outdated, nor, for that matter, the claim that it has nothing to do with Marxism.

Accordingly, discussing the practical implementation of socialism, I will spell out the need to create a system of self-managed firms and have them freely operate in markets within a state-controlled economy.[15]

The main contribution to the literature on producer cooperatives is the insight that a system of self-managed firms gives rise to a new mode of production (see Jossa 1978; Nove 1986; Schweickart 2002, 2011; Jossa 2010a, 2010b) and that the revolution sparked off by the transition from a system of capitalistic firms to a system of cooperatives would be fully consistent with Marx's theoretical approach.

My claim that democratic firm management is tantamount to socialism and fully consistent with Marxism is supported by my belief that Marx and Marxists rated work as the true foundation of all human actions, both theoretical and practical.[16]

In my estimation, an attentive analysis of the *Economic and Philosophical Manuscripts* of 1855 suggests a non-statist interpretation both of Marx's approach and, primarily, of Marxism. Unfortunately, the integral text of this important work was published in its original German version no earlier than 1932, which means it was unknown to those Marxist classics (Kautsky, Plekhanov, Lassalle, Gramsci and Lenin), who are responsible for establishing the canon for a statist interpretation of Marx's socialism. In this connection, it was argued that their fragmentary knowledge of Marx's actual thought would have misled even the greatest of all geniuses (Schaff 1965: 11). As is well known, the picture of Marx that emerges from the *Manuscripts of '44* is that of a humanist (see Bloch 1838–1947, 1968; Bigo 1953; the contributors to Fromm's 1965 anthology; and Orfei 1970; as well as Althusser for a dissenting view), and there can be little doubt that a socialist system founded on democratic firm management has much more in common with humanism than with a statist system.[17]

As a result, an additional aim of this book is to disprove Althusser's claim (see Althusser 1965: 8) that the spontaneous ideology of the workers' movement, which, left to itself, could only produce utopian socialism, trade unionism, anarchism and anarcho-syndicalism, is strongly antithetical to a centrally planned economic system such as Marxist socialism, because the latter,

> presupposing as it does the massive theoretical labour of the establishment and development of a science and philosophy without precedent, could only be the work of men with a thorough historical, scientific and philosophical formation, intellectuals of very high quality.

As I will argue in greater detail further on, late in life even Lenin reached the conclusion that a democratic firm system, though certainly linked to anarcho-syndicalism, could well be reconciled with Marx's view of the historical process.[18]

In my estimation, a socialist revolution would bring the French Revolution to its logical conclusion. Hence, I reject Chevalier's view of a socialist revolution as even more radical and dangerous than its French antecedent, a movement that, due to an onslaught of principles such as private ownership and loyalty to one's home country, would ultimately jeopardise tradition and sweep away the existing social order (see Chevalier 1949: 373). In contrast, I champion the idea that its ultimate effect would be to pave the way for the Fourth Estate to secure the same full rights that the Third Estate conquered for itself during the French Revolution.[19]

4. Preliminarily, it is worth clarifying that the producer cooperative theorised in the recent economic literature is a firm that is run by workers, but whose hierarchical structure is headed by elected managers (who may be chosen from among non-members and, once appointed, may opt for membership).[20] Although decision-making powers are ultimately vested in the workers, this right is not exercised on a day-to-day basis, since responding to a changing business environment requires prompt decisions made by single individuals. Indeed, the prerequisite for the efficient operation of a firm is not the good will and dedication of amateurs, but the expertise of professional managers who are well-trained in business organisation issues, market research techniques and the sophisticated accounting strategies typically adopted by large-size firms (see Bauer 1963: 39).[21]

Apparently unlimited, in practice the decision powers of the members cover a small number of areas, which, though important, do not interfere with the actual operation of the firm's business (e.g. passing resolutions to appoint managers, authorise major investments or, eventually, admit new members). In apportioning functions between themselves and their managers, the partners of a cooperative should act in accordance with the principle that 'the people in whom the supreme power resides ought to do of themselves whatever conveniently they can; and what they cannot well do, they must commit to the management of ministers' (see Montesquieu 1748, vol. II: ch. 1).

This is consistent with the main aims of democratic firm governance: vesting in workers the task of making decisions on particularly weighty options, apportioning the firm's surplus among them and – most importantly – devising democratic management modes that may induce an efficient state mechanism to deprive capital of all power.

With reference to the ability of a democratic system to reverse the capitalistic capital–labour relationship (a point that will be analysed in-depth below), let us emphasise that while in capitalistic systems it is capital owners that pay workers a fixed income, in a system of democratic firms it is capitalists that earn fixed incomes – i.e. interest on capital.

An additional major point is that the minor role of meetings of workers in running the firm's core business does not prevent them from performing major political functions: electing delegates to parliamentary assemblies or defining the overall guidelines for a centralised plan.

Economic theorists are agreed that self-managed firms should be free to carry on business in the market in line with private utility calculations. In Ward's seminal 1958 article, they are said to work towards maximising average worker income through the adoption of distribution rules ensuring that the revenue available for distribution to workers will increase in proportion to rises in the firm's aggregate revenue. Such revenue amounts to the balance between the firm's income from the sale of its products and its outlays, mainly the cost of raw materials and semi-finished articles and the interest and taxes respectively payable to providers of funds and the state. The incomes earned by the workers cannot be categorised as wages or salaries, since they are not associated with an employment contract current with third parties. Unlike wages or salaries, they fluctuate over time in accordance with the firm's income profile: indeed, with reference to the ability of a democratic system to reverse the capitalistic capital–labour relationship (a point that will be analysed in-depth below), let us emphasise that while in capitalistic systems it is capital owners that pay workers a fixed income, in a system of democratic firms it is capitalists that earn fixed incomes – i.e. interest on capital.

In Sertel (1982) and the greater part of the later literature, self-managed firms are said to work towards maximising the workers' well-being by boosting their incomes, reducing the strain entailed in production activities and making their work more agreeable.

An additional preliminary point to be made is that the pay rates of member-workers are linked to their respective job descriptions, in terms that each hierarchical level is assigned a coefficient reflecting the percentage of the firm's income to which the workers concerned are entitled as long as they stay with the cooperative and which they forfeit upon leaving it. While it is true that these coefficients should ideally be devised at the centre, they may also be fixed at firm level provided they are laid down before the firm is started up. It is assumed – let this be repeated – that the income assigned to each member is commensurate with the revenue earned by the cooperative.[22]

As mentioned above, the market-based operation of producer cooperatives does not, in itself, rule out large-scale state intervention in the economy, but this is just an option, not a distinctive characteristic of a system of democratic firms.

5.   To understand my line of reasoning, it is convenient to start from Vanek's distinction between two types of self-managed firms (see Vanek 1971a, 1971b).

One type is the so-called WMF (worker-managed firm), which self-finances its investments and is not allowed to use loan capital. In this type of firm, senior and younger workers are paid the same incomes irrespective of the circumstance that while the former may have helped finance corporate investments by accepting income reductions in previous years, the latter are likely to have contributed little or nothing to the firm's self-financing. As partners leaving the firm are not entitled to any portion of the firm's past self-financings, it is clear that the savings used to finance the WMF's investments belong to the firm and not to the partners. This is why both the real and financial assets of WMFs are said to be 'assets not owned' by the members.[23]

Our emphasis on the preliminary notion that the WMF's investment resources belong to the firm goes to disprove the widespread misconception that the WMF is owned by the workers and that its assets are ultimately the property of its partners. However, as the question of ownership titles is both complex and hazy, for the purpose of our investigation the essential point is not so much the issue of the ownership of the firm, as the rights that the partners of the firm have and the rights that they lack. In the literature, there is general agreement that the individual partners of a WMF are in no case entitled to require the reimbursement of the firm's investment resources.

The second type of self-managed firm, the LMF (labour-managed firm), uses loan capital. In it, income from capital is distinct from income from labour, since the firm pays its partners both labour incomes and interest on the amounts it has borrowed from them. In this case, the partners financing the firm hold credit instruments negotiable on financial markets and those who prefer to save remain the owners of the resources they have accumulated.

On occasion, Vanek has described this type of firm as a cooperative financed from outside; and the distinction between self-financing firms and firms financed from outside has become customary in the relevant literature. On closer analysis, however, this distinction is not correctly drawn: in fact, LMFs are fully entitled to ask the partners to finance them and the 'ban on self-financing' only entails that, prior to earmarking corporate (i.e. internal) funds for investment financing, the firm is obliged to issue instruments of credit (backed by those funds) in favour of the individual partners. Consequently, a correct way of setting the WMF against the LMF is to say that whereas in WMFs capital incomes are in no way separated from labour incomes, in LMFs the partners receive an income from paid employment and those (whether partners or not) who have financed the firm receive the customary interest on the amounts they have made available to the firm.

As happens in WMFs, workers leaving an LMF are not entitled to any portion of the value of the firm's assets, but those who have financed the firm with their savings will continue to receive interest on the amounts contributed, even after they have left the firm.

As I shall show further on, the LMF should be prioritised over the WMF, because the claim that in a system of cooperative firms it is labour that hires capital (and not vice versa) – a central idea I will be developing throughout this book – is only applicable to cases in which labour incomes are strictly separated from capital incomes.

6.   The potential of a cooperative system for implementing a new mode of production is confirmed by the success story of the Mondragon Group. The gas stove manufacturing establishment that was to become the first firm of the 'Mondragon Group of Cooperatives' was set up in the Basque Country in Spain in 1956. Ever since, the group has grown into a colossus joining over 260 cooperatives with an aggregate headcount of more than 100,000 workers (99 per cent of whom are working members). Today, it is the leading conditioning equipment producer in Spain, the third largest Spanish industrial group in terms of headcount, the seventh largest Spanish group in terms of turnover and the ninth largest concern in the world in terms of sales. Its member firms were formally joined into the Mondragon Cooperative Corporation (MCC) in 1991, fifteen years after the death of the group's original founder, Don Josè Maria Arizmendiarrieta. Most of the group cooperatives operate in industry, particularly the electric household appliances, machine tools and automotive sections. Despite the recent downsizing of Eroski, the group distribution business, the overall dimensions of the group have been steadily on the increase. Numerous analyses of the organisational aspects and record of experience of the Mondragon Group have emphasised the high efficiency levels of its member businesses (see Thomas and Logan 1982; Bradley and Gelb 1983; Foote 1991; Kasmir 1996; MacLeod 1997; Cheney 1999).

Each Mondragon Group cooperative vests in its workers the power to vote at meetings and, hence, full managing powers. All the members are holders of the same number of interests and exercise their decision-making powers in accordance with a complex system combining processes specific to direct and representative democracy.

The keystone of the Mondragon system is the group bank (Caja Laboral Popular), which was set up in 1959 with the mission of boosting employment by supporting the establishment of new cooperatives. The aggregate headcount of the Caja's approximately 350 branches exceeds 150,000 persons.

Workers wishing to join a Mondragon cooperative are required to make a contribution in an amount commensurate with the approximate yearly income of a worker in the lowest pay-rate bracket, but the initial payment is just five per cent of the total and the remainder may be paid in under a multi-year investment plan, which is often funded through a financial agreement entered into with the Caja Laboral. New entrants are entitled to become members within a certain timeframe and the aggregate number of non-members at any time may not exceed 5 per cent of the total headcount.

A major problem faced by Mondragon right from the onset was the need to neutralise the strong resistance that is customarily put up against the birth of any non-capitalistic large-size business enterprise. Significantly enough, the birth of a strong system of cooperative firms is not only opposed by extreme liberalists and, generally, people at ease within the present social order, but even by trade unionists fearing that their power position would be greatly eroded by the proliferation of producer cooperatives to the detriment of capitalistic firms. This is why the Mondragon movement has traditionally distanced itself from trade union organisations (see Kasmir 1996: 23).

Although the cooperative firm model endorsed in this book departs in some respects from a typical Mondragon cooperative, the success of this group is a clear sign that a system of cooperative firms may lead to the establishment of a new mode of production.

7. Chapter 1 expatiates on the opinions of Marx and Engels concerning producer cooperatives. It remembers how: (1) Marx, on several occasions, praised cooperation as a movement whose generalised growth would give rise to a new mode of production; and (2) Lenin, in a 1923 article entirely concerned with this subject, described cooperation as a major organisational step in the transition to socialism and went so far as to equate it with socialism at large. 'Cooperation is socialism', he declared.

Considering Marx's and Engels's views and Oskar Lange's description of self-management as the springboard for pressing the working class into positive action, the book provides evidence that democratic worker management of firms amounts to socialism – and the only form of socialism possible today.

One of the founding ideas behind this book is that Marxism is not incompatible with orthodox political economy and that the prerequisite for an exacting analysis of a new mode of production is a simultaneous focus on mainstream economics and Marxist theory. This is the main subject of Chapter 2, which is followed up by an analysis of various points of orthodox economic theory conducted with the dual aim of highlighting major advantages of a system of producer cooperatives and fleshing out the characteristics of a producer cooperative not affected by the main faults of those in existence in the Western world. In my estimation, most of the shortcomings of existing cooperatives discussed in the literature would effectively be remedied if cooperatives were organised in accordance with the principles laid down by mainstream economists.

A full analysis of these shortcomings lies outside the scope of this book. Consequently, in Chapters 3, 4 and 5, I will only enter into discussion of financing difficulties, the tendency to under-invest and employee shirking – the main defects analysed in the literature over these past fifty years.

Based on the reflections developed in the opening chapters, in Chapter 6, I will be discussing a number of organisational details, which are assumed to help producer cooperatives fight off competition from capitalistic companies.

Chapters 7 to 9 highlight positive points of cooperative firms. With reference to unemployment and alienation – two major themes that are analysed in-depth – let us mention that Chapter 8 and Chapter 9 include my conclusion that unemployment and alienation would be greatly reduced in a system of self-managed firms. Additional advantages are discussed in Chapter 10. As cooperation is of benefit to the community at large, cooperatives are often described as 'public goods'.

Considering Marx's and Engels's views and Oskar Lange's description of self-management as the springboard for pressing the working class into positive action (see Lange 1957: 157), the book will both try to establish if the pro-cooperation movement may become the guiding principle and new pole star for a genuine leftist movement[24] and, at the same time, provide evidence in support of my main point – i.e. the claim that democratic worker management of firms amounts to socialism – and the only form of socialism possible today.[25]

A major focus point of discussion is the transition from capitalism to the form of socialism advocated within it. The claim that a system of producer cooperatives is a new mode of production requires pinpointing the main aspects of this transitional process and deciding if such a transition can be expected to come about. Accordingly, Chapters 11 and 12 expatiate on Marx's, Engels's and Gramsci's descriptions of the transitional period and a number of related issues. In the subsequent chapter, I raise a question that, despite its exceptional bearing on the issue of the transition, has not yet been satisfactorily answered: what is the basic contradiction of capitalism?

My concern in this book is with Marxism, not the correct interpretation of Marx's theoretical approach. This requires re-examining Marxism from a new perspective. In other words, inasmuch as it is true that any bounce forward of the revolutionary movement entails coming to terms with previous defeats and out-growing them, now that the Soviet planned system has finally collapsed, Marxism can be viewed in a different light and in full agreement with the statement of Jacques Derrida (1993: 78) that 'Marxism remains at once indispensable and structurally insufficient: it is still necessary but provided it be transformed and adapted to new conditions and to a new thinking'.[26] This further review of Marxist themes will be conducted in the subsequent chapters, specifically in Chapters 14 and 15.

For my part, I reckon that the importance of reviewing the literature on employee-managed firms in a Marxist key lies in bringing to the foreground a number of advantages that the mainstream economic literature dealing with this category of firm has been found to understate.[27]

The terms cooperative, self-managed, employee-managed, worker-run, employee-controlled and democratic firm are used as synonyms.

8. This book contains further developments of the author's research on socialism and a resume of the author's research results on this subject. Many pages are translations, revisions or reproductions of pages written in articles and essays published over the span of about thirty years.[28]

Notes

1 For an excellent review of Hansmann's approach, see Cuomo (2006).
2 'The concept of economic democracy seeks to extend democracy of the political arena to the domain of production. This, of course, directly contradicts the logic of capitalism' (Gunn 2012: 5).
3 An altogether different business model is Vogt's 'liberal capitalist firm', where workers, though still wage-earners, enjoy (some) more freedom in seeing to their duties than is customary in traditional capitalistic businesses (see Vogt 1996).
4 As mentioned by Gould (1985: 204), even such a major author as Rawls has failed to point out that equal access to certain social and economic conditions is a necessary prerequisite for political freedom.
5 This idea is shared both by Cohen and Rogers (1983) and Bowles and Gintis (1986).
6 As shall be seen below, a democratic firm system requires production and distribution to be democratically organised.
7 As soon as the capital–labour relation is reversed upon the establishment of a workers' democracy, class struggle ebbs down, in my opinion, because workers appropriating the firm's surplus tend to become savers and, hence, potential capital income earners, while traditional capital gain earners, capitalists, are deprived of all their power. Conversely, in his approach, class struggle and class divisions persist until the newly introduced system becomes a fully-fledged communistic society (see McConnell 1949: 39).
8 In this connection, I feel in synch with Simone Weil, who thinks that distortions produced by corruption, preconceived ideas and other such evils make it difficult to apprehend the truth and that identifying misrepresented ideas and focusing on the lives of men, their passions and their interests is what really counts (see Weil 1955: 157).
9 Scholars denying the equation of socialism with the centralised planning system established in the Soviet Union include, among others, Marcuse (see Marcuse 1958: 70–74, 81–83, 156–157 and other writings) and the Marxist historian Pedrag Vranicki (1965: 348), who describes socialism as the progressive assertion of corporate management modes in stark conflict with the bureaucratic practices specific to Stalinism (see Vranicki 1965: 348). Interestingly, Bernstein's revisionism was instigated by his hostility to the omnipresence of the 'providential' interventionist state and sympathy for the democratic management of firms (see Angel 1974: 117).
10 In particular, with reference to farmers' cooperatives, it is often argued that over the past fifty years the application of insights contributed by information theory, agency theory, the theory of social and economic organisation, property rights theory, as well as transaction costs theory has resulted in considerable progress (see, *inter alia*, Cook *et al.* 2003; Chaddad 2012: 446).
11 Economic democracy – what Bauer used to term 'guild socialism' – is ultimately 'an extension of the basic principles of British democratic government from the political to the economic area' (Bauer 1920: 204).
12 The market socialism model that Chilosi and Nuti hold has failed is a system that was

launched in some countries in an abortive attempt to rectify the faults of the Soviet central planning model by reviving markets.

13 The movement for worker control in enterprises – Garson wrote (1973: 469) – 'is the central issue of class struggle in our generation'.

14 This is what Anweiler wrote in 1958 (472); and in 1973, Trower remarked that the pendulum of democracy had stopped swinging the other way and was now swinging in the direction of the establishment of democracy in the firm (1973: 138). The situation today will be discussed in the closing chapters of this book.

15 The first producer cooperative was established in France and carried on business from 1834 to 1870 (see Dreyfus 2012: 42).

16 This view is shared by numerous scholars, prevailingly of the left (see, for instance, Weil 1934).

17 One major characteristic of Marxist literature is that the type of revolution to be fought is never described in detail. This is equally true of Marx's *Capital*, of Lukàcs's *History and Class Consciousness* and of a much-praised work such as Hyman's *Industrial Relations: A Marxist Introduction* (see Gall 2012: 144–146).

18 As matter of fact, it has been repeatedly emphasised that this idea is far from widely shared today. At this stage, it suffices to mention that several theorists, including Webb (1891) and Gibson-Graham (2003), do not trace the roots of democratic management to Marxism. Significantly enough, the trade union organisation battling for self-management in France (C.F.D.T.) has occasionally denied any Marxist affiliation (see Rosanvallon 1976).

19 According to Perrotta (2006: 353), capitalistic businesses mainly differ from cooperative firms in their attitudes towards labour (i.e. issues such as wage levels, living and working conditions and the rights of workers).

20 All the directors are usually members of the producer cooperative, both in Italy and the United States, where non-working members may not exceed a pre-fixed total. In France, no more than one-third of the board members may be chosen from among non-members. No members are allowed to serve on the boards of the plywood cooperatives operating in the United States.

21 See, for example, Dahrendorf (1959: 430–440). The distinction between reporting and managing functions is held to be essential in any firm and, generally, any social organisation, regardless of the formal structure of its hierarchy (see Dahrendorf 1959: 381).

22 When the income level of each firm is given, the pay rates of the members with equal qualification of different firms will, admittedly, diverge as a result of competition, but I do not see why the practice of considering the different competiveness levels of individuals and firms when fixing pay rates (by democratic means) should be rated as non-democratic. After all, compared to payroll inequalities between the workers of capitalistic companies, those between the members of one and the same cooperative would be much less significant (see Adams 1963; Goodman 1974; and von Siemens 2011). For more on this subject, see, for instance, Jossa (1992).

23 In point of fact, this shortcoming is not confined to the WMF. In the LMF, capital goods do not become the property of individual partners and those who save do not, by virtue of this, become owners of real or financial assets.

24 In-between the participation of workers in decision processes within the firm and full self-management there are a gamut of possible intermediate steps (see Gunn 2011) that cannot be addressed in a book that is only concerned with the case in which decision-making is vested solely in workers.

25 A trenchant saying by Trower (1973: 138) runs: 'If freedom is our goal, industry will only become democratic when it is governed by those working in it'. In a just society – Rousseau wrote (1755: 88) – 'no one citizen should be rich enough to buy another, and no one so poor as to be obliged to sell himself'. Inasmuch as this is true and capitalism is an unjust and oppressive system, it must be spelt out in bold letters that

whenever the Left confines itself to demanding decent homes, healthy holidays and mass-produced commodities on the mere pretext that plenty of workers still live in hovels, cannot afford to spend their holidays in seaside resorts and have to do without personal cars, it is actually accepting inequality with resignation and putting up with oppression.

(Mallet 1963: xvii)

26 This opinion is shared by Schaff (1965: 256), who thinks it far from surprising or exceptional that changes in circumstances should necessitate revisiting Marx's thought. In Lichtheim (1965: 203), we read that 'we cannot enter even briefly into the history of the liberal age (which was also the age of Marxian socialism) without becoming aware that its unifying concepts are no longer quite the same as our own'.

27 The renowned theorist on economic systems Giovanni Arrighi once wrote (2007: 10) that 'historical sociology must be taken more seriously than political economy'. Conversely, in this book, I intend to show that the prerequisite for a correct assessment of the comparative advantages and defects of capitalism versus socialism is some background knowledge in political sociology and economics.

28 Specifically, in these books and articles: 'Sulla teoria economica dell'impresa autogestita', *Rivista Internazionale di Scienze Sociali*, January–March 1983; 'Sul problema del sottoinvestimento delle imprese gestite dai lavoratori', in *AISSEC*, V Annual Scientific Convention, Pavia, 14–16 December 1988; *The Economic Theory of Socialism and the Labour-Managed Firm* (co-authored with G. Cuomo), Edward Elgar, Cheltenham, 1997; 'Marx, Marxism and the Cooperative Movement', in *Cambridge Journal of Economics*, 2005a, vol. 36, n. 1; 'How Cooperative Firms should be Organised from the Perspective of Today's Economic Theory', in *Politica Economica*, 2008a, vol. 24, n. 3; 'Unemployment in a System of Labour Managed Firms', in N. Salvadori, A. Opocher (eds), *Long-Run Growth, Social Institution and Living Standard*, Edward Elgar, Cheltenham, 2009a; 'Alchian and Demsetz's Critique of the Cooperative Firm, Thirty-Seven Years After', in *Metroeconomica*, 2009b, vol. 60, n. 4; 'Gramsci and the Economic Theory of the Labour-Managed Firm', in *Review of Radical Political Economics*, March 2009, vol. 41, n. 1; 'Gramsci, The Economic Theory of Cooperatives and the Transition to a Socialist Economy', in *Solidarity Economy Net*, April 2009, vol. IV; *Esiste un'alternativa al capitalismo?*, manifestolibri, Rome, 2010; 'The Democratic Road to Socialism', in *Rivista Internazionale di Scienze Sociali*, July–September 2010, n. 3; 'Investment Funding: The Main Problem Facing Labour-Managed Firms?', in *Economia e Politica Industriale*, 2010, vol. 37, n. 2; 'Le contraddizioni del capitalismo e il loro possibile superamento', in *Studi e note di economia*, 2011, n. 1; 'Sulla definizione del socialismo', in *Rivista di Politica Economica*, January–March 2012, vols I–III; *Per un marxismo nell'epoca della globalizzazione*, manifestolibri, Rome, 2012; 'Cooperative Firms as a New Production Mode', in *Review of Political Economy*, 2012b, vol. 24, n. 3; 'A System of Self-Managed Firms as a New Perspective on Marxism', in *Cambridge Journal of Economics*, 2012c, vol. 36, n. 4; 'Alienation and the Self-Managed Firm System', forthcoming in *The Review of Radical Political Economics*, 2012a; 'The Key Contradiction in Capitalism', forthcoming in *Review of Radical Political Economics*; 'Marx, Lenin and the Cooperative Movement', forthcoming in *Review of Political Economy*.

1 Marx, Lenin and the cooperative movement

1 Introduction

On several occasions, Marx praised cooperation as a movement whose generalised growth would give rise to a new mode of production. At different times in his life, he even seems to have been confident that cooperatives would ultimately supplant capitalist firms altogether. In a 1923 article entirely concerned with this subject, Lenin described cooperation as a major organisational step in the transition to socialism and went so far as to equate it with socialism at large. 'Cooperation is socialism', he declared (Lenin 1923a). In *L'Ordine Nuovo* (1919–1920), Gramsci described workers' councils as milestones on the road to socialism.

Despite these authoritative endorsements, ever since the days of the Paris Commune the cooperative movement has received little attention from Marxists. In point of fact, this should come as no surprise, since the type of cooperative that has made headway in history is a firm where workers are 'their own capitalists' (Marx 1894a: 571) and is consequently at odds with the claim that producer cooperatives give rise to a genuine form of socialism.

Meanwhile, modern economic theory has provided evidence that the pure cooperative is Vanek's LMF – a firm that self-finances its investments entirely with loan capital and strictly segregates labour incomes from capital incomes. And as the workers of such a firm can hardly be described as 'their own capitalists', this disproves the view of most Marxists that cooperatives are an intermediate form between capitalism and socialism.

What are the implications of these reflections? Considering that Marx, Lenin and Gramsci looked upon cooperation as a new mode of production that supplants capitalism, Marxists can be divided into two distinct groups: those who identify socialism with a state-planned command economy and those who equate it with a system of self-managed firms – although neither group has been able to provide conclusive evidence that Marx actually accepted one or the other of these systems.

Furthermore, there is general agreement that Marx's concern was mainly with methodology (as argued in Chapter 1) and that his fragmentary writings about the economic system of the future do not constitute a fully-fledged doctrinal system (see Balibar 1993: 169).[1]

With all the caution required by these considerations, I do think it possible to argue that an efficient system of producer cooperatives would give rise to a socialist order capable of superseding capitalism in full harmony with Marxist thought. In this chapter, quotes from Marx and from Lenin's 1923 article on cooperation will be utilised, in order to refute the widely shared, yet incorrect assumption that Marx and Lenin rejected cooperation, even as a mode of production for the transitional period.

The argument, in this chapter, is that the late emergence of an economic theory of producer cooperatives is one of the reasons why Marxists continued to neglect not only cooperation as such, but even the passages from Marx and Engels, in which a system of producer cooperatives is described as a new mode of production.

2 Marx's approach to producer cooperatives

In the *Inaugural Address* (1864), Marx wrote:

> But there was in store a still greater victory of the political economy of labour over the political economy of property. We speak of the co-operative movement, especially of the co-operative factories raised by the unassisted efforts of a few bold 'hands'. The value of these great social experiments cannot be over-rated. By deed, instead of by argument, they have shown that production on a large scale, and in accord with the behest of modern science, may be carried on without the existence of a class of masters employing a class of hands; that to bear fruit, the means of labour need not be monopolised as a means of dominion over, and of extortion against, the labouring man himself; and that, like slave labour, like serf labour, hired labour is but a transitory and inferior form, destined to disappear before associated labour plying its toil with a willing hand, a ready mind, and a joyous heart.
>
> (Marx 1864: 11)[2]

In the third volume of *Capital*, he also argued:

> With the development of co-operatives on the workers' part, and joint-stock companies on the part of the bourgeoisie, the last pretext for confusing profit of enterprise with the wages of management was removed, and profit came to appear in practice as what is undeniably was in theory, mere surplus-value, value for which no equivalent was paid.
>
> (Marx 1894a: 513–514)

Both these quotes leave no doubt that Marx looked upon an all-cooperative system not only as feasible, but as bound to assert itself in history, as a new mode of production that would wipe out hired labour and a system where privately owned means of production – capital – would cease being used to enslave workers. In such a system, he claimed, workers would no longer be exploited and, even more importantly, would be freely and willingly working for firms owned by them.

The system of producer cooperatives envisaged by Marx was a market system that makes workers 'their own masters' (Mill 1871: 739) and deprives capital owners of the power to make decisions in matters of production.[3] In Marx's opinion, this system is 'in accord with the behest of modern science' and, inasmuch as it is a new mode of production arising within the older mode of production and supplanting it, it is even more efficient than capitalism.[4]

Both the equation of an all-cooperatives system with a new mode of production and its assumed potential for outperforming and superseding capitalism are underscored in numerous often-quoted passages from *Capital*. On pages 570–571, for instance, Marx describes joint-stock companies as firms that will lead to the abolition of the capitalist mode of production 'within the capitalist mode of production itself'. Further on, he also argues:

> The co-operative factories run by workers themselves are, within the old form, the first examples of the emergence of a new form, even though they naturally reproduce in all cases, in their present organization, all the defects of the existing system, and must reproduce them. But the opposition between capital and labour is abolished there, even if at first only in the form that the workers in association become their own capitalists, *i.e.* they use the means of production to valorise their labour. These factories show how, at a certain stage of development of the material forces of production, and of the social forms of production corresponding to them, a new mode of production develops and is formed naturally out of the old [...]. Capitalist joint-stock companies as much as cooperative factories should be viewed as transition forms from the capitalist mode of production to the associated one, simply that in one case the opposition is abolished in a negative way, and in the other in a positive way.
>
> (Marx 1894a: 571–572)

One of the reasons why Marx forcefully endorsed the introduction of cooperatives and the abolition of hired labour even in a system remaining purely mercantile in nature is that (from the perspective of a critic of capitalism) producer cooperatives realise such a basic component of political democracy as economic democracy. Indeed, Marx, Marxists and other critics of the existing social order concordantly rate political democracy as merely formal when power remains firmly in the hands of capitalists – i.e. when capital is still the economic power holding everything in its sway.

3 Cooperatives as starting points for state planning and the role of the state

In Marxian terms, cooperative production is not an end in itself, but 'a lever for uprooting the economic foundations upon which rests the existence of classes'

(Marx 1871: 334) and a means of organising the domestic production system in line with an all-inclusive plan. This can be clearly inferred from Marx's comments on the experience of the Paris 'Commune':

> The Commune, they exclaim, intends to abolish property, the basis of civilization! Yes, gentlemen, the Commune intended to abolish that class-property which makes the labour of the many the wealth of the few. It aimed at the expropriation of the expropriators. It wanted to make individual property a truth by transforming the means of production, land and capital, now chiefly the means of enslaving and exploiting labour, into mere instruments of free and associated labour [...]. But this is Communism, 'impossible' Communism! Why, those members of the ruling class who are intelligent enough to perceive the impossibility of continuing the present system – and they are many – have become the obtrusive and full-mouthed apostles of co-operative production. If cooperative production is not to remain a sham and a mare; if it is to supersede the capitalist system; if the united co-operative societies are to regulate national production upon a common plan, thus taking it under their control, and putting an end to the constant anarchy and periodical convulsions which are the fatality of Capitalist production – what else, gentlemen, would it be but Communism, 'possible' Communism?
>
> (Marx 1871: 335)

In Marx's view, inasmuch as the Paris Commune 'supplied the Republic with the basis of really democratic institutions', it could be looked upon as 'the political form, at last discovered, under which to work out the economical emancipation of Labour' (Marx 1871: 334) and bring about 'the expropriation of the expropriators'. And Engels made it clear that 'the Paris Commune demanded that the workers should manage cooperatively the factories closed down by manufacturers' (Engels 1886: 389).

In this connection, Easton has rightly argued (1994: 162) that Marx 'sees cooperatives as the economic corollary of the "really democratic institution" of the Commune' and that 'in his view of the state he sees cooperative production not as a matter of simple negation of the existing capitalist system, but rather as a dialectical transcendence that negates as it preserves'.

In his critique of Bakunin's *Statehood and Anarchy*, Marx provided the following explanation of the phrase 'organisation of the proletariat as the dominant class':

> It means that the proletariat, instead of fighting individual instances against the economically privileged classes, has gained sufficient strength and organization to use general means of coercion in its struggle against them; but it can only make use of such economic means as abolish its own character as wage labourer and hence as a class; when its victory is complete, its rule too is therefore at an end, since its class character will have [disappeared].
>
> (see Marx 1875b: 519)

Today, when the interests of workers are endorsed by political parties capable of securing the support of the majority of the people, the 'general means of coercion' required to combat the economically privileged classes and abolish hired labour could well be a single act of Parliament prohibiting wage labour altogether. When asked if private property could be abolished by peaceful means, Engels replied that 'it is to be desired that this could happen, and Communists certainly would be the last to resist it' (Engels 1847a: 349), but he added that where the dominant class should halt such progress through the use of violence, the proletariat would be pressed into fighting a revolution (Engels 1847a: 349–350).

The work from which these passages have been taken, the *Principles of Communism*, was written at roughly the same time as the *Manifesto*. To explain the differences between these two texts, Engels said that on writing the *Manifesto*, they had resolved to expound their shared ideas about the road towards communism only to the extent they had thought it expedient to make them public (see Engels 1847a: 114, as quoted in Lawler 1994).

The role of democracy in fostering the advent of socialism is also described in the following excerpt from Engels (1895a: 515–516):

> *The Communist Manifesto* had already proclaimed the winning of universal suffrage, of democracy, as one of the first and most important tasks of the militant proletariat, and Lassalle had again taken up this point. Now that Bismarck found himself compelled to introduce this franchise as the only means of interesting the mass of the people to his plans, our workers immediately took it in earnest and sent August Bebel to the first, constituent Reichstag. And from that day on they have used the franchise in a way which has paid them a thousand-fold and has served as a model to the workers of all countries.

Marx's praise of cooperation is to be viewed in light of his belief that legal relationships and political organisation systems have their roots in material production relationships. As discussed in the previous chapter, a 'civil society' that is organised as a system of producer cooperatives is one where capital is no longer the economic power holding everything in its sway and where those owning substantial property are prevented from imposing their will upon the rest of the population. The commodities manufactured by democratically managed cooperatives cease to be, in the first place, an external object unrelated to our work and turn into the product of free choices made by workers in association.

4   Lenin's 1923 article

At this point, I will try to establish what Lenin thought of a system of producer cooperatives.

In *Life of Lenin*, Fischer (1964, vol. II: 957) reports that after the introduction of the New Economic Policy (NEP) (as a response to the libertarian rebellion in

Kronstadt), Lenin read a great many books on the cooperative movement and used the resulting insight to dictate an article ('On Cooperation'), which appeared in the *Pravda* on 26 and 27 January 1923 and proved to be 'so innovative as to take the whole party by surprise' (Boffa and Martinet 1976: 240). Concerning this article, Lunacârskij commented that many of the slogans launched by Lenin were at first received with puzzlement and rated as absurd, though later on they were found to be rich in valuable implications (see Strada 1980: 117).[5]

Following the advent of Stalin, this article fell into oblivion both inside and outside the USSR and although it marks a turning point in Lenin's political thinking, it is little known even today.[6] As it includes both his conclusion that 'we have no way out but to admit that all our opinions on socialism have radically changed' and his straightforward equation of socialism with cooperation, a correct appraisal of its bearing on the evolution of Lenin's thought would reveal if Lenin's radical change of opinion actually induced him to lose faith in central planning and identify socialism with cooperation late in life.

In his 1923 article, Lenin remarked that the burgeoning role of the cooperative movement within the framework of the 'New Economic Policy' was a clear indication that the task lying before them, at once simple and complex, was to organise the bulk of the population into cooperatives. In essence, he wrote, what we actually need

> is to organize the population of Russia in cooperative societies on a sufficiently large-scale, for we have now found the degree of coordination of private interest, of private commercial interest, with state supervision and control of this interest, that degree of its subordination to the common interests which was formerly the stumbling block for very many socialists.
>
> (Lenin 1923a: 1797–1798)

And as the core idea behind the NEP was the need to leverage the private profit motive in the construction of a socialist system,[7] there can be little doubt that he was prefiguring an increasing recourse to cooperation. Let us add, however, that Lenin made the establishment of a socialist system dependent on two prerequisites – i.e. both the public ownership of cooperatives and a party-controlled state organisation working in the interests of the working class.

However, the moment Lenin reached this conclusion, he also realised that the views concerning the very nature of socialism had undergone radical change. Now – he argued – 'we are entitled to say that the mere growth of cooperation ... is identical with the growth of socialism' and 'at the same time, we have to admit that there has been a radical modification of our whole outlook on socialism' (Lenin 1923a: 1802).

Cooperation, he continued, 'which we formerly ridiculed as huckstering', constitutes the social regime we have to support by any means. As soon as those advocating a transition to communism seize power, 'cooperation under our conditions nearly always coincides fully with socialism' (see Lenin 1923a: 1797–1803).[8]

Accordingly, this article is clear evidence that by 1923 Lenin had come to think of cooperation not as a component of the NEP, but as the regime that better than any other could help establish a real and proper socialist order.[9] We look at cooperation – he wrote – from a perspective that has so far been underrated – i.e. 'the standpoint of transition to the new system by means that are the simplest, easiest and most acceptable to the peasant' (Lenin 1923a: 1798).

> But this again is a fundamental importance. It is one thing to draw out fantastic plans for building socialism through all sorts of workers associations, and quite another to learn to build socialism in practice in such a way that every small peasant could take part in it. That is the very stage we have now reached.
>
> (Lenin 1923a: 1798)

As cooperation 'is adjustable to the level of the most ordinary peasant', at last we are in a position to argue that 'there are no other devices needed to advance to socialism' (Lenin 1923a: 1799). Consequently, in Lenin's later approach, cooperation is the right road for the edification of socialism at last discovered.[10] 'Owing to the special features of our political system' – Lenin wrote – 'cooperation acquires an altogether exceptional significance, so much so that it is possible to say' – let us repeat this – 'that it coincides fully with socialism' (Lenin 1923a: 1801–1802).[11]

Concluding, in 1923, Lenin no longer believed that nationalising means of production was a necessary assumption for the edification of communism. 'Our state apparatus' – he wrote in a later article (Lenin 1923b: 357) – 'is so deplorable, not to say wretched, that we must first think very carefully how to combat its defects'.[12]

5 Bucharin's analysis of Lenin's article

Lenin's article was interpreted by Bucharin in the following way.[13] The guiding principle against which Bucharin tested Lenin's article was the belief that the initial post-revolutionary stage – i.e. socialism – was to be strictly kept apart from communism – the hoped-for end-stage and acme of the revolutionary process. Moreover, he clearly emphasised that in the initial post-takeover phase, the victorious revolutionaries would have to postpone planning and rely on markets and cooperation instead. From Bucharin's perspective, the assumption of lasting success of the revolution was an economic growth rate commensurate with those recorded in capitalist countries. He had read the writing by the liberalist von Mises that started the well-known debate on planning in the 1930s (which he quoted) and remarked that backward economic units were being integrated into the burgeoning economy of the state in a variety of different ways, but principally via the market (Bucharin 1925b: 160). The deferral of planning, he argued, was made necessary by the fact that any strategy founded on coercive top-down commands was bound to prove abortive (Bucharin 1925b: 159). And as he held that the most significant plus point of the NEP was to have lifted the ban on private initiative and placed peasants and the middle classes in the service of socialism, he suggested holding on to this strategy in future as well. After a long drawn-out confrontation with the remnants of private capital and sizeable gains in economic power, he wrote, they were progressing towards planning, and despite the awareness that this process would take time to complete, he was confident that the state would induce both those economic entities that were already working in unison with the Party and, so far, agonistic players to espouse and advance the Party's cause, whether they liked it or not (Bucharin 1925b: 160).

In Bucharin's view, this new course had been made possible by the fact that the Soviets were by now well-established and that risks of a return to capitalism were consequently remote. He rated this course as an improvement over both pre-war communism and their one-time belief that central planning was to be introduced within a possibly tight timeframe. Concluding, he admitted that their long-held idea that the victorious proletariat would have to do away with markets promptly after the takeover, put an end to capitalism almost overnight and introduce planning as soon as possible was a misconception (Bucharin 1925b: 161).

Bucharin rates this new course as a departure from the NEP, whose launch he perceived as a temporary step backward within a slow and lengthy process.

In sum, Bucharin appears to have welcomed the new ideas expressed in Lenin's 1923 article, because they fell in with his own. Discussing Lenin's concern that the rate of growth of the post-revolutionary economic system might prove rather slack, he remarked (1923a: 161) that the strategic plan underlying Lenin's article on cooperation – a testament of sorts – differed sharply from the plan behind the NEP. On realising that the stoutest enemies of socialism – the lower middle classes and the peasantry – were not easily involved, Lenin had dropped his advocacy of central planning and conceived the idea of using the mediation of large capitalists, especially public sector licensees (1923a: 162). In other words, had resolved to try and create an anti-middle-class bloc in between the proletariat and large capitalists. The innovative points of his 1923 article were an alliance of workers and peasants against large capitalists and, generally, the remnants of private capital[14] and the description of cooperatives as socialist firms in consequence of the fact that they were 'founded on land and on means of production which are the property of the State, i.e. of the working class' (1923a: 163).

6 Recent analyses of Lenin's article

Let us repeat that Lenin's 1923 article has been largely ignored ever since Stalin's rise to power.

One exception is Valentino Gerratana, who provides a short overview of Lenin's later writings and suggests re-examining this article in conjunction with them (Gerratana 1970: 259–264). Unfortunately, Gerratana fails to pinpoint the exact links between such a review and Lenin's declared reconsideration of his previous beliefs.

The argument that Lenin's advocacy of cooperation is closely associated with the NEP, the scheme that Lenin perceived as a temporary 'retreat', is barely more convincing, since the passages where Lenin equates socialism with cooperation make no mention of any move backward (see Medvedev 1980: 558–559).

An additional reference to Lenin's later thought is found in Massimo Salvadori's article 'Lenin e i soviet', where Sovietism is described as a practical scheme designed 'to facilitate the access of the masses to public life' (Salvadori 1972: 56), rather than 'an ideology or a socio-political state organisation scheme to be juxtaposed with less markedly "leftist" conceptions of socialism' (Salvadori 1972: 53).

Actually, Salvadori's argument that Lenin neither looked upon Soviets as revolutionary bodies in their own right (Salvadori 1972: 62), nor on Sovietism as a method for organising economic and social life can at most be applicable to the years before 1923, when Lenin repeatedly mentioned the opinion of the Bolsheviks that there was 'nothing so silly as railways to the railwaymen and tanneries to tanners'. The thorough reconsideration of the essence of socialism documented in Lenin's article would rather suggest the opposite conclusion. In 1923, when Lenin equated socialism with democratic firm management, he was doubtless proposing a different social and economic organisational scheme.

From a recent monumental history of communism by Cortesi (2010: 533), we learn that late in life, looking back on the Bolshevik Revolution in retrospect, Lenin found that the resulting social order was characterised by a compound of pre-modern and excessively advanced aspects and had undergone radical change in the decade immediately before (Cortesi 2010: 533). In Cortesi's words, Lenin's self-directed criticism casts a blot on his reputation as a man who steadily and lucidly pursued his goal without wavering (Cortesi 2010: 533). After a critical reconsideration of the past, Lenin abandoned his one-time identification of socialism with central planning, turned his attention to markets and claimed that pending the advent of communism (which is never as much as mentioned in his 1923 article) socialism could be attained through the establishment of a system of cooperatives operating in markets.

As I will show in greater detail further on, Lenin's puzzling self-criticism can be traced both to his status as the main theoretician of Soviets, 'of the transfer of all state power into the hands of workers, soldiers and peasants'[15] and, above all, to misgivings concerning a totalitarian involution of the state apparatus, which haunted him during the last years of his life (Cortesi 2010: 545). 'Although the implementation of the scheme underlying State and Revolution was out of the question in the post-revolutionary years' – Cortesi argues (2010: 546) – 'it would be a gross mistake to ignore the close link between Lenin's poignant awareness of the risk of bureaucratism and the beliefs he held in 1917, i.e. the unifying thread in his theoretical approach'.[16]

Though not entirely beside the mark, both Cortesi's interpretation of Lenin's reconsideration of his past as a sign of consistency and his reference to *State and Revolution* fail to shed full light on the point I am discussing. One step in the unitary evolution of Lenin's thought is the 1920 text entitled *Left-Wing*

Communism: An Infantile Disorder, which is wrongly held to be 'principally aimed against Gorter and Pannekoek, the spokesmen for council communism' (Negt 1979b: 322). Actually, its main aim is to disprove the alleged existence of two communist parties 'arrayed against each other', a party of leaders intending to steer the revolutionary struggle from the top and create a dictatorship of the proletariat, and a mass party conceiving of revolution as an upsurge from the bottom and wanting to establish the dictatorship of the proletariat as a class (Lenin 1920a: 1398). In Lenin's view, the antithetical groups were, on the one hand, those altogether inimical to the idea of a party-led revolutionary struggle and, on the other, those wishing the revolution to be steered by a strong and well-organised party supported by the masses and conceiving of the takeover of the proletariat as a class, not party, dictatorship.[17] As for factory councils, in the 1920 article, Lenin unconditionally endorses Soviet power as an idea that 'has emerged throughout the world and is spreading among the proletariat of all countries with extraordinary speed' (1920a: 1389). He denounced their 'false use by the Mensheviks, who went bankrupt because of their inability to understand' their role and significance and concluded that 'the work of the Party is carried on through the Soviets', which are 'democratic institutions the likes of which even the best of the democratic republics of the bourgeois world have never known' (1920a: 1403).

On closer analysis, therefore, Lenin's 1920 article was doubtless aimed against who failed to recognise the huge contribution of an efficient organisational effort to the success of the revolution, not against Pannekoek as the spokesman for council communism. Similarly, while Rosa Luxembourg is certainly among the targets, Lenin was not censuring the theorist of workers' councils. His criticisms were rather aimed at the person who made the lucid remark (as early as 1905) that 'the elimination of democracy ... is worse than the disease it is supposed to cure: for it stops up the very living source from which alone can come correction of all the innate shortcomings of social institutions' (Luxemburg 1905: 594–595) and was 'the first to recognise the seeds of the future involution of Soviet society both in Lenin's notion of the party and in other aspects of his approach' (see Negt 1979b: 321).

Bearing in mind the direction in which Lenin's thought was heading, the self-critical tone of his 1923 article is to be viewed in association with his 'political testament', the text in which he predicted the feared bureaucratic degeneration of the Party and can thus be read as a partial conversion to Luxembourg's ideas. Quoting Lukàcs (1924: 83):

> the Soviet system does its utmost to relate human activity to general questions concerning the state, the economy, culture, etc., while fighting to ensure that the regulation of all such questions does not become the privilege of an exclusive bureaucratic group remote from social life as a whole.

As I will show in greater detail further on, the 1923 article points to a certain measure of continuity within the theoretical approach of Lenin, the theoretician of the death of the state. Fears of a bureaucratic involution of the Party induced Lenin to proclaim that a system of producer cooperatives operating in markets under the lead of the Communist Party would both realise socialism and inhibit risks of an anti-democratic involution. Due to his faith in the Party, he was confident that as long as the Communist Party remained well established and firmly in power, these cooperatives, far from fostering a return to capitalism, would work towards the full attainment of socialism within a market economy and would therefore help establish a democratic form of socialism exempt from the risks of involution. It is worth remembering that the NEP envisaged a greater role for the Soviets (see Anweiler 1958: 469).

7 Delving deeper into the issue

What is our final interpretation of Lenin's article? Although I basically share Bucharin's interpretation of the 1924 article, I wish to lay greater emphasis on the reflections that led Lenin to turn from an advocate of central planning into a supporter of cooperation. On the one hand, the novelty of Lenin's 1923 article lay in his move away from the idea of state socialism – a form of socialism that takes over from capitalism a strong concentration of firms and manages the economy from the centre; on the other, the novelty lay in the insight that socialism can be implemented by establishing a system of cooperative firms operating in the market. Until then, Lenin had looked to Soviets as the preferred tool for exercising worker control over capitalistic factories,[18] but by 1923 he had realised that worker control was to be exercised by empowering workers to run production establishments. In his maturity, Lenin prefigured the idea of contemporary producer cooperative theorists: a system of democratic firms amounts to a socialist order.

On closer analysis, though, Lenin's 1923 article is less innovative than would appear at first sight. His belief in the need for socialist firms to operate in a market economy for a long time and his theorisation of the Soviet system as a tool for the transition to socialism both predate the revolution. And after the October Revolution, he welcomed 'the gradual transformation of these councils from revolutionary tools to the agents of the newly-established state power' (Anweiler 1958: 402). In July 1920, he included the following paragraph in his 'Theses on the fundamental tasks of the Second Congress of the Communist International':

> Concerning the Socialist Party of Italy, the Second Congress of the Third International considers that the criticism of that party and the practical proposals submitted to the National Council of the Socialist Party of Italy in the name of the party's Turin section, as set forth in *L'Ordine Nuovo* of May 8, 1920, are in the main correct and are fully in keeping with the fundamental principles of the Third International.
>
> (see Leonetti 1971: 14–15)

To our knowledge, however, even in the period before the revolution, when he unconditionally supported Soviets, he never defined the exact role they were expected to play in post-revolution production processes. He wrote:

> To say that the Soviets have anywhere in Russia ever enjoyed 'full power' is simply ridiculous. Full power means power over all the land, over all the banks, over all the factories.... The Soviets have never had full power. And the measures they have taken could not result in anything but palliatives.
>
> (Lenin 1957–1970, vol. XXVI: 101)

Unfortunately, Lenin's words fail to shed full light on the actual role of Soviets in socialism. In Carr (1953: 474–475), we read that

> following the revolution there were material risks of a conflict between 'state control' and 'worker control' in the field of industrial policy. If the true meaning of 'worker control' was placing administrative tasks in the hands of the central congress of soviets and its managing committee, it was just a synonym for nationalisation.... Conversely, if its true meaning was placing control into the hands of factory committees or soviets, its implementation was likely to interfere both with state control and with any planning policies designed to reverse the anarchical character of capitalistic production processes.

For a long time, Lenin failed to state his opinion on Soviets clearly (see Salvadori 1972: 54–55, 59).

Conversely, he was the first to clearly distinguish between socialism and communism and to emphasise the need to construct socialism out of the very bricks of the bourgeoisie. Discussing the control issue in a well-known 1917 article (Lenin 1917b), he maintained that far from complex (as was generally assumed), the control issue was actually 'very easy and quite practical', since 'the principal measure, the chief method to introduce control' is 'uniting the population according to profession, purpose and work, branch of labour, etc.' (1917b: 802). 'Bureaucracy must be abandoned for democracy' – he wrote – and 'the initiative of workers and other employees must be drawn on; they must be immediately summoned to conferences and congresses; a certain proportion of the profits must be assigned to them, provided they institute overall control and increase production'. In addition to this, he recommended abolishing the principle of commercial secrecy (1917b: 810–811).

In matters of competition and incentives, before the revolution Lenin suggested that the competitive race was to be steered by the socialist state:

> Far from extinguishing competition – he wrote – socialism for the first time creates the opportunity for employing it on a really wide and on a really mass scale, for actually drawing the majority of working people into a field of labour in which they can display their abilities.
>
> (Lenin 1917c: 386)

Further on, in the same article, he added:

> Competition must be carefully organised among practical operators, workmen and peasants. Every attempt to establish stereotyped forms and to impose uniformity from above [...] must be combated.... All 'communities' – factories, villages, consumers' societies and committees of suppliers – must compete with each other.
>
> (Lenin 1917c: 393)

As regards this connection, Meyer (1957: 220) has argued that Lenin thought of emulation 'as a tool to oblige work-dodgers to work for the state' and that 'the fact that people had to be forced to see to their work came as a hard blow both to proletarian aspirations and previous socialist theorists'.

In *The Impending Catastrophe* (1917e), Lenin made it clear that while the pre-revolution political apparatus was to be thoroughly changed following the revolution, the envisioned nationalisation of the economic apparatus would not 'deprive any "owner" of a single kopek' (Lenin 1917e: 804). In his opinion, capitalists were to be stripped of all power, while the institutions and organisational bodies of the older system were to be maintained.

There is general agreement that the assessment of workers' councils is strictly dependent on the uses to which they are assigned at each stage in history (see, for instance, Chitarin 1973: 15–16; Negri 1974: 95–98). Our approach so far suggests that both before the revolution and at the time he wrote his 1923 article Lenin believed that post-revolution factories would have to operate in a market economy for a long time, while the gradual dismantlement of Soviets was imposed by the central decision processes associated with the introduction of the dictatorship of the proletariat and war communism.[19] Significantly enough, the resolution passed at the first pan-Russian conference of workshop committees just a few days before the revolution (17–22 October 1917) runs as follows: 'Only when workers seize control of capitalist firms and gain a true understanding of their goals and social weight will they create the assumptions for self-managing these firms efficiently'. At that time, Lenin believed in the future of worker control. The prevailing climate in the country, Massari comments (1994: 73), the disappearance of factory owners and the enthusiasm kindled in workers by the awareness of their newly-gained power further heightened such expectations. In a practical manual published in December 1917, self-management and the maintenance of the decision-making powers of Soviets are clearly said to be the prerequisites for worker control.

Hence, there are reasons to assume that Lenin's discouragement of Soviet rule in the post-revolutionary period is to be traced to an adverse record of experience[20] and, especially, to the awareness that an advanced democratic organisation was not easy to establish in a besieged country (see Anweiler 1958: 433). Lenin took a firm stand against revolutionary socialists, anarchists, revolutionary communists and popular communists – i.e. the factions who were pressing for the prompt establishment of a council system and workers' republic and who accused him of betraying the socialist principles of the October Revolution, because times were not ripe and both the civil war raging at home and the international situation were fraught with risks.[21]

Lenin's stout opposition to factory councils immediately after the revolution can hardly be denied. As Anweiler states (1958: 446):

> The victory of the Bolsheviks resulted in changes in the very rationale behind councils: from radical democratic institutions and tools for proletarian self-government, the Russian councils had turned into the instruments used by the party elite to steer the masses. Concepts such as 'the party as a steering organ' or 'soviets as transmission belts' are in stark conflict with the plan to create self-governing masses and cancel the distinction between 'top' and 'bottom' that Lenin had launched in 1927 and popularised through the Bolshevik propaganda apparatus. In the early post-revolutionary period, the soviets were no longer looked upon as the springboard for the hoped-for self-governed economy.

Significantly, Section 7 of the *General Instructions on Worker Control* published in the *Izvestia* on 13 December 1917 ruled: 'The Control Commission has no part in running firms and is not responsible for their operation or performance: factories remain firmly in the hands of their owners!' (see AA.VV. 1970: 29).

In the light of the evolution of Lenin's thought, his 1923 article marks a return to his initial, impassioned advocacy of Soviets, a return that was made possible by the awareness that the country's economy was now tolerably stable, that power was firmly in the hands of the workers' party and that central planning could consequently be done without.

Those doubting the conversion of Lenin to the socialism = cooperation identity may nevertheless object that his real scheme was to organise peasants (the last surviving bourgeois class) into cooperatives and restrict hired labour to industry (the sector that Lenin held to have been organised along socialist lines, even during capitalism). This scheme envisaged the advancement of socialism through the dialectic juxtaposition of a capitalist sector (farming) with a genuinely socialist sector (industry), the organisation of the former into cooperatives and the latter into large state-owned concerns and a well thought-out strategy to ensure the final predominance of industry over farming (see Preobrazhensky 1925; Lorenz 1974: 770).[22] In point of fact, although this argument is supported by some of Lenin's earlier writings, it conflicts with Lenin's explicit statements (in the 1923 article) that the NEP had determined 'a radical modification in our whole outlook on socialism' and that 'cooperation nearly always coincides fully with socialism'.[23]

In point of fact, considering the paramount position gained by the Russian cooperatives of the time in both the wholesale and retail trade sectors, there are no reasons to assume that Lenin was planning to confine the creation of cooperatives to the farming sector only.

In short, the reason why Lenin equated a system of cooperatives with socialism was his belief that these firms would combine and reconcile the private profit motive with state regulation, which he deemed to be a necessary step in the transition to communism.

8 Different readings of Lenin's 1923 article

Those doubting the conversion of Lenin to the socialism=cooperation identity may nevertheless object that his real scheme was to organise peasants (the last surviving bourgeois class) into cooperatives and continue to use hired labour in state industry. The scheme envisaged was the advancement of socialism through the dialectic juxtaposition of a capitalistic sector (farming) with a genuinely socialist sector (state-owned industry), with the organisation of the former into cooperatives and the latter into large state-owned concerns and a well thought-out strategy to ensure the final predominance of industry over farming (see Preobrazhensky 1925).[24] This seems to be confirmed by a passage where Lenin argues that 'they look down on cooperative societies, failing to appreciate their exceptional importance ... from the standpoint of transition to the new system by means that are the *simplest, easiest and most acceptable to the peasant*' (Lenin 1923a: 1798 [emphasis in the original]). An even clearer passage runs as follows:

> Success in the practical work that now lies ahead will depend largely on the establishment, through the medium of commodity exchange, of proper relations between urban industry and agriculture. It will depend on the ability of the co-operative societies, by steady and persistent effort, to clear the way for the development of commodity exchange and to take the lead in this field. It will depend on their ability to collect the scattered stocks of commodities and to secure the production of new ones. In the long run, the practical solution of these problems is the best way to achieve our aims, namely, to restore agriculture and, on that basis, to strengthen and develop large-scale industry.
>
> (Lenin 1921e)

In my opinion, this argument conflicts with Lenin's explicit statements (in the 1923 article) that the NEP had resulted in 'a radical modification in our whole outlook on socialism' and that 'cooperation nearly always coincides fully with socialism'. Provided it is true that cooperation nearly always fully coincides with socialism, it is difficult to understand why industry as a whole and the service sector should not be organised into cooperatives.

A similar line of reasoning underlies a different, though radical, criticism that may be levelled against our approach. Understating the power of the petty bourgeoisie, Lenin thought that the parties to class struggle were workers and large capitalists only. In 1918, he wrote:

> All of us very well realise that there can only be one alternative in our class struggle: recognition either of the rule of capital or of the working class. We

know that all the attempts by the petty-bourgeois parties to form and pursue their policy in the country are doomed to failure before they even start. We have clearly seen and experienced several attempts by various petty-bourgeois parties and groups to push through their policy, and we see that all attempts by intermediate forces are bound to end in failure.

(Lenin 1918e)

As a result, concerning the prospect of conciliation with cooperatives, he argued:

Comrades, the workers' co-operatives are today faced with extremely important economic and political tasks. Both the one and the other are now part and parcel of the economic and political struggle. In respect of the immediate tasks I want to underline the meaning of 'conciliation with the co-operatives'. This conciliation, mentioned so frequently of late in the papers, radically differs from the conciliation with the bourgeoisie, which is nothing short of treachery.

(Lenin 1918e)

Bearing in mind this passage, it is worth remarking that Lenin (see Lenin 1921e) drew a clear-cut distinction between workers' cooperatives (large-size firms) and producers' cooperatives (associations of farmers or petty non-agricultural producers). In the mind of the great revolutionary, conciliation with workers' cooperatives was out of the question, because it would have entailed an agreement with big capitalists.

In point of fact, workers' cooperatives no longer existed at that time, because they had been merged with the Soviet state at the instigation of Lenin himself (see Lenin 1918e), and this may explain why Lenin did not mention workers' cooperatives in the 1920 article (Lenin 1920b), where he wrote that 'all types' of cooperatives, 'not only consumers', but producers', credit, and other coopera-tives should, by appropriate stages and with due care, be amalgamated into a Central Union of Consumers' Societies'.

In essence, this is Cohen's point in a 1973 book where he argued (see Cohen 1973: 143) that Lenin's 1923 article was concerned with trading businesses, rather than producer cooperatives (as was assumed in later years).

Dissenting from Cohen, I wish to emphasise a conflict between this approach and Lenin's explicit acknowledgement – in the 1923 article – that 'we have no way out but to admit that all our opinions on socialism have radically changed'. Considering that back in 1918 Lenin wrote (Lenin 1918e) that 'the whole of society must become a single workers' co-operative' and that 'to establish this type of co-operative ... is the condition for the victory of socialism', there is no reason to argue that in 1923 he had reconsidered his previous convictions. In other words, since the conclusion that all firms were to be organised as workers' cooperatives operating independently of the central power structure predates 1923, I do not see why he himself should have categorised his 1923 article as absolutely innovative.

However, even if one accepts this second interpretation, there is a high probability that Lenin would have endorsed the establishment of cooperatives of any size if only he had had knowledge of the possibility of setting up firms freed from capitalist control (as are Vanek-type LMFs).

This reflection is very important because, even if we accept the idea that in 1923 Lenin did not think socialism to be compatible with large-size cooperatives, it is difficult to deny that he would have endorsed LMF model cooperatives (which disempower capitalists), irrespective of size.

The claim that the cooperatives envisaged by Lenin were firms allowed to retain at least part of the residual is supported both by the fact that the NEP was Lenin's own brainchild and by a passage that reads:

> by adopting the NEP we made a concession to the peasant as trader, to the principal of private trade; it is for this reason (contrary to what some people think) that the cooperative movement is of such immense importance. All we actually need under the NEP is to organise the population of Russia in cooperative societies of a sufficiently large scale, for we have now found the degree of coordination of private interest, of private commercial interest, with state supervision and control of this interest, that degree of its subordination to the common interests which was formerly the stumbling block for very many socialists.

(Lenin 1923a: 1797)

Additional quotes in support of this approach include: 1) the passage running 'we went too far when we reintroduced the NEP, but not because we attached too much importance to the principal of free enterprise and trade – we went too far because we lost sight of the cooperatives' (Lenin 1923a: 1798); and 2) the passage where Lenin, speaking of cooperation, underscored the need to make its socialist meaning clear to all (1923a: 1798). Why did Lenin endorse free enterprise and trade, if not to suggest that industrialists and tradesmen were to be empowered to retain at least a portion of the earnings from their enterprises? And what socialist function is cooperation expected to perform if not entitling workers to run their firms in place of capitalists?

For a final and conclusive answer to these questions, we may refer to an article dating as far back as 1917 (see above), where Lenin spelt out in bold letters that 'the initiative of workers and other employees must be drawn on ... a certain proportion of the profits must be assigned to them' (Lenin 1917e: 810).

9 The rationale behind Marxist criticisms of cooperation

The question to be answered at this point is why cooperation, though endorsed by Marx and Engels, is usually thought to be unsuited to securing the transition to communism.

Marx's scant concern with cooperation in the period after the collapse of the Paris Commune is certainly one reason, and the long string of failures experienced by the cooperative movement from the mid-seventies onward doubtless played a non-negligible role (see Bernstein 1899: 149–152). As is well known, Marxism has traditionally been viewed as a form of 'scientific socialism' – a theory that does not 'preach' the advent of communism, but 'predicts' it as an unavoidable event.[25] Producer cooperatives that fail to head towards a major performance are not effective tools for furthering the advent of communism. 'The cooperative form', Kautsky wrote, 'can only be implemented sporadically and imperfectly and will never become the prevailing form' (Kautsky 1892: 109).

This idea was shared by a well-known Italian Marxist in the early twentieth century. With reference to the 1860s and 1870s, Enrico Leone remarked that the pressure of lasting defeat and a critical review of the past induced Marx to reconsider his view of the transition period and to drop his advocacy of cooperatives at least temporarily. He stopped thinking of cooperatives as tangible proof that profit-oriented businesses could be changed into firms working towards the advancement of society and re-emphasised the side-effect of changing workers into 'their own capitalists' (see Leone 1902: 287). Hence, it is possible, though not certain, that Marx lost faith in cooperation.

The assumption that Marxists moved away from cooperation after the conversion of Kautsky and Lassalle to statism is somewhat more convincing. From then on, Marxists began to equate socialism with nationalised means of production and, following the Bolshevik Revolution, they systematically relied on state-owned firms, rather than cooperatives (see, among many others, Preobrazhensky 1926: 17, 218ff. and 238ff.).

While it is true that loss of faith in cooperation is likely to have played a major role in determining the turn to statism, a passage from the *Manifesto of the Communist Party* (513) would suggest that the decisive factors were theoretical criticism levelled by Marxists against cooperation:

> We may cite Proudhon's *Philosophie de la Misére* as an example of this form. The Socialistic bourgeois want all the advantages of modern social conditions without the struggle and dangers necessarily resulting therefrom. They desire the existing state of society, minus its revolutionary and disintegrating elements. They wish for a bourgeoisie without a proletariat. The bourgeoisie naturally conceives the world in which it is supreme to be the best; and bourgeois Socialism develops this comfortable conception into various more or less complete systems.

This excerpt would seem to suggest that Marx and Engels thought of a system of producer cooperatives as a form of 'conservative or bourgeois socialism'. However, before deciding if this is true, it is worth asking ourselves if the system concerned is one where the bourgeoisie can exist without the proletariat or the proletariat without the bourgeoisie and whether the criticisms in the above-quoted excerpt are really aimed against producer cooperatives. And in as much as a bourgeois society is a social order characterised by capitalist relations of production –

i.e. an order where the owners of production means are the ruling class, which keeps workers in subjection and represents 'the world ruled by it' as a world destined to last forever – both these questions have to be answered in the negative.[26]

Nonetheless, Webb, Rodbertus and Bernstein flatly denied the socialist essence of cooperation and defined it as nothing but an intermediate form between capitalism and socialism (see Bernstein 1899: 154–155).

An additional explanation for the scant attention given to the aforequoted Marxian excerpts is probably the late emergence of an economic theory of cooperatives. As the first theoretical study of producer cooperatives was published by Ward as late as 1958, it is possible to assume that existing cooperatives failed to head towards major success, because they were not run in accordance with effective economic principles (see Vanek 1971a, 1971b).

Discussing the distinction between WMF and LMF cooperatives, Vanek (1971b: 187) provided the following explanation of his claim that WMFs are doomed to fail by their very nature:

> In my opinion,... the arguments presented hereafter are so powerful in explaining the shortcomings of traditional or conventional forms of producer cooperatives and participatory firms that they offer an ample explanation of the comparative failures of these forms in history ever since they were first conceived of by the writers of the eighteenth and nineteenth centuries. The development of this analysis was to me personally most gratifying. It had always puzzled me how it could have been possible that a productive organization based on cooperation, harmony of interests and the brotherhood of men, so appealing and desirable on moral and philosophical grounds, could have done so poorly when subjected to a practical test. It seems to be that we now have both an explanation and a way of remedy.

Ideological reasons are likely to have played a major role in diverting interest away from cooperation and deferring its theoretical study in time.

Defining cooperatives in his own (and Marx's) time in a 1865 study and discussing the distinction made by economists between the main sources of wealth, land, capital and labour, Walras argued that individuals tend to accumulate ever greater quantities of all three types of wealth, until, in due course, they gradually become owners of land, capital and labour. Carrying this point to extremes, Walras went so far as to describe economic progress as the road towards a fuller access of individuals to all categories of wealth and, in particular, of workers to the ownership of capital (Walras 1865: 14).

Accordingly, he mentioned two main characteristics of cooperatives:

1. in terms of scope, a tendency towards creating venture capital which is indivisible because owned by all the members; and
2. in terms of the source of their resources, the fact that this venture capital is formed of wage deductions.

(Walras 1865: 5–6)

He concluded that, in essence, cooperation was a tool to enable workers to acquire capital through saving (see Walras 1865: 7).

Walras's approach suggests an additional reason why Marxists have seldom concerned themselves with cooperation. His valuable analysis of cooperation in his own and Marx's time may both explain why Marx described cooperatives as firms where workers were 'their own capitalists' and why later Marxists, arguing with Korsch that cooperatives would breed a system defined as 'producer capitalism', did not deem it worthwhile to work towards the establishment of another form of capitalism.

This conclusion provides an opportunity to stress how the insights provided by economic producer cooperative theory may help disprove the criticisms of Marxists. As mentioned in the introduction, following the publication of Ward's 1958 article, economists drew a distinction between two types of cooperatives, WMFs and LMFs, and made it clear that LMFs, unlike WMFs, self-finance their investments and segregate labour incomes from capital incomes. For the purposes of this book, this distinction is decisive. If we describe the LMF as the 'ideal type' of producer cooperative, we are also in a position to show that cooperatives are truly socialist firms – the subject of our next few chapters.

But there is more to this. As mentioned before, whereas Lenin's view of the post-revolutionary social order reflects his belief that socialism and communism were to be kept apart, central planning can be upheld only by those who look upon socialism and communism as equivalent systems.

The clearest analysis of the differences between socialism and communism is owed to Durkheim. Ever since Plato, Durkheim wrote, communism has been an ideal that countless philosophers have upheld, in order to come to terms with the timeless issue that private property generates egoism. A quote from *Socialism and Saint-Simon* (1928: 27) runs: 'the fundamental communist idea – everywhere the same under scarcely different forms – is that private property is the source of selfishness and that from selfishness springs immorality'. Over the span of history, communistic systems have been theorised whenever a philosopher found that the times were ripe to receive his message. In the intervals between one and the subsequent theorisation, the communistic ideal remains dormant, but even in periods when it is brought to the forefront of attention, it is too speculative to exert much influence. The fact is that egotism is so deeply rooted in human nature that it simply cannot be eradicated at the exhortation of a philosopher. As a result, any call for communism and the associated regeneration of the world has at best the effect of an impressive sermon preaching the Word. Unlike communism, socialism is a realistic call for a new social order that arises in connection with certain social trends underway in a given period of time. It is not designed to cure the world from a timeless disease such as immorality, but to deal with situations of utter social distress that must not be tolerated or declared to be beyond remedy. Communism is to socialism as the sacred is to the profane.

Nevertheless, communism and socialism do have much in common: both of them prioritise society over the individual at least to some extent, caution against the risks for society stemming from the private profit motive (or economic particularism) and lay much emphasis on the fact that self-love is no guarantee for a just social order. On closer analysis, however, they are designed to fight different forms of particularism: a communist condemns private property as anti-social and rejects it altogether; from the perspective of a socialist, risks stem from 'the individual appropriation of large economic enterprises which are established at a specific moment in history' (Durkheim 1928: 39). In other words, whereas communism preaches the suppression of economic interest, socialism suggests eradicating the dominion of one class over the other through the socialisation of capital.

On closer analysis, therefore, communism and socialism are not different forms of one and the same doctrine, and they should not be looked upon as two facets of the same coin. To emphasise their concordant opposition to excessive individualism while understating the radical differences that keep them apart would be misleading. This is why a review of the origins of communism is of little help in tracing and explaining the history of socialism and why communism should be analysed separately from socialism. Whereas the beginnings of communism go as far back as the time of Plato, socialism is a reaction away from capitalism. In the opinion of Durkheim (see 1928: 41), the rise of large-scale industry was a necessary assumption for the birth of socialism, because 'it was necessary, on the one hand, that economic activities assume more social importance and, on the other, that social activities assume a more human character'.

As mentioned above, it was his awareness of the differences between socialism and communism that induced Lenin to suggest implementing socialism by establishing a system of cooperatives – i.e. a system where the private profit motive would not be demonised. Turning to Stalin, centralised planning and Marxism in the twentieth century, it is a plain fact that he opted for centralised planning and disregarded the communism-socialism distinction. And while it is true that Stalin took no single step in the direction of true communism and virtually consigned communism to the dustbin of history, in the minds of the people a centrally planned system came to be looked upon as communism proper. This is why twentieth-century Marxists took exception to the appeal to self-interest inherent in socialism and Lenin's idea of socialism as cooperation fell into oblivion.

10 Conclusion

In this chapter, I have argued that Marx and Lenin strongly endorsed the creation of a system of cooperative firms and have backed up this claim with quotes that speak for themselves. As far as Lenin's 1923 article is concerned, I have argued that it marked a significant turning point in the evolution of his thought. The experience of wartime communism had taught Lenin that Soviets could not be reconciled with central planning and this newly-gained insight had induced him to defer the implementation of his one-time plan to replace monopoly capitalism with a centrally planned economy. The Soviets discussed in his 1923 article are bodies that carry on business in a market economy and, consequently, are the exact counterpart of the producer cooperatives studied by modern economic theorists.

Concluding, Lenin's neglected 'testament to posterity' suggests that socialism can be implemented by creating a system of self-managed firms that operate in markets under the guidance of the Communist Party. The fact that Lenin's article uses insight from the post-revolution period adds to its importance, in that it shows that Lenin's idea of socialism was 'shaped by the struggle for socialism and can be further developed by reference to this struggle' (Lukàcs 1924: 91). As mentioned above, these ideas were rated as inacceptable and were put aside after the rise of Stalin to power. At that point, socialism came to be identified with the centrally planned economic system whose changing fortunes span the whole of the twentieth century up to the present.

Notes

1 In this connection, we may cite the maxim that the Italian philosopher Francesco Guicciardini enunciated in his *Ricordi* (1512–1530), namely 'futuris contingentibus non est determinata veritas'.
2 The *Inaugural Address* of 1864 has been described as the rough draft of a political economy of labour (see Balibar 1993). From Lichtheim (1965: 114–159), we learn that Marx defined a nationwide system of producer cooperatives created with state aide as basically socialist in nature, despite the absence of such an essential component as the socialisation of means of production (a goal whose inclusion in the programme of the international would have been strongly opposed by the bulk of French delegates).
3 In Marx's approach, in addition to challenging the capitalistic social order, workers perform a positive role: they work towards self-organising themselves in manners recalling those suggested in Flora Tristan's *L'Union Ouvrière* – a book that is mentioned by Engels in *The Holy Family* (1845: 21–31) and which Marx himself had certainly read (see Massari 1974: 82–83).
4 Several Marxist authors are agreed that this new mode of production will be a direct offshoot of capitalism. Among them, Offe points to a structural mismatch within capitalist society between new sub-systems and structural elements, which are functionally at odds with the logic of capital valorisation (see Offe 1972a: ch. 3).
5 Strada's comment (1980: 125) is also interesting in this connection: 'Lenin often strikes us as being an experimenter who does not adopt a rigid plan, but proceeds by subsequent adjustments'.
6 It is neither mentioned in Lukàcs' *Lenin* (1924) or Meyer's *Leninism* (1957), nor in Tonini's *Cosa ha detto veramente Lenin* (1967), Deutscher's *Lenin* (1970) or the collection of Lenin's articles about the construction of socialism published in Italy in 1972 and the history of Marxian economics by Howard and King (1989).
7 'Egoism is too essential to human nature to be uprooted from it – as desirable as that might be', Durkheim wrote,

> [w]hen, therefore, one inquires under what circumstances it could be extirpated, one cannot but be aware that he places himself outside reality, and that he can produce only an idyll whose poetry can be pleasing to the imagination, but which cannot pretend to be in the realm of fact.

(1928: 38–39)

8 It is evident that Lenin was not concerned with the ownership of means of production, but with social relations of production. And this is why he looked upon the cooperative regime as 'the socialist regime'.

9 As is well known, Lenin described the NEP as 'State capitalism' and held it to be superior to war communism (see Lenin 1921a, 1921c: 200–201, 1922b, 1922d: 1745–1746). It is also for this reason that cooperation is superior to the NEP and amounts to socialism.

10 Accordingly, Hegedüs is wrong when he claims (1980: 538–539) that in Lenin's theoretical approach cooperatives 'carry a lesser weight, in terms of their contribution to the implementation of the values of socialism, than state-owned firms'.

11 In *Antidühring* (1882: 281), Engels described cooperatives as 'transition measures to the complete communistic organisation of society'.

12 Stalin (1940: 10) described Leninism as 'Marxism of the era of imperialism', but this definition refers to the time when Lenin thought that socialism would be a natural outgrowth of monopoly capitalism and imperialism, not the time during which he wrote his 1923 article.

13 Lenin's opinion on Bucharin is well known:

> Bukharin is not only the greatest and most valuable theoretician in the party; he is also rightly considered the favourite of the whole Party, but his theoretical views can be classified as fully Marxist only with great reserve, for there is something scholastic about him.
>
> (Lenin 1922c: 1775)

14 The fact that Bucharin shared this idea emerges from an article dated 15 January 1925 (Bucharin 1925a: 116), where he wrote that the aim to be pursued by any means was to create a worker-peasant bloc and ensure proletarian hegemony within the bloc. Actually, this idea had been first expressed by Lenin even before 1923 – for example, when he wrote: 'the main thing now is to advance as an immeasurably wider and larger mass, and only together with the peasantry' (Lenin 1922a: 1742; see also, Lenin 1921b: 318–320, 1921c: 197–199).

15 See Lenin (1957–1970, vol. XXV: 14).

16 On the subject of a unifying thread in Lenin's thought, see also, Chitarin (1973: 16–17).

17 Pannekoek took exception to Lenin's idea of a party that would prove able to take the lead in a revolution. Specifically, *with respect to the working classes in the countries of developed capitalism*, in Western Europe, 'matters were entirely different since they were expected to become masters of production and, hence, to regulate labour, the basis of their lives, themselves'. However, he also added that 'such an aim cannot be attained by an ignorant mass, confident followers of a party presenting itself as an expert leadership'. *With respect to the working class in Russia in 1917*, he owned that 'Russian revolution could be victorious only because a well-disciplined, united Bolshevik party led the masses, and because in the party the clear insight and the unyielding assurance of Lenin and his friends showed the way' (Pannekoek 1938: 128–129).

18 Full worker control over capitalistic factories is the situation where the factory is still the property of capitalists, but where workers are empowered to make a full, exact and comprehensive census of the commodities produced and the way the relevant profits are distributed (see Lenin 1957–1970, vol. XXI or vol. XXVI: 91).

19 In October 1917, Lenin wrote: 'when the State will be a proletarian state, when it will be an instrument of violence exercised by the proletariat against the bourgeoisie, we shall be fully and unreservedly in favour of a strong state power and of centralism' (Lenin 1917d: 254). Actually, this phrase induces us to think that he had changed his mind and that some time before he used to think differently.

20 A quote from Lewin (1969: 18) runs: 'Factory committees, workers' councils, worker control, genuine bodies which had spontaneously arisen from the revolutionary thrust sparked off by the seizure of power ... generated nothing but chaos which threatened to bring the country's production apparatus to a standstill'.

21   The Bolsheviks were facing a real dilemma: if, in line with their political plat-
form, they reduced their control on soviets in order to favour the growing
involvement of the masses in administrative and governmental processes, there
was the risk that these might come under the influence of the opposition.

(Anweiler 1958: 451)

All the same, the violent repression of the Kronstradt revolt at the orders of Lenin and
the Bolsheviks can barely be justified. Its instigators, who were stout supporters of the
council system, proclaimed that the Soviets, not the Constituent Assembly, were the
bulwark of workers (see Anweiler 1958: 466). In an article published in the *Isvestija*
during March 1921 (quoted in Anweiler 1958: 467), we read:

> Through the October revolution, the working class hoped to acquire its freedom.
> The result was a condition of even greater serfdom of human personality. Power
> has been transferred from the police officers in the service of the monarchy to the
> hands of usurpers – communists – and the result is that instead of obtaining their
> freedom workers are now terrorised by the Ceca.... Its better to die than live
> under this communistic dictatorship.... Kronstadt is the trumpet call for the third
> revolution, which will help workers shed the newly-imposed chains and clear the
> way for the construction of socialism.

In this connection, Anweiler commented (1958: 468) that the anti-Bolshevik nature of
this revolt 'was, at the same time, clear evidence of the cleavage between Bolshevik
dictatorship and the ideal origins of council power'.

22 This approach is also recommended by Nove (1980: 625–626) and, in part, by Martinet, who finds in Lenin's later writings, and especially his 'famous article on cooperation', 'major interesting suggestions and an overall attitude which calls for respect'.
In this article, Lenin describes cooperation, which he previously despised as a typical
component of bourgeois culture, as 'a precious tool for the advancement of socialism
and the only tool that may help convert peasants to socialism and, more generally,
induce the masses to participate in the management of the economy' (Botta and Martinet 1976: 31).

23 Bucharin held Lenin's 'political testament' to be contained in his last five articles,
entitled *Pages from a Diary, On Cooperation, Our Revolution, How We Should Reor-
ganise the Workers' and Peasants' Inspection* and *Better Less, but Better* (Cohen
1973: 139). All these writings show that the older Lenin still rated socialism and communism as different forms of social organisation, but had come to equate socialism
with democratic firm management. When Lenin expressed the wish to 'build communism with the hands of non-Communists', Bucharin made it clear that the non-
communistic hands – for instance, cooperation – mentioned by Lenin were socialist,
not capitalist, hands (see Cohen 1973: 140–141).

24 This approach is also recommended by Nove (1980: 625–626) and, in part, by Martinet, who finds in Lenin's later writings, and especially his 'famous article on cooperation', 'major interesting suggestions and an overall attitude which calls for respect'
(see Botta and Martinet 1976: 31).

25 In Tucker (1961), Kautsky's remark that theorists of scientific socialism rated class
struggle, the victory of the proletariat and the advent of socialism as ineluctable developments (Kautsky 1907: 202) is denied at least for the period after the publication of
the *Economic-Philosophical Manuscripts* in Russian (1927) and German (1932).
Nonetheless, the interpretation of Marxism as a worldview that sees socialism as
unavoidable is still widely accepted.

26 In an interesting book, Screpanti has recently emphasised that 'the basic institution of
capitalism is the contract of employment' (see Screpanti 2001: 258). If this holds true,
a system of producer cooperatives has nothing to do with capitalism (see also, Screpanti 2002).

2 Is Marxism compatible with modern economic theory?

1 Introduction

My claim that a system of producer cooperatives may give rise to a new post-capitalistic mode of production poses the need to establish how this system would work and whether or not it may offer a comparative edge over capitalism. For this purpose, we can refer to a large body of literature that appeared after the publication of the seminal contributions of Ward, Vanek and Meade mentioned in the introduction. As these writings fit within 'orthodox' economic theory, the reader may ask himself if it is admissible to make reference to them in an analysis of socialism and Marxism. In my estimation, this preliminary question can be answered in the affirmative, since Marxism and orthodox economics, though antithetical in many respects, are doubtless scientific theories and, as such, are reconcilable (as I will be discussing at length in this chapter).

In point of fact, this view is far from generally shared. In Pasinetti's words (1984: 15):

> Yet Marx's overall arguments were not easy to challenge. The obvious procedure would have been to question the premises. But this is precisely what was difficult. Marx's premises were exactly the same as those of Smith and Ricardo, *i.e.* of established economics. If only one could find an economic theory that made no reference to labour, no reference to means of production, possibly even to production itself ... that would surely be the sort of thing that a frightened Establishment could not but most warmly welcome. Marginal utility theory provided precisely that.[1]

Hobsbawm (1982: 38–39) has argued that ever since the 1950s, the line separating what is Marxist from what is not has been progressively blurred[2] as a result of the tendency of left-leaning intellectuals to include Marxism in mainstream educational syllabuses and instigate lively academic debate (see also Kliman 2010: 66; Rodinson 1969: 9).[3]

In the wake of Althusser, some scholars have highlighted an epistemological break between an anthropological phase and a scientific phase – i.e. the years when Marx wrote the *Economic-Philosophical Manuscripts of 1844* and his mature years when he worked on his labour theory of value, historical material-ism and the notion of modes of production. And while I reject such a clear-cut distinction, I do endorse Althusser's warning that to downgrade dialectical method to a reversed Hegelian approach would be a gross mistake. In fact, the use of Hegelian dialectic is the reason why many orthodox political economists deny the scientific standing of Marxism. The non-Marxist scholar Bronfenbren-ner (1967: 115) defined Marx as 'the greatest social scientist of all time', but Marx's status as a scientist is far from universally recognised.

In short, I agree with Schumpeter (1954: 9) and other economists (see, for instance, Leontief 1937: 84) that despite the strong Hegelian imprint in all of Marx's works (see, for example, Tucker 1961; Berlin 1963), the description of Hegelism as the keystone of Marxism would amount to debasing its scientific standing, and this can only mean that the fundamentals of a Marxist approach can be correctly understood and apprehended without regard to Hegel's dialectic.

Korsch's view of the role of dialectics in Marx departs from both Althusser's and Schumpeter's. As pointed out by Rusconi (1968: 109–110) and Colletti (1979: 48–49), in *Marxism and Philopsophy* Korsch identified three distinct stages of development within Marxism. The earliest of these, he argued, stretched from about 1843 to the publication of *The Manifesto* and was the period when Marx acted as a dialectical thinker advocating immediate revolution and emphasising the importance of revolutionary subjectivity. The second – i.e. the period after the abortive Paris revolution of 1848 and the dissolution of workers' organisations – was characterised by signs of regression, which are clearly recognised in *Capital* and persisted right to the end of the century. Those years, Korsch argued (1931: 134), were marked by 'a separation of theory from praxis' in Marx's thought, by a primary concern with economics rather than philosophy and by a gradual progression from dialectics to a scientific approach; deterministic elements became ever more prominent, and revolution was described as necessitated by objective laws. The third phase marked a return to philosophy and dialectics – a move that Korsch endorsed. Korsch described socialism as scientific when, purged of the typical limitations of bourgeois science and idealism, it heads towards a dialectically materialist worldview (Korsch 1923: 6).

Korsch's line of reasoning can be set against Benedetto Croce's still widely shared argument that science is inextricably bound up with positivism and con-sequently shares its limitations. However, it should also be viewed against the background of the argument (Przeworsky 1995: 168; 1998) that only an obscur-antist can postulate the existence of a distinctly Marxist philosophy of science, allegedly relieving Marxists from the obligation to adopt the criteria governing the evaluation of other theories.

Concerning the orthodox scientific method, I share Veblen's view that it is highly restrictive and wish to emphasise that orthodox economists would have much to gain from a stronger focus on sociological, philosophical and non-falsifiable notions, as well as other elements of Marx's method.

This poses the need to offer a correct interpretation of Marx's method – a need that has become ever more pressing since Lukàcs proclaimed that the novelty of Marxism lay exclusively in its method (see Lukàcs 1923: 1–2; Engels 1859; for a dissenting view, see, for instance, Carver 1984; Liss 1984: 16; Farr 1984: 217).

In the words of Danilo Zolo (1977a), a major epistemological error in which the socialist theoretical tradition remained caught up for some fifty years is now a thing of the past. This mistake – Zolo clarifies – was the tendency to find fault with received analytical procedures and even formal logic, to reject the method of the 'bourgeois sciences' in favour of an anti-bourgeois 'materialistic' and 'historical-dialectical' conception of society and nature, to equate neo-positivism with political conservatism and to claim that the only correct interpretative approach to bourgeois society was a dialectical procedure shaped by the principles of Marxism and the workers' movement (see Zolo 1977a: 4).

To refute the objections of mainstream economists towards the idea that Marxism is a science, we have to demonstrate that its method is not incompatible with traditional scientific methodology. The issue of dialectics becomes crucial in this connection. The power of scientific socialism to dismantle the limits of bourgeois science and create assumptions regarding a dialectic-materialistic worldview has already been mentioned. Hence, it is time to ask ourselves if the use of dialectics is actually what distinguishes Marxism from orthodox science and what exactly is meant by it. The central role of dialectics in Marx's thought and in Marxism can hardly be denied. Concerning its exact meaning, Marx wrote:

> if ever the time comes when such work is again possible, I should very much like to write two or three sheets making accessible to the common reader the rational aspect of the method which Hegel not only discovered but also mystified.
>
> (Marx 1858: 249)

Unfortunately, he never translated this plan into practice, and this may explain why his dialectical method is still being interpreted in a variety of different ways (see Bhaskar 1991; Reuten 2009: 28).

In part, these diverging interpretations of Marx's notion of dialectics can be traced to different views concerning his theory of knowledge. Some see Marx as a rationalist, believing that reality must be apprehended through the exercise of reason, without regard to sensorial perception. Others characterise him as an empiricist, thinking of cognition as the result of sensorial observation and requiring the use of the inductive method of natural science. Others still think of Marx as a pragmatist, believing that ideas and concepts are nothing but aids to knowledge and that cognition requires the backing of experimental evidence (see Easton 1970: 402).

H.G. Backhaus, one of the main instigators of the Mega 2 edition of Marx's works, holds that Marx's theoretical approach can be interpreted in two different ways: as a theory concerned with analysing the contradictions affecting a mode of production and as a method for the diachronic analysis of the developments of an economic system. In his opinion, Marx was not fully aware of this distinction, and this may explain why the dialectical approach is no longer prominent in Marx's later works (see Backhaus 1997; Fineschi 2008: 24–28). As I will be arguing in the next section, in our estimation, dialectics should rather be described as a logic-historical method.

2 Dialectics as the analysis of a totality with real oppositions

In Marxian theory, production, distribution, exchange and consumption are perceived as links of a single chain – i.e. the different facets of one unit. Commenting on this point in a youthful work on historical evolution, Lukàcs wrote that Marx, much like the German philosophers and chiefly Hegel, conceived of world history as a homogeneous revolutionary process consistently geared towards the attainment of freedom. The very core of Marx's conception of history, he argued (Lukàcs 1968a: 34), is the supremacy of totality – i.e. the pre-eminence of the whole over its artificially detached parts. In this connection, Rovatti (1973: 125) points out that ever since Lukàcs published *History and Class Consciousness*, commentators have concordantly endorsed the view that the true aim of Marx's critical approach was to proceed from a fragmented view of the structure of capitalism to an approach highlighting a *totality* conceived of as consistently moving forward in a single direction.

Let us repeat that Lukàcs was one of the first to highlight the totality-focused perspective of Marx's dialectical method. He wrote (see Lukàcs 1923: 35–36): 'it is not the primacy of economic motives in historical explanation that constitutes the decisive difference between Marxism and bourgeois thought, but the point of view of totality'. Here Rusconi (1968: 49) specifies that Lukàcs rated the 'totality perspective' not only as a speculative aid, but as a real and proper 'critical method for the interpretation of society' and 'a criterion used to make history intelligible'. Negt (1979a: 350) endorses Lukàcs's view that the totality notion is the key element distinguishing the Marxist from the bourgeois worldview (see also, Balibar 1993: 98). According to Lukàcs, however, the totality perspective is closely bound up with Hegelian dialectic.

In view of the declared purpose of this book, I wish to emphasise that dialectics may be practised in accordance with a non-Hegelian method that even the most orthodox thinkers would probably rate as acceptable. In particular, a form of dialectical thinking that mainstream thinkers may accept is the method of the 'interpenetration of opposites', which is concerned with 'reconciling contradictions' (see Sowell 1985: 28–35) or highlighting a sudden change or reversal of circumstances, which until then had been perceived as fixed and given (Luporini 1966: 155; 1974: ix).[4]

Using the phrase 'unity of differences' to describe mutual relationships, in *Capital* Marx argues (see Marx 1867: 199) that 'the independence of the individuals from each other has as its counterpart and supplement a system of all-round material dependence' (1867: 202–203). Lenin, who looked upon dialectics as the most intriguing of all philosophical issues (see Meyer 1957: 19), defined it as 'a tool capable of disclosing links between one thing and all the others' (1957: 21).

A dialectical analysis of 'interpenetrating opposites', which explains that capital (viewed as a social relation) requires of necessity hired labour and that hired labour can only exist in the presence of capital, far from necessitates abandoning the non-contradiction principle – and this is precisely the crucial point.

Viewed as the analysis of 'interpenetrating opposites', as 'a theory of how to discover interconnections in nature and society' (Hodges 1967: 118), dialectics helps expand 'our notion of anything to include, as aspects of what it is, both the process by which it has become that and the broader interactive context in which it is found' (Ollman 2003: 13), as well as the awareness that in any dialectical interactions, whether mutual or between unequal poles, the 'dominant determination runs from one pole to the other'. Indeed, without this, 'the dialectic characterizes the mutual conditioning of the poles, their relational consistency, but does not reveal a dynamic movement in the system that they constitute' (Laibman 2007: 4). On closer analysis, this is tantamount to arguing that the dialectical method reveals a close-meshed network of links and interactions in a context where everything, far from being fixed or unchanged in space or time, is perpetually in motion and subject to change, birth and death and where the typical contradictions and conflicts of society take centre-stage (see, for example, Labriola 1902: 22; Bronfenbrenner 1967: 118; Gallino 1987: 219–220; Volpi 1989: 29; Sherman 1995: ch. 1) with the double warning that: (1) this interpretation is only acceptable if we think of real, not merely logical contradictions (as clarified in Colletti 1974, 1980); and that (2) only contradictions that 'express the true essence of movement' can appropriately be described as dialectical (Lukàcs 1956: 92).

The idea that dialectics cannot do without a totality assumed to be moving on without pause is both correct and widely shared. Hegel (the leading authority in this field) once wrote that non-systematic thought cannot qualify as scientific and that any content is only justified when viewed as part of a whole (Hegel 1830: paragraph 14). As pointed out by Lefebvre (1968: 106), in Hegel the 'identity of reality and the rational is neither accomplished over or done with, nor ideal, indeterminate and yet to be; he intercepts history at the point where it brings about this union' (an acknowledgement of the dialectical unity and the solution of contradictions).

The main effect of totality-focused dialectics is to magnify the impact of causality on the context, in terms that its individual components will be perceived as different, depending on the totality that they are part of from time to time. The end result is a compound of effects impacting on the elements by which the system is constituted (Karsz 1974: 131).

Althusser, too, was convinced that simultaneous focus on a problem and the surrounding totality was the prerequisite for addressing and solving a problem dialectically (see Karsz 1974: 130), but he claimed that this was only applicable to Marx's method. Hegel's, he argued, was antithetical to the non-contradiction principle and 'completely dependent on the radical presupposition of a simple original unity which develops within itself by virtue of its negativity' and 'only ever restores the original simplicity and unity in an ever more "concrete" totality' throughout its development (Althusser 1965: 175).

The paramount place of totality in Marx's approach has to do with his particular view of history and dynamics, but Althusser specifies that 'the structure of the whole must be conceived before any discussion of temporal sequence' (see Althusser and Balibar 1965: 105).

Schaff (1974: 18) holds that the all-importance of the totality notion in Marxism sheds light on affinities between Marxism and structuralism, since the prime criterion governing any of the cultural movements of the Structuralist family (in the natural, human and/or social sciences) is the need to look upon each research object as an integral whole.

The primacy of the totality perspective in Marx's system is also revealed by close links between the notion of ideology, historical materialism and the concept of modes of production (see, for instance, Bidet 1998: 179).

In conclusion, the idea of dialectics as a totality-centred analysis method goes to support the argument that the differences between the Marxist and orthodox scientific methods are certainly appreciable, but not such as to nullify the scientific essence of Marxism.

Galvano della Volpe, one of the scholars who drew a clear-cut distinction between the dialectical methods used by Marx and Engels, argues that Marx worked out an alternative dialectical method that can be described as 'scientific or analytical', as well as characterised by the so-called 'concrete-abstract-concrete circle'. More precisely, della Volpe thinks of dialectics as a method of analysis capable of displaying a movement from the concrete to the abstract and back again to the concrete – a model that he holds to be compatible with the non-contradiction principle (see della Volpe 1964). For my part, I deny that Marx's method is to start out from the concrete in order to reach the abstract and then to retrace his steps back to the concrete and agree with Gruppi (1962: 159) that the concrete-abstract-concrete model is much more restrictive than the totality-focused approach and might ultimately impoverish, if not altogether nullify, the dialectical approach.

3 More about two different views of dialectics

In 1958, Norberto Bobbio emphasised the distinction between two notions of dialectics. 'Faced with two conflicting entities', he wrote,

> we may either opt for the 'compenetration-of-opposites' (or mutual-interaction) method or for a method founded on the 'negation of the negation'. When the former is adopted, both entities are kept firm and are assumed to mutually condition each other; when the latter is adopted, we assume that the first entity is cancelled by the other at a first stage and the second by the third at a subsequent stage.
>
> (Bobbio 1958: 347)

Concerning these antithetical methods, Badaloni argued (1962: 110) that the former was the method of Marx the mature economist and scientist, while the latter was the method of the younger Marx.

Bobbio's argument is in line with the already mentioned distinction between Hegel's dialectic, which Sichirollo (1973: 149) describes as 'the world as it appears in discourse', rather than a method, and the Marxist dialectical method, which we accept and which does not rule out the non-contradiction principle.

With respect to the diverging interpretations of Marx's dialectic, Luporini (1963a: 352) raised the question whether the phrase '(Marxian) reversal of Hegelian dialectic' was intended to suggest that Marx had reversed Hegel's speculative *system* in order to lay bare the rational core – i.e. the dialectical *method* – or the idea that this reversal was to be accomplished *within* the dialectic itself. Luporini himself correctly declared himself in favour of the former option.

Casting this reflection in different words, let us repeat that there is a clear-cut distinction between Hegel's dialectical approach and the Marxist approach, which I endorse. Indeed, whereas the former, which is no method, emphasises 'the union of opposites' irrespective of the fact that 'this result of speculative thinking is nonsensical to the understanding' (Hegel 1831: 14), the latter is a method that does not negate the validity of the non-contradiction principle. Both Bobbio (1958: 343–346) and Dal Pra (1972: viii–x) are agreed that the latter approach was preferably used by Marx in his mature years.

Although the Marxist thinkers quoted include the Hegelians Lukàcs and Korsch, the core idea behind our reflections so far is that Hegel's totality and contradiction notions are antithetical to the corresponding Marxian notions.

All the same, there is no denying that Marx did occasionally use a Hegelian dialectical method. As pointed out by Hudis (2000), this clearly emerges from his demonstration that capitalism cannot be suppressed by simply abolishing private property. The suppression of capitalism, Marx argued, was just the first negation that required a second – i.e. the negation of the negation – specifically, the negation of capital. The need to distinguish between the *first* negation – negation in general – and the *second* negation – or negation of the negation – was first suggested by Hegel, who described the first as concrete, *absolute* negativity and the second as nothing but *abstract* negativity (see Hegel 1831: 134). In line with this distinction, in *Capital* we read:

> The capitalist mode of appropriation, which springs from the capitalist mode of production, produces capitalist private property. This is the first negation of individual private property, as founded on the labour of its proprietor. But capitalist production begets, with the inexorability of a natural process, its own negation. This is the negation of the negation.
>
> (Marx 1867: 929)

An additional illuminating remark is found in the postscript to the second edition of volume I of *Capital* (1867: 103): 'The mystification which the dialectic suffers in Hegel's hands by no means prevents him from being the first to present its general forms of motion in a comprehensive and conscious manner'.

In contrast with Adorno and Habermas, who hold that the dialectical approaches of Marx and Hegel are both at odds with formal logic (see Habermas 1963: ch. iv), other authors (including Cingoli 2005: 129) have argued that Hegelian dialectics was preferably practised by Engels, rather than Marx.

However, the reflections developed above and the quotations from authors approaching Marx from different angles induce us to re-emphasise that our belief that dialectics is compatible with formal logic is mainly supported, not so much by any critical analysis of Marx's actual writings, as by the idea that the interpretation of Marxism that we accept is compatible with science.

4 Marxism as a scientific approach

Our line of reasoning so far and the quotations I have been utilising aim at backing up our argument that Marxism is a scientific approach in the sense suggested by Galvano della Volpe (in *Logic as a Positive Science*) and Zolo (1977b: 47–48).[5] Accordingly, if the view of analytical Marxists that Marx's method differs in no way from the method of orthodox economics is not acceptable, the idea that the scientific character of Marxism is to be denied on account of its method is even less acceptable. 'Marx's works' – Farr (1984: 217) remarked – 'are clearly shaped by the scientific outlook of the nineteenth century', and this is what Marx himself openly claimed. When a reviewer of *Capital* argued that Marx's work was simply intended to prove, 'in a strictly scientific manner', that certain social relationship patterns lie in the nature of things, Marx wrote (see the postscript to the second edition of his work): 'Whilst the writer pictures what he takes to be actually my method in this striking and [as far as concerns my own application of it] generous way, what else is he picturing but the dialectical method?' (Marx 1867: 102).

On the subject of the methodological issue, it is worth mentioning Paci and Gruppi, two scholars who try to stop the 'dialectics versus science' debate once and for all by arguing, respectively, that Marxism is 'a scientific historical approach *to material history* and, hence, the study of objective contradictions' (Paci 1962: 1869 [emphasis in original]) and that it is simply inadmissible to reduce the historical method of Marxism – a discipline concerned with the scientific analysis of social fact – to the mere method of logic (Gruppi 1962: 196).

The question is: did Marx actually confine his use of dialectics to historical analyses?

While I do not deny that dialectics has a place in the historical analysis of social processes, our research aim in this book is to decide whether it is appropriate to extend its use to scientific analysis proper – i.e. to studies that, though addressing specific facts, are designed to enunciate universally valid laws. Is Paci right – we asked ourselves – when he claims that a scientist – for instance, a political economist – will give no thought to the issue of dialectics when he/she extracts an object of investigation from its context and chooses an abstract scientific approach in dealing with it (Paci 1962: 189)? Answering this question in the negative, let us conclude that the true, strong point of Marx's approach to political economy is his use of (non-Hegelian) dialectics, even in the analysis of the laws of motion in capitalism – i.e. when enunciating universally valid laws. This process of thought leads us to argue, in full agreement with Bensaïd (2002: 204), one major plus point of Marxist economic theory, compared to orthodox science, is exactly the practice to which mainstream economists tend to take exception – i.e. his use of the dialectical method, both in the analysis of historical facts and the enunciation of general theories.

5 The strong and weak points of traditional Marxist theory

In the light of our reflections so far, at this point I will try to pinpoint the plus points and defects of Marxism compared to orthodox economics. As things stand today, the received view that they are antithetical scientific approaches results in loss for either of them: orthodox science has to do without the renewed vigour that would stem from closer links with Marxism; Marxism loses consensus the more it engages in head-on confrontations with orthodox theory. According to Harvey (2010: 240), 'the repression of critical and radical currents of thought or, to be more exact, the coralling of radicalism within the bounds of multiculturalism […] or cultural choices, creates a lamentable situation within the academy'; and Lukàcs argued that the task of a Marxist was to glean useful teachings from the whole of Western literature (1970: 137).

Hence, it is time to ask ourselves what ultimate contrast there is between Marxism and orthodox economic theory today. Let us spell out in bold letters that the originality of Marx's thought does not lie in the labour theory of value (a value theory that Marx took over from Smith and Ricardo), but first and foremost in its analytical method and, second, in theories and notions that Marx proved able to fuse into an organic whole: notions such as modes of production, alienation, class struggle, ideology, historical materialism; processes such as the growing concentration of capital and the way capitalism arose and grew, as well as the contention that the collapse of capitalism will be precipitated by its own internal contradictions.[6] As argued by Isaac Deutscher (1970: 215), Marxism tells us how capitalism works and will come to an end and, first and foremost, offers a convincing explanation of the links binding individuals to their fellow-beings and their own and other classes, as well as their relationships with, and attitudes towards, the technological means in use in their time. As Veblen put it:

> Taken in detail, the constituent elements of the system are neither novel nor iconoclastic, nor does Marx at any point claim to have discovered previously hidden facts or to have invented recondite formulations of facts already known; but the system as a whole has an air of originality and initiative such as is rarely met with along the sciences that deal with any phase of human culture.[7]

(1906: 299)

In the words of Aron (1970: 178), the true essence of Marxism is the theory of the capitalistic mode of production, which in turn is closely associated with historical materialism (for a similar view, see Rodinson 1969: 13–18; Godelier 1982: 332). Whereas before Marx historians used to concern themselves primarily with political events and religious or philosophical ideas, the primary concerns of Marx's approach to political history or the history of ideas were analysing prime causes and the agents behind them, as well as the interrelations between man, nature and a horde of actors grouped into castes, orders and classes.[8]

A key idea of Marxism already mentioned above is the notion of modes of production. Marx described a mode of production as a social organisation in which one prevailing production model intended as a compound of productive forces and relations of production confers significance on the system as a whole (see Luporini 1966: 170).

Our belief that nothing stands in the way of reconciling Marxism with orthodox economics leads us to argue that the transfer of historical materialism, modes of production, alienation or other Marxist key notions to mainstream economics would far from invalidate the basic core of this scientific discipline. The true reason why mainstream economists still perceive Marxism as antithetical to their discipline is that they refuse to acknowledge the relevance of the notion of modes of production. In contrast with their belief that the main determinant of human economic behaviour within all age groups is the minimum cost principle, Marx, like Polanyi after him, held that this purely economic principle could only explain economic behaviour in capitalistic systems and that dissent over this specific point resulted in two different definitions of the essence of political economy (Cangiani 2011). In my view, this contrast might also be satisfactorily resolved provided neoclassical economists resolve to acknowledge the validity of the notion of modes of production, confine the applicability of their theoretical approach to capitalism and thereby take a decisive step towards ending this conflict without renouncing the fundamentals of their scientific discipline.

Our line of reasoning justifies the claim that the correct economic definition of revolution is 'a change in the production mode' and that the description of Marx's approach to economic revolution is far from 'course or abstract' (Burke 1981: 86) or 'perplexing, to say the least' (Basso 2008: 160). Nonetheless, the received view is that revolution entails of necessity a sudden cataclysm (Kirman 1991: 476), a *violent* change in current circumstances or, in short, a radical non-evolutionary change (see Settembrini 1973: 6; Geary 1974: 92–93; Burke 1981: 85–86).

The idea of revolution as the advent of a different mode of production is so crucial to Marx's thought as to suggest the argument that the potential for giving rise to a new mode of production is the only criterion of validity against which the Marxist essence of a theory should be tested. Today, Ragionieri argues (1965: 36), 'it is generally assumed that the core idea behind Marxism is the insight that the capitalistic economy is historically determined and has self-bred an antagonistic power battling for the establishment of socialism'. And this is exactly the core issue I am discussing in this chapter: no one holding that capitalism is bound to last forever will ever become a good Marxist (see, for example, Luxemburg 1908).

In the estimation of Abendroth (1958: 77), Marx and Engels consistently strove to come to terms with the problem that the actions of man in society, though autonomously devised, tend to evolve in directions other than those that had been – and could be – anticipated and end up shaping the subsequent behaviour of mankind. As a result, Abendroth holds that the aim of making men masters of their history will not be achieved unless and until this situation is reversed. Interestingly, his conclusion that this 'core issue of Marxist thought' makes Marxism 'as topical as ever' (1958: 78–79) is fully in line with my idea that Marxism as a theory of revolution has lost none of its topicality.

This subject is discussed by Abendroth in a well-known 1967 book whose main working hypothesis can be summed up as follows. In the Stalinist and fascist epochs, the fairly moderate post-WWI revolutionary wave of the 1920s was halted by a counter-revolutionary movement, which precipitated the defeat of Marxism conceived of as a mass phenomenon. Finding themselves thrown 'off-stage', Western Marxist intellectuals reacted to this change in circumstances by giving themselves up to rhetorical exercise and abstaining from practical action – a clear sign that they no longer anticipated the materialisation of socialism (see Anderson 1976: 35ff.). Let me add that during this process, Western Marxism gradually acquired the connotations of a philosophical, rather than economic, movement (see Blackledge 2004: 60). Around 1980, Anderson's faith in the final advent of socialism was also badly shaken. In the minds of numerous authors, the retreat into mere philosophising produced a dual impact on the American left: first, it resulted in the adoption of specialist theoretical jargon, which proved impenetrable to non-academics; second, it produced a horde of speculative analyses, which were little related to the crucial social and political events of the time (see Jacoby 1987: 158; Blackledge 2004: 147). It is worth repeating that no theoretical approach can qualify as Marxist if it rejects the idea of revolution and is not inspired by the wish to change the world.

As Meyer appropriately puts it (Meyer 1994: 317), the vitality of Marxist thought rests on the prospect of social change. Consequently, if the twenty-first century proves to be a period of steady social stability, it is probable that Marxism in all its forms will be perceived as irrelevant and will die out. In contrast, where no stability is achieved, social thought will necessarily be influenced by Marxist ideas or any other ideas perceived as further developments of Marxism.

6 Marxism as science: a critique of Lucio Colletti's approach

The reflections that I have been developing so far may help us reverse Colletti's argument that Marxism is no science.

Colletti starts out from the idea that Marx's method of analysis is Hegelian dialectic, which he holds to be in stark conflict with the non-contradiction principle – the true founding stone of scientific investigation. Conversely, I have provided evidence that dialectics can be interpreted in manners that do not conflict with science. This does not mean that Colletti thinks of Marxism as a philosophical, rather than scientific, discipline. As he himself concedes,

> no scientific branch, whether economics, philosophy, history, jurisprudence or government theory, is in a position to accommodate Marxism within itself, though none of them would be safe from its incursions where it should resolve to place it within a different branch.

> (Colletti 1979: 48)

Colletti's argument that Marxism cannot do without Hegelian dialectic is mainly based on his belief that the true core element of Marx's approach – i.e. alienation theory – necessitates the acceptance of dialectics in its Hegelian form (see Lissa 1982: 254). In support of this contention, he writes: 'Indeed, the cause of alienation is the fragmentation of what was once united, i.e. the rupture of, or split in, an original whole' (Colletti 1979: 47). On closer analysis, though, what Marx described as alienated is work that is undertaken under pressure of external compulsion, rather than for purposes of self-realisation – and this notion of alienation is not necessarily related to dialectics.

From my perspective, Colletti's argument that Marxism is no science because of an excessive use of value judgments is equally unacceptable for two reasons: first, the critical-normative viewpoint is doubtless compatible with a strictly scientific approach; second, this idea was effectively criticised by Hilferding (quoted by Colletti himself) years ago. In particular, refuting the received view that 'politics is a normative doctrine ultimately determined by value judgments' and 'since such value judgments do not belong within the sphere of science, the discussion of politics falls outside the limits of scientific treatment' (1923: 5), Hilferding objected that a Marxist will rate politics as scientific provided that it 'describes causal connections' and that 'the task of scientific politics, i.e. of a political method capable of describing causal connections, is to disclose the causal factors which determine the willed decisions of the various classes of society'. In his opinion, this justified the conclusion that 'the practice of Marxism, as well as its theory, is free from value judgments' (1923: 5–6).

Colletti's counter-argument – i.e. the contention that Marxists think of history as vouchsafing the passage from capitalism to a superior social order 'occupying a higher position on the value scale' (see Colletti 1979: 39) – can also be reversed without difficulty in terms that Marxists may well be assumed to believe, like Schumpeter (1942), that socialism is a necessary offshoot of capitalism, not because of a higher position on the value scale, but for scientific reasons.

Concluding, it is worth emphasising that the scientific character of Marxism or any of its modern variants has been called into question in scholarly studies by Soldani (see, in particular, Soldani 2001, 2007) on the grounds that Marxism has failed to keep pace with the latest developments in modern scientific methodology, specifically the long-standing rejection of epistemological realism.

Whereas Marxists still look on the social system as called upon to confirm or refute the explanations of reality we have been offering – Soldani argues – today the idea that society and its historical evolution fall outside the domain of theoretical investigation is no longer accepted. Social history, it is argued, is the chronicle of the more or less rational actions made by individuals. As such, it cannot be analysed without regard to the actions of its social actors and it cannot, by its very nature, be viewed as external or unrelated to their material behaviour. Within society, empirical phenomena are nothing but thought that materialises under the circumstances prevailing from time to time. Development processes are neither external to those observing them, nor self-standing. Concluding, Soldani emphasises the urgent need to rethink both the Marxist conception of history and its approach to knowledge overall.

Soldani's critique has been appropriately refuted in an in-depth review by Dell'Ombra (2008), to which the reader is hereby referred. In my estimation, Soldani's constructivist interpretation of the scientific method in a capitalistic society appears to be marred both by subjectivism and by an excessive emphasis on the active role of knowledge, which ultimately undermines the validity of science overall, not only of Marxism. More specifically, Soldani holds that the circumstances under which the apprehension of reality becomes possible never actually materialise in today's society, since capitalism generates blindness – a conclusion this book frankly rejects as excessively radical.

7 Conclusion

In the introduction to this chapter, I quoted Hobsbawm's argument (1982: 38–39) that 'the line separating what is Marxist from what is not is now blurred'. All the same, it is a fact that even today the 'reconciliation' of Marxism with modern economic theory is far from close at hand. The use of the term 'reconciliation' is only designed to stress the need to conduct a more exacting comparative analysis of Marxism and orthodox thought with respect to the scientificity of their respective analysis methods. It goes without saying that the aim of such attempt should never be, in the words of Derrida (1993: 44), 'to play off Marx against Marxism so as to neutralise, or at any rate muffle, the political imperative in the untroubled exegesis of a classified work'. The prerequisites for the acknowledgement of the scientific essence of Marxism are – let this be repeated – clearing away a few Marxist tenets that are undeniably antithetical to the recognised canons of modern science and persuading orthodox academics to abandon Popperian falsificationism and, generally, abstain from the use of methods that may prevent them from appreciating the complexities of reality. As Kühne puts it (1974, vol. II: 313), the precondition for a dialectical confrontation between Marxists and orthodox economists to prove fecund is mutual concessions from either front.

In sum, in this chapter I have tried to demonstrate that only those thinking of the labour theory of value and Hegelian ontological dialectics as the fundamentals of Marxism and of Hegelian dialectics as antithetical to science can share the idea of an insoluble contrast between Marxism and economic science. An additional aim of this chapter was to argue that even where Marxism, for the sake of 'reconciliation' with orthodox economic theory, should actually renounce Hegelian dialectic and the labour theory of value as a price theory, its considerable cognitive potential would nevertheless remain intact. In the words of Levine (1984–1988: 16), the greater the consensus on fundamentals, the greater the probability that a debate will prove constructive. Disagreement over fundamentals makes it virtually inevitable that those holding different opinions will refuse to listen to each other. Advocates of socialism and capitalism will, in any case, refuse to listen to each other on grounds of their confrontational political beliefs. Mutual incomprehension and void debate lie in the nature of things.

One point that was purposely left outside the scope of this chapter is the analysis of Marx's actual thought, specifically with regard to dialectics. In other words, this chapter's concern was principally with Marxism, rather than with a correct reading of Marx's writings.

Today, Marxism comes in a number of different versions and even orthodox mainstream economics falls into numerous schools whose basics are often difficult to reconcile. It is widely argued that Marx's writings, especially those sketching the economic system of the future, contain fragmentary theoretical approaches, instead of offering fully developed theories. In point of fact, this is consistent with Marx's own saying that methodology only is what really matters. In fact, this finding is all but new. Back in 1899, Bernstein argued that Marx and Engels's writings could be used to demonstrate anything and everything, and Kautsky warned that it was impossible to position absolute reliance on every one of Marx's words, because his sayings were often mutually contradictory (Kautsky 1960: 437).

More precisely, my working hypothesis in this chapter was to demonstrate that the use of a rigorous scientific method capable of shedding light on the complexities of reality is the prerequisite for an exhaustive comparative study of Marxism and orthodox economic science. As pointed out by Meek (1972: 171–175), ever since marginalism developed into the logic of rational choice theory, the starting point for any comparative analysis of Marxism and marginalism has been the insight that both of them endorse the view of economic behaviour as ultimately rational.[9]

However, any such comparative analysis requires the expunging of weak points and enriching one with the strong points of the other. In particular, if the point designed to enrich orthodox economic theory is the idea of a new mode of production – as some have lately begun to think – the comparative study of these two theoretical approaches is likely to prove a highly rewarding exercise.

Notes

1 For recent analyses of the differences between mainstream economics and heterodox economics, see Lee (2011a, 2011b), Mearman (2011) and Garnett Jr. (2011). Lee characterises mainstream and heterodox economics as non-comparable and maintains

that both draw their fundamental right to exist from academic liberty and intellectual pluralism. Mearman holds that mainstream and heterodox economics are difficult to define and that any strict distinction between them is consequently unwarranted. Garnett proposed an alternative view of academic pluralism that is more conducive to the flourishing of heterodox economics.

2 In an earlier essay, Hobsbawm argued that historians also had always drawn a clear-cut distinction between 'Marxists' and 'non-Marxists' and had concerned themselves preferably with the former group, but had unduly widened it through the inclusion of a wide selection of authors. As a matter of fact, he argued, this distinction is absolutely necessary; otherwise, a history of Marxism would be difficult to write and, where written, would hardly make any sense (Hobsbawm 1979: 61).

3 This is why an attentive Marx expert such as Rubel argued that terms such as 'Marxian' or 'Marxist' lacked any sound basis (see Rubel 1974a: 20–21).

4 In this connection, the great theorist of world systems, Immanuel Wallerstein, has argued (2006: 14) that 'the division of knowledge into distinct boxes – disciplines – is an obstacle, not an aid, to understanding the world'.

5 Endorsing the scientific standing of Marx's work, Vilar claimed that in 1845 Marx and Engels started working together daily, thanks to their shared belief that political economy was the only modern scientific discipline with a truly scientific matrix and that this necessitated rejecting the inconsistent approaches to society that philosophers had been offering so far. In later years, however, Marx and Engels included history among the objects of their scientific speculation (see Vilar 1978: 66–68). It is worth emphasising, however, that Marx was, and remained, a philosopher and that throughout his life he consistently refused to adopt the speculative methods of natural science (see, *inter alia*, Mészàros 1978: 134; Agazzi 1984).

6 For a well-reasoned opinion to the contrary, see Grossmann (1983).

7 In the opinion of Kautsky, for instance, the key ideas of Marxism were the materialistic conception of history and the role of the proletariat as the driving force behind the socialist revolution (see Geary 1974: 85).

8 A typical statement by a historical materialist (see Panzieri 1958: 107) that sheds light on central ideas discussed in this book runs as follows:

> Since there is no way of distinguishing the worker as a citizen battling for his political ideas from the worker seeing to his duties in the factory, it is simply unconceivable that the latter, having been used up, oppressed and crushed by his master, should undergo any change once he has left the workshop. The political battle of the workers' movement is simultaneously fought in the workshop and on every terrain within society. However, the main battlefield is and remains the factory, the very core of capitalistic power, and it is there that the worker is called upon to negotiate and assert his power. The issue of worker control is hence closely bound up with the need to revive revolution as a solution to the issue of antagonism within the factory.

9 Several authors are agreed that Marx practised methodological individualism (see, specifically, Oppenheimer and Putnam 1958: 17; Elster 1985; Screpanti 2007: 102–103; and a body of writings by Marxist rational choice theorists); some are prepared to admit that Marxism is compatible with methodological individualism (see, for example, Goldstein 2006); lastly, a considerable number of 'analytical Marxists' (including, *inter alia*, Roemer) think Marxism to be compatible with neoclassical thought (see Tarrit 2006). As mentioned in Faucci (2010: 94–95), the idea that Marxism is compatible with marginalism was even shared by Benedetto Croce. In contrast, Carver has argued that Marx rejected methodological individualism (see Carver 1984: 225–226).

3   The problem of investment funding in labour-managed firms

1 Introduction

This chapter starts the review of the producer cooperative theory produced by economists writing in the wake of the studies of Ward (1958), Vanek (1970) and Meade (1972). One of its aims is to argue that a cooperative financing itself through bonds will neither cease being an LMF as a matter of course nor automatically run the risk of under-investing. It is also argued that an LMF-type firm will not necessarily tend to make high-risk investments, since the link binding the members of an LMF to their firm is closer than that between shareholders and capitalistic firms. I will start out from the difficulties and defects of cooperatives discussed in the literature and use the resulting insight as an introduction to the analysis of an organisational pattern assumed to enable producer cooperatives to bring about a new mode of production. Three main criticisms – financing difficulties, under-investment and the assumed difficulty of watching worker-members at work – will be examined in this and subsequent chapters. Additional supposed shortcomings will be briefly mentioned in Chapter 5.[1]

There is widespread agreement that the severest shortcoming is difficult investment funding. The above-mentioned distinction between LMFs and WMFs is crucial to a correct understanding of both my line of reasoning and conclusion that no particular funding difficulties actually stand in the way of the growth of this movement (see Albanese 2003; Tortia 2007; Jossa 2007b).

2 The funding difficulties of producer cooperatives

Economists have long argued that the severest obstacle to the self-driven growth of an employee-managed firm system in a capitalistic economy is the so-called 'collateral dilemma' (Vanek 1970: 318): working-class operators without any property of their own are often unable to lodge the collateral that potential providers of funds require as a form of security to back repayment of their loans. This means that there are funding difficulties in producer cooperatives.

While this is certainly true, it is worth distinguishing between the funding difficulties of LMFs and those of WMFs. As risk-taking is a sure sign of the operator's confidence in the success of an enterprise, outside capital providers tend to grant more loan capital to firms that self-finance large portions of their investments; often, the interest rates charged increase in an inverse ratio to the self-financed part of a firm's investments.[2] And in line with the 'increased risk principle' theorised in Kalecki (1937; see also, Baumol 1953; Stiglitz 1969), the risks taken by owners of firms increase in direct proportion to the part of the firm's investments that is funded with loan capital. As a result, if the firm is an LMF, financing its operations solely with loan capital, the risks taken by its members are likely to be maximised, since the firm will only obtain loans at fairly high interest rates. These are the reflections that led Drèze to emphasise (1989: ch. IV; 1993: 257–262) that the risks associated with fixed-rate loan capital in capital-intensive or high-risk cooperatives may greatly erode, if not altogether nullify, the incomes of workers in the event of a downturn in the firm's business.[3] According to Drèze, capital-intensive firms and firms in high-risk business sectors are often compelled to use risk capital, and joint-stock companies – he noted – emerged and made rapid headway in capitalistic systems exactly because they offered means of effectively solving problems in these two critical situations.

Economic theorists have drawn attention to an additional major point with a distinct bearing on LMFs: if the cooperative is a limited liability firm, its members may venture into particularly risky investments on the assumption that, while the success of a risky investment will step up their earnings, in the event of a failure they can leave the firm without honouring their obligations to external providers of funds (see Drèze 1976; Schlicht and Weizsäcker 1977; Gui 1982, 1985; Eswaran and Kotwal 1989; Putterman *et al.* 1998: 886–897; Pittatore and Turati 2000: 27). This fear on the part of financers, it is argued, adds to the difficulties that LMFs whose members do not invest their own resources in the firm are seen to face when it comes to borrowing funds to finance their investments.

The question now is: are these objections really as weighty as they may appear at first sight?

3 Possible solutions to the funding problems of LMFs

Consistent with the reflections in the previous section and with Vanek's approach, before discussing the financing difficulty issue with special focus on LMFs, we have to answer the question: how can the members of an LMF gain access to credit?

As mentioned in the introduction, to self-finance itself, an LMF can issue bonds and offer them for purchase to its partners. This self-financing case can be broken down into two sub-cases, depending on whether the firm's bonds issues are allotted to the members entirely or in part (in which case, the rest is offered to the general public).

Either decision may give rise to conflicts of interests, because it requires a majority resolution by the members. In the former sub-case, a conflict is likely to arise over the rate of interest the securities will have to bear: since any increase in the capital income assigned to these securities will produce a pro-rata decrease in the member's labour incomes, there will obviously be dissension between those wishing to remunerate the bonds with a greater or lesser part of the firm's revenues. Moreover, in either sub-case, there will be differences of opinion concerning the proportion of the global issue to be allotted to the members. Those intending to increase the firm's investments are likely to prioritise self-financing, while others might be altogether averse to self-financing or wish to minimise the self-financed proportion and maximise the surplus available for distribution. In my estimation, however, although these conflicts of interests are surely material enough, they are far from insurmountable obstacles to the viability of an LMF issuing bonds for member financing.

Methods of providing more effective security to external financers would redouble the advantages of self-financing. One such method would be the rule that interest on the members' bonds is to be paid out only after external loans have been remunerated. Under this rule, bonds issued by democratic firms would fall into two categories: (1) internal bonds – i.e. bonds for distribution among the members issued at the direction of the manager or by a majority resolution of the members; and (2) external bonds – i.e. bonds for subscription by third parties in general (external financers and members). Preference rights would only attach to those bonds that are freely offered to the general public (see Cuomo 2003).

In Chapters 6 and 9, I will show that there are solid reasons for arguing that self-managed firms should be owned by the state as the ultimate obligor for their debts. Indeed, as lenders would derive formidable security from such an arrangement, it is often argued that an all-cooperatives system is only conceivable on condition that the firms concerned are declared to be state property.

4 Equity financing

An additional preliminary point is deciding whether the members of worker-run firms facing financing difficulties should or should not be authorised to issue voting or non-voting equities. On this point, it is worth specifying right from the start that equity issues are reasonable only if the proportion of profit to be allotted to them is fixed upon their issuance. Voting-equity financing is the rule in the mixed worker and capitalistic-controlled system of cooperative firms theorised by Meade (1989). However, although this mixed solution was doubtless devised with intent to tackle the funding issue, Meade's is not a system of worker control proper. Moreover, as a cooperative issuing voting equities tends to be gradually turned into a capitalistic firm, the best solution is to restrict analysis to models of employee-controlled firms that do not adopt this form of member financing.[4]

Turning to the case of a cooperative resolving to issue non-voting equities or variable rate bonds (see, *inter alia*, Nutzinger 1975: 181; Drèze 1976: 1133–1135; Vanek 1977: 226–228; McCain 1977: 365; Jay 1980; Gui 1982: 267; Thomas 1990: 17ff.; Thomas and Defournay 1990; Major 1996; Waldmann and Smith 1999), it is worth clarifying that this option is not at odds with the logic behind self-management, albeit in its strictest or narrowest form. Indeed, just as profit-sharing agreements with workers are occasionally used in capitalistic systems, so income-sharing agreements with capitalists should be an option in a system of self-managed firms.

Non-voting equities are fully in line with Drèze's approach to the funding issue – namely, his proposal that firms should enter into 'financing agreements' that would transfer all risks from the firm's partners to its financers. In this connection, Drèze (1989, 1993) draws attention to 'implicit contract theory' – i.e. the finding that workers in capitalistic firms (who are less prepared to share risks with capitalists) usually enter into tacit contracts entailing acceptance of lower wages in exchange for the employer's commitment not to reduce wage levels in periods of crisis (i.e. in exchange for the fact that it is employers that run the risk of a crisis). If workers under capitalism deem it in their interests to renounce part of their earnings in order to self-insure themselves against the risk of fluctuations in their incomes – Drèze contends – the same should be applicable to a labour-managed economy, where workers might find it expedient to change their variable incomes into fixed incomes by executing contracts with providers of funds and thus transfer business risks onto capitalists.[5]

However, as this proposal may sound exceedingly radical and, as thus, suggest the absence of a proper solution to the funding problems of labour-managed firms, it is probably convenient to approach the problem from a different viewpoint and to state that a firm experiencing funding problems should be authorised to issue non-voting equities.

The issuance of non-voting equities is another case in which incentives for members and incentives for outside capital providers might turn out to be mutually exclusive. The members of a cooperative, raising funds by issuing non-voting equities or quasi-shares, may resolve to launch investment projects designed to make work more agreeable without generating any appreciable monetary gains. Possible options include in-house crèche and kindergarten facilities, workplace embellishments, new machinery to alleviate work and so forth (see, *inter alia*, Waldmann and Smith 1999: 247; Nuti 2000: 95–96), but also investments aimed to safeguard employment levels within the firm. Second, the members might decide to conceal the profits of the investment and use them to finance new investment projects, instead of making them available for distribution (see Wolfstetter *et al.* 1984; and Waldmann and Smith 1999: 267).

To minimise the first of these risks, Major suggests including the value of fringe benefits in the residual used as a basis to calculate the yield of the bonds (see Major 1996: 557); to avert problems altogether, others recommend linking the yields of the quasi-shares to the industry-wide index (see Waldmann and Smith 1999). However, in either case, it is fair to admit that the solution proposed would neither be easy to implement, nor effectively outweigh this risk.

Opponents of the non-voting-equity financing hypothesis also draw attention to the risk of conflicts of interests between simple working members and workers who are also financers. Examples in point are particularly risky high-income projects that might jeopardise the firm's current employment levels or financial performance. Under such circumstances, worker-members financing the firm can be assumed to be voting for the investment in contrast to simple working members, with the result being investments that one or the other member category does not deem in its best interests.[6]

Addressing the case of variable-income securities entirely and exclusively allotted to the members of the firm, Hansmann pointed to an additional potential risk: the conflicts of interests that are likely to arise between owners of greater or lesser stakes in the firm when it comes to passing the resolution needed to fix the capital-income/labour-income distribution ratio (see Hansmann 1996: 90).

The option of variable-income non-voting-equity financing is often held to be open to the additional objection that LMF securities would have no market if the members were free to resolve not to pay any dividends on them and their outside capital suppliers were prevented from reversing such a resolution. On closer analysis, however, this objection is effectively refuted by my initial proposal that the proportion of the profits to be allotted to such equities be fixed upon their issuance.

One further problem requires proper consideration at this point: the moment when the workers have assigned part of the cooperative's income to equity owners, they will, quite naturally, tend to take a further step forward in this process – e.g. they will tend to issue voting equities to apportion business risks and firm control functions between themselves and their financers. The problems stemming from such a decision have been highlighted by several authors. To confine the firm's risk profile within socially optimal levels, risk capital providers might require some control over the firm's management. As there is little doubt that the workers' determination to attract risk capital would induce them to grant financers a certain measure of control, the resulting external control over an LMF would impair the democratic nature of its management and thereby set off a piecemeal return to capitalism (see Gintis 1989; Bowles and Gintis 1993: 35; Drèze 1993: 257–262; Putterman 1993; Dow and Putterman 2000; Putterman *et al.* 1998: 886–887; Dow 2003).

In conclusion, the above-mentioned weighty counterarguments seem to suggest that this financing mode is not the ideal solution.[7]

5 Are LMFs likely to venture into particularly high-risk investments?

At this point, we may ask ourselves whether the members of a democratic firm, being exclusively remunerated out of the residual, will actually prioritise high-risk investments and, if so, whether this alleged risk propensity stems from the awareness that where an investment should fail (instead of generating the expected boost in income), they could leave the firm without meeting its obligations with creditors (see Drèze 1976; Schlicht and Weizsäcker 1977; Gui 1985; Putterman *et al.* 1998: 886–897). A necessary corollary is the conclusion that the assumed risk propensity of democratic firms would expose providers of outside capital to particularly high risks. In other words, whereas capitalists investing risk capital in a public company are able to control its managers and stop them from engaging in exceedingly risky operations, financers of an LMF have no means of preventing managers (who are controlled by the firm's working members) from venturing into particularly risky investment projects. And the control over the company's management is held to provide sufficient assurance to the financers of a public company.

The same argument can be set out starting from the fact that borrowing costs are largely dependent on the different amounts of information to which creditors and debtors respectively have access and that information asymmetries are all the more important in dealings with limited-liability firms. In situations where liability is limited, free riding is a material risk, since borrowers may be tempted to launch high-risk investments on the assumption that they will cash all profits and transfer losses onto creditors.

In my opinion, this assumed disadvantage for external financers of an LMF is fairly negligible. For one thing, while the shareholders of a public company have ample scope for portfolio diversification, the members of an LMF not only depend on a single firm for their labour and capital incomes, but have little scope for diversifying their investments. And this is one reason why the members of a cooperative make cautious investment choices and tend to prioritise low-risk investment projects.

Second, the main concern of the working members of an LMF is to make their incomes as safe and stable as possible, which means they will prioritise less risky investments than those typically opted for by the managers of public companies in a capitalistic system. This argument was already introduced in Section 3, but can now be applied to a different context. As mentioned before, decision-makers in capitalistic firms tend to act in the exclusive interests of the owners, without regard to the interests of workers: an investment with an appreciable income potential will therefore be made, even though it may jeopardise the jobs of many. In labour-managed firms, instead, decisions on single investments or preferred investment categories are made by the workers (or by the managers they have appointed) with due regard to both their expected returns and the anticipated impact on employment levels within the firm. And this rather bespeaks the assumption that workers will opt for less risky business projects.

The idea that the partners of a cooperative are more risk-averse than those of capitalistic firms has become commonplace in the literature (see Jensen and Meckling 1979; Bonin *et al.* 1993; Doucouliagos 1995; Dow 2001, 2003; Park *et al.* 2004; Birchall and Ketilson 2009; Melgarejo *et al.* 2010; Gunn 2011: 325; Birchall 2012; Bouchon *et al.* 2012).

The opposite view is endorsed by Hansmann. Analysing the pros and cons of employee-managed firms and, specifically, the fact that workers can only work for one firm at a time and derive extremely variable incomes from the firms they control, Hansmann wonders if this will actually make these firms rather risk-averse. In his view, this assumption is contradicted by experience, given that many cooperative firms (e.g. in the plywood industry, in farming and in banking) carry on business in capital-intensive industries, make high-risk investments and earn extremely variable incomes. Hansmann's conclusion is that the considerable risks of dismissal faced in capitalistic firms induce workers to look upon cooperatives as the lesser danger, even in high-risk industries; this, he argues, is why cooperative firms often opt for high-risk investments (see Hansmann 1996: 57, 71–72, 78–79).

Concluding analysis of this point, we can neither endorse the position of those who see LMFs as more risk-averse than their capitalistic twins (see Gintis 1989; Bowles and Gintis 1993: 35; Putterman *et al.* 1998: 886), nor the opposite assumption that labour-managed firms show a marked propensity for high-risk investment projects.

6 A supplementary analysis of the financing difficulties of LMFs

As the voting equity hypothesis was ruled out in Section 5, it remains to be decided whether an LMF that adopts bond financing will necessarily face serious financing difficulties.

Compared with providers of funds to public limited companies, those financing a democratic firm are at odds, since they cannot choose between shares or bonds, and this is an all but minor disadvantage. However, if the assumption of a lesser risk propensity of democratic firms is accepted, the resulting disadvantage would be offset by a lower risk profile.

But there is still another argument that needs to be addressed. As (in the theoretical, pure case) cooperatives remunerate loan capital prior to labour, financers of LMFs face lesser risks than providers of funds to limited companies, in which labour is remunerated prior to capital. In capitalistic firms, workers receive their wages month after month, as production activities progress, whereas loan capital is remunerated after longer intervals of time and risk capital only appropriates the residual. In cooperatives, instead, it is workers that rank last in terms of remuneration.[8] As a result, loans granted to cooperative firms are, in this respect, safer than loans to public limited companies;[9] and this goes to refute the assumption that cooperatives face particularly serious difficulties raising investment funds.[10]

This is not in conflict with my starting remark that cooperatives do face funding difficulties, since few of their members own property to offer as collateral to potential providers of funds. For this and other reasons to be discussed further on, it is best to compare medium- to large-sized cooperatives with limited liability companies, such as public companies. As these companies are liable to creditors only for the value of what they have invested, this more than counterbalances the alleged handicap inherent in the fact that the members of cooperatives are usually property-less.

Let us repeat that these reflections so far suggest that cooperatives do not face particularly serious funding difficulties. Further on, this preliminary conclusion will be backed up by analyses of competition, insolvency risks and ownership structure, as well as notes on risk diversification options and Schweickart's interesting proposal to apportion available savings among LMFs. The first three of these points will be dealt with in the next couple of chapters, while the last two are addressed in this chapter.

7   Risk diversification in democratically managed firms

Today, portfolio diversification is a means of hedging uncertainties associated with stakes in enterprises carrying on particularly high-risk business activities. Shares are one way to achieve this end. In a capitalistic system, investors entitled to residual claims on the profits of a company may diversify their investment portfolios by purchasing equities of companies with different risk profiles. The same is not true of a system of democratic firms, where a worker living on the residual of his firm is bound to that particular firm and cannot diversify his labour investment by working simultaneously for more than one firm. On closer analysis, though, a very simple institutional measure would enable the partners of democratic firms to participate in the lives and business activities of more than one firm at least indirectly: a number of cooperatives might join to form a 'second-level cooperative' – i.e. a firm whose members are not individuals, but cooperative firms themselves.[11]

The member cooperatives would staff the second-level firm with part of their own working members and would receive shares of the second-level cooperative's income in proportion to the number and qualifications of the workers seconded by each of them. Moreover, to spread risks, the second-level cooperative's revenues would have to be distributed to the affiliates.

The funding methods of the second-level cooperative would be the same as those of its first-level affiliates, but the resulting pyramid of firms would reduce funding difficulties, since the affiliates would finance the second-level cooperative either with direct capital contributions or with loans backed up by collateral lodged by it. A second-level cooperative negotiating a financing agreement would act in the name, and for the account of, the whole group, and the resulting business differentiation within the group would reduce both the aggregate risks of the group and those taken by the financers of the second-level cooperative's individual investment projects.

Thanks to these second-level cooperatives, ordinary LMF-type firms resolving to venture into high-risk business activities or launching large-scale manufacturing projects which would otherwise be outside their reach would automatically have access to a risk-spreading mechanism comparable to the portfolio diversification strategies available to investors in capitalistic countries.

Now that the funding problem objection has been satisfactorily refuted, we may ask ourselves why existing cooperatives are mostly the WMF-type. One explanation is that financing difficulties are highest at the start-up stage. When the firm is still small and lacks fixed assets or other investments to use as collateral in raising outside loan capital, the solution is usually the establishment of a WMF – a firm that uses the greater part of its earnings for self-financing purposes. However, it is worth specifying that once a cooperative has been created as a WMF, it is all but easy to turn it into an LMF at a later stage.

8 Schweickart's approach to the funding issue

To dispel any remaining doubts regarding the potential of a system of producer cooperatives for solving the financing difficulties stifling its growth, we may cite a model that David Schweickart developed specifically for this purpose.

In this model, a system of democratic firms operates under a scheme envisaging stringent public control over the way that the savings and investment fund are distributed. As is well known, publicly controlled investments are specific to the socialist tradition. In the 1930s, during the debate on economic calculation in socialism, Maurice Dobb (in part in the wake of Keynes) spoke of investment choices Rmade in markets as 'acts of faith par excellence' (since managers are constantly unaware of what others are doing) and 'both arbitrary and short-sighted (because they entail a systematic underrating of future needs and, hence, a tendency towards underinvestment)'.[12] These and other reasons, he concluded, necessitated exercising state control over investments.

Using these and the insights of previous theoreticians of public investment control, Schweickart developed a model designed to achieve two main aims: (1) abolish capital incomes; and (2) devise fairer regional investment patterns. For purposes of readability and because my aim is only to offer an additional solution to the funding difficulties of cooperatives, I will skip some points of his public investment control theory, including the suggestion that capital incomes be altogether abolished.

In Schweickart's model, investment control is implemented as part of public investment financing (on which I concur), in terms that investment funds are both raised and distributed by the state, while non-public institutions are prohibited from accepting savings from citizens. The funds sourced from the general public are used to issue public equities carrying interest at market rates. As far as public investment allocation is concerned, Schweickart suggests both investment control and a specific investment apportionment scheme providing for the appropriation of savings, first to regions and subsequently to firms.

In short, Schweickart suggests that the investment fund should be apportioned among regions in direct proportion to their respective population sizes (the 'fair share principle') for two main reasons:

1. because the state is called upon to redress market imbalances; and
2. because saving is not viewed as a particularly virtuous action (as are abstinence, patience and so forth).

The idea of adopting the fair share principle in allocating the investment fund to different regions is perfectly in line with the principle that state funding is a public service, which entails that citizens should be granted equal access to public services in both quantitative and qualitative terms. By way of example, it is one of the founding principles implied in the Italian Constitution, which rules (Section 3) that 'all citizens have equal social dignity and are equal before the law' and vests in the Republic the task of 'removing any economic and social obstacles that may materially encroach upon the freedom and equality of all citizens and thereby inhibit the full development of their personalities'. Nowhere in the Italian Constitution – let us add – is there a principle stating that citizens shall have access to public services in proportion to their personal income or the average income level of the region where they live – and this, no less than Section 3, amounts to an implied ruling that citizens should have access to public services on equal terms.

But how should the 'investment fund' that regions receive from the central government be allocated or used? On the one hand, there is central planning, which Schweickart rejects, because he is critical of the very idea of substituting planning for the working of the market; on the other, there is the allocation of the entire investment fund to a network of banks empowered to conduct business in line with capitalistic criteria (Schweickart 1993: 72; 2002: 50–51).

Ruling out both these radical options, Schweickart opts for a system 'between these extremes' (Schweickart 2002: 51). As mentioned before, the general principle he upholds is the 'fair share' criterion, concerning which he makes it clear that before apportioning the fund among regions, the government would have to earmark part of the collected funds for the functions and non-decentralised public services performed and provided by various levels of government and that before apportioning the fund among firms, it would have to make key decisions regarding the part of the investment fund to be allocated for public capital investment. At the regional and municipal levels, part of the funds would be used to provide public services to the regional and local communities and the rest would be managed by a system of public banks.

An additional point to be clarified is the criteria that are to govern the apportionment of the aggregate resources among banks. In Schweickart's approach, the share allocated to each bank is to be commensurate with the number and size of the firms to which it provides funds, its own efficiency level as reflected in bottom-line results and, above all, its track record in creating new jobs using the allocations received.

Banks would be organised as non-profit institutions. Representatives of the bank's own in-house staff would serve on each bank council, along with those of the firms funded by it and with representatives of the community's development planning agency. Banks would be public institutions required to allocate their funds in line with democratically devised criteria. Profitability is one criterion, but only one. In particular, they would be expected to prioritise financing applications from firms adopting employment-boosting business strategies (Schweickart 1993: 74–77; 2002: 53–56).

In my opinion, some points of Schweickart's interesting model need revising. For one, a country where savings bear no interest would be obliged to stay away from world markets. Second, I think it more convenient to allocate the investment fund to the regions based on pure efficiency criteria. Provided that these variants were introduced, even liberalists would probably rate Schweickart's model as acceptable. Non-liberalist aspects of this model include the rule that savings should flow entirely to the state and the criterion of apportioning resources among regions in proportion to the size of the population. As this second rule is based on the idea that each citizen is entitled to receive the same amount of public services, even a liberalist is likely to subscribe to it without difficulty.

The points that have the greatest bearing on the subject of this book are nationalised savings and their allocation by the state, since this would enable the government to enforce equitable distribution criteria and include democratic firms among beneficiaries. As Schweickart's model provides for public banks, these might be obliged to adopt credit-rating criteria intended to prioritise project viability over firm solvency.

Concluding, both the nationalisation of savings and public investment control might help tackle the investment-funding problems of cooperative firms and award resources to disadvantaged regions, whose stumbling blocks have traditionally been insufficient saving levels and inadequate capital accumulation.[13]

9 Final reflections

The ultimate conclusion of this line of reasoning is that there are no reasons to assume that a well-organised democratic firm would necessarily face particularly serious financing difficulties. Basically, this is also Hansmann's conclusion:

> If an employee-owned firm needs capital primarily to purchase assets that are not firm-specific, the firm can usually borrow it on reasonable terms. While it is true that the resulting leverage may impose substantial risks on the members of employee-owned firms, it is a fact that these are often prepared to bear a relatively large amount of risk. In fact, employee-owned firms are surprisingly common in comparatively capital-intensive industries that employ fungible assets.
>
> (1996: 75)

Further on, Hansmann also argues (1996: 77): 'It seems, then, that the costs of obtaining capital cannot by themselves explain prevailing patterns of employee ownership either within or without the industrial sector'.[14]

Nonetheless, one major question is still open: if LMFs are actually exempt from the financing difficulties faced by most existing cooperatives, why do firms not organise themselves as LMFs? An answer to this question would require an exhaustive discussion of the complex relations between producer cooperative theory and the cooperative movement – an analysis that lies outside the scope of this book and should be developed in a paper purposely focused on this specific point (see *inter alia*, Dow 2003; Jossa 2007b).

One reflection, though, is certainly opportune. The LMF-type firm discussed in this book is a model that was developed in the theoretical literature published in the wake of the path-breaking contributions of Ward and Vanek and has little, if any, similarity with real-case scenario cooperatives.

As a result, this book is to be viewed as a distinctively theoretical approach with few, if any, links to the empirical literature on the cooperatives of the Western world.

Notes

1 To keep this book a reasonable length and, in part, because the last word on this issue seems to have been said, I will skip the issue of the perverse supply curves of cooperatives raised by Ward in 1958. For an exhaustive analysis and partial refutation of this objection, see Bonin and Putterman (1987: ch. 7) and Cuomo (2010).

2 In a 1993 paper discussing the reasons why cooperatives tend to be comparatively few in any modern economic system, Gui points to difficulties in attracting capital or qualified business managers and the greater impact of a satisfactory level of 'performance in the team' on the success of a democratically managed firm versus a capitalistic company (see also, *inter alia*, Mygind 1997; Vaughan-Whitehead 1999: 42). For a different view, see Hansmann's study of firm ownership structures and management modes (1996: 4) and its main finding that 'the capital intensity of an industry and the degree of risk inherent in the industry both play a much smaller role than is commonly believed in determining whether firms in that industry are investor-owned' (Hansmann 1996: 4).

3 Quoting Drèze (1993: 254), the funding issue is 'central to understanding why labor management does not spread in capitalistic economies'.

4 Meade's proposal is analysed in-depth in Cuomo (2010: ch. VII).

5 Dréze himself used the words 'paradoxical' and 'surprising' to describe his conclusion that the workers of an LMF can indifferently opt for either a financial agreement or a labour agreement. In the former case, they would fix the dividends owed to financers in given circumstances; in the latter, they would define their own workloads and wage rates in the same situations (see Drèze 1989: 92–93; 1993: 260). In a perfect competition environment, both these agreements would ensure the same results. In a situation of uncertainty and imperfect markets, the actuals-versus-budget balance would be charged to financers in one case and to workers in the other.

6 Unlike other conflicts of interests, 'this is not a conflict between principal and agent, but one opposing principal to principal' (Nuti 1997: 135).

7 Major obstacles stand in the way of equity financing in Eastern European countries: first, banks seldom provide loans to investors wishing to buy securities without having the necessary cash on hand; second, given the scarce bottom-line results of firms and their resulting inability to distribute dividends, it would take years before any returns on such investments can be expected to accrue (see Kalmi 2000: 6–7). All the same, workers in those countries have traditionally practised equity investing.

8 A different case is that of Italian cooperatives, whose members are hired workers. Based on Law n. 142/2001, the workers' wage claims are classed as priority claims and are consequently to be settled prior to any others (on this point, see Reito 2008).

9 'The residually remunerated resource suppliers can be thought of as "insuring" the suppliers of resources for some of their risks' (Zafiris 1986: 37).

10 In addition to, or instead of, lodging collateral, the firm might allow outside capital providers to inspect its operations and accounting records (see Bonin and Putterman 1987: 63–64).

11 This idea is based on the experience of the Spanish 'Mondragon' group and was suggested to me by Gaetano Cuomo (see also, Smith and Ye 1987; Gunn 2011: 325).

12 Dobb's approach to the consumption-investment option and the possibility of determining the investment rate and interest rate simultaneously (see Dobb 1939, 1955a), though acute, is no longer acceptable today, at least in its original formulation.

13 Schweickart's approach was analysed in-depth in Jossa (2004d).

14 Far from facing any funding difficulties, the 'Mondragon Group of Cooperatives' has constantly managed resources in excess of its actual requirements. To date, its group bank, Caja Laboral Popular (CLP), has been able to finance all group businesses. Based on a 1994 report, its financial resources would be enough to fund sixteen groups of the size of the existing one (see Lutz 1997: 1413–1414).

4 Under-investment in labour-managed firms

1 Introduction

This chapter offers an analysis of the already mentioned under-investment issue – i.e. the assumption that a self-managed cooperative makes fewer investments than its capitalistic twin. This issue was first raised in connection with the problem of the partners' attenuated property rights in their cooperative.

Although it is true that the aims of the managers may differ from those of the partners, for the purposes of this analysis I will skip this element of complication and assume instead that the relevant decisions – i.e. investment choices – are made directly during a general meeting. An additional convenient assumption is that the workers are perfectly 'homogeneous' in terms of work input, but differ greatly with regards to the consumption versus saving option.

Our model firm is the so-called egalitarian cooperative, where the partners of a given category are assigned the same pay rate, regardless of within-firm seniority (regardless, I repeat, of whether they have accepted income reductions to help finance the firm over a number of years or have contributed little or nothing to its self-financing).

The starting point for all extant research on the investments of self-managed firms has been the fact that the partners lack individual property rights to the firm's capital goods or assets – an aspect common to LMFs and WMFs.[1] As I will show further on, the most important point is that the individual partners are not entitled to claim repayment of the sums they have provided to the firm for purposes of self-financing – a typical aspect of WMFs.

2 The under-investment issue

The typical structure of worker-managed cooperatives may explain why analyses of the supposed tendency to under-invest[2] start out from the assumption that the partners of a WMF make their investment decisions with the awareness that on leaving the firm they will neither be entitled to the returns on such investments, nor be paid back the amounts they make available to the firm on passing self-financing resolutions.

This is why numerous theorists have emphasised the severe conflict of interests arising between partners expecting to leave the WMF soon (on reaching retirement age or for other reasons) and partners intending to stay on. Under-investment is the direct result of this conflict of interests, since workers about to leave the firm (and forfeit their right to a share of the firm's income) will hardly be prepared to renounce part of their current income and are likely to vote against fresh investments.[3]

With specific regard to the system of property rights that used to be in force in ex-Yugoslavia, analysts of the investment issue in WMFs generally assume that the value of the capital stock accumulated by the firm cannot be reduced; that is to say, that it is not within the powers of the firm to disinvest and distribute a larger portion of its income among the partners (in fact, under Yugoslav law, manufacturing equipment could be sold, provided the corresponding proceeds were used to purchase new capital goods and/or depreciate existing manufacturing equipment). As will be shown below, the ban on disinvestment is not directly associated with the joint ownership of corporate capital goods (which is specific to WMFs). In theory, nothing can prevent a WMF from distributing a larger share of its income by selling its manufacturing equipment or abstaining from depreciation. All the same, in the literature, it is customary to take for granted that a WMF resolving to invest is not in a position, so to say, to retrace its steps: the capital stock it has accumulated can be further increased, but not reduced.

As a result, investments that would appear advantageous to a capitalistic firm may not be perceived as such by a WMF, due to an additional reason besides the conflict of interests between those leaving the firm before the expiration of the project's useful life and those expecting to stay on until the capital goods to be purchased are worn out or become obsolete. A capitalistic firm (or the cooperative allowed to disinvest) depreciating its capital stock is free to decide whether to use the relevant proceeds to replace the equipment when worn out, distribute them in the form of profits or use them for financial investments. In contrast, to avoid reducing its capital stock, a WMF will always be obliged to use the proceeds of the depreciation process to replace worn-out equipment. And as no firm is in a position to rule out future downturns in business, in connection with each investment, a WMF faces a greater risk, which is one major reason for the lesser investments made by WMFs.

To clarify the difference between the above mentioned two under-investment tendencies, we may add that while it is true that both are caused by attenuated property rights, in the former case it is the individual partner that forfeits his right to a share of the returns on the firm's investments, whereas in the latter it is the workers' collective as a whole that loses the right to be repaid the sums used for self-financing the firm and is prohibited from distributing them among the partners. The tendency to under-invest is often termed the 'Furubotn-Pejovich effect',[4] regardless of whether it is caused by both of the above reasons or merely one.

In analytical terms, the tendency to under-invest can be explained based on a comparison between the cooperative firm and its capitalistic 'twin'. As is well known, the precondition for a capitalistic firm to purchase a machine of price C_0, which is expected to yield an annual sum R for a period of T years, is that the present value of the expected future income is greater than C_0. Hence, equilibrium will be reached when:

$$RL_t \sum_{t=1}^{T} (1+r)^{-t} = C_0 \tag{1}$$

where RL is the annual gross income from the investment, r is the interest rate (assumed to be constant) and a worn-out asset is assumed to have no value.

With reference to the first of the two causes of under-investment in WMFs, it is argued that a WMF in which the decision-makers expect to remain with the cooperative for an average number of years equal to P (where $P<T$) will purchase the same asset only if:

$$RL_t \sum_{t=1}^{T} (1+r)^{-t} = C_0 \tag{2}$$

As a result, a WMF's tendency to under-invest will exceed the corresponding level of its capitalistic 'twin', only if the period of time the partners expect to stay on, on average, is shorter than the life of the investment (and the tendency to under-invest is obviously all the greater, the less the partners expect, on average, to remain with the firm).

This type of analysis is found in numerous studies of the under-investment issue. However, if we ask ourselves if this line of reasoning is correct, it is worth highlighting that the issue has not been properly posed and, especially, that insufficient attention has been given to the fact that an investment, once made, is generally renewed.[5]

3 The tendency for under-investment in the WMF

In the literature, it is customary to distinguish between two schools: the School of Vanek (or the Cornell University School), which seems to have theorised only the first of the two tendencies to under-invest;[6] and the School of Furubotn and Pejovich (or the Texas School), which has mainly concerned itself with the second of the two tendencies.

A WMF is not necessarily prohibited from disinvesting. In fact, as the capital goods of a WMF are purchased with the firm's 'own' savings, they must be the property of the firm and there are no reasons to assume that the firm – i.e. the workers' collective – should not be entitled to sell its own capital goods.[7] The obstacles to investment arising from the ban on disinvestment might easily be removed by simply lifting this ban. And the findings of the Texas School show that this would considerably reduce under-investment.

Before discussing the first of the under-investment hypotheses, it is worth clarifying that the time horizons of workers, which greatly impact investment decisions, are largely dependent on the decision-making method – i.e. whether decisions are made by the managers in an attempt to reconcile their own interests with the propensities of the partners or, conversely, by all of the partners in a general meeting. In addition to this, the decisions are also dependent on the polling system adopted.

To make things simple, let us assume that investment decisions are passed by majority resolutions at a general meeting and that only one investment at a time is put to the vote. In such a case, the time horizon influencing the investment decision will not be the average number of years the decision-makers expect to stay with the cooperative (as is often maintained in the relevant literature),[8] but rather the shortest time prospect among the time prospects of those whose votes determine the formation of a majority in favour of the decision. In a cooperative with 100 partners, a majority in favour of the decision will therefore be formed on condition that fifty partners think that the investment is convenient. Assuming that the partners are arranged in a decreasing order, beginning with the one expecting to stay with the firm longest and going on with those expecting to stay on for fewer and fewer years, the decisive time prospect for the formation of a favourable majority is that of the partner ranking fifty-first in this classification.

An additional factor which greatly influences the decisions of the partners is the employment-boosting/de-staffing effect of a project. Indeed, even an investment with a high income potential might not appear advantageous to the partner fearing to lose his job in consequence of it.[9]

A major assumption implied in current analyses of the investment issue is that the sums invested will be reimbursed to the partners when the investment project has been completely implemented. In fact, although nothing prevents the cooperative from disinvesting, at the end of the plant's useful life the firm it is unlikely to do so if the project has proved successful. In a market economy, a standard or medium-successful firm expects to expand its market outlets and grow steadily over time, so that only firms facing great financial difficulties will usually disinvest.

In the light of the above, it is possible to say that the partners of a cooperative are perfectly aware that investments will usually be renewed and that the distribution of depreciation expenses to the partners is the exception, even in situations where it is permitted by law. As a rule, the proceeds of depreciation will be used to renew, replace or re-purchase the plant or other worn-out capital goods. In other words, the partner of a cooperative knows that once an investment decision has been made, he will receive his share of the returns provided he stays with the firm and that he will not get back his share of the investment, even if the life of the project should prove to be fairly short.[10]

Unlike the partners of a cooperative, investors in capitalistic companies can both expect to cash the returns on their investment and have the invested sums reimbursed at any moment. In order words, every partner of a cooperative knows that as long as he works in a cooperative, he will be in a position to receive the income from his work, the profit (or surplus) earned by the firm and the income from the capital he has invested in the cooperative, but, at the same time, he also knows that the moment he leaves the firm, he will no longer be entitled to any share of the firm's profits and will also forfeit his right to any increases in value of the corporate assets that the firm is likely to accumulate over the years. Only if the firm is the LMF-type will he continue to collect the returns on the capital invested in the firm. This means that, *ceteris paribus*, the returns on every single penny that has been invested in a cooperative fall short of the returns cashed by the owners of a capitalistic firm. This contradicts the claim of those authors who contend that when assessing the worth of the project, the partners of a WMF will only consider the cash flow that the project is expected to generate in the period they will remain members; and as this period may be less than the economic life of the project, they will evaluate it over a truncated planning horizon and, *ceteris paribus*, will consequently reduce its Net Present Value.[11]

Hence, in line with Vanek's approach, but departing from the findings of other authors, my conclusion is that the temptation to under-invest is latent in the minds of all the partners of a WMF, including those expecting to stay with the cooperative for many years to come and regardless of whether the assumption of the ban on disinvestment is introduced or skipped.

Assuming that every partner of a WMF is aware that he will never recover the sums invested in the firm (and that the only way to benefit from them is to stay on and cash the returns on the investment), in the case under review the time horizons of all the partners will be shorter than the economic life of the investment. Consequently, as the sum invested is deemed to be 'forfeited', every partner will be willing to make the investment on the condition that:

$$RN_t \sum_{t=1}^{P} (1+r)^{-t} > C_0 \tag{3}$$

where *RN* is the net return on the investment and *P* the period of time the individual partner expects to stay with the cooperative.

In contrast, in a capitalistic firm, production capacity is maintained by setting aside funds for depreciation (so that the additional returns on the investment become a permanent form of income) and an investment is made when:

$$RN_t \sum_{t=1}^{\infty} (1+r)^{-1} > C_0 \tag{4}$$

Under the assumptions made above, the wish to under-invest is always lurking in the minds of the partners of a WMF, and under-investment is likely to reach levels exceeding those usually estimated in the relevant literature.[12]

4 The under-investment issue in the LMF

At this point, I will examine the corresponding behaviour of an LMF, a type of firm to which the current literature ascribes no tendency to under-invest (see Vanek 1971a: 193–195; Ellerman 1986: 63).

From the above reflections, it follows that the only, though far-reaching, difference between the investment choices of a WMF and those of an LMF is that those made in the latter are influenced by the awareness that the partners who have invested in an LMF take away the sums they have provided to the firm.

As mentioned before, assuming that the investment project will be renewed and that interest accrues on the sums at the current rate, the partners will cash the returns on their investment exclusively during the time they stay with the firm. As a result, each partner will vote in favour of an investment project only if:

$$RNN_t \sum_{t=1}^{P} (1+r)^{-t} > 0 \tag{5}$$

where N reflects interest payments and RNN is the income earned by the firm, net of both depreciation allowances and interest paid on the invested capital. As argued before, the firm will implement the project only if more than 50 per cent of its partners will find it worthwhile.

In contrast, a capitalistic firm will approve the investment project if:

$$RNN_t \sum_{t=1}^{\infty} (1+r)^{-t} > 0 \tag{6}$$

This seems enough to justify the argument that LMFs, too, will show a tendency to under-invest when the partners do not expect to stay in the firm for an indefinite period of time.

Whereas a comparison of (3) and (4) with (5) and (6) may suggest equal levels of under-investment in both of these types of cooperative firm, in fact there is a major difference between them. The net income of a WMF is income net of depreciation, while that of an LMF is income net of depreciation and interest paid on the invested sums; from this, it clearly follows that the partner of a WMF (knowing that on leaving the firm he will forfeit the interest on his investment) will have a lesser incentive to invest than the partner of an LMF (who knows that he will always keep the interest on the sums invested in the firm and, on leaving, will only lose his share of the income net of the interest paid).

This result, though at variance with the usual findings of the literature (see Jensen and Meckling 1979: 481–484; and, for an even more correct perspective, Ellerman 1986: 65), is fairly simple. As a rule, investment both yields an income flow and increases the value of a firm. When making an investment project, a capitalistic firm will consider both of these effects, whereas a pure cooperative firm (the LMF) will only consider the net income that would flow from the investment. This, however, implies that the partner of an LMF will perceive an investment as less advantageous than it is for a capitalistic firm in the same situation.

Let us repeat that this result is both simple and consistent with the nature of an LMF, a firm whose partners do not own the capital goods they use (see Jossa

1986; also, see Chapter 6, this volume) and which clearly separates income earned on capital from income earned through work. The question is: who cashes what an investment may yield above the current rate of interest in a pure labour cooperative? And as this yield cannot go to capitalists, since these stay outside the firm (given that all of the capital is borrowed), it will go to the workers throughout their periods of membership. As far as net worth increases generated by the investment are concerned, it is clear that as soon as the partners leave the firm, they forfeit any right in them (see Flakierski 1989: 65).

Departing from Vanek, my conclusion is that both the LMF and the WMF may under-invest, but that this tendency may be counteracted by the opposite tendency – i.e. over-investment, which will be discussed in the next two sections.

5 Under-investment and defence of the job

The tendency of self-managed firms to under-invest has been denied in a number of studies that have not been given sufficient attention. Setting out from the increases in firm size and headcounts that investment produces, some researchers have argued that where the workers' target is not only maximising per capita income, but also making jobs as safe as possible, investment in a self-managed firm – for the very reason that it is made in the interests of those whose jobs may be at risk – tends to exceed the corresponding levels in capitalistic firms.

This argument can be further developed. Work in a self-managed firm may be associated with a number of advantages – e.g. participation in the firm's decision-making processes, a more pleasant working environment and others that will be entered upon in greater detail further on. To this extent, as long as an investment may reduce the risk of job loss, it also extends these advantages over time by creating new jobs, strengthening the firm and lowering risks of bankruptcy (see Uvalic 1986a: 399–401; 1986b: 21–22).

In analytical terms, the tendency of a WMF to over-invest is expressed in the following way. Let us assume that an investment yields an amount R per year for an infinite number of years and that the partners expect to stay in the firm for P years if the investment is not made and for Q years if the investment is made (where $Q > P$, as the investment makes the job safer). If partners attach value S to the greater safety and amenity of the job, then a WMF will invest when:

$$RN_t \sum_{t=1}^{Q} (1+r)^{-t} + S_t \sum_{t=1}^{Q} (1+r)^{-t} > C_0 \qquad (7)$$

where C_0 is the price of the machinery. Comparing (7) with (4), it may well be the case that a WMF will be found to over-invest.

Let us repeat that most of the points discussed in this section are hardly ever touched upon in the literature, in terms that the main subject on which authors tend to expatiate is the assumption that the fear of failures and the resulting lay-off risks may induce the partners of cooperatives to authorise fewer investments (see Jensen and Meckling 1979; Connock 1982; Drèze 1993; Doucouliagos 1995; Dow 2003). In other words, in evaluating the extent to which an investment is, or is not, in the interest of a given partner, one must assume that the investment will not have the effect of reducing employment, since an investment that will result in a substantial increase in the firm's net income might not appear advantageous to the partner fearing to be deprived of his job in consequence of it.

6   Investment in human capital and the cooperative firm

As I have said, the minor fear of unemployment is not the only reason why the partners of cooperatives tend to stay on with their firms. As decisions in cooperatives are passed by majority votes,[13] the individual workers have an added incentive to commit themselves to the firm, because any dis-utilities that could possibly arise are such that the worker of a cooperative, more than the worker of a capitalistic firm, can remove them through a sort of voice effect. Whereas the dissenting worker of a capitalistic firm just has the option of leaving, in a cooperative firm he can voice his dissatisfaction and participate in the subsequent decision-making process. If this is true, jobs in the cooperative firm will tend to be tailored to the partners' needs, and this will clearly augment their commitment to the firm and reduce quitting – i.e. reduce the number of workers leaving voluntarily.

Inasmuch as this is correct – i.e. if quitting is actually less frequent in cooperative firms – an important consequence for investment arises. So far, the analysis of investment in self-managed firms has been confined to investment in fixed assets. In actual fact, firms also invest in human capital, and when this is the case the time horizons of both capitalistic and cooperative firms span the period of time the workers can be expected to continue working for the firm.

It has long been recognised that the fear of quitters may induce capitalistic firms to under-invest in human capital. And while it is true that an efficient outcome will only be reached if workers and the firm share the risks and benefits of investment in human capital, in point of fact neither of them can be sure that the working relationship will last long enough to take advantage of all the expected gains from the investment. In fact, even in the case of firm-specific human capital, workers quitting their jobs will reduce the benefits the firm expects to draw from its investment in human capital.

As mentioned before, to the extent that quitting rates depend, among other things, on working conditions, in cooperative firms, which make decisions by a majority vote, Hirschman's voice mechanism is likely to prevail.

In contrast, when the quitting rates of a cooperative firm are lower for this particular reason, both the benefits expected from investment in human capital and, accordingly, investment in training will increase.

In short, the whole argument can be posed as follows. When deciding on an investment in human capital, both cooperatives and capitalistic firms will consider whether it is in their best interests to produce an asset over which the individual worker retains full property rights. As this particular aspect of the property rights regime can never be modified, the firm, in discounting the benefits expected to flow from its investment, will include the probability of unwelcome resignations. If the relevant interest rate is the same for both types of firms, but the quitting rate differs, so that the quitting rate of a cooperative firm is lower than the quitting rate of a firm maximising profit, then, as a consequence, the cost of investment in human capital that a cooperative firm is willing to bear will be higher for a given time horizon and interest rate.

If the above argument holds, the tendency to under-invest is much reduced (or even eliminated), as investment can be considered as the sum of both investment in fixed assets and investment in human capital.

The greater propensity for investment in human capital may also have a different explanation. As it is difficult to see the purpose of pooling generic (i.e. non-specific) resources into a firm, some theorists today tend to assume that firm-specific resources are one explanation for the very existence of firms. Capital and labour resources are classed as firm-specific if they decrease in value on being moved from one firm to another.

The property rights based model of the firm theorised by Grossman, Hart and Moore (GHM) is based on the initial assumption that property is tantamount to control and on two additional assumptions: the idea that a firm is to be equated with the capital assets that it owns (Grossman and Hart 1986: 692) and the argument that 'ownership confers residual rights of control over the firm's assets' (Hart and Moore 1990: 1120). Moreover, considerable emphasis is laid on the insight that the owners of given assets are fully and exclusively entitled to prevent third parties from making any use of them and that the essence of ownership is the owners' title to dispose of the assets from which they draw the payoffs of their business. This exclusive disposition right may indirectly lead to control over human capital.

In GHM's theoretical model, the primary importance of rights of control is to determine the relative power positions of the parties to a labour relation and, accordingly, the distribution pattern of a firm's surplus and its incentives to invest in physical and human capital. This influence explains why business mergers may produce two antipodean results: a greater incentive for the purchaser of the other firm to invest in physical and human capital; and, conversely, the loss of the right to invest on the part of the owner of the purchased firm. Workers, for their part, will give more consideration to the goals of an agent whom they know to be in control of the assets that are their work implements.

Commenting on this model, Stiglitz rightly concluded that the true essence of ownership was not the right to appropriate the residual, but the residual rights of control over the relevant assets: title to use assets of every kind and nature for any purposes not specifically provided for in a contract is only vested in the owner, which is tantamount to saying that an owner who is not contractually obliged to make specified actions is free to use all the assets of which he has control for the purposes he will deem most expedient from time to time (see Stiglitz 1994: 165).

This line of reasoning may help explain the basic difference between capitalistic and cooperative firms in matters of surplus and incentives. Upon the transformation of a capitalistic firm into a cooperative, the firm's control rights over the relevant capital assets are transferred from the one-time owners to the workers' collective with unpredictable results in terms of efficiency. And this is an explanation for the greater propensity for human capital investment observed in cooperatives (see McCain 1992: 213–214; Jossa and Cuomo 1997: 277–281).

7 Are producer cooperatives biased against innovation?

An additional issue to be discussed at this point is the assumed scant innovation focus of cooperatives – a problem that is closely associated with the under-investment issue and is held to explain why cooperatives are particularly numerous in comparatively asset-light industries.

The main reasons why producer cooperatives are thought to be less innovation-focused than capitalistic companies are listed below (for additional details, see, for instance, Jensen and Meckling 1979; Ben Ner 1988; Gintis 1989; Bonin *et al.* 1993; Drèze 1993; Doucouliagos 1995; Dow 2003; Maietta and Sena 2010):

1. The funding difficulties faced by cooperatives often prevent them from adopting capital-intensive technologies.
2. Cooperatives often have less qualified managers and, consequently, managers with a less pronounced innovation focus.
3. Considering the high risks involved in innovation projects (by their very nature), the members of cooperatives, who are usually risk-averse, tend to abstain from introducing any.
4. As cooperatives are usually smaller than their capitalistic twins, they mostly have smaller research and development departments and fewer resources for investment in innovative schemes.
5. Due to the awareness that bankruptcy risks are remote, the managers of cooperatives avoid engaging in head-to-head competition.

The first three objections are effectively refuted by the demonstration (see above) that cooperatives are not necessarily risk-averse, do not face insurmountable financing difficulties and may well have able managers.

As for the fourth, size-related objection, further on I will argue that a government intending to implement a form of market socialism should primarily enforce benefits in favour of large-sized firms – a reflection that strips this objection of all its weight.

The only argument for a reduced innovation focus of cooperatives that seems to be left is, thus, the assumed lesser involvement of cooperatives in the competitive race as a result of remote insolvency risks. And although this objection is fairly insignificant in itself, it is worth countering it by reference to an interesting idea by Adam Smith, according to whom innovation processes are often instigated by personnel engaged in production independent of research and development departments. To the extent that Smith is right, in consequence of their greater interest in the positive performance of their firm, the worker part-ners of a cooperative are likely to prove much more proactive than the hired workers of a capitalistic company.

8 Concluding remarks

The following conclusions may be drawn from the analysis I have made:

1. A tendency to under-invest may exist both in WMFs and LMFs.
2. As investments, once made, are usually reiterated or renewed, there is an argument to say that this tendency is stronger than usually highlighted in the current literature.
3. As a result of the reiteration or renewal of investments, the tendency to under-invest operates (in LMFs and WMFs), even when the partners expect to remain in the cooperative for longer, on average, than the life of the single investment.
4. Both in WMFs and LMFs, the tendency to under-invest is dependent on the period of time that the partners expect to remain with the cooperative, but is not dependent on the life of the individual investment.
5. In both types of cooperatives, there is a tendency to over-invest, which is caused by the wish of the partners to make their jobs in the cooperative as safe as possible.
6. In both types of cooperatives, there is a tendency to over-invest, which is the effect of the partners' right to participate in the firm's decision-making processes and the resulting stronger commitment of the workers to the firm.[14]
7. There is nothing to suggest that under-investment would tendentially exceed over-investment.

The findings of this chapter are in line with my recommendation that coopera-tives be organised as LMFs, rather than as WMFs. Other advantages of the former type of cooperative will be mentioned and discussed further on.

Notes

1   Pursuant to a law passed in Yugoslavia in December 1953 to enforce provisions gov-erning the management of corporate fixed assets, the workers' collective had a 'right of use' upon the firm's capital goods.
2   For Vanek's analysis of this subject (which differs greatly from that of Pejovich and Furubotn dealt with further on), see Vanek (1971a, 1971b).
3   In line with early research on this subject, we set out from the assumption that self-financing cooperatives are not allowed to borrow any capital from banks. Though contradicted by Yugoslav practice, this assumption is recurring in studies (of firms that self-finance themselves, both with corporate funds and external credit) designed to demonstrate that external financing added to the problems faced by self-managing

firms (see Furubotn and Pejovich 1973: 280–281). Some researchers (for instance, Stephen 1980) have shown that this assumption had only been introduced for simplicity purposes.

4 See Pejovich (1975: 262ff.), Furubotn and Pejovich (1970a, 1970b) and Furubotn (1976, 1980).

5 For an exhaustive analysis of under-investment in cooperatives, see Cuomo (1997, 2010: ch. 4).

6 As has been made clear, in none of his writings has Vanek made the assumption that self-managed firms cannot disinvest (see, on this point, Zafiris 1982: 65–66; Uvalic 1986a: 390–391, 413, fn. 6).

7 In point of fact, Furubotn and Pejovich are not concerned with WMFs in general, but with socialist – i.e. state-owned – WMFs. In their opinion, insofar as the firm receives its capital goods in usufruct from the state, it cannot be empowered to sell them and distribute the relevant proceeds among its partners. As mentioned by Stephen, in Vanek, the ban on investment is also associated with the 'collective nature of investment' (see Stephen 1984: 69; 1978); however, here, Stephen probably misinterprets Vanek's line of reasoning.

8 See Vanek (1971a: 175; 1971b: 188).

9 See Connock (1982: 288).

10 Hence, Vanek's assumption that the duration of an investment is infinite (see Vanek 1977: 187) appears fairly realistic, while the contention that he traces underinvestment to the assumption that capital goods last forever is not correct. Such criticisms have been set forth, among others, by Zafiris (1982: 56–59) and Stephen (1984: 79).

11 See Stephen (1984: 68).

12 In an analysis of the literature, Ellerman has pointed to the widespread, though incorrect, belief that under-investment is caused by the fact that 'workers who leave the firm before the asset has been fully depreciated are forced to "forfeit" the non-depreciated portion of the asset, which they nevertheless "paid for" with their reinvested earnings' (Ellerman 1986: 63).

13 For the benefits to the production process coming from implementing voting procedures, see Drèze (1989: 31–35); for arguments against the desirability of having majority rules, see Furubotn (1978).

14 An in-depth analysis of the under-investment issue is developed in Bonin and Putterman (1987: ch. II)

5 Alchian and Demsetz's critique of labour-managed firms

1 Introduction

In this chapter, I will examine a criticism of employee-managed firms that is inherent in the theory of the firm of Alchian and Demsetz (AD) and is generally rated as the most solid objection against these firms. Ever since the appearance of AD's analysis in 1972, it was almost concordantly held to offer a convincing and exhaustive explanation of the reasons why capitalistic firms outnumber and out-perform cooperatives in any free market economy. Numerous points raised for discussion in later years ignited a divisive debate, which is worth discussing here.

In my opinion, AD's critique of cooperatives is bound to crumble under the weight of the numerous objections that it comes in for. Hence, the decision to provide a comprehensive overview of these criticisms and try to establish the bearing they have on this debate.

2 Cooperatives in Alchian and Demsetz's theory of the firm

First and foremost, AD's pioneer contribution is a theory of the firm explaining why associations of producers of the type we name 'firms' arise. AD's starting proposition is that firms are mainly created because team production is more efficient than individual production – i.e. because the aggregate output of a team exceeds the arithmetic sum of the individual outputs that the team members would generate if each of them were to work on his own.

At a certain point in their article (1972: 77), we read: 'It is common to see the firm characterized by the power to settle issues by fiat, by authority, or by disciplinary action superior to that available in the conventional market. This is a delusion'. Indeed, in the opinion of these authors, a firm draws its origin from contracts and its authority and disciplinary powers are strictly determined by the clauses of agreements freely negotiated between parties in the marketplace. An entrepreneur telling his employees what to do is comparable to the individual consumer ordering the commodities he needs from a grocer's and ceasing to buy his provisions from that supplier if his orders are not satisfactorily performed.[1] To look at the manager as continually engaged in organising, directing or assigning workers to individual tasks within the firm is misleading, for the entrepreneur's real task is to negotiate contracts on terms that will prove accept-able to both parties (see also, Nozick 1974: 160ff).[2] If this is true, where does the difference between the employer/employee relationship and the corresponding customer/grocer relation lie? In fact – as AD answer – a firm is: (1) a team that carries on production activities; and (2) an organisation in which a central agent enters into contracts with all of the remaining team partners.[3]

To discourage employee shirking, each firm establishes a specific corporate function responsible for supervising and monitoring the performance of indi-vidual team partners. This is the task of the entrepreneur or monitor, the above-mentioned central agent who hires and dismisses team partners, enters into contractual agreements with them and sees that they all perform their tasks to the best of their abilities. But who will monitor the monitor? In 'classical' capitalis-tic firms, this problem is solved by empowering the central agent to appropriate the balance between revenues and costs, since this creates an incentive for the entrepreneur to discipline team work at a high level of efficiency. As AD put it, the reason why the classical capitalistic entrepreneur is allowed to appropriate the firm's profit – i.e. the difference between revenues and costs – is not so much the greater risk proneness of those who go into business (as Knight assumed in his celebrated 1921 contribution)[4] as the consideration that this is the most appropriate way of remunerating a person who is monitoring and measuring the commitment of the team partners to their tasks.[5]

In short, AD's central proposition is that the entrepreneur is he who takes upon himself the task of watching team partners at work upon and that a fair remuneration for this task is an income that increases in direct proportion to the performance of the team.[6]

AD hold that this explains why firms more often tend to organise themselves along capitalistic than cooperative lines (see AD 1972: 786). If profit – they argue – were equally apportioned among workers, instead of being entirely appropriated by the person in charge of watching others at work, workers would be induced to work both harder and better, but the monitor would have less incentive to perform his tasks properly. As a result, productivity losses from a lower level of control would probably exceed the gains from the reduced benefits that individual workers would draw from working less or less hard.[7] Even more so, in a firm that apportions all profits among workers (as is the rule in coopera-tives) and does not adopt a specialised monitoring function, AD hold it reason-able to assume that productivity levels would slow down, despite the greater interest of workers in the efficient functioning of their firm (see also, Jensen and Meckling 1979: 485).[8]

On closer analysis, AD far from deny that cooperatives might be a viable solution under certain circumstances. A case in point, they argue, is small-sized firms; especially in firms where a fairly small number of partners are 'actively' engaged within the team (and aware of their major contribution to the results of the team's joint work), experience has shown that profit-sharing and a participa-tory organisational structure may carry noticeable advantages. Another reason why profit-sharing is a particularly appropriate solution in smaller firms is the fact that mutual control is both easier and more effective when production activities are carried out by a fairly small number of participants.[9]

3 A critique of Alchian and Demsetz's approach

AD's idea that the entrepreneur/employee relationship vests in the former just as much power as is wielded by a party entering into contracts in the marketplace has been called into question by theorists who consider the firm a hierarchical structure where specific investments are all-important. According to these authors, AD's view that firing an employee is, to a manager, tantamount to switching over to a different supplier (at least from the perspective that interests us here) is not correct, since the costs involved in finding a new job are far higher than those necessary to obtain fresh orders (see, for example, Williamson 1986: 67–70; Dahl 1985: 114–116; Gould 1985: 206–208).

As argued by Ronald Coase (1960), AD's approach would be correct if no transaction costs were entailed, but in the absence of transaction costs there would be no firms at all, and all business operations would be directly transacted in the marketplace.

This suggests a very general argument that can be expressed in the following manner. As mentioned before, if transaction costs were nil, there would be no firms. However, this amounts to saying that 'in the absence of transaction costs', firms would become unnecessary and that 'any enterprise will operate efficiently regardless of how rights to participate in its management decisions may be assigned' (Mc Cain 1992: 206).

One additional criticism of the idea that the employer exercises no power over workers is found in a number of analyses showing that certain forms of monitoring associated with the division of labour and other organisational patterns are not only adopted for reasons of efficiency, but also in an effort to maintain and strengthen the employer's authority (Marglin 1974; Braverman 1974; Edwards 1979; Putterman 1982; Bowles 1985).[10] Howard and King argue that:

> [w]age-labour relationships are one area in which Marx discusses the role of coercion as a coordinating device within fully developed capitalistic systems. His argument hinges on the fact that employment contracts cannot be specified for all contingencies, so that the terms of exchange of labour services for wages are contestable and conflict is endemic.[11]
>
> (2001: 796)

Be that as it may, the main point I wish to discuss in this chapter is the monitoring issue, for this is what AD hold to be the main obstacle to the establishment of cooperative firms. According to Jensen and Meckling's agency theory (1976, 1979: 470–471), a firm is 'a nexus of contracts' and agency is the relationship whereby one person, termed the principal, directs his agent to perform a task for his account.[12] To reduce the inevitable divergence between his own interests and those of his agent and confine the resulting losses, the entrepreneur uses the agency contract and the monitoring function. Agency costs include the costs of monitoring, those of co-interesting the agent in the proper performance of the contract and the resulting loss; and the agency contract and the monitoring function are the tools used to minimise such agency costs.

Do these reflections support AD's contention that an agency contract between the owners of a capitalistic firm and its managers will vouchsafe a higher level of efficiency than that obtainable in a cooperative?

Before answering this question, let us make clear that the problem facing cooperatives, though surely one of corporate governance, differs from other corporate governance issues, since it arises not so much from the separation of property from control as from a multiple control (or multiple usufruct) structure. When the monitoring function is vested in a plurality of individuals – it is argued – each monitor has little incentive to see to his tasks efficiently, because he knows that while incurring total monitoring costs, he will only appropriate a fraction of the greater income generated by his effort; the resulting inducement to free riding will be all the stronger, the more that the control or usufruct structure is fragmented. But is this really the main drawback on the proliferation of cooperative firms?

In situations where all the workers engage in monitoring – as is concordantly assumed to be the case in cooperative firms – the first objection[13] to AD's analysis is as follows: compared to the central monitor cashing the whole residual, individual partners will doubtless have a lesser incentive to perform their monitoring function at a high level of efficiency, but whereas in a capitalistic firm this function is vested in one or a few specialised monitors, in a cooperative it lies with all the partners – and a hundred pairs of eyes are far better than one. In other words, in a cooperative where all the partners engage in monitoring, none of them are specifically responsible for this function, but all of them will nonetheless be watching others at work out of self-interest in their dual capacity as monitors and residual claimants (see, for example, Miller 1993: 306; Hansmann 1996: 70). And there is no evidence that a single monitor, however strong his incentive, will perform this function better than a plurality of monitors with a lesser incentive. Those performing the monitoring function in democratic firms without a designated monitor are residual claimants – and this is probably what counts most.

With reference to the issue of monitoring costs, it is worth emphasising that reciprocal partner monitoring entails no costs for the firm, since this can do without personnel specifically hired for the monitoring function. In the simplest case scenario, each worker will be monitoring the one next to him: each worker processing raw materials or semi-finished products can quality check the materials conveyed to him by others without incurring appreciable costs; no video camera will be needed to watch people taking a coffee break, since those working beside them will record the fact at no cost.[14]

Moreover, there can be little doubt that the disapproval of fellow partners may act as a powerful deterrent to shirking, especially because free riding is perceived as a far more odious practice among peers than in employer-employee relations, in which workers have traditionally played cat and mouse with employers.

Lastly, as shirking is an infectious disease, there are reasons to assume that the partners of a democratic firm will have an incentive to work hard, in order to set an example for others to follow.

In their in-depth analysis of the monitoring issue, Bowles and Gintis shed light on many distinct 'effects'. In their opinion, the monitoring issue is first of all an instance of 'market failure' associated with the non-measurable nature of worker commitment and the resulting difficulty to word employment contracts in such a way as to specify all the facets of the job descriptions of individual employees. The typical strategy of a capitalistic firm in a competitive labour market is to adopt pay rates well above the 'reservation wage', to appoint specialised monitors and to use the threat of dismissal as a means of eliciting the desired levels of commitment. In contrast, to deal with drawbacks from incomplete work contracts, cooperatives adopt the strategy of leveraging the self-interest of their workers as 'residual claimants' by co-interesting them in the production process. In this way, they create an inducement to greater commitment and obtain levels of efficiency that in capitalistic firms are generally unknown (see Bowles and Gintis 1994: 210).

The greater commitment to work stemming from the workers' status as residual claimants is what Bowles and Gintis term 'direct residual claimancy effect'.[15] This effect is maximised in small-sized firms, because in larger cooperatives the workers know all too well that only a small fraction of the excess income generated by their higher work effort will ultimately be distributed to them.

According to Bowles and Gintis, there are other reasons, besides the direct residual claimancy effect, that may account for the greater efficiency of cooperatives compared to their capitalistic twins. One of these is the considerable commitment of workers who feel that their status as co-owners of their cooperative makes them responsible for the firm's performance. There can be little doubt that people working on their own derive more satisfaction from work than those in employment or that partners identifying with their firm fear dismissal more than workers in capitalistic firms. Both these factors suggest that levels of commitment in cooperatives are likely to exceed those in capitalistic firms. At first sight, this process, or 'participation effect', may seem to fall in with the direct residual claimancy effect, but on closer analysis it differs from it, as I will show further on (see Bowles and Gintis 1993: 27–28).

Second, those making decisions in common with others feel responsible for such joint decisions and will maximise commitment out of a feeling of loyalty (see, for example, Oakeshott 1978; Horvat 1982; Birchall and Simmons 2004a, 2004b). Hence, the process that, borrowing Hirschmann's language, can be termed the 'loyalty effect'.

Third, the workers of a cooperative firm can cross-monitor each other at a high level of efficiency. Let us repeat that the costless information on the work of fellow partners to which the partners of a cooperative have access enables them to judge if those working beside them are seeing to their tasks with adequate commitment. This process, which Bowles and Gintis (1993: 28) term 'reciprocal monitoring effect', is confirmed by a number of field surveys (see Gunn 1984; Fitzroy and Kraft 1986; Craig and Pencavel 1993).

The combined result of the effects defined by Bowles and Gintis is to determine that the lesser effort of some may be perceived as detrimental to the interests of the partners; in other words, that the free riding criticism may turn out to be unrealistic.[16]

As shown above, one major criticism of AD's free riding hypothesis has to do with the subject of reciprocity – a major theme on which both Fehr and the Zürich School have provided special focus. Sen (1994) and Hart (1995: 681) have argued that even in a capitalistic firm, the production process can be termed a merit good, since workers draw various benefits or disadvantages from the success or failure of their firm. As suggested by the experimental findings of the Zürich School, reciprocity is a component of human action with a major impact on efficiency (see Fehr and Schmidt 1999; Crivelli 2002: 37, 40). However, because of inherently closer cross-relations between the modes of conduct of the individual workers of a cooperative, in this type of firm the impact tends to be much stronger than in firms organised along capitalistic lines.

As a result of the greater relevance of the reciprocity principle in cooperatives, individualism preferably describes the typical conduct in a capitalistic firm. Mutual confidence is crucial to the smooth performance of the production process of a cooperative and is heightened by the successful attainment of the partners' common aims. Very often, the feeling of solidarity binding the partners of a cooperative to each other may induce them to work even harder than their mere self-interest would dictate. Emulation is no less important and, unless it degenerates into rivalry or mutual distrust, it will induce the partners to work towards boosting productivity. Lastly, the partners tend to identify with their cooperative much more strongly than the workers of a capitalistic firm and are thereby refrained from any forms of opportunistic conduct.

The major importance of mutual confidence in cooperatives determines that control, which is born of mistrust, may diminish the satisfaction that those watched at work draw from their proper conduct (which is designed to deserve the confidence placed in them). Falk and Kosfeld (2004) have provided evidence that excess control of the kind typical in capitalistic firms may even prove counterproductive, in terms of slowing down productivity or making work more toilsome. Mutual trust, Zamagni (2005: 54) argues, may add to the self-esteem of those in whom it is placed and may thereby reduce risks of free riding (on this point, see also, Weitzman and Kruse 1990; Kandel and Lazear 1992). These reflections are in line with Bowles and Gintis's criticisms of AD's approach.

4 Further criticisms of Alchian and Demsetz's analysis

The decisive objection against AD's analysis is implicit in Veblen's theory of the evolution of entrepreneurship. Based on this, expanding markets and increasing business volumes have made it impossible for the owner-entrepreneur to supervise all of the firm's processes entirely on his own, and this accounts for the gradual substitution of impersonal standard wage contracts for the previous individual agreements between the owner-entrepreneur and each of his workers. In Veblen's opinion, the result of this evolutionary process is the piecemeal migration of the monitoring function from the entrepreneur to experts specifically trained for this function (see Veblen 1923: 105). And as it is clear that cooperatives can hire salaried monitors no less than capitalistic firms, this objection comes to AD's approach as a deadly blow.

In other words, the most forceful objection to AD's critique is the argument that the partners of a cooperative are free to appoint a monitor if they feel this to be in their best interests – as the experience of Israeli kibbutzim or the Mondragon cooperatives in Spain confirm (see Putterman 1984: 173; Elster and Moene 1989b: 28; Sacconi 1992). Whereas the free riding issue poses the need for a cooperative firm to appoint a manager with a strong incentive to discipline the partners' work, in itself it far from provides evidence that cooperatives are doomed to inefficiency only because they have no officer specifically assigned to the monitoring function. In the opinion of Eswaran and Kotwal (1989: 162), the insight we ultimately derive from AD's approach is the need for a cooperative to appoint and effectively remunerate a monitor – an argument that does not rule out the possibility that capital could be hired by labour.

The point of AD's critique of cooperatives still to be addressed is the status of the monitor. Must he necessarily be a 'residual claimant' – i.e. an individual entitled to cash the whole balance between costs and revenues – or can he be paid a fixed salary?

The argument that only a manager paid with a residual claim will perform the monitoring function to a satisfactory level is disproved by practical experience. In limited companies, the monitoring function is vested in managers, whereas the 'residual' – the profit earned by the company – is distributed to the shareholders (on this theme, see, for example, Putterman 1990: 168; Mazzoli 1998: 153–154). To counter this objection, AD argue that managers refrain from shirking their duty to monitor and measure the team partners' commitment to work by the competition they face from managers both inside and outside the company. In other words, in the opinion of AD, control over the monitors of a limited company is ensured by the shareholders' right to dismiss and replace shirking managers (see Alchian and Demsetz 1972: 788). Inasmuch as this is true, the answer to their objection is that nothing would prevent a cooperative from firing its monitor if the partners should find that he is failing to see to his duties to their full satisfaction.

AD themselves make it clear that the prospect of appropriating the firm's profit is by no means the only inducement to efficiency for a manager. An additional, but equally powerful, incentive is competition. To make a career, a manager is required to further the interests of his current employer and make a name for himself as an able professional. A manager causing loss to his company by failing to eradicate employee shirking would ruin his reputation and would hardly be offered employment by any other company (see, for example, AD

1972: 781–783, 788; Alchian and Allen 1983: 188). However, the manager competition hypothesis can doubtless be extended from the capitalistic to the cooperative firm.

In short, the above reflections far from support the need to pay a manager a variable income or assume that a cooperative paying managers a fixed salary will necessarily underperform.

Turning to situations in which it is difficult to watch individuals at work or measure the share of the team output attributable to each of them, Holmstrom (1982) has argued that incentive and monitoring difficulties of this kind can be solved by entering into a collective contract with a team and making the disbursement of the contractual fee conditional on an aggregate team output commensurate with a level that is attainable in a non-shirking environment. However, although this practice would afford dispensing with the monitoring function altogether, in the ordinary course of business it is the exception and there are reasons to believe that, by its very nature, it would be more easily adopted in a cooperative than a capitalistic firm.

In sum, AD's idea that want of a specialised monitoring function is the main drawback responsible for the lower productivity levels of cooperatives is objectionable in a considerable number of respects (see also, Cable and Fitzroy 1980; Putterman 1984: 172–175; Bonin and Putterman 1987: 46–54; Faccioli and Scarpa 1998: 70–72; Bruni and Zamagni 2004; Zamagni 2005).

The argument that the free-riding hypothesis regarding team work can barely explain why labour is usually hired by capital and not vice versa is amply confirmed by comparative studies of monitoring costs in capitalistic versus cooperative firms whose findings point to negligible differences between the two (see Morse 2000).

5 The case of professionals and artists

The argument that partnerships are the ideal form of association for professionals has been mentioned before. AD trace it back to the difficult measurement of the individual contributions that professionals make to the overall performance of the team and the fact that monitoring hardly makes sense in such a situation. This line of reasoning was countered by Hansmann's objection that 'it is relatively easy to assess the quality of a lawyer's work, in part because the work product frequently consists of written documents produced by that lawyer alone' (Hansmann 1996: 70).

On closer analysis, though, Hansmann's argument is marred by a misinterpretation of AD's analysis. He sets out from the assumption that a single pair of eyes specifically assigned to the monitoring function is outperformed by more pairs of eyes not purposely mandated to such effect (a view that I share), but ascribed to AD the idea that the partners of a cooperative will deal with the shirking problem much more efficiently than the specialised monitors of a capitalistic firm, due to their sheer number and the strong incentive to perform this function at a high level of efficiency. The strong incentive of each partner of an employee-managed firm to watch all the others at work, he wrote, 'has led many to argue' – most conspicuously by Alchian and Demsetz in a well-known article – 'that employee-owned firms are particularly likely to arise when monitoring employees is unusually difficult' (Hansmann 1996: 70).

In fact, this is not AD's position. AD did present partnerships as particularly numerous in fields such as the professions and the entertainment industry, where they held monitoring to be particularly difficult, but they did not speak of the greater efficiency of a hundred pairs of eyes compared to one. In their opinion, in situations where monitoring is difficult, it is more sensible to rely on people concerned with increasing output out of self-interest than on a specialised monitor. In a partnership formed of a small number of professionals, they argue, the desire of each partner to add to his earnings will result in an added incentive to efficiency, despite the awareness that it is difficult to monitor his actual rate of work (see AD 1972: 790).

As Hansmann puts it, to account for the tendency of professionals to be joined in partnerships, we have to bear in mind that they preferably provide direct services to clients, instead of intermediate services to firms. This, they argue, results in great mobility, for a professional will retain his customers upon switching over to a different firm and will be less reluctant to leave the current partners of his team and join with others in establishing a new partnership (see Hansmann 1996: 72).

Another explanation of the viability of cooperatives of professionals in Hansmann's approach is the considerable homogeneity of their labour force. On closer analysis, this explanation, too, has to do with the monitoring issue: although the members of a partnership have little, if any, coercive power over their peers, they surely can watch them at work more efficiently than they would be able to do so in respect of individuals assigned to different jobs from their own.

An additional related subject is the argument of those that hold that the efficiency of 'peer' monitoring increases in proportion to the quality content of a job. The quality content of a service is less easy to appraise than its quantitative content, and this may explain why top-down monitoring, which is less 'pervasive' than peer monitoring, is also less effective when applied to higher-level services (see Faccioli and Scarpa 1998: 72–73).

6 On the length of the working week

Turning to the 'second postulate of classical theory', we may now raise the following question: will the working week in a system of democratic firms be longer or shorter than it is in capitalistic firms? My answer to this question will provide a suitable introduction to further reflections on AD's approach.

Viewed in combination, the greater satisfaction deriving from own-account work in cooperatives versus employment in a capitalistic firm and the workers' title to appropriate the fruit of their labour would seem to suggest that cooperatives may prolong the working day, in order to boost their earnings. In fact, there is no evidence that more hours would be worked in an all-cooperatives system than in a capital-managed one.

In Keynes' opinion, in capitalistic systems, 'the second postulate of classical theory' is not applicable for a number of reasons: first, in unionised contexts, the optimal length of the working day or week is not bargained for by individual workers, but by trade unions for their account; second, employment levels and the length of the working day or week are mainly a function of aggregate demands for goods and services; and, above all, labour mismatches are frequent in any capitalistic economy. On the contrary, the second postulate does apply in a cooperative allowing its partners to freely fix their optimal working days. Consequently, since the workers of capital-managed businesses are prevented from fixing the optimal length of the working day, while those of labour-managed firms enjoy this right, it would appear that there are no reasons to assume that more hours will be worked in either system.

These provisional findings require the support of an in-depth analysis.

7 A mathematical formulation

Let

$$x = x(\bar{K}, L\bar{e}) \tag{1}$$

be the production function of the firm's only output, where L is the number of workers employed, $\bar{e}$ stands for their average production effort, K is assumed to be given and the number of workers employed and their aggregate production effort are perfect substitutes. If

$$U_i = f(y_i, e_i) \ (i = 1 \dots L) \tag{2}$$

is the utility function of the individual i, which depends on the income that the individual earns (y_i) and his level of effort (e_i), and if the function is assumed to be both additive and linear, the individual's optimal level of effort will be the level that maximises

$$U_i = \frac{P_x X - R}{L} - D_i(e_i) \tag{3}$$

where R is the interest payable on loan capital and D is the disutility of work.

The average effort of the firm's workers is:

$$\bar{e} = \bar{e}_{n-1} + \frac{e_i - \bar{e}_{n-1}}{n} \tag{4}$$

where e_i is the level of effort of the worker considered and $\bar{e}_{n-1}$ is the average effort of the remaining workers. The solution obtained when (3) is maximised using (1) and the constraint (4) is a Nash equilibrium for the situation in which each worker can freely determine his effort on the assumption that the rates of work of the rest are given. The result is:

$$\frac{p_x X'(Le)}{L} = D_i'(e_i) \tag{5}$$

where we assume that the part of the firm's profit earned by each partner is unrelated to his individual effort and that the income earned by the firm is equally apportioned among the partners of the cooperative.

Here, (5) shows that the commitment of a partner of a cooperative acting in accordance with individualistic profit calculations will be the level at which the marginal disutility of work equals the marginal productivity of his tasks, divided by the number of partners in the cooperative.

A Pareto social optimum would instead be obtained if:

$$p_x X'(Le) = D_i'(e_i) \tag{6}$$

Comparing (5) with (6) on the assumptions set out above, we find that:

1. The effort expended by each worker comes considerably short of the level that would maximise the benefits for the partners of the cooperative. This is because each partner is fully aware that, while accepting the whole disutility of a greater production effort, he would only receive the fraction of the corresponding benefit obtained by dividing the marginal productivity of his effort by the number of partners of the cooperative.
2. The effort expended by each worker diminishes in an inverse proportion to the number of partners in the cooperative. This obviously depends on the fact that L increases in proportion to the number of partners entitled to the excess income generated by those working harder than the rest.

Though certainly a severe criticism of cooperation as such, these findings far from support AD's argument that capitalistic firms are more efficient than cooperatives. In a capitalistic firm, a Pareto optimum would only be achieved if workers were free to determine the optimal length of their working week and their levels of effort, which is definitely not the case. In capitalistic firms, the working day and week are predetermined and managerial control over workers prevents the latter from determining their individual levels of effort (Keynes held that the 'second postulate of classical economics' was not applicable to capitalistic firms, see Keynes 1936). Moreover, whereas in a cooperative firm any increased effort on the part of a worker does generate an increase in income – though this is, at times, minimal – in capitalistic firms, wage levels are predetermined and, hence, unrelated to the productivity levels of the workforce. As a result, a worker's added effort will not result in a corresponding pay increase.

The only use to which the model described above can be put is a comparative analysis of the respective equilibrium situations of a cooperative firm and a hypothetical 'capitalistic' firm, where, *by absurdum*, workers are imagined not to be watched at work and the 'second postulate of classical economics' is assumed to apply.

At this point, we may ask ourselves what would happen in a specific situation – i.e. if the marginal disutility of work in a cooperative is assumed to be zero and the 'capitalistic' firm with which the equilibrium condition of our cooperative is compared is 'unmonitored'.

Comparing (5) – i.e. the equilibrium solution for the cooperative firm on the assumption that $D(e_i)=0$ – with (6) – i.e. the equilibrium level of our (unmonitored) 'capitalistic' firm in a situation of perfect competition – the marginal labour productivity level of the cooperative is found to be zero, while that of the 'capitalistic' firm will constantly be above zero; and as marginal productivity levels are inversely related to the rates of work used, the cooperative will generate a higher income.

This finding is at odds with the assumption that levels of effort in a cooperative are lower than those in a capitalistic firm allowing its workers to freely determine the length of their working week and the level of their production effort, and this finding holds both for the situation where

$$D_i'(e_i) = 0$$

and for each case in which:

$$D_{i,c}'(e_i)L < D_{i,p}'(e_i) \tag{7}$$

where $D_{i,c}'$ is the marginal disutility of work in a cooperative firm and $D_{i,p}'$ is the corresponding value for a 'capitalistic' firm (see Cugno and Ferrero 1992).

The implications of this finding for the worker commitment measuring and monitoring issues raised by AD are apparent.[17]

8 Final reflections

The greater part of the reflections developed above are in synch with the idea of Robertson and Dennison (1924: 121) that the main problem in cooperatives is the 'management issue', for it is difficult to deny that – given the tendency of cooperatives to distribute their income equitably among all the partners – few cooperatives are in a position to pay the high salaries that able managers can expect to earn in capitalistic firms.

Whenever a group of people resolve to work as a team – we may add – the partner outperforming the others in initiative and organisational skills will inevitably take the lead. The crux of the matter is that such a person has no incentive to establish a cooperative and share power and earnings with others. He will prefer to found a capitalistic firm, where he will hold all authority and, if sole owner, appropriate the whole of the surplus (Jensen and Meckling 1979; Abell 1983; Leete-Guy 1991: 69; Jossa and Cuomo 1997: 317; George 1997: 59–60). A case in point is the Basque 'Mondragon Group of Cooperatives', which was often left without top managers, the officers called upon to ensure the company's growth (see Zabaleta 1986: 29).

In the opinion of some, one way to overcome the 'management issue' is to choose managers preferably from amongst non-partners and thereby further the development of a market for managers. Another way is to ignite competition between capitalistic firms and cooperatives and then encourage the transformation of capitalistic firms into cooperatives through a purposely designed taxation system. The rationale behind this idea is the classification of cooperative firms as 'merit goods'.

Notes

1 The idea that neither the employer nor the employee are obliged to protract their contractual relationship indefinitely induced AD to argue that long-term employment contracts are not an essential attribute of the firm (see Alchian and Demsetz 1972: 777). Yet Williamson has shown that later on, Alchian changed his mind on this point (see Alchian 1984: 38–39; Williamson 1985: 53, fn. 11; Williamson 1986: 241–242).

2 This amounts to a criticism of Coase's theory of the firm, which is shared by Hart (see Hart 1989), but was dropped by Alchian at a later stage. In the words of Arienzo and Borrelli (2011: 58), over the past couple of years, 'the employment contract has turned, from a relationship between unequals, into a relationship between individuals negotiating a commercial deal on equal terms'.

3 According to some authors, cooperatives are hybrids blending market attributes with hierarchical mechanisms (see Valentinov and Fritzsch 2007; Menard 2004; Chaddad 2012), but while this is probably applicable to farming cooperatives, it does not extend to producer cooperatives operating in industry.

4 Models that vest monitoring functions in those least risk-averse were proposed by Kihlstrom and Laffont (1979) and Eswaran and Kotwal (1989).

5 Demsetz himself revealed that the greater part of his and Alchian's line of reasoning in the 1972 paper was based on suggestions drawn from Knight (Demsetz 1988c: 163–164, fn. 6).

6 In Demsetz's words, the main aim of the 1972 paper was to relate different firm organisation modes to different monitoring requirements (see Demsetz 1988c: 153). From the perspective of those who hold AD's main contribution to be the 'who will monitor the monitor' issue, the answer is appointing a residual claimant with a self-monitoring incentive – i.e. concerned with monitoring at a high level of efficiency (see Eswaran and Kotwal 1989: 162). Does this necessarily entail appointing a residual claimant? This issue will be addressed later.

7 On the scant efficiency of shareholder control or control by a large group of persons, see Hart (1995: 682–683).

8 Jensen and Meckling's view (1979) that a democratic firm structure may weigh on efficiency by weakening managers and their authority over the partners by whom they are appointed was theorised by Bernstein back in 1899: upon the abolition of the capitalistic ownership structure without concomitant organisational changes, Bernstein argued, the firm's organs would dissolve through loss of their common convergence point (see Bernstein 1899: 159).

9 Before I proceed to analyse AD's approach, it is worth mentioning the opinion of some authors that the lesser incentives to work in cooperatives are unrelated to the

control issue. Whereas in capitalistic firms incentives to work are generated by the fact that workers receive an income commensurate with their marginal product, in cooperatives worker incomes depend on the way the firm's residual is apportioned among the partners (see, for instance, Williamson 1980). However, as I will argue further on, Williamson's approach is hardly acceptable.

10 Bowles's argument in this well-known essay is that shirking is both congenital to human nature and greatly dependent on the way production is organised. To account for the greater efficiency of employee-managed firms, he highlights the lesser incentive to the shirking of workers who do not feel that they are being exploited, compared to those of a capitalistic firm, in which business is not carried on in the workers' interests.

11 The correct approach is that those who have no option but to do what is crucial for their subsistence or welfare cannot be assumed to be free (see, *inter alia*, Cohen 1978).

12 Disputing the definition of the firm as 'a nexus of contracts', Screpanti (2004) and Zamagni (2005) have rightly argued that the capitalistic firm is first and foremost 'a nexus of employment contracts' and that theoreticians of the 'nexus of contracts' mistake employment contracts for the myriad other agreements entered into by firms, as if they were the same. This argument is perfectly in keeping with the reflections above.

13 In this chapter, I am only dealing with criticisms relevant from an economic perspective. Political or psychological objections, such as Weisskopf's assumption of a deep mistrust of democracy, behind these approaches are not addressed (see Weisskopf 1993: 131). A far more comprehensive objection is that AD's monitoring theory lies open to the same criticisms that AD raised against Coase (see Hart 1989): it is not clear why team production and monitoring issues should be addressed within the firm, instead of via the market mechanisms.

14 Analysing plywood production in cooperatives versus capitalistic firms, Greenberg (1986: 43–44) noted that compared to the single monitor in the former, the latter tended to have up to six or seven monitors.

15 The main point on which Reich and Devine (1981), as well as Bowles and Gintis (1993), provided focus is the idea that sharing profits with workers reduces incentive costs and external monitoring requirements.

16 In the opinion of some, the critical factor determining if central monitoring outperforms mutual monitoring or vice versa is the technological content of the tasks involved (see Putterman 1984: 173–174).

17 For further details on this subject, see Sen (1966), Israelsen (1980), Ireland and Law (1981) and Aage (1995).

6 On the rational organisation of labour-managed firms

1 Introduction

In the debate on employee-managed firms, economists have often stressed the need for more detailed information on the institutional context that each author refers to. 'Much of the economic literature on the labour-managed firm' – Jensen and Meckling argued (1979: 475) – 'suffers from failure to specify clearly the institutional arrangements which the authors have in mind'; and the situation remained much the same in later years (see, *inter alia*, Bonin and Putterman 1987: 1–3). For example, several authors maintain that self-managed producer cooperatives generically 'reverse' the traditional capital–labour relation, but they do not specify that this applies only to cooperatives organised in line with Vanek's LMF-type. Considering the differences between capital and labour discussed in Dow's book (Dow 2003; see also, Skillman and Dow 2007), this generic claim does not provide the background knowledge required for a correct understanding of the institutional aspects of a labour-managed system. With this in mind, in this chapter, I wish to illustrate an organisation mode that is likely to ensure the efficient running of employee-managed firms.

For the purposes of this study, it is worth emphasising that while the reference system in this book is one that is predominantly composed of cooperative firms, the greater part of the approach can be extended to cooperatives carrying on business in capitalist systems.

2 Efficiency aspects of self-managed firms

The argument that only self-interest oriented cooperatives can be efficiently run will sound like an evident truth to any economist. The reason why I emphasise this notion is that Article 45 of the Italian Constitution restricts tax benefits to cooperatives classed as non-profit organisations. The rejection of the open door principle – another apparently self-evident prerequisite for the efficient running of a cooperative – also needs underscoring, because it is one of the mainstays of the cooperative movement.

A much more complex issue is the argument that a labour-managed firm intending to purchase capital goods has to borrow money capital. Based on majority resolutions passed by the partners, firms should be free to self-finance their investments on the condition that the partners are allotted bonds in the aggregate value of the distribution that would have been made if the relevant earnings had not been retained. In other words, the firm must be the LMF-type theorised by Vanek, which strictly segregates labour incomes from capital incomes when distributing its profits. The allotment of bonds to partners (as explained in Chapter 3) is necessary both to avoid under-investment and give security to external providers of funds. The bonds may be marketable or non-marketable and the differences between the two cases have been discussed by Zevi (2003) and Tortia (2005, 2007).

Our emphasis of the need to allow self-financed firms to allot bonds in the amounts of the partners' respective contributions to the firm's self-financing is justified by Vanek's initial distinction between self-managed firms, which do not self-finance themselves (LMFs), and self-financing firms (WMFs), as well as his claim that these tend to under-invest. Considering the major role of self-financing in many employee-managed firms, to prevent LMFs from self-financing, their investments would mean dooming the better-performing type of cooperative to failure. As a result, both types of cooperatives would be marred by severe short-comings: the LMF would be unable to secure the capital needed for its growth, whereas the WMF would tend to under-invest.

As mentioned above, the ideal organisational model for a cooperative is one that provides for the division of workers into categories based on training pro-grammes and examinations and for the distribution of the firm's income to the workers by reference to the coefficient assigned to each individual category, preferably at the central level. Here, it is worth adding that this arrangement would offer the additional advantage of making income distribution both fairer and more democratic.

An additional prerequisite for the efficient operation of a self-managed firm – the appointment of one or more managers – has also been mentioned before. The objection that joint decision-making by a council is the main obstacle to the growth and proliferation of cooperatives was first raised by John Stuart Mill. Back in 1871, Mill argued (745) that one-man management by the bearer of a specific interest was more advantageous than business conducted in association and that a single decision-maker created the assumptions for the attainment of goals that would otherwise be beyond reach, due to differences of opinion between the partners and time-consuming collective decision-making processes. Compared to a group of people, he added, a competent single entrepreneur freed from the control of a board was much better able to take balanced risks and adopt costly improvements. The idea that cooperatives have difficulty electing efficient managers has recently been put forward in a number of studies (including Thomas and Logan 1982; White and White 1988; Meek and Wood-worth 1990; Bartlett *et al.* 1992; Morris 1992; Kasmir 1996; Chaves and Sajardo 2004; Spear 2004; Basterretxea and Martinez 2012) and must be discussed here to complete the analysis of the AD's arguments. The idea is based on the grounds that:

1. As a rule, the salaries paid to the managers of cooperatives fall short of those paid to the managers of comparable capitalistic companies for a number of reasons.
2. Due to their medium to small size, cooperatives are usually unable to hire professionally qualified managers.
3. Most of the managers employed by cooperative firms are non-members who fail to develop a cooperative spirit and have difficulty establishing positive relationships with their subordinates.

But are these objections really convincing?

Such a simple move as the election of fully empowered managers would effectively sidestep the objection concerned. If the question involved simply deciding if workers as such are as qualified as shareholders to run their firms – Dahl wrote with regard to the option of representatives elected by the workers – the answer would be that they are much more qualified (see Dahl 1989: 331).[1]

On closer analysis, though, the question of the comparative abilities of workers versus shareholders to choose competent managers is just one point. Bernstein was among the very first to argue that the supposed non-viability of self-managed firms stems from the conflict between economic democracy and the need for discipline within any business enterprise. 'In the operation of a firm, where friction is the rule and unemotional resolutions are to be taken at all hours, day after day' – he wrote (1899: 158) – 'it is simply inadmissible for a manager to be employed by those managed and his office to be dependent on their whims'.

Bernstein's objection is far from irrelevant and is paralleled by Einaudi's later argument that 'able proactive managers will leave the enterprise the moment a workers' council is established' (1920: 688). Nonetheless, the fact remains that the decision-making problems associated with any form of business conducted in association necessitate both electing a manager and providing him with full powers. The scant cogency of Bernstein's objection is proved by experience, because the cooperatives that vest full authority in their managers are usually run efficiently enough.

A different critique is found in Lepage (1978: 98–103), who holds that managers freed from the control of capitalists are likely to prioritise their own over the interests of their workers in making choices. This criticism recalls Alchian and Demsetz's claim that capitalists are better able to control firms than workers.

These efficiency-related objections have been controverted by the findings of an accurate survey that has recently provided evidence that the managers of cooperatives are far from inefficient (see Basterretxea and Martinez 2012). For the purposes of analysis, however, the preceding reflections suggest that the medium to large cooperative is likely to be the more efficient type. As a rule, smaller cooperatives lack the resources that would be needed to hire professional managers and it is in them that decisions are often made jointly by the partners (though one of them invariably acts as leader).

In view of my research goals, the need to use medium to large firms as a reference frame must be spelt out, because it disproves the widespread assumption that large firm dimensions conflict with the cooperative nature of a self-managed firm (see, for example, Birchall 2000).[2]

As is well known, advocates of the paramount role of worker involvement in the decision-making processes of a cooperative tend to argue that size is inversely related to efficiency (see, for instance, Sapelli 1982: 71–73). While numerous authors hold that small-sized cooperatives are more efficient, thanks to stronger reciprocal relationships and increased trust between partners, in my opinion: (1) cooperatives face formation difficulties; and (2) large-sized employee-managed firms that vest full authority in their managers do not come in for the greater part of the criticisms levelled against cooperation. This point has also been mentioned before and will be examined further on in greater depth.

A point that I only mention in passing is the criticism that any firm is, by its very nature, an authoritarian structure, and that this extends to socialist firms as well, entailing the dual need, for every medium to large firm, to elect one or more managers and adopt an organisational structure vesting powers both in managers and a variety of intermediate functional levels. In this connection, 'the basic argument is that contractual enforcement of an efficient solution is impossible, either because complete contracts cannot be designed, or because the amount and quality of labour agreed upon cannot be observed or verified' (Vogt 1996: 40).

3 The ownership issue

The subject to be addressed at this point is the view concerning the ownership of an employee-managed firm. The idea that attention should be deflected from the (once paramount) ownership issue to the far more relevant control issue has been suggested in a wealth of recently published economic studies (see, *inter alia*, Zamagni 2005: 16–17), but while this reflection is certainly appropriate, it would be a mistake to underrate the continuing relevance of the ownership issue.

The first thing to say is that the liabilities of an LMF must first and foremost be debts of the partners. Otherwise, upon a downturn in business, they might leave the firm, without honouring their financial obligations to creditors. Second, many authors think that neither the firm's capital goods nor its stock inventories can be owned by the partners for two main reasons: because, as a rule, a partner is not entitled to dispose of his/her shares in the firm's capital goods; and, second, because partners leaving the firm can either ask to retain their credits or have them refunded, but have no title in any portion of the firm's tangible property. Ever since Roman times, an ownership right has been construed as an *ius utendi et abutendi*, and this entails that a person who is not entitled to dispose of an asset is not its rightful owner.

A way out of this stalemate is offered by Vanek's argument that the owner of a producer cooperative must necessarily be the state (see Vanek 1970), and this necessitates clarifying that the right of the partners to freely operate the firm's assets empties the relevant public property of much content. One major effect of the public ownership of self-managed firms is the formidable security offered to providers of funds by the state's role as obligor of last resort for any corporate debts. Indeed, some authors have gone so far as to argue that an all-cooperatives system is only conceivable if the labour-managed firms are publicly owned (see, for example, Barsony 1982).[3]

In point of fact, a system of cooperative firms with publicly owned means of production may be constituted of two different types of firms. One type, which we will term the LMF1, is a firm holding capital goods under a licensing agreement entered into with the state, the owner of such means; the other type, which we will term the LMF2, is a firm whose capital goods are freely purchased, but which become the property of the state once they have been bought. This should not strike us as surprising if we bear in mind that LMFs that self-finance their investments are obliged to allot bonds to the members in the aggregate value of the income that each of them would have earned where the relevant profits had been distributed (as mentioned in the Introduction).[4]

A fundamental implication of the public ownership principle is that cooperatives are not allowed to alienate their capital assets, unless they intend to purchase replacement assets of at least equal value. The rationale behind this ban is clear enough: the partners cannot be authorised to retain the proceeds of the sale of capital assets that are actually state property. In other words, capital goods may only be alienated in situations where the resulting proceeds are to be used to pay off debts or replace obsolete capital goods, but never for purposes of distribution to the members.[5]

In Vanek's approach, a system of labour-managed firms where production means are publicly owned amounts to a socialist system.[6] For my part, I share the idea that a system of labour-managed firms is a socialist system, but from my perspective the actual management of firms by the working class would be a far more important breakthrough than the public ownership of production means.[7]

An additional, major reflection is that tangible assets that can neither be assigned to the partners, nor to the firm's financers must necessarily belong to the firm. Thus, the resulting picture is a rather anomalous construct, in which the firm's liabilities are classed as debts of the partners, and tangible assets and stock inventories are categorised as the property of the firm.

Our analysis of ownership rights offers a welcome opportunity to clarify post-default or post-winding up scenarios. As soon as a business crisis seems to be looming, one or more partners might resolve to leave the cooperative in the hope that the decision of the remaining partners to keep the firm going will relieve them of their contractual obligations and shift them onto those resolving to stay. As a result, any exit application by one or more partners will oblige those who stay to face the option of carrying on the firm's business at the cost of taking over the outgoing partners' debts or having the firm liquidated. In the latter case, the outstanding debts of the firm will have to be honoured by all the partners, including those asking to leave.

Besides filling the gap in self-management studies that was pointed out in the opening paragraph, the clarifications just provided will both shed light on points that economic cooperation theorists have not yet sufficiently entered upon and help confute an often-quoted objection by Jensen and Meckling, as I will be doing in the next paragraph.[8]

In contrast with my opinion, Di Quattro (2011) thinks that cooperatives are the property of their members. In addition to this, he argues that cooperatives should both pay their workers' wages and salaries and distribute the surplus to them in proportion to the quota of property held by each of them. Accordingly, he argues (2011: 534), in market socialism 'market prices are used as accounting devices or efficiency indicators, but not to distribute income', because interest and profits are distributed to shareholders, who socially own the means of production, and thus 'interest and profit incomes coexist with egalitarian aims'.

For my part, I strongly dissent from Di Quattro. The reflections so far have clearly shown that in market socialism the income-from-employment and profit categories are cancelled since they are the components of the incomes earned by the members of democratic firms, while the interest income category is retained since it constitutes the income (purged of the profit component) that capitalists continue to earn.

4 Jensen and Meckling's critique of cooperatives

In a well-known 1979 paper (reprinted in Prychitko and Vanek 1996), Jensen and Meckling suggested that modern producer cooperative theorists had mainly concerned themselves with a category of employee-managed firm which is nowhere found in the real world: a type of enterprise they termed 'the pure rental firm'.

The main characteristic of this type of firm, they argued, is that

> all claims on the firms themselves are held by employees, but there is no market for such claims; that is, employees have claims on current net revenues which they cannot sell to anyone else because eligibility for claims is conditional on employment and the right to become an employee is not legally for sale.
>
> (1996: 477)

At first sight, this description of the labour-managed firm, which Jensen and Meckling are said to have drawn from Vanek and Meade, would seem to be correct, but their subsequent remark that 'what is unique about the pure-rental economy is that firms are forbidden to hold claims or rights in durable productive resources like those held by individuals' (1996: 477) is in conflict with my approach to property rights in LMFs.

To account for Jensen and Meckling's assignment of all rights to the partners instead of the firm, we may refer to a subsequent passage in which they mention the prevailing view that rights in the firm attach to workers, as long as they work for the firm. However, Jensen and Meckling's initial identification of the pure rental firm with the LMF is subsequently contradicted by an entry between brackets defining the pure rental firm as one that rents its capital goods[9] – i.e. as an altogether different firm from the usual LMF.

In point of fact, the true reason as to why Jensen and Meckling preliminarily equate the pure rental firm with the labour-managed firm discussed in the economic literature and subsequently describe it as a firm renting all its capital goods is that they have misconstrued the current notion of the labour-managed firm. In all probability, from the LMF's use of loan capital, they failed to draw the obvious conclusion that a firm purchasing physical capital goods with borrowed funds becomes the owner (not lessee) of the assets it has purchased. Indeed, their argument that 'what is unique about the pure-rental economy is that firms are forbidden to hold claims or rights in durable productive resources like those held by individuals' will only hold true on the highly implausible assumption that the firm rents physical capital goods. And this explains why they describe LMF as a category of self-managed firm that is nowhere found in the real world.

As a result, it is inappropriate to describe the LMF as a pure rental firm. Far from renting physical capital goods, the LMF is a firm that borrows money capital. The reflections that I will be developing over the next few paragraphs are evidence that the main criticisms against employee-managed firms are not applicable to the LMF as configured by us.

5 Further reflections on criticisms levelled against self-management

Under-investment, funding difficulties, monitoring and control issues are just some of the problems that the institutional organisation mode just described can effectively help address.

In Chapter 3, I have tried to show that LMFs do not necessarily face the funding difficulties that critics of self-management hold to be its main shortcoming. Here, we have to refute an additional objection, which was raised by Jensen and Meckling:

> It seems to us unlikely that outside investors will voluntarily entrust their funds to a labour-managed enterprise in which the workers maintained complete control and the investors were allowed to hope that the worker-managers would behave in such a way as to leave something for them, the residual claimants.

> (1979: 487)

Undoubtedly, this is a weak point of employee-managed firms, for while the shareholders funding a limited company exercise control over the company's operations, providers of funds to cooperatives are deprived of this control, since they are not part of the firm's staff. But is this a decisive critique against LMFs? My answer would be a straight yes if LMFs were denied the self-financing option – i.e. if we had not made it clear that the best possible solution is a system of LMFs that are empowered to adopt self-financing resolutions. Upon the adoption of the organisation mode we are endorsing, even members about to leave an

LMF – we have said – would be concerned with the firm's future success, since they would retain their bonds after their exit.

On the subject of control, Jensen and Meckling (1979: 488–489) complained that no suggestions for tackling this problem in cooperative firms could be found in the relevant literature.

> No one has specified a well-defined set of procedures for solving the decision-making problem within the firm when the preferences of the workers are not all identical. As a rule, it is simply assumed that the workers will have a common set of preferences and that no conflicts will arise in translating these into operational policies at the firm level.
>
> (Jensen and Meckling 1979: 488–489)

For my part, I think that this objection is not applicable to firms that elect and vest full authority in a manager and where important decisions are made by passing majority resolutions. The manager is expected to act in the interests of the partners of the cooperative and will be dismissed if a majority of the partners are dissatisfied with his/her choices.

An in-depth analysis of the high costs associated with difficult decision-making in cooperatives was provided by Hansmann in a celebrated 1996 book concerned with existing Western cooperatives in place of the model cooperative developed by economic theorists. In my opinion, for the reasons explained above, if the decisions in cooperatives are made by managers that are allowed full freedom of action, the issue raised by Hansmann will be ruled out by definition.

The under-investment issue is dealt with in a wealth of studies whose authors have generally emphasised its relevance for WMFs, but not for the LMF. A major point – let me repeat this – is that the time horizon issue raised by Furubotn and Pejovich would be promptly solved if a self-financing cooperative, to avoid being turned into a WMF, should allot its partners bonds in the amount of the earnings that would otherwise have been available for distribution.

Inasmuch as it is true that the under-investment issue can be ruled out, the growth rate of a system of cooperatives – the main efficiency indicator – would not fall short of the rate recorded in a capitalist system.

Let us add that under the organisational arrangement described above, the partners of an LMF will both be liable to third parties for the firm's debts and have claims against the firm in their capacity as financers of part of the firm's investments – not to mention the fact that on leaving they will be relieved of their debts to third parties without forfeiting their claims against the firm.

Another advantage of the organisation mode we are describing is to avert a frequent malpractice in public sector cooperatives (e.g. those in ex-Yugoslavia): the risk that the partners should 'devour the firm', in terms of dismantling it, selling its machinery and equipment and distributing the relevant receipts among themselves. And the reason is that workers liable for their debts can hardly be supposed to dismantle their firm – i.e. the source of income that would enable them to honour their obligations.

These reflections may also explain why this organisation mode would help solve the portfolio diversification issue. As is well known, one major weakness of employee-managed firms is difficult risk diversification: whereas shareholders of public limited companies – i.e. those entitled to manage enterprises – are in a position to diversify their investment portfolios at will, in a system of cooperatives those entitled to manage enterprises can only work for one firm at a time. In the system just described, however, the bondholders of LMFs will have the option of diversifying their portfolios by selling their bonds to third parties and purchasing bonds of other firms. This does not apply to WMFs, which are self-financing firms that do not allot any bonds and whose partners are consequently prevented from diversifying the returns on their investments.

As far as the capital assets maintenance problem is concerned, it is worth mentioning that while the partners planning to leave a WMF within a short time-frame will hardly deem it expedient to bear the cost of properly upgrading the firm's capital assets, the exiting partners of the LMF will be interested in the success of their ex-firm even after their exit, because they retain the bonds that they were assigned upon the adoption of self-financing resolutions.

The last criticism to be discussed is a somewhat more complex one. Capitalist firms working towards maximising profit – it is observed – concomitantly tend to maximise the revenues of society as a whole (and in perfectly competitive conditions, this may lead to a Pareto optimum). The same does not apply to the self-managed firm for two reasons. First of all, assuming that a self-managed firm should actually maximise average worker incomes in line with Ward's original theoretical approach, the average domestic income level would not be simultaneously maximised, because of a mechanism determining that return on investment is levelled out. Second, if the firm strives to maximise, not average worker income, but – in line with what is mainly assumed today – benefits for the workers, the result will be a fall in the GDP caused by lesser incentives to work (see Williamson 1980). At that point, the resulting fall in the aggregate domestic income would impose cuts in public spending and cause an adverse impact on firms (e.g. firms would no longer enjoy the benefits flowing from increased public spending on education and so on).[10]

On closer analysis, though, this criticism is objectionable, both because it is far from true that capitalism maximises incentives to work and also because there are reasons to assume (as mentioned above) that even though income is not maximised in the short run, the rate of growth of a system of self-managed firms would not fall short of the corresponding rate of growth of a capitalist system.

6 Obstacles to the creation of producer cooperatives

Although the above mentioned criticisms are those most frequently discussed in the literature, there are authors who highlight additional shortcomings – for instance, the objection that new cooperatives are difficult to establish.

Brisk firm creation is, quite obviously, a major need in capitalist systems, and even more so in a system of democratic firms (see, for example, Meade 1972:

420–421; 1979: 787; Jensen and Meckling 1979: 478–479). Yet there are reasons to argue that odds at the formation stage of a cooperative far exceed those faced by the founders of a capitalist firm. As is well known, a capitalist firm is set up when one or more persons of large means resolves to hire personnel on the assumption that the collateral they are able to lodge will help them raise more capital in case of need. A person with capital resources and organisational talents will hardly deem it convenient to found a cooperative and share corporate powers and revenues with others. Such a person is likely to opt for a capitalist firm, in which he will both hold all power and, as long as he remains sole owner, keep all the firm's profits for himself (see, for example, Dow 2003: 17; Gunn 2006: 346). Those emphasising this point also draw attention to the fact that the proposer of a cooperative investment project is not entitled to appropriate all the resulting revenues for two reasons: (1) because he has to share the net earnings from his project with the other partners; and (2) because on leaving he will forfeit his claim to the income that the firm is likely to earn in the future, thanks to his initiative. According to Ben Ner, a new firm can opt for the cooperative form, provided its founding partners meet the following four requirements: they must be able to (1) define both a business concept and the associated action plan; (2) face the risk of losses; (3) raise capital; and (4) cover start-up expenses. The same author also made it clear that the odds are against workers (compared to capitalists) in all these areas (Ben Ner 1987: 289–290). As suggested by two well-known theorists of the cooperative movement:

> as soon as a capitalist raising capital for a profit-oriented business project starts carefully weighing the comparative advantages of different legal forms, he is likely to set up a limited partnership or company, while the establishment of a cooperative will barely enter his estimate of advantages.
>
> (Riguzzi and Porcari 1925: 5)[11]

Hence the conclusion that only persons without financial means or appreciable entrepreneurial talents may think of founding a cooperative.[12]

Nevertheless, while there is no denying that the scant propensity of investors to lend capital to property-less operators is a major drawback to the growth of the cooperative movement, it is a fact that most existing LMFs are viable enough (see Section 7).

The reflections developed above would seem to suggest that a system exclusively composed of democratic firms is barely the ideal solution and that policies for the enforcement of such a system would prove abortive. Advocates of the cooperative ideal will probably be agreed that a better (or probably necessary) solution would be to leave the formation of small firms (e.g. those with headcounts below ten or twenty) to individual initiative and restrict government aid to firms above a given dimensional threshold.[13] The experience of the Mondragon cooperatives has shown that work relations tend to deteriorate in firms that employ 1,000 members or more (Thomas and Logan 1982: 178–182).

The most authoritative analysis of the implications of difficult firm creation in the cooperative sector is the 1970 book by Vanek. In a chapter on specific draw-backs to the growth of the cooperative movement, Vanek suggested that govern-ments could make up for formation difficulties by building industrial sheds and making them available to cooperatives. Although Vanek's proposal deserves careful consideration, I am inclined to think that the above-mentioned firm cre-ation difficulties would be better solved in a system where efficient small-sized cooperative firms would be freely competing with capitalist firms and medium to large cooperatives, only (considering their classification as 'merit firms'; see, further on, Chapter 10) would be eligible for tax benefits and subsidised rate loans. Eligibility for tax benefits should obviously be made conditional on the ability of the cooperative to generate 'external economies' – i.e. benefits for the community at large. And it goes without saying that many economists, irrespective of political faith, are agreed that the criterion of granting benefits to firms that can be catego-rised as merit firms obeys a pro-competition rationale, rather than a statist one.

7 Non-distributable reserves

Despite the findings of this comparative analysis of the abilities of public limited companies versus equal-sized cooperatives to attract financing (see Chapter 2), it is a fact that a cooperative that self-finances itself as mentioned above (i.e. by allotting to its partners bonds in the aggregate value of its undivided profits) would find it more difficult to obtain external financings than one allocating all its profits to the non-distributable reserve. As a result, it is necessary to examine this issue in greater depth.

Non-distributable reserves perform a variety of functions, including the pro-vision of security to outside financers. This is why I now ask: if a cooperative that self-finances itself in the manner mentioned above and leaves its non-distributable reserves intact, would it continue to reap the benefits that coopera-tives draw from such reserves?

The answer might be in the affirmative if the bonds concerned were declared to be inalienable. On closer analysis, though, this option would only apply to situations in which the partners plan to stay on with the firm, since it would be unreasonable to allot inalienable bonds to workers who are out of the coopera-tive. Hence, there are two alternative solutions: (1) allotment of inalienable bonds for the period that the partners continue to stay with the firm; or (2) alloca-tion of part of the profits to the non-distributable reserve.

Coming to an additional function of these reserves, several authors have noted that workers today are hardly keen on running cooperatives, since they do not want to accept variable incomes in place of fixed wages and salaries. When this issue arises, non-distributable reserves may perform the important function of making the incomes of the partners more stable, in terms that producer coopera-tives might resolve to pay their workers a minimum, fixed pay rate.

It goes without saying that nothing stands in the way of the adoption of this solution, provided the firm continues to earn enough profits while paying the wages and salaries owed to its workers. Conversely, as it cannot be ruled out that some cooperatives will be operating at a loss, to avert risks of bankruptcy and, simultaneously, guarantee the workers a fixed minimum income, the aggregate amount of the cooperative's non-distributable reserves should always be enough to cover the form's fixed personnel costs, even in the event of a downturn in business.

This situation is governed by Section 2545ter of the new Italian Civil Code, which rules that 'non-distributable reserves may be used to cover losses only after the reserves allocated for purposes of capitalisation or for allotment to the partners upon the dissolution of the firm have been entirely used'.

8 Conclusion

There is little denying that throughout the fifty-year debate on employee-managed firms, authors have seldom thought it necessary to dwell at length on the type of organisation they were addressing and have therefore provided strongly contrasting approaches. This is why I resolved to provide a somewhat detailed description of a specific organisational structure that would both ensure the efficient running of producer cooperatives and come in for less severe criticism. The aim in this chapter was to argue that a well-organised system of cooperative firms would not be marred by many of the shortcomings highlighted in the current literature.

Of note, this chapter also included criticism of a well-known article by Jensen and Meckling, which, to my knowledge, has not yet been raised.

Notes

1   On this point, see Kahana and Paroush (1995).
2   Whereas Sylos Labini holds small-sized cooperatives to be 'barely viable' (2006: 34; see also, 2004: 105), a study by Poletti dated 1905 sets forth the opposite view.
3   Pareto (1893: 59) has emphasised that public ownership of means of production bears the difficulty of distinguishing between different categories of goods. On closer analysis, though, while it is true that a building may indifferently be used for residential or production purposes, it is easy to object that an asset will only be turned into a capital asset when it is used to produce marketable goods.
4   This means I disagree with von Mises (1951), according to whom privately owned means of production are a necessary assumption for the existence of markets, because a system with publicly owned capital goods lacks incentives for an efficient use of such assets.
5   Hence, Nuti is wrong when he claims (see Nuti 1992: 151) that 'only if the partners of a cooperative were authorised to retain part of the increase in the value of their assets would they become entrepreneurs proper' and that this 'would change cooperative firms into privately-owned businesses'.
6   In the opinion of Dobb (1969: 141–142), to equate the gist of a socialist economy with anything other than the social ownership of production means would result in a break with the socialist tradition of the past century (see also, Sweezy 1963: 330; Landauer 1959, vol. I: 5; Wiles 1962: ch. 1; Dobb 1970: 50–51; Kornai 1971: 337–338).

7 In this connection, Berle and Means (1932) and other theorists of the ownership/ control separation in capitalism have argued that market socialism would cease to be an alternative to capitalism the moment that capitalists are deprived of their former control over firms.

8 My reflections in this section do not rule out that there are reasons to argue that cooperative firms may and should be privately owned (see Wolff 2012: 141–142).

9 The exact wording of the entry on page 479, is 'one in which all capital goods are rented'.

10 For this criticism, see, specifically, Lepage (1978: 103–110).

11 The assumption that start-up capital-raising problems are by far the main barrier to firm creation is confirmed by the history of the cooperative movement and endorsed by numerous economic theorists (*inter alia*, Cole 1953, vol. I: ch. 14, 24; 1954, vol. II: chs 5, 9; as well as Putterman 1982: 150–151; Zangheri *et al.* 1987; Gunn 2006: 35).

12 Olson (1965) has suggested that the obstacles to the establishment of jointly owned organisations and the costs and efforts to set them going far exceed the resulting benefits.

13 These ideas are shared by Schweickart (2005), who suggested that a sector of small-sized capitalist firms is a necessary prerequisite for the proper working of a socialist system, both at the initial stage and, probably, throughout its lifespan.

7 An in-depth analysis of the advantages of democratic firms

1 Introduction

At this point, it is convenient to start a review of the advantages of self-managed firms.

There is general agreement that a major collective benefit of economic democracy is the fact that people who are free to pursue their interests are happier than those acting on somebody else's instruction. As will be shown further on, this is certainly one, though not the greatest, advantage of cooperation.

A correct approach would be to distinguish between benefits flowing from any single cooperative and those specific to an all-cooperatives system only. However, in part because most of the above-mentioned benefits are also applicable to cooperatives conducting business in a capitalist economy (albeit to extents strictly commensurate with the number of cooperatives in existence), I will abstract from this distinction in this chapter, examining solely those benefits that would be ensured by an all-cooperatives system.

Birchall, for instance, has quite appropriately emphasised his surprise at observing that this aspect of the problem is rarely covered in the literature (see Birchall 2012: 270–271).

2 The advantages of cooperation from the perspective of John Stuart Mill

The best-known authors who unreservedly extolled the cooperative firm by emphasising its potential for creating solidarity and beneficial effects on human character are probably John Stuart Mill and Alfred Marshall.

Mill looked upon cooperation as the organisational form that best meets the interests of the working classes. 'I cannot think' – he wrote – 'that they will be permanently contented with the condition of labouring for wages as their ultimate state. They may be willing to pass through the class of servants in their way to that of employers; but not to remain in it all their lives' (Mill 1871: 760–761). It is apparent that Mill shared the socialist view that worker emancipation may be achieved through association – i.e. through the creation of cooperatives abolishing salaried labour, granting workers the status of partners and allowing them a say in their management.

Besides this basic reflection, the main idea that Mill had in mind when praising the cooperative firm was associated with competition and the way it impacts upon human nature and happiness. In his opinion, increased productivity levels were not the main advantage of a system of cooperative firms. Underscoring the impetus to production that stems from cooperative modes of work, he rated this advantage 'nothing compared with the moral revolution in society that would accompany' cooperation, namely

> the transformation of human life, from a conflict of classes struggling for opposite interests, to a friendly rivalry in the pursuit of a common good to all; the elevation of the dignity of labour; a new sense of security and independence in the labouring class; and the conversion of each human being's daily occupation into a school of the social sympathies and the practical intelligence.
>
> (Mill 1871: 789–790)[1]

Mill approved of competition as a means of discouraging indolence, inducing individuals to improve and reinforce their inborn abilities and providing both a selection criterion and rules to govern rates of pay. Especially in his younger years, he severely criticised those socialists who were inimical to the idea of the market as a major inducement to work and the governing criterion for income distribution. This is why he criticised Owen for setting up self-contained communities with scant incentives to production. On closer analysis, however, competition in a labour-managed firm system differs from competition in capitalism.

The positive effect of cooperative production on human character is a major point of Mill's analysis of the cooperative movement in his day and a specific, well-known cooperative firm (the Rochdale Society), which had been experiencing rapid growth ever since its foundation in 1844. These cooperatives, he wrote, clearly show that shared interests have prompted a feeling of solidarity amongst the partners and have thereby helped improve their characters. Mill went so far as to contend that cooperatives were 'a course of education in those moral and active qualities by which success alone can either be deserved or attained' (Mill 1871: 791). In another passage, he also discussed the distinction (re-proposed by Marshall in later years) between base motivations behind economic activity (to be put to the best possible use for want of anything better) and motivations based on lofty feelings (which he typically ascribed to cooperative firms).

In Mill's opinion, both political economy and political science overall were to be grounded in a thorough knowledge of the laws that determine and govern human character. Even more so, the main idea Mill had in mind when planning to write a treatise on ethology (a project he later abandoned) was that a thorough knowledge of the evolution of human character was a prerequisite for the creation of a social science proper and that this, in turn, required elaborating a science of character (see Mill 1871: xvi–xvii; see also, Becattini 1989: 135–136).

3 Marshall's idea of the cooperative firm as an agent-moulding character

Like Mill, Alfred Marshall analysed the impact of economic organisation on character. Defining the essence of economic science (see opening pages of *Principles of Economics*), he also defined its two main goals:

> It is on the one side the study of wealth, and on the other, and more important side, a part of the study of man. For man's character has been moulded by his every-day work, and the material resources which he thereby procures, more than by any other influence unless it be that of his religious ideals; and the two great forming agencies of the world's history have been the religious and the economic.
>
> (Marshall 1890: 1)

An even more significant excerpt from a work written in 1897 reads as follows:

> Social science or the reasoned history of man, for the two things are the same, is working its way towards a fundamental unity; just as is being done by physical science, or, which is the same thing, by the reasoned history of natural phenomena. Physical science is seeking her hidden unity in the forces that govern molecular movement: social science is seeking her unity in the forces of human character.[2]
>
> (Marshall 1897: 299–300)

The idea that human character is not given from the outset, but is thoroughly shaped by the environment and its economic structure is already expressed in Marshall's early writings. In one of them, for example, we are told that 'we scarcely realise how subtle, all pervading and powerful may be the effect of the work of man's body in dwarfing the growth of man' (Marshall 1873: 105–106). In the *Principles*, on the subject of the relative importance of the main two factors in world history, Marshall states that, compared to religious factors, whose influence is more intense, economic factors act themselves out by the day and hour, throughout the greater part of a man's life; for a man's mind is absorbed by matters associated with his business even when he stops working and, as is often the case, sets out to plan future actions (see Marshall 1890: 2).

The decisive part played by work in shaping man's character led Marshall to contend that the main task of a social thinker was to suggest institutional reforms that would enhance the best qualities in man, namely the 'high' motivations he equated with ethics. In Marshall's view, the shaping principles of capitalism are the profit motive and individualism, the main springs of 'base motivations'.

The foregoing may explain why Marshall exalted the ethical motives behind the cooperative movement (see Marshall 1890: 306) and its main goal, namely 'the production of fine human beings' (Marshall 1889: 228). In his opinion, cooperation was characterised by high aspirations and the wish to enhance what is best in man and educate him to collective action – i.e. to work jointly with others for the achievement of shared ends. Its direct aim was 'to improve the quality of man itself' (Marshall 1889: 228).

This idea returns in a passage from *The Economics of Industry*, where Marshall and his wife praise the personality of Owen, his 'boundless faith in the ultimate goodness of human nature and the possibility to mould noble characters, his deeply-felt desire to bring to the fore the best qualities of men by trusting in them and appealing to their reason' (Marshall and Marshall 1881: 271–272).

In the start-up phase, the cooperative movement is sure to come up against major difficulties, but it holds within itself the seeds of growth, since education helps workers see to their interests and teaches them the moral strength needed for the joint pursuit and attainment of their political goals (Marshall 1925: 228).

4 Additional advantages of economic democracy

From the benefits of democratic firms discussed by these two major authors of the past, this chapter will now proceed to discuss the advantages highlighted in more recent theoretical contributions.

The following is a tentative list of the advantages that democratic firms are ascribed in the literature:

1. the pleasure the partners derive from own-account work;
2. wresting power from capitalists;
3. a powerful impulse to political democracy;
4. major firm efficiency gains from worker involvement in production processes;
5. a stop to exploitation and degrading alienated labour;
6. the tendency of labour incomes to increase in proportion to boosts in labour and capital productivity;
7. more investments in human capital;
8. a positive influence on the characters of workers and stronger community feelings;
9. softer competition and reduced insolvency risks;
10. declines in structural unemployment and the disappearance of classical and Keynesian unemployment;
11. marked downward trends in class conflict and wage hikes and the resulting slowdown in inflation;
12. improved income distribution;
13. an end to external firm control and, hence, to the sway of multinational corporations;
14. reduced monopoly building;
15. lower environment pollution levels and reduced production of hazardous materials;
16. lesser risks of power abuse and fraud;

17. economic efficiency gains from a lesser need for state intervention; and
18. the eclipse of the current paramount role of the economic factor in the evo-
    lution of society.[3]

As mentioned above, in this chapter, the analysis will be restricted to a few interrelated advantages of cooperation. Minor and more obvious benefits not analysed in this chapter will be dealt with further on. Specifically, the unemployment
and alienation issues will be discussed in the next chapter and in Chapter 8. The
subject of Chapter 9 is the bounce forward in democracy afforded by the suppression of capitalist power.

5 Efficiency gains afforded by cooperative firms

Alfred Marshall argued that one of two basic advantages of cooperation is
the ability to make the most appropriate use of 'capacity for work' – a
resource that in capitalist systems is awfully wasted. 'In the world's history' – he
wrote – 'there has been one waste product, so much more important than all
others that it has a right to be called "The Waste Product": it is the higher abilities of many of the working classes' (Marshall 1889: 229). Indeed, this tendency to waste labour is even observed in capitalism, the production mode that
more than any others is shaped by self-interest, by a concern with putting
available resources to the best possible uses and by the tendency to minimise
waste. At first sight, this may strike us as singularly surprising, but actually it
is the obvious result of the fact that workers (unlike inert materials lacking a
will of their own) are responsive human beings whose reaction to conflicts
between their own and their employers' interests is to resist exploitation, work
sluggishly and slow down their effort to exactly that level that will avert risks of
dismissal.

However, waste of labour is not specific to capitalism. All of the production
modes that have arisen during various stages of world history, from slavery to
capitalism, had one thing in common: they invariably stripped workers of the
product of their labour by assigning them to tasks whose benefits were reaped by
others. In other words, over the span of world history the best energy of workers
have been 'wasted' for want of just those incentives that would have induced
them to engage in work to the best of their abilities.

At the opposite end of the spectrum are the partners of a cooperative, since
their title to appropriate the earnings from their work and their responsibility for
the firm's operations are strong inducements to streamline production and
increase output.

As will be explained in greater detail further on, an additional explanation for
the labour productivity edge of cooperatives is the fairer income distribution
they guarantee, because workers entitled to shares of the firm's profits are likely
to be both more collaborative and more pro-active. Two additional reasons
accounting for the higher labour productivity rates of cooperative firms include
greater focus on human capital building and less frequent dismissals. Indeed,

risk of dismissal interferes with interpersonal relations and acts as a disincentive to working towards the success of the firm.

One objection against the assumed productivity edge was raised by Williamson *et al.*, who claimed that incentives to work are less strong in cooperatives. These authors pointed to promotion and earning the employer's esteem as a powerful stimulus to greater dedication and contrasted this advantage of capital-managed systems with a major drawback of democratic firms: the strong incentive to shirk stemming from the awareness that only part of the surplus revenue generated by the greater work input of one partner is actually cashed by that partner. In a cooperative of n partners assigned to equal tasks, this part is but $1/n$ – which means that incentives to production in labour-managed firms increase in an inverse proportion to firm size. In contrast, Meade (1972: 403), Blumberg (1968) and Conte (1982) have argued that even in larger cooperatives, worker involvement may generate benefits in terms of stronger motivation.

A different argument against the labour productivity edge of democratic firms is associated with the insight that worker solidarity is a reality in capitalist businesses as well. In a well-known 1982 paper, Akerlof argued that the aversion to the idea of wage cuts on colleagues may induce the workers of a capitalist firm to step up their rates of work above pre-set input standards. In this way – he suggested – they will make good for the damage entailed in paying the same wage rate to the less performing part of the workforce. A firm in these circumstances is likely to remunerate such a 'gift' by continuing to pay the same wage rate to all its workers, without raising the standard expected to be met by better-performing staff partners. The relevance of Akerlof's argument is confirmed by empirical evidence that average labour productivity levels exceed pre-set standards in many capital-managed businesses (see Baker *et al.* 1988; Gibbons 1998).

On occasion, worker solidarity in labour-managed firms may produce the opposite effect, in terms of inducing hard-working staff partners to slow down their rates of work for fear of embarrassing their fellow workers (on this point, see the findings of Prandergast's 1999 overview of the literature on the perverse effects of incentives, as well as Tortia 2008a, 2008b: 87–88).

Combining Akerlof's argument with Prandergast's findings, it is possible to argue that the gains from incentives to boost labour inputs and from stronger inter-partner solidarity in labour-managed firms may be outweighed by Akerlof's solidarity effect.

A well-known experimental study conducted by Elton Mayo has shown that the involvement of workers in the firm's decisions may effectively boost productivity levels. Mayo's experiment is a landmark in sociological literature. Many authors who reviewed its research findings have suggested that the considerable productivity gains recorded at the Hawthorne Works during the tests had actually been brought about by the promotion of many of the workers involved to higher positions in the firm (the so-called 'Hawthorne effect'). However, Blumberg (1968) and others have provided convincing evidence that they were mainly, though not solely, owing to the involvement of the workers in decisions related to work conditions.

More recently, the argument that worker involvement in decision-making may lead to labour productivity gains has been confirmed by numerous empirical research findings. Cases in point include Jones and Backus (1977); Bellas (1972); Defourny *et al.* (1985); Estrin *et al.* (1987); Weitzman and Kruse (1990); Levine and Tyson (1990); Sterner (1990); Estrin and Jones (1992, 1995); Defourny (1992); Thomas and Logan (1982); Bartlett *et al.* (1992); Doucouliagos (1995); Levine (1995); Craig and Pencavel (1995); Gui (1996); Ben Ner *et al.* (1996); Tseo *et al.* (2004).

Conversely, the finding that capital-managed businesses tend to outperform cooperatives was reported in Hollas and Stansell (1988) and Faccioli and Fiorentini (1998); for somewhat ambiguous results, see Fitzroy and Kraft (1987) and Berman and Berman (1989).

Similarly, a comparative analysis of the two categories of firms conducted by Estrin in 1991 reported conflicting results: a negligible productivity differential when headcount was used as a proxy of labour input and a considerable underperformance of cooperatives when total hours worked by blue collars were used as a measure of labour input.

Two noticeable surveys of this same subject were performed by Jones and Pliskin in 1991 and by Bonin *et al.* in 1993.

On closer analysis, though, these surveys seem to have little relevance to the approach in this paper, because in the lead-up to when economists at last picked up employee management as a research goal, cooperatives organised themselves along lines that are at odds with the theoretical model to the point of impinging upon labour productivity. Especially in Italy, where 'profit-oriented' cooperatives are outlawed by the provisions of Article 45 of the Constitution, it would barely make sense to appraise the productivity levels of these firms using the theoretical producer cooperative model as a benchmark.

With reference to the pleasure that the partners draw from their work in cooperative firms and the scant regard of the managers of capitalist firms for the preferences of their workers, Ben Ner (1988: 293–294) has remarked that when each worker was asked to state the type of job description he would like to be assigned to, the power of the workforce within the firm would increase well above levels deemed acceptable by their employers. In contrast, in cooperatives, nothing prevents the partners from freely stating their preferences, and this adds both to their satisfaction at work and, presumably, to their individual productivity levels.

Inasmuch as it is true that the productivity rates recorded in cooperatives exceed those of capitalistic firms, the workers of the former should also earn higher incomes. With reference to existing cooperatives, this assumption is confirmed in Bartlett *et al.* (1992) and Burdin and Dean (2009), but is contradicted by the findings of a survey conducted by Pencavel *et al.* (2006).[4]

6 Income distribution in democratic firms

While the productivity gains associated with cooperation are likely to boost worker incomes above the corresponding levels in capitalist systems, we may now ask ourselves if income distribution patterns will prove more or less fair.

As mentioned before, in this model, the profits earned by democratic firms will be distributed among workers based on 'coefficients' – i.e. pre-fixed per cent shares of the firm's residual – as determined at the central level. However, as each group is likely to include individuals with different production capabilities, it can be assumed that each firm will adjust the centrally fixed coefficients in line with its individual organisation pattern. And there are reasons to assume that the socially determined distribution pattern substituted for the current market-determined pattern will bring about a social order that is more just (see Castoriadis 1975).

The 'sacrifice-based criterion' is a socially determined distribution method that was theorised by Albert and Hahnel in numerous essays and analysed and discussed, among others, by Panayotakis (2009). Does the phrase 'socially determined distribution' still make sense after this qualification?

In a system of cooperative firms, differences in worker income levels will be observed both within the same firm and between different firms. By their very nature, within-firm worker income differences are socially determined when they are centrally fixed, though in this case – let this be repeated – the inborn inequalities between the workers of each category may induce firms to award individual workers higher or lower coefficients than those that are centrally fixed. As firm-level coefficients voted by the workers at meetings must be fixed with due regard to market conditions, it is more appropriate to say that they are socially determined only in part, since the social essence of the state's and the partners' decisions is attenuated, though not entirely nullified, by external market pressures. This conclusion is supported by empirical experience: in existing cooperatives, the highest pay rate is rarely fixed at over three or four times the lowest coefficient.

In contrast with the neoclassical rule that prices – including those of the factors of production – are determined by the law of supply and demand in every market economy, there are reasons to argue that socially determined distribution coefficients will tend to reduce inequalities. As a matter of fact, supply and demand do not obey the same rationale: whereas demand for labour is determined by an individual firm's needs and considerations, supply is not solely determined by market factors and, at any rate, it fluctuates over considerably longer timespans. As firms are in a position to hire fresh workers whenever they need them, demand for labour fluctuates in accordance with the conditions prevailing in markets from time to time. On the contrary, labour supply is much less volatile, both because it is mainly dependent on the specialisations in which workers have been trained and because it is socially conditioned. As a result, it is inadmissible to say that the prices of factors of production are determined by the law of supply and demand as are those of commodities. In a system of cooperative firms there is ample evidence – Paul Krugman wrote (2007: 7) – 'that institutions, norms, and the political environment matter a lot more for the distribution of income – and that impersonal market forces matter less' than economic manuals might lead you to believe (see also, *inter alia*, Fleetwood 2006; Di Quattro 2011: 533–537).

Let us assume that distribution coefficients are determined by the social choices made both by Parliament and by the partners of firms at their meetings, and that, in so doing, neither of them had regard to the conditions prevailing in markets. A priori, there are no reasons to assume that once a given distribution pattern has been socially determined, demand for one or the other category of workers will equate with the corresponding supply level.

But what would happen in situations of disequilibrium in a single labour market? When supply for a given job description exceeds the corresponding demand, firms will be in a position to hire the most qualified workers and the long-term unemployed will have no way out but to switch to different jobs. Above all, based on an analysis of the trends in various labour markets, young people in search of a first job will tend to shun those qualifications for which supply systematically exceeds demand. Conversely, when demand exceeds supply, firms will have difficulty finding workers with suitable qualifications. In the long run, however, the market would develop its natural response, in terms of inducing new entrants to choose those job descriptions for which prospects of employment are greatest.

In point of fact, as a result of the educational system and the practice of employment through competitive examinations, such spontaneous market responses do not entirely cancel out the socially determined nature of distribution. Competitive examinations are, by their very nature, a tool that balances out labour supply and demand. And the role played by the educational system in determining the professional choices of the young is well known and does not require further discussion here. In many respects, the educational system and competitive examinations are designed to attain the same goal.[5] In other words, if the public hand works towards regulating the supply of labour in manners that will determine the desired adjustments to demand, the pay rates assigned to factors can be fixed at levels that social conscience will perceive as fair.[6]

How should we rate the spontaneous tendency of a labour-managed system to create distributive inequalities? As mentioned before, in a market economy, the decisions that determine pay gaps between different firms are the result of spontaneous tendencies. And producer cooperative theorists have made it clear that pay gaps between cooperative firms would be even more marked than they usually are in capitalist firms.

An additional relevant reflection concerns the coefficients that would be fixed for managers. Considering that worker incomes would be higher than in capitalist systems, one might assume that managers, viewed as the latest surviving representatives of the class of capitalists, would be assigned lower pay rates. This assumption was refuted by Korsch, based on the empirical observation that the greater part of the revenues earned by capitalist firms are not assigned to the managers, but distributed to shareholders. Consequently, as capitalists would lose this source of income, the pay rates of managers may well be as high as in capitalism. Indeed, this would be perfectly in line with the nature of firms that, in legal terms, are run by the workers, but whose efficient running is actually dependent on the abilities of their managers (Korsch 1922: 33–34).

To conclude this analysis of distribution, I will mention an important objection. As the workers of democratic firms have to take all the risks attached to production, it is argued, some of them are probably not satisfied with the variable incomes they earn as a result of the varying fortunes of their firms (see, for instance, Ben Ner 1987, 1988: 295–296).

To refute this objection, it may be argued that the best way to organise a democratic firm is to assign the partners a fixed pay rate below the firm's anticipated average revenues and allocate the surplus to a reserve that can subsequently be disbursed, in order to offset falls in revenue possibly recorded in the event of downturns in business.

A different, though usually much criticised, solution would be a social fund that the state might accumulate by taxing corporate profits and use to supplement distributions by firms in temporary financial distress.

A closing and fairly obvious observation is that even though distribution coefficients are socially determined, the state must play a part in terms of levying taxes and awarding subsidies designed to correct excessive inequalities (just as happens in capitalist systems).

As a result, I do not agree with those who argue that in a system of labour-market firms, the law of markets will invariably perpetuate those appalling inequalities that to-date, more than ever, afflict humanity (see Derrida 1993: 110).[7]

One effect of the greater distributive equality typifying a system of labour-managed firms is a reduced tendency for saving, which in turn determines slacker growth rates (see Chalkley and Estrin 1972).

7 Internal controls and firm size in a system of democratic firms

An additional advantage to be discussed in this chapter is reduced monopoly building.

The cross-holding structure of group companies is both anti-democratic and extremely unfair, because it enables holders of comparatively small stakes to control large business sectors and creates the ability for the holding company to appropriate the profits of any of its subsidiaries by simply passing a majority resolution to this effect. For this reason, the 'one man one vote' principle is a major advantage of a system of labour-managed firms, because it determines a less systematic control of firms by other firms.

To a large extent, the substantial shadow cast over world politics by the business world is one of the effects of the proliferation of multinational corporations, and the growing political power of firms is the main driving force behind the advancement of post-democracy. Another advantage of lesser external firm control to be mentioned here is, therefore, the potential for sweeping away multi-national corporations from an all-cooperatives system.[8]

Does the less systematic control of firms by other firms mean that average firm size in an all-cooperatives system will exceed the average size of capitalist businesses today?

Vanek laid considerable stress on the tendency of cooperatives to commensurate firm dimensions with the size of the plant (see Vanek 1970: 273). As is well known, when the production unit of a capitalist firm reaches its dimensional optimum, the company feels encouraged to implement an endless set of plant enlargements and upgrades, on the assumption that this will generate comparable rises in profits; and this is how monopolies arise. In contrast, a cooperative tends to upgrade its plant as a result of the entry of new partners and to leave per capita incomes roughly unaltered. As a result, it is hardly surprising that capitalist firms are, on average, larger than cooperatives.

In the opinion of Gordon (1976), the main driving force behind firm concentration in capitalism is not the prospect of economies of scale, but the process he terms 'qualitative efficiency' – the objective of the ruling class to keep in check the working class and exercise full control over production. Indeed, by replacing living labour with 'dead labour' (i.e. labour with capital), capital concentration makes for tighter capitalist control over production processes and leaves workers with less and less scope for opposing employer decisions. It is the typical response of the ruling class to labour's struggle for fairer income distribution patterns.

Two benefits of lesser firm concentration in cooperative systems are a downward trend in advertising expenditure (see Steinherr 1975) and an appreciable drop in transport costs: if nine firms operate in a given industrial sector in place of a single monopolist – Vanek considered (2006: 18) – the distance to be covered in supplying consumers assumed to be evenly spatially distributed will decline by one-third of the previous total.

In sum, the smaller average size of cooperatives compared to capitalist firms goes to reduce the weight of monopolies in labour-managed systems. And in Vanek's view, this is probably the most important benefit of a democratic firm system and, arguably, one whose scope is far from confined to the domain of economic theory (Vanek 1993: 90).

8   Levels of competition in democratic firms

At this point, we may ask ourselves if the reflections so far have a bearing on inter-firm competition. Competition may vary greatly in intensity, and it is doubtful that escalating competition will always add to the well-being of a community. In fact, the cut-throat competition that small-sized firms in any country face today from corporate giants and Indian or Chinese firms with minimal labour costs shows that the actual competitive environment of a globalised world is exceedingly aggressive. The fear of losing out in the global competitive race causes uncertainty and stress and increases *pari passu* with the degree of competition. Provided it is properly regulated, competition is a powerful driving force of the economy, but whenever it is left without proper government, it turns into a destructive force. According to Stiglitz (1994: 276), nothing supports the view that market economies, where competition is particularly stiff, are more efficient than those where competition is softer.

Levels of competition are determined by ethical, social and government-driven mechanisms. It is well known that Max Weber traced competition to the Calvinistic ethic and that the competitive race is viewed with greater favour in countries such as the United States than elsewhere.

Marx (1857–1858: 38) defined competition as 'the free development of the mode of production based upon capital; the free development of its conditions and of its process as constantly reproducing these conditions'. In free competition, he argued,

> it is capital that is set free, not the individuals. As long as production based on capital is the necessary, hence the most appropriate, form for the development of society's productive power, the movement of individuals within the pure conditions of capital appears as their freedom.
>
> (1857–1858: 38)

Further on (1857–1858: 40), his conclusion was that:

> hence, on the other hand, the absurdity of regarding free competition as the ultimate development of human freedom, and the negation of free competition as equivalent to the negation of individual freedom and of social production based upon individual freedom. It is merely the kind of free development possible on the limited basis of the domination of capital. This type of individual freedom is therefore, at the same time, the most sweeping abolition of all individual freedom, and the most complete subjugation of individuality to social conditions which assume the form of objective powers, indeed of overpowering objects – objects independent of the individuals relating to one another.

Based on Marx's line of reasoning, it is possible to argue that the crux of the matter is not so much excessive competition, as the circumstance that it is still 'the free development of the mode of production based upon capital'. In other words, inasmuch as competition in the service of capital is one thing and competition in the best interests of consumers and workers quite another, if competition in a democratic firm system is actually found to be the latter type, it would be a valuable mechanism deserving effective protection.

This begs the question: will competition in a system of cooperative firms be more or less aggressive than in capitalism?

The absence of external firm control and multinational corporations from an all-cooperatives system and, in general, the already mentioned lesser tendency to monopoly building explain why in such system firms would engage in competition more freely than they are currently doing in capitalism. The tendency of cooperatives to confine dimensional growth to just that size that will maximise efficiency is an additional factor working in the same direction.

The reduced aggressiveness of competition in an all-cooperatives system can also be traced to the apportionment of corporate profits among all partners, a fact that is likely to attenuate the strong incentive to ever stiffer competition, which in capitalism is primarily due to the appropriation of the profits by a single individual.

Third, competition in an all-cooperatives system would be less aggressive, since the incomes of workers with equal skills do not tend to level out (see Montias 1976: 255–256). A cooperative aiming to maximise per capita incomes has no incentive to recruit workers prepared to accept pay rates below those compatible with its average income level. As is well known, such a firm tends to hire partners when marginal productivity is above its average income.

Accordingly, workers in such a system will enjoy a greater and, even more importantly, different freedom to choose between work and non-work. To clarify this point, it is worth considering that a firm that is not interested in hiring workers willing to accept lower pay is one that knows all too well that it is not at risk of losing its current workforce solely because its pay rates fall short of those paid elsewhere.

In the next chapter, I will also show that a less aggressive type of competition offers the added advantage of reduced insolvency risks.[9]

Notes

1   According to Bataille, any undertaker:

> has a clear idea of categories of people that have a bearing on its business (proletarians, intermediaries, accountants, technicians), but ignores individuals as far as it can. No such thing as the warmth of close interpersonal relations will bind together those who are caught up in its internal cogs: a firm is spurred on by glacial greed, employs heartless labour – and has as its only god its own growth.
>
> (1976: 64)

2   While it is true that personality is the result of social relationships (Heller 1980: 51), it seems fairly obvious that social science must mainly focus on the agents that shape human personality.

3   On the subject of the advantages of cooperatives overall, see Birchall (2012). It is worth noting that Birchall's opinions on producer cooperatives strongly diverge from the approach in this book.

4   Wolff (2012: 156–158) shares the idea that the main obstacle to the creation of a system of a self-managed firm run by workers in full autonomy is not the alleged lower productivity levels of democratic firms.

5   The idea that distribution may be socially determined is at the basis of the movement for participatory economics promoted by Albert (see Albert 2003).

6   Departing from this approach, Miller (see Miller 1989: chs 6, 7) maintains that in a self-managed firm system, distribution is determined by the market, but that suitable corrective actions by the state might raise its level of social acceptability well beyond that prevailing in capitalist systems.

7 The top executives in major U.S. corporations sometimes draw paychecks of hundreds of millions of dollars, often 300–400 times the pay of their employees (cf. Baker 2012: 376).
8 Hence the comment of Crouch (2003) that this insight would have induced first-generation revolutionaries to campaign for the abolition of capitalism.
9 Lepage (1978: 91–98) expatiates on the claim that in matters of monopoly building and competition, cooperative firms are constantly at a disadvantage.

8 Labour-managed firms and unemployment

1 Introduction

Though widely shared, the claim that cooperative firms tend to hire fewer workers than capitalist firms is not supported by the findings of any reliable analyses. Discussing this point, this chapter will separately address the two main types of unemployment theorised in the literature: 'classical' unemployment and Keynesian unemployment. The aim is to show that a system of cooperative firms would reduce both of these types of unemployment for a number of reasons.

Structural unemployment has already been dealt with in Chapters 2 and 3.

A necessary preliminary statement is the view (see, *inter alia*, Ward 1958; Ireland and Law 1982: 82) that a system of employee-managed firms has no labour market, since demand for labour is unrelated to the current pay rate. On closer analysis, however, this argument is barely convincing, because in individual firms labour supply is a function of the applicable pay rate, and firms do offer jobs.

2 Classical unemployment

As is well known, in mainstream theory, unemployment is often traced to high labour costs. This chapter will outline three well-known theoretical approaches to high-wage unemployment, namely:

1. efficiency wage theory;
2. insider-outsider theory; and
3. path-dependence theory.

In relation to these three approaches, this chapter will try to show that none of them are an option in a democratic firm system that, by definition, incurs no labour costs.

To start with, I will sum up the main points of efficiency wage theory as reported by Yellen (1984), Stiglitz (1986) and Weiss (1990). According to these authors, wages may be deliberately kept high when firms want to induce their personnel to work hard and with great commitment. Indeed, as Akerlof and others put it, workers who are well-paid feel rewarded and tend to remunerate the 'partial gift' of a higher pay rate with the 'partial gift' of greater commitment to their tasks. This is what is meant by incentive effect (see, among others, Akerlof 1982, 1984; Burow and Summers 1986). The second major finding of this theory is the turnover effect, which traces high wages to the efforts of firms to retain the personnel they have – i.e. to avoid incurring the substantial training and other costs associated with hiring new workers (see, among others, Stiglitz 1974, 1985; Hall 1975; Schlicht 1978; Salop 1979). The selection effect, which is said to stem from the wish of the firm to attract and retain the best workers available (see, among others, Weiss 1980; Malcomson 1981), is held to be an even more important factor. These three effects concordantly entail fixing the equilibrium wage above the level at which labour demand would equal labour supply.

Both capitalist and employee-managed firms tend to attract and retain the best labour force available and avert the personnel turnover and other costs associated with replacing the existing workforce with new hires. However, unlike capitalist firms, democratic firms cannot attain these ends by increasing the wages of their partners, since these earn, not wages proper, but a pre-fixed percentage rate of the firm's income. Neither can they attract given workers by allowing them a greater rate of their residual than the pre-fixed coefficient, since this would automatically necessitate reducing the rate assigned to other workforce categories.

Moreover, while the discipline effect stemming from the fear of lay-offs is certainly no less an option in democratic firms than in capitalist ones, no discipline effect can be generated by increasing the income levels of the partners of a cooperative and no high-wage unemployment of the type suggested in efficiency wage theory is consequently envisaged in a worker-managed economy.

As far as the insider-outsider approach is concerned, it conceives of the labour market as split into two parts and assumes wage levels to be determined by insiders only. As the dominant position of insiders is generally explained with high lay-off and hiring costs, the existence of trade unions is not an essential prerequisite for the validity of this theoretical approach. An additional point to be emphasised is that outsiders do not automatically become insiders on first joining a firm. As lay-offs are generally governed by the 'first in, first out' rule, it is only those who have been working for the firm for some time that can feel safe from lay-off risks when wages begin to rise. And this is why wages will often soar to levels far above those that would guarantee full employment.

The main rationale behind this theoretical approach is that cooperation within the manufacturing process increases in proportion to the team spirit prevailing within the firm. In the opinion of Lindbeck and Snower, this may account for the observation that even in periods of high unemployment workers face little competition from other workers prepared to put up with lower pay rates. The reason why firms seldom deem it expedient to replace existing workers with others ready to accept lower wages, they argue, is the fear that insiders resenting this unfair practice may prove less cooperative with the newcomers. Lindbeck and Snower have claimed that even outsiders refrain from underbidding on the assumption that they would be harassed by insiders and treated as scrabs intending to 'steal other people's jobs'. In other words, lack of cooperation from insiders may greatly affect the productivity rates of newcomers, which means that not only workers, but even firms will assume that wage cuts are not in their best interests (see Lindbeck and Snower 1982, 1985, 1986a, 1986b, 1988a, 1988b; Lindbeck 1993). In the opinion of Solow (1990: 37), this formidable finding accounts for the greater part of classical unemployment from high wages.

As is well known, one major point of Ward and Vanek's producer cooperative theory is the argument that workers oppose the hiring of new partners for reasons of self-interest – i.e. to prevent cuts on their incomes. At first sight, this would appear to back up the assumption that the insider-outsider approach can be extended to a system of democratic firms. In fact, as incomes in producers' cooperatives are determined by the market, insiders in these firms can hardly be assumed to step up their incomes to levels that would stand in the way of the entry of more workers.

The point that I wish to highlight here is that even in the insider-outsider approach, unemployment is associated with high labour costs. This is, in itself, enough to rule out that this kind of unemployment is an option in a system of democratic firms.

Turning to the path-dependence theory, one major assumption behind this approach is that the rate of growth in money wages tends to be fixed at exactly that level at which the earnings of the existing workforce can be maximised without entailing lay-offs of insiders or new hires. In other words, based on this theory, it is assumed that those in employment drive up wages to levels at odds with the creation of new jobs (see Blanchard and Summers 1986, 1987, 1988).

The favourable reception of this and the previous two theoretical approaches (along with others not mentioned in this chapter) is ultimately responsible for the widespread opinion, in economic thought, that high wages are the main cause of unemployment.

There is general agreement that high labour costs are one of the causes of labour market rigidities (see Nickell 1997; Siebert 1997; Layard and Nickell 1999).

Compared to a capitalistic system, in a system of cooperatives, the labour market is likely to be more flexible for two main reasons: one, because the absence of trade unions would rule out those rigidities that are caused by the impact of union action; and, second, because partners assuming that the low competitiveness levels of their firms are caused by a lack of flexibility might work towards reducing rigidity. Again, the decisive point is this: in no case would labour market rigidities cause unemployment. Indeed, as worker incomes in a system of cooperatives are paid out of the firm's residual, any rigidities undermining the competitiveness of a cooperative would determine cuts in worker incomes, rather than employment levels.

A preliminary conclusion possible at this stage is that a democratic firm system would offer the far from negligible advantage of doing away with all such unemployment as is traced to high labour costs by these theorists.

3 Keynesian unemployment in a cooperative system

Keynes established a close link between the systems he termed the 'cooperative economy' and the 'natural economy', but although his line of reasoning on this point is not easy to follow, it is clear that his description of a cooperative economy closely recalls the current idea of a system of producer cooperatives or labour-managed firms. In the 1933 draft of what was to develop into *The General Theory*, distinguishing between 'cooperative economies' and 'entrepreneur economies', he maintained that the former system was not subject to fluctuations in aggregate demand and was governed by Say's law. This conclusion induced him to argue that involuntary unemployment is typical of a market economy founded on hired labour.

In the opinion of Keynes, the 'second postulate of classical theory' is applicable to a cooperative economy, and workers in such a system will choose to continue working, as long as the marginal productivity of labour exceeds its marginal disutility level. In the wake of Karl Marx, Keynes argued that the nature of production in the real world is not, as 'classical' economists assumed, a case of C-M-C' – i.e. of exchanging a commodity for money, in order to buy another commodity – but an instance of M-C-M' – i.e. a situation where money is exchanged for commodities with the aim of making more money. The belief that the second postulate of classical theory is valid in a cooperative economy induced Keynes to state that one major difference between a cooperative economy and an entrepreneur economy is that the former, unlike the latter, is characterised by the C-M-C' pattern – i.e. the principle of exchanging commodities or working for money for the purpose of acquiring other commodities.

This is an additional reason why Keynes argued that overproduction crises, while frequent in capitalist economies, are impossible in systems such as barter or cooperative economies that adopt production systems of the C-M-C' type.[1]

Is Keynes's line of reasoning correct?

In my opinion, as the investment function of a democratic firm does not substantially differ from that of a capitalist firm, Say's law is not applicable to a labour-managed economy, where aggregate demand is subject to fluctuations (see Jossa and Cuomo 1997: ch. 10). On the contrary, as a result of the validity of the second postulate of classical theory in a system of democratic firms, involuntary Keynesian unemployment in such a system will be inexistent.

At this point, I will try to establish what would happen in a system of democratic firms that are subject to the second postulate (in the way clarified in Chapter 4), but not to Say's law. How would a cooperative firm respond to a fall in aggregate demand?

In a system where Say's law does not apply and where national income is determined in Keynesian terms, each fall in aggregate demand will reduce the aggregate number of hours worked. However, when lay-off decisions are adopted by the workers themselves at meetings or, at any rate, in their interests, it is difficult to imagine that the workers will be prepared to fire each other. Indeed, especially in the event that lay-offs were decided by drawing lots, the fear of being drawn would induce the partners to vote against lay-offs. Consequently, there is every reason to believe that in the case of a fall in aggregate demand, a democratic firm, instead of dismissing its workers, will opt for a shorter working week. No involuntary unemployment will ensue wherever this happens: all the workers already in employment will retain their jobs, though all of them will work fewer hours.

Hence, it comes as no surprise that in their analysis of lay-off resolutions in cooperative firms, Vanek (1969), Steinherr and Thiesse (1979a, 1979b) and Brewer and Browning (1982), who did not credit the partners with feelings of mutual solidarity, concordantly reached the conclusion that, in the case of a fall in aggregate demand, workers of a democratic firm would not find it convenient to authorise any lay-offs.[2]

4 Reduced bankruptcy risks in democratic firms

As mentioned before, remoter insolvency risks are an additional major advantage of a system of cooperative firms. As is well known, a company faces insolvency when its costs exceed revenues. Hence, the absence of the largest cost item – wages and salaries – from a democratic firm system would greatly help confine insolvency risks.

An additional argument is relevant in this connection: if pay levels in a democratic firm fall below the average for the system, the partners will tend to leave the firm. However, due to the aversion to the entry of newcomers postulated by the theoretical model cooperative, the exiting partners are likely to have difficulty getting better-paying jobs elsewhere. As a result, while risks of insolvency will generally be remote, workers earning pay levels below the system's average will face the serious inconvenience of having to put up with meagre incomes.

In other words, the downward trend in insolvencies is the result of a major difference between capitalist and employee-managed firms: in the former, workers take precedence over capital providers, since they cash their wages and salaries on a monthly basis; in the latter, the partners participate in the 'residual' and although their incomes may be paid out in monthly instalments, they are determined only after the whole of the firm's costs, including capital charges, have been duly settled.

Let us add that these arguments in support of low bankruptcy frequency are only relevant to the theoretical cooperative model in which workers earn variable incomes. In actual fact, it is well known that existing cooperatives mostly pay their partners fixed wages and salaries.

In a system where incomes may be zeroed, workers must evidently enjoy some measure of protection, but this goal calls for state intervention in the economy and is a point to be discussed further on.

Remote bankruptcy risks are mutually interrelated with lower risks of dismissal, another typical characteristic of cooperatives. As mentioned before, a cooperative may respond to declining demand by reducing working hours instead of laying-off part of the workforce. On the other hand, since lay-offs are the exception because of lesser insolvency risks, employee-managed firms offer the additional advantage of making jobs both safer and longer-lasting.

As for competition, which in capitalist systems is often very tough, it is greatly cooled off as a result of reduced insolvency risks (as mentioned in the previous chapter). A firm that is aware that it will not go bankrupt is free to resolve not to engage in competition at all. For instance, provided the partners are prepared to accept lower incomes, the firm may decide to grant them more free time by reducing daily working hours or the working week. In such a situation – i.e. when bankruptcy risks are not looming – competition, even though sharp, will not be an evil, since individual firms will have the option of engaging in the competitive race or, conversely, reducing incomes.

5 Kalecki's approach to full employment

Coming back to efficiency wage and discipline-effect theory, its authors may have drawn it from a 1943 article by Kalecki, which is often rated as 'deservedly famous' (see, *inter alia*, Salvati 1981), but which they hardly take the trouble of quoting. Kalecki's theory is discussed in a separate section, because it includes a cogent argument in support of the employment-boosting potential of a labour-managed system. Kalecki's starting point is the fact that despite a wish to secure wider markets for their goods, industrialists often oppose demand-boosting public spending policies that would increase employment just because they are inimical to public intervention. To account for this apparent inconsistency, Kalecki mentions three main reasons that may explain their resistance to employment-boosting spending policies:

1. an aversion to public intervention in the economy in general;
2. a strong dislike of measures purposely designed to regulate employment levels and the labour market; and
3. the social and political changes associated with long periods of full employment.

Let us emphasise right now that a cooperative system would hardly oppose public intervention. As soon as the government ceases to be perceived as the expression of the capitalist class, the workers of democratic firms operating in a class conflict-free context would not only deem it in their interests not to oppose public intervention in the economy, but would even welcome any such intervention, provided that its aim is to further full employment.

Specifically, Kalecki's comments on the arguments against public spending mentioned in points 1 and 2 are as follows.

To a large extent – he argued – employment levels in a *laissez faire* system are positively related to trust, since economic crises are often caused by a lack of confidence in the future development of the economy and concomitant falls in private investment. As a result, capitalists are indirectly able to exercise powerful control over government policies. Any moves that may interfere with this feeling of confidence should be carefully avoided for fear of depressing the economy (Kalecki 1943: 166). It is possible to add that one major effect of the close link between confidence and employment is to hold workers and their unions back from stepping up their demands on the assumption that entrepreneurs, alarmed by the risk of strikes and excessive rises in labour costs, may respond by cutting investment resources. Kalecki's conclusion was that a generalised belief in the power of the government to increase employment at will would deprive industrialists of their control over government policies (for in periods of faltering confidence, the government would be in a position to try and restore a climate of trust through public spending).

Kalecki's comments on point 3 are even more forceful. Assuming that the government could efficiently handle the opposition of the industrial class, he argued, 'the social and political changes likely to be triggered by the maintenance of full employment would promptly fuel fresh protests from the business world' (Kalecki 1943: 168). Consistent with this rationale, modern efficiency wage theorists have made it clear that no discipline effect will result from lay-off risks in conditions of full employment, since workers losing their jobs would easily find employment elsewhere. Moreover, in long-term full employment conditions, trade unions would gain in power, workers would look to the future with greater confidence and the working class and its union representatives would step up their demands.

In Kalecki's opinion (1943: 168), brisk demand in markets – the prerequisite for full employment – doubtless adds to profits, but as industrial operators value order in the workplace even higher than rewarding bottom-line results, in the short term (at least) they will put up with slack demand and lesser profits, so long as this enables them to secure control and trim down demand for higher wages.

To the extent that Kalecki's line of reasoning is correct, the added strength the working class is assumed to gain during boom periods goes towards refuting Marx's argument that the revolutionary thrust of the working class is inversely related to levels of prosperity. Hence, is not surprising that Kalecki's line of reasoning has been described as 'a direct refutation of Marx's argument that thriving trade and industrial activities weaken the confrontational spirit of workers' (Morley-Fletcher 1986: xiv).

6 Unemployment and the Phillips curve

The argument that a system of cooperatives is likely to ensure full employment may receive confirmation from the debate on the Phillips curve.

The idea that the short-term Phillips curve is decreasing – i.e. that wage rate and unemployment levels are inversely related – is a widely accepted macroeconomic principle. There is less agreement concerning the long-period Phillips curve, because Tobin (1972) and others hold its slope to be decreasing, even in the long run.

As a rule, a decreasing Phillips curve entails that unemployment and inflation are two antithetical ills and that there is no way of reducing one without increasing the other. And as inflation is always perceived as a danger, it has long been customary to shape monetary policies geared towards controlling inflation, even at the cost of rises in unemployment. As a result, it is possible to argue that unemployment is often the effect of economic policies, which drive up unemployment for the sake of inhibiting inflation.

Today, there is widespread agreement that a vertical long-period Phillips curve identifies an equilibrium income level at which inflation and deflation are both ruled out. However, while monetarists hold that this level is the NRU – a natural rate of unemployment, which is generally assumed to be voluntary (i.e. caused by the search for jobs) – most Keynesians argue that this equilibrium income level is a NAIRU ('non-accelerating inflation rate of unemployment'), at which unemployment is, for the most part, involuntary.

The Phillips curve with a NAIRU reflects social conflict between capital and labour and has been elucidated, among others, by Rowthorn (1977) and Carlin and Soskice (1990). It rests on the assumption that the equilibrium income level at which prices neither increase nor diminish is attained when the unemployment level at which wage-driven price increases make up for productivity-driven price drops. From this perspective, equilibrium unemployment is involuntary, because the bargaining power of unions increases at each rise of unemployment and wages are driven up to levels beyond those that would be compatible with labour productivity rates of growth. In such a situation, the full employment hypothesis becomes unrealistic, because the deflationary policies necessitated by the need to slow down the wage and price spikes sparked off by the added power of organised workers would promptly result in more unemployment.

From the foregoing, it follows that one major advantage of a system of cooperative firms is the non-applicability of the Phillips curve. In the absence of wages, any rise in incomes would reduce unemployment without driving up monetary wages and prices in their wake. And in a conflict-free context, the government would be in a position to shape both expansionist monetary and fiscal measures and employment-boosting policies without igniting the social conflicts that trigger inflation.

In short, in the light of the Phillips curve theory, Kalecki's 1943 argument can be reformulated in line with the idea that the absence of levels of conflict that ignite inflation (and oblige the government to put in place deflationary policies) enables a system of cooperative firms to work towards full employment through expansionist policies.

In even more general terms, it is possible to argue that full employment would be the rule in a cooperative system. Given the absence of a Phillips curve, it would no longer be necessary to put up with rises in unemployment for the sake of reducing inflation, for unemployment and inflation would cease to be antithetical ills, and the government would always be free to launch employment-boosting policies.[3]

7 A comparison of this chapter's findings with those of the literature

The prevailing opinion, in the literature on democratic firms, is that worker control tends to increase, rather than reduce, unemployment. Most authors trace this conclusion to the assumed fundraising difficulties of democratic firms that were dealt with and denied in Chapter 2.

According to other authors, unemployment in a labour-managed economy would rise, because firms would tend to under-invest and, thus, create fewer jobs – an assumption refuted in Chapter 3.

A somewhat more convincing argument in support of the unemployment problems of a system of self-managed firms is found in the already mentioned 1958 article by Ward, where short-term equilibrium is shown to require a higher capital–labour ratio in labour-managed firms compared to capitalist ones. From this, it obviously follows that where the two systems should be assumed to have equal capital accumulation levels, unemployment would be higher in a system of democratically managed cooperative firms.

Ward's argument loses most of its cogency as soon as one considers that the findings of dynamic analyses should have prominence over his static comparison of the employment levels recorded when the two systems are assumed to have equal amounts of capital available. As soon as it is demonstrated that capital is accumulated at different rates in the two systems that are compared, his finding becomes nearly irrelevant.

The conclusion that a system of producer cooperatives will increase, rather than reduce, unemployment is also supported by the idea that the supply curve of a cooperative operating in a perfect competition environment may have a decreasing slope. As is known, Ward's theory on the 'perverse' slope of the supply curve has lost much of its former clout as a result of severe criticisms raised by numerous authors in later writings (see, among others, Domar 1966; Sen 1966; Berman 1977; Miyazaki and Neary 1983). The idea that every upsurge in demand generates fewer jobs in a labour-managed system than in a system of capitalist firms, therefore, will hardly prove this chapter's approach wrong.

Inasmuch as a labour-managed economy is exempt from both classical and Keynesian unemployment and tends to accumulate capital at a brisker pace than the system in adoption today, it seems reasonable to assume that unemployment levels would decline after the transition to the new system.

8 Conclusion

This chapter has tried to answer the question as to whether unemployment levels in a system of producer cooperatives would exceed those prevailing in capitalist systems. For this purpose, three main types of involuntary unemployment have been examined:

1. high-wage unemployment;

2. Keynesian unemployment; and
3. structural unemployment.

These have been examined in a comparative analysis of these two systems. The third form of unemployment mentioned above was dealt with in Chapters 2 and 3, so only the remaining two types of unemployment were discussed in some detail in this chapter.

Summing up the findings for a democratic firm system, it is possible to say that the first type of unemployment is not applicable by definition, and that the same can be said of Keynesian unemployment, since the applicability of the second postulate of classical theory to a self-managed economy rules out the existence of involuntary unemployment.

As for structural unemployment, the main reason why this form may be assumed to soar to higher levels than those of capitalist systems is that the capital–labour ratios of democratic firms tend to increase in the short run. However, Chapters 2 and 3 have shown that LMF-type firms would not tend to invest less than capitalist firms.

An important argument in this chapter is that governments are more likely to act as employers-of-last-resort in systems of self-managed firms. And this seems to be an additional and fairly weighty argument in favour of the idea that the democratic management of firms would tend to eradicate involuntary unemployment (in this connection, see, among others, Aspromourgos 2000).

Notes

1 In this vein, an interesting quote from Joan Robinson (1941: 236) runs that 'whatever part of their profits the capitalists do not consume they invest' and that, for this reason, Marx (much like Keynes) thought that 'the problem of effective demand does not arise'.
2 In the opinion of Ward (1958), implied, though widely accepted, rules require that no majority resolutions should undermine the solidarity feelings linking worker to worker. This contention was countered by Robinson (1967). As a matter of fact, in ex-Yugoslavia, both hiring and lay-off criteria were generally fixed by workers' councils.
3 Wolff (2012: 126) argues that full employment in a self-managed system might be guaranteed by a purposefully established state body, whose functions he cursorily outlines.

9   Alienation in a self-managed firm system

1 Introduction

Continuing the in-depth analysis of the advantages of cooperative firms, this chapter will provide evidence that alienation – a central notion in Marx[1] – is reduced, though not entirely eradicated, in a system of LMF-type cooperatives. In other words, this chapter will set out to demonstrate:

1. that the effect of the authentic revolution sparked off by the introduction of self-management would be to reduce alienation in full keeping with Marx's theoretical approach; and
2. that central planning does not eradicate alienation.

The potential for reducing alienation is, hence, an additional major advantage of the system under analysis in this book.

For the purposes of this discussion, in this chapter, self-managed firms will be assumed to be the LMF-type.

2 The fortunes of alienation theory over time

The changing fortunes of the *Economic-Philosophical Manuscripts of 1844* and the elaborate approach to alienation they include can be traced to the varying attention that Hegelian fundamentals have received in academic debate over time.[2] Marx's notion of alienation had been ignored for years when Lukàcs (1923) thrust it into the spotlight of academic attention by disentangling it from the mazes of Marx's *Capital* (several years before the posthumous publication of the *Manuscripts* themselves). One explanation for the interest aroused by the contribution of Lukàcs is the widely shared assumption, during those years, that the defeat of the Social Democratic Party in Germany had in part been caused by the abandonment of Hegelian philosophy and the turn to a positivistic vision of Marxism instigated by Karl Kautsky (see Basso 1971: 18–32). Traditionally, each turn to reformism in socialist movements has been associated with a rediscovery of positivism; hence, it is possible to say that the ground for the enthusiastic reception of the *Manuscripts* of 1844 was prepared by the Hegelian approach to Marx that Lukàcs, Korsch and Gramsci instigated within the growing anti-reformist climate of the early post-WWI years.[3] (One must, however, note that, according to Fineschi (2013: 5), the new edition of Marx's works has shown that the *Economic-Philosophical Manuscripts of 1844* simply do not exist, because they seem to be a series of sketched notes.)

Objecting to alienation as a notion, Louis Althusser (1965) highlighted a sharp split between Marx's maturity and his early years, when he had not yet accepted the labour theory of value or enunciated his theory of historical materialism and production relations. Moreover, in Althusser's opinion, a central notion of *Capital* such as fetishism was unrelated to the notion of alienation that Marx took over from Feuerbach when he was fairly young. A scholar who expressed comparable opinions even before Althusser is Daniel Bell (1962).[4]

In later years, instead, alienation and fetishism were often closely associated with each other, and today they are looked upon as central themes of Marxian thought, both by those who rate them as closely interlocked and those who sharply set them apart as two different notions. Holloway (1992: 152) has argued that 'the three volumes of *Capital* ultimately revolve around the subject of fetishism', while Sève (2004: 27–28) has remarked that an analysis of Marx's mature works highlights the use of hundreds of words (associated with alienation) that we rated as fallen into utter disuse (cf. also Sowell 1985: 27; McGlone and Kliman 1996; Favilli 2000: 203; Carver 2008). The idea of a unitary thread linking Marx's early and mature approaches to the issue of alienation is endorsed by Tucker (1961: ch. 11), Schlesinger (1965), Avineri (1968), Mészàros (1970), Catephores (1972), Ollman (1976), Schaff (1977), Balibar (1993: 108) and others. According to Musto (2010: 339), in Marx's approach, fetishism is a specific aspect of alienation.

Despite the generalised view that Marx held on to alienation theory right to the end, however, there is no reason to assume that his approach to alienation in the *Manuscripts* of 1844 overlaps with that of his mature years. Sève (2009: ch. 10) and others see the older Marx as preferably concerned with capitalist alienation, rather than alienation in general. Musto (2010: 338–340) holds that one of the best descriptions of alienation is found in the paragraph of the first book of *Capital*, entitled 'The fetishism of commodities and the secret thereof'. Compared to Marx's earlier approach, he argues, this description offers a more accurate definition, both of the notion as such and of actions to eradicate it.

3 Different forms and levels of alienation

The necessary starting point for any correct analysis of alienation is Marx's conception of man (Ollman 1976: 131ff.). As is well known, from the observation that values and modes of being in capitalism differed sharply from those in non-capitalist societies, Marx deduced that the essence of man could only be grasped by examining social production relations, because 'man and society are no separate notions; rather, man is intrinsically connoted by his social essence' (Luporini 1955: 4).[5] However, he also wrote that 'industry is the real historical relationship of nature, and therefore of natural science, to man'; further on, he also stated that by looking upon industry as the exoteric revelation of man's essential powers, one could gain an understanding of the human essence of nature or the natural essence of man (Marx 1844a: 303). And this amounts to admitting the existence of a natural essence of man. The idea that the above quote conveys, indeed, is that man is basically one with nature and 'just as society itself produces man as man so is society produced by him' (Marx 1844a: 298).[6]

Marx identifies four main forms of alienated labour. The first of these is the alienation of the worker from the product of his work. In capitalism, a worker has no say over the amount or composition of the output of his work. The product is an object that acquires an existence of its own, which is external to the worker and, thus, alien and hostile to him. The more the worker increases his output, the more he finds himself under the sway of capital. A second form is the kind of alienation deriving the worker from his production activity. The work input of a hired worker does not belong to the worker himself, but to another person; it is forced labour from which he draws no satisfaction. Only when eating, drinking or lying in bed does the worker feel human. At the same time, the worker is alienated from his own species. A man who undertakes work for the sole purpose of satisfying needs, as a means of subsistence, becomes indistinguishable from an animal and is consequently alienated from his species as well. Lastly, hired labour is alienated from the worker by the capitalist, in terms that it does not belong to the worker and is discharged under the dominion of another man, the capitalist, in a state of coercion.

In Marx's approach, alienation comes not only in different forms, but also at different levels. Some of these are common to a variety of social organisation modes, while some are specific to capitalism only. In general terms, from the foregoing, it can be deduced that the categories of work to be described as 'alienated' are all the production activities not primarily aimed at meeting human needs, those aimed at earning necessary means of subsistence and, even more generally, those conditioned by external constraints.[7] With this wide meaning, any work done in a system characterised by productive specialisation – the division of labour – is alienated.[8] Those finding pleasure in their work tend to diversify their activities, switch between jobs and eschew over-specialised occupations,[9] whereas the division of labour strips workmen of the intellectual potential inherent in any work process.

In a different, though equally wide and comprehensive sense, alienation comes about in association with the working of markets, where its roots are impersonal mechanisms whose effects can hardly ever be planned or wilfully contrived. The main alienation-generating market mechanism is competition, which impels people to behave in manners they would probably shun if they were not obliged to vie with competitors. A capitalist market necessitates higher degrees of specialisation than a competition-free environment. Overall, market-related alienation is the effect of scarcity and the resulting need to act under compulsion and renounce freedom of choice.

Any activities undertaken for income-earning purposes may be described as 'alienated' and this characterisation can be rated as a core assumption behind

Marx's entire theoretical approach. Speaking of the worker, Marx raised the query:

> Is this 12 hours' weaving, spinning, boring, turning, building, shovelling, stone-breaking, regarded by him as a manifestation of life, as life? Quite the contrary. Life for him begins where this activity ceases, at the table, at the tavern, in bed.
>
> (Marx 1849: 34)

And in *Grundrisse*, with reference to a tradesman or professional, he spelt out in bold letters that the exchange relation confronts us like a power that is external to producers and independent of them.

> The social character of the activity, as also the social form of the product and the share of the individual in production, appear here as something alien to and existing outside the individuals; not as their relationship to each other, but as their subordination to relationships existing independently of them and arising from the collision between indifferent individuals.
>
> (Marx 1857–1858: 94)

Fetishism is one aspect of market alienation or, in the opinion of some, an overlapping notion. Fetishism is the process whereby interpersonal relations within production and exchange processes take on the characteristics typical of relations between commodities – i.e. a false perception of reality. In a market economy, production is controlled by private operators producing goods for their mutual requirements. On closer analysis, however, private producers are only formally autonomous: whenever one of them steps up the production volume of a given article, the resulting drop in prices will impel other producers of that article to reconsider their original decisions. And social relations that generate interdependencies of this sort end up resembling relations between things, rather than interpersonal relations.[10] Men as consumers are dependent on markets, where they are at the mercy of their products.[11]

A less general, but even more compelling definition of alienation is 'work which is subject to the sway of capital'. In Marx's *Manuscripts of 1844*, he stated:

> the more the worker exerts himself in his work, the more powerful the alien, objective world becomes which he brings into being over against himself, the poorer he and his inner world become, and the less they belong to him.... The alienation of the worker in his product means not only that his labour becomes an object, an external existence, but that it exists outside him, independently, as something alien to him, and that it becomes a power on its own confronting him. It means that the life which he has conferred on the object confronts him as something hostile and alien.
>
> (Marx 1844a: 211)

Similarly, in *Grundrisse*:

> No extraordinary intellectual power is needed to comprehend that, if the
> initial situation assumed is that of free labour arising from the dissolution of
> serfdom, or wage labour, the only way in which machines can originate is in
> opposition to living labour, as property alien to it and hostile power opposed
> to it, i.e., they must confront labour as capital.

(Marx 1857–1858: 577)

Dissenting from Althusser, Elster argued that the dominion of dead labour over
living labour, the subjection of labour to capital and the idea that production
means are an alien power holding workers in their sway are the most important
points with which Marx concerned himself in his mature years (see Elster 1985:
102). The worker's estrangement from the commodities he has created – Elster
wrote – is closely related to his spiritual alienation. To produce commodities is
to create a need for them – a need that is often frustrated in the capitalist production context. The link here is a fairly transparent one. In contrast, the reason why
the estrangement of workers from production means should cause alienation is
much less easy to grasp, since it is hardly possible to maintain that workers need
production means in one way or another. Nonetheless, although this form of alienation is certainly less evident, it has even more far-reaching implications. It
reflects the crucial structural fact that the worker is stripped of his claim on the
entire value of his product and its effect is to further exacerbate the worker's
commodity-related alienation. Dispossessed of production means, workers have
no control over the work process as a whole and are consequently unable to
realise their work potential to the full (see Elster 1985: 103). According to Elster,
a major assumption of Marxism is the idea that life is rewarding when it is
founded on self-realisation, rather than passive consumption. Indeed, in Marx's
approach, the severest form of alienation originates from the estrangement of
people from their creative faculties and may either magnify or stifle a desire for
self-realisation; and this is the reason why the ideal of self-realisation in work is
an immensely valid guiding principle for industrial and political reform (see
Elster 1989: 297).[12]

  As a rule, Marxist authors distinguish between different forms of alienation,
but not between different *levels* of alienation; very often, they also fail to identify
or discuss possible causes or ways to fight it. In particular, there is no agreement
on the assumption that Marx held scarcity to be its main cause.[13] Tucker, for
instance, has criticised those Marxists who assume that alienation is to be traced
to the 'despotism of physical needs' and has argued that life needs are not the
cause, but just an expression of alienation. He writes:

> And given his own underlying premise about the inherently creative nature
> of man, it could hardly be otherwise. A being who spontaneously tends to
> be productive might well experience self-activity in work that he performs
> for a living. Thus, a carpenter might derive creative satisfaction and a

personal sense of fulfillment from the carpentry by which he lives ... there is no necessary connection between self-alienation and the need to work for a living.

(Tucker 1961: 137)

Whereas Tucker held Marx to blame alienation on dependence on money (Tucker 1961), in actual fact alienation in Marx is traced to more than one reason, including the subjection of labour to the power of capital. As a result, the argument that dependence on money is the sole cause of Marxian alienation is not correct.

This begs the question: what is to be gained from an analysis of different levels of alienation?

Tracing capitalist alienation to hired labour is tantamount to claiming that the establishment of a self-managed firm system without hired labour would sweep away the primary form of alienation.[14] As mentioned above, in a democratic firm system, the capitalist capital–labour relation is reversed, since workers cease being bought by owners of production means and become buyers of means of production themselves. As a result, democratic firms are an effective means of counteracting that form of alienation that stems from the subordination of labour to capital.[15] 'The worker', Marx wrote,

actually treats the social character of his work, its combination with the work of others for a common purpose, as a power which is alien to him; the conditions in which this combination is realized are for him property of another. ... It is quite different in factories that belong to the workers themselves, as at Rochdale.

(Marx 1894a: 178–179)[16]

The lower labour division levels required by a system of cooperative firms are one further explanation for the claim that alienation would be less marked in such a system.

An additional point to be emphasised is that alienation is stronger in workers compared to capitalists:

The propertied class and the class of the proletariat present the same human self-estrangement. But the former class feels at ease and strengthened in this estrangement, it recognises estrangement as its own power and has in it the semblance of a human existence.

(see Marx and Engels 1845: 36)

Alienation is an objective phenomenon, a fact. Workers under capitalism are always alienated, even though they may experience no 'feelings' of alienation (see Schacht 1970: 154ff.).

4 Alienation and revolution

But how can mankind be relieved from alienation? In the *Manuscripts of 1844*, communism is described as the social organisation mode that roots out alienation. Hence, my decision to establish if alienation theory may offer clues for defining the type of production mode one can expect to arise upon the abolition of capitalism. In this connection, let me observe that the contours of this future social order can only be deduced from the bulk of Marx's writings, since Marx is known to have provided few, if any, descriptions of the 'inn of the future'. For example, the faults and contradictions of capitalism addressed within the framework of crisis theory may offer a number of insights into Marx's ideas of the social order that would arise out of the ashes of capitalism. In my opinion, however, it is alienation theory and, specifically, the analysis of individual forms of alienation that can help better prefigure how the social order of the transition from capitalism to communism will be organised. Analysing the *Manuscripts of 1844*, Althusser (1965: 136) wrote: 'Setting out from the key notion of estranged labour, Marx solves the inner contradictions of political economy by thinking of it and then rethinking the bulk of political economy through it'; and, years before, Cornu (1949: ch. 6) had suggested that the alienation concept was the core idea based on which Marx had developed his new approach to the course of history and communism, and this major turn in the evolution of his thought was evidenced by the *Manuscripts of 1844*.[17]

Inasmuch as my line of reasoning so far has been correct, it is barely to be doubted that the revolution sparked off by a move from capitalism to self-management would sweep away all such alienation as currently stems from the dominion of capital over labour. As mentioned above, however, alienation comes in different forms and at different levels, and self-management would not root out those forms of alienation that are related to the working of markets and shortage of commodities. These forms of alienation can only be cancelled by a second revolution intended to suppress markets straightaway. This claim is consistent with the idea that the introduction of socialism was to be the first step of the process and that the second step, the establishment of communism, was to be deferred until after the necessary assumptions were created by the resulting surge in production levels.

A problem still to be addressed in greater depth is the reason why markets would continue to generate alienation even in a democratic firm system. As has been made clear, the alienation-generating factor is external compulsion on production activities. In capitalist systems, a major form of compulsion stems first and foremost from competition, so that businessmen unable to shape organisational modes for cutting costs face insolvency. In other words, insolvency is the penalty for all those who are unable to stand up to external competition in markets, and the ultimate implication of this is that production is far from free.

Compared to a system of capitalist firms, a system of democratic firms greatly reduces insolvency risks. Insolvency is the effect of the pincers in which firms are caught up when costs escalate and prices tumble down under the pressure of competition from more efficient rival firms. And as the labour costs of self-managed firms are nought by definition, in the absence of upward price spirals triggered by labour costs, the strain caused by these 'pincers' would be greatly reduced (see Jossa 2010: 82–85). Hence, it is possible to conclude that markets in democratic firm systems would be a near proxy for those theorised by neoclassical economics, in terms that they would actually afford scope for free choices. By way of example, in democratic firms, workers prepared to put up with lower incomes may reduce the working week to three days and thereby avert insolvency risks.

The one form of alienation that democratic firm management is unable to cancel is commodity fetishism, which Marx held to affect every market economy.[18]

As a result, irrespective of the degree of freedom assumed to reign in the markets of a self-managed system, there will be no means of eliminating that form of alienation that is related to markets.

The question to answer at this point is whether the suppression of the sway of capital over labour can be followed up by a dismantlement of markets at least by degrees, if not from morning to night. Clues on this point may come from the 'debate of the 1930s' on price systems in planned economies. This debate made it clear that neither prices nor markets or the associated incentive systems can be abolished as long as commodities are available in limited amounts.

Concluding, from Marx's approach and the conclusions of this debate, it follows that two revolutions are necessary:

1. a first revolution to reverse the capital–labour relation and root out the sway of capital and the alienation it carries in its track; and
2. a second revolution to realise the Marxian ideal of a communistic society by solving the scarcity issue and abolishing markets straightaway.

5 A critique of Bigo's approach

In this section, I will try to establish if central planning entails the elimination of alienation by its very nature. The most relevant contribution here is an analysis by Bigo.

In Bigo's approach (1953: 111), the attempt to split the road to communism into two distinct steps was one of the thorniest issues Marx faced. His aim – Bigo argued – was to provide evidence that communism would sweep away alienation in man, while retaining some forms of value, at least at the first step. Indeed, '[t]he goal that Marx had set himself was actually a very difficult one' (1953: 111).

What kind of solution did Marx work out, according to Bigo?

Far from maintaining that communism was likely to be implemented within a short timeframe, he postulated a very slow process during which inequalities and social constraints would be gradually dismantled. Mars's solution for the transition period was to retain private property and hired labour and to introduce centralised planning. As Bigo puts it, Marx had no option but to admit – and this is the crux of the matter – that over the span of the transition period, the capitalist factors to be retained – private property as an institution, wages and salaries as its necessary assumptions and the resulting right to freely dispose of such incomes – would stop generating alienation, because alienation was a condition connoting trade exchanges only (see Bigo 1953: 111). In other worlds, from Bigo's perspective, the introduction of planning alongside persisting capitalist remnants eliminates alienation, because it eliminates exchanges between capitalists and workers and between private producers and consumers.

Bigo's argument is that the cause of Marxian alienation was neither hired labour nor the valuation of commodities by reference to abstract values or the existence of money, but the fact that prices were determined by the interplay between consumers and competing manufacturers (instead of being fixed at the end of a decision-making process).

In Bigo's opinion, this is the reason why a mature Marxian work such as the *Critique of the Gotha Program* postulates the creation of a centrally planned system allowing for joint ownership of production means – i.e. a social order where products would no longer be interchanged between manufacturers. Quoting Marx:

> Within the collective society based on common ownership of the means of production, the producers do not exchange their products; just as little does the labour employed on the products appear here as the value of these products, as a material quality possessed by them, since now, in contrast to the capitalist society, individual labour no longer exists in an indirect fashion, but directly as a component part of the total labour.[19]
>
> (1875a: 85)

In Marx's view, such a centrally planned economy would rise from the ashes of capitalism still 'stamped with the birth-marks of the old society from whose womb it emerges' (Marx 1875a: 95), workers would receive vouchers reflecting the hours worked and would then exchange these vouchers for commodities in amounts equalling the value of the hours worked. Accordingly, they would ultimately be remunerated with the same amount of labour that each of them has contributed to society.

At this point, we have to ask ourselves if Bigo's line of reasoning is correct. Would the introduction of planning actually do away with alienation during the transition period, as Bigo assumes?[20]

The centrally planned system that Marx had in mind when he wrote the *Critique of the Gotha Program* is basically the system that ruinously collapsed wherever it was established – namely, in the Soviet Union, as well as in eastern countries. All the same, for the purposes of this book, it is interesting to explain Bigo's theoretical error.

As was made clear by the debate of the 1930s, Bigo is wrong when he assumes that markets can somehow be imitated or used without the concomitant introduction of competition. An additional unconvincing argument is his claim that alienation would be cancelled under conditions where markets and money would continue to exist in the absence of competition. In point of fact, the one precondition for sweeping away alienation is putting an end to scarcity, as mentioned above. However, Bigo's main error is to have assumed that alienation could be cancelled, despite retaining hired labour working at the commands of the planner. If the aim is to induce workers to generate the output levels expected of them, there are but two options: introducing competition or the commands of a planner. There is no third option.[21] In either case, labour would not be free, but alienated.

Marx also thought that the strongest form of fetishism was linked to money:

We have already seen, from the simplest expression of value, x commodity A=y commodity B, that the thing in which the magnitude of the value of another thing is represented appears to have the equivalent form independently of this relation, as a social property inherent in its nature. We followed the process by which this false semblance became firmly established, a process which was completed when the universal equivalent form became identified with the natural form of a particular commodity, and thus crystallized into the money-form.

(Marx 1867: 187)

Now, a centrally planned economy that retains money will retain the strongest form of fetishism as a matter of course.[22]

The conclusion is that Bigo's approach is wrong for a number of reasons, including the undeniable fact that nowhere in the *Critique of the Gotha Programme* did Marx claim that this centrally planned system was expected to cancel alienation within a few days of the end of capitalism.[23]

6 Cooperation and human personality

Both Mill and Marshall made it clear that the beneficial influence of cooperative firms on the personalities of workers was closely associated with the alienation issue. This is why I will briefly come back to this point here.

As is well known, in his celebrated *VI Thesis on Feuerbach* (1845), Marx wrote: 'the essence of man is no abstraction inherent in each single individual. In its reality it is the ensemble of social relations' (Marx 1845: 4). And in the much celebrated preface to *A Contribution to the Critique of Political Economy*, he emphasised that 'the mode of production of material life conditions the general process of social, political and intellectual life. It is not the consciousness of men that determines their existence, but their social existence that determines their consciousness' (Marx 1859: 20–21).[24] One may not share Marx's radical opinion on this point, but the idea that human character is strongly influenced by production relations will be easily accepted, even by non-Marxists.

Even before Marx, the idea that human 'character' is shaped by the environment and by social institutions was strongly endorsed by Robert Owen in a well-known work on the new society of his day (Owen 1816) and in various later works (see Bronowski and Mazlish 1960: 486). From his experience of industrial life in Manchester, the ruthless behaviour of factory-owners in his day and the rush for enrichment during the Industrial Revolution, Owen held the conviction that spreading greed, inhuman behaviour and the deterioration of morals were caused by the factory system. It was this that led him to propose new forms of social organisation intended to counteract a competition-based system whose ultimate goal was profit-making.

It is well known that Owen's approach was a major influence on Mill and Marshall. Owen's ideas returned in a seldom-quoted book written by Wright Mills more than sixty years ago, in order to argue that the left should work towards humanising society by socialising means of production. It was in the workshop, more than in the electoral district – Mills wrote – that 'the new man' of a free society was to be developed. In his opinion, it was for this reason that unions had to make it their task to battle for control over work (Mills 1948: 258).

In more recent years, George Bataille wrote that the factory knows those forces that may serve its purposes – proletarians, middlemen, accountants, engineers – but tends to ignore men; no feelings of sympathy link men to men once they get caught up in its gears, the factory is moved on by boundless greed, is devoid of compassion in its use of labour and looks to only one god: its own furtherance (Bataille 1976: 64). Even more recently, the economist Hahn has argued that the founding principle of capitalism is in stark contradiction with the main ethical values of the Judaic Christian system, which exalts virtues such as benevolence and sympathy towards one's neighbours, condemns greed – particularly greed for wealth – and teaches us not to accumulate treasures on earth. Under this ethical system, seeking pecuniary remuneration as a primary goal and thereby failing in one's duty of solidarity towards fellow-beings is not considered to be worthy of admiration. And yet – Hahn concludes – this is exactly what is asked of people working in a capitalistic system (see Hahn 1993: 10).

As mentioned above, cooperatives are expected to help create feelings of mutual solidarity among people. To the extent that it is true that the workers of a cooperative share a common fate and that production activities are organised in such a way that the whole workforce will benefit from the efforts of a single member to add to his/her income, it is possible to assume that an all-cooperatives system would expand the realm of human altruism and induce workers to become less self-centred.

This is what Meade wished to emphasise when he described the functioning of his *Agathotopia*, a society based on principles of cooperation:

> The typical Agathotopian has a more cooperative and compassionate attitude in his or her social behavior than is the case at present in the United Kingdom, where we have, alas, been subject for so many years to such a regime of devil-take-the-hindmost and grab-as-much-money-as-quickly-as-possible. This suggests that there is some positive feedback between social institutions and social attitudes.
>
> (Meade 1989: 8–9)

As is well known, the main dichotomy discussed in sociology is the distinction between society and community that Tönnies drew in order to contrast pre-capitalist rural society with capitalist society. Tönnies saw the former character-ised by strong interpersonal connections between family members and neighbours and the latter characterised by individualism, as well as by contractual relations determining that interpersonal links are either dissolved or mediated by the market. In his opinion, individualism and contractual relations give rise to a form of instrumental rationalism, economic calculation, which became the central notion of the work of Max Weber. In Weber's approach, rationalisation is the process whereby man, outgrowing tradition and the belief in magic, starts looking at the world with disenchantment. In his view, it is identified with modernisation and 'the spirit of capitalism' and marks a turn to the better that is perceived not only in economics, but also in religion (the Reformation) and politics (bureaucra-tisation). At the same time, however, Weber diagnosed the risks associated with excessive rationalisation – i.e. an adverse impact on human interrelations and loss of the values that shaped the Jewish-Christian civilisation. He wrote:

> The fate of our times is characterised by rationalisation and intellectualisa-tion and, above all, by the disenchantment of the world and precisely the ultimate and most sublime values have retreated from the public sphere either into the netherworldly realm of mystical life or into the brotherliness of the immediate relationships between individuals.
>
> (1919: 41)

For the purposes of my line of reasoning, Weber's approach suggests that the dichotomy between society and community theorised by Tönnies is relevant not only to the distinction between feudalism and capitalism, but also to that between capitalism and the form of socialism I am discussing in this book (and this is an additional argument in support of the socialist essence of a worker-managed firm system). As I have tried to show in this chapter, in self-managed firms, aliena-tion and fetishism are reduced and community feelings are greatly enhanced, since workers are aware of their shared fate and know that the effort of anyone of them will generate benefits for the others as well. Lastly, as a result of the workers' less individualistic outlooks and the attention given to the profit motive and considerations of maximum well-being, instrumental rationality plays a lesser role in these firms, and this has a major beneficial effect on the personali-ties of men and women.[25]

Let us specify in passing that Marxism, Christian philosophy and existential-ism differ greatly in their respective approaches to alienation (see Prucha 1965).

7 Conclusion

In this chapter, I have tried to make the following points:

1. Democratic labour-managed firms reduce the main cause of alienation.

2. Bigo's claim that alienation is cancelled by central planning is unwarranted.
3. The cooperative firm tends to improve the personalities of those who work in it.

My reflections go towards reinforcing the idea that the establishment of a democratic firm system would amount to a consistently Marxian anti-capitalist revolution. However, the main aim of this chapter was to highlight that one of the main advantages of a socialist system founded on self-management is its potential for greatly reducing alienation.

Notes

1 According to Kühne, 'The real starting point of the Marxian system is not, as is often thought, the theory of exploitation, but Marx's criticism of the dehumanisation or "alienation" under capitalism' (1972: 313). Tucker, for his part (1961: 99), describes self-alienation as 'the fundamental category of Hegelianism' and argues that Marx 'came to see alienation everywhere' as 'a phenomenon pervading every single sphere of human life' (1961: 102); years before, Rubin (1928: 5) had argued that alienation and fetishism are at the basis both of Marx's entire economic system and his theory of value. The importance of the *Manuscripts of 1844* and alienation theory for a correct interpretation of Marx was also emphasised by Ernst Bloch (1938–1947: 46) on the assumption that Marxism was 'nothing but the struggle against the dehumanisation which culminates in capitalism'. In the words of O'Brien (1981: 411):

> For Marx the aim of society was not, as it is true of capitalist systems, the maximisation of production and consumption. Marx was not unconcerned about the conquest of poverty, but he was still adamantly opposed to consumption as a supreme end. Marx was mainly concerned with the creation of that type of society in which man could be truly human, free and independent. Capitalist systems, on the other hand, robbed man if his freedom and his independence, and made him, in a word alienated – alienated from all that truly mattered.

For concordant views, see also, Korsch (1967) and Colletti (1969: 353).
2 Although I agree with Kauder (1968: 270) that 'the alienation concept of the young Marx is the legacy of Hegel and the Hegelian left', it is interesting to mention that some trace the origins of Marx's alienation theory not to Hegel, but to Adam Smith (see Fay 1983). An interesting historical analysis of the notion of alienation is developed in McLellan (1978).
3 Interestingly, when Lukàcs read the *Manuscripts of 1844*, he reconsidered some of the opinions he had expressed in the detailed analysis of reification and alienation included in his well-known 1923 book entitled *History and Class Consciousness* (on this point, see Bolaffi 1978: 7–11).
4 In 1942, Sweezy wrote (13): 'it was during the next two years, mostly spent in Paris and Brussels, that he broke with his philosophic past and achieved the mature point of view from which he was to write his later economic works'.
5 According to Cornu (1955), Marx's claim that the essence of man is realised in his relations with the environment goes back to Feuerbach, though Feuerbach identified the environment with nature, rather than with society.
6 Production activity is a tool that man consciously uses to control his environment. Marx terms the dialectical interaction between mankind and nature 'objectivisation' and criticises Hegel for failing to draw a distinction between 'objectivisation' and 'alienation' (see Elliott 1979: 350–351).

7 In the words of Kant (1797: 85–86), 'every rational being exists as an end in himself' and is not merely 'a means to be arbitrarily used by this or that will'.

8 The division of labour, which prevents workers from making free choices, is either caused by the existence of interchange or the commands of a planner – i.e. by the pressure of material conditionings. Accordingly, the argument that no alienation will be caused by the division of labour in the absence of interchange (see, *inter alia*, Roberts and Stephenson 1970, 1975) does not sound particularly convincing. In a Soviet-type centrally planned system without interchange, for instance, the division of labour does generate alienation, because it is the result of external commands.

9 The idea that the division of labour makes work degrading was shared by numerous eighteenth-century writers, including Smith, Ferguson, Millar and Wallace (see West 1969: 137).

10 Conceived of as a wrong perception of reality, fetishism generates two main effects: first, it deludes workers into believing that freedom and equality are possible; and second, it encourages workers and capitalists to adapt to impersonal social processes (see Elliott 1979: 353).

11 'The objective conditions essential to the realization of labour' – Marx wrote (1863–1866: 35) – 'are alienated from the worker and become manifest as fetishes endowed with a will and soul of their own'. Quoting this passage, Bedeschi appropriately commented (1972: 213) that 'this process, which falls in with alienation, is nothing but the materialisation of the fetishistic consciences or illusions of economists'.

12 In a well-known monograph about alienation theory, Mészàros wrongly equated Marxian alienated labour with wage labour straightaway (see Mészàros 1970: ch. 4).

13 Mészàros (1970: 313) and Elliott (1979: 351) distinguish between two aspects of alienation: the idea of dispossession – i.e. the worker's loss of control over nature and production activity; and the fact that man is confronted by a *hostile* power, which makes his life purposeless. Although Elliot describes the former aspect as alienation and the second as estrangement, he owns that these two terms are, in many respects, synonymous (Elliott 1979).

14 Let us mention, in this connection, that both Kant and Fichte postulated a contrast between the way we are and the way we should be, and that the young Marx was attracted by the Hegelian notion that knowledge and historical evolution will help solve this contrast (see Tucker 1961: 74–75).

15 For an interesting and exhaustive analysis of this point, see Reich and Devine (1981).

16 In an outline of different levels of alienation, Sobel (2008) contends that alienation will outlast the end of capitalism and extend right into the early phases of the new social order.

17 From Cornu's perspective, Marx's emphasis on the realisation of the essence of man in society amounts to a call for suppressing just that system, capitalism, which negates the human condition by generating alienation.

18 In the opinion of Braybrooke (1958), provided a hired worker accepts his status and is made conversant with what is being produced and the purposes of the relevant production activities, he would hardly be more strongly alienated in capitalism than in a self-managed system. In my opinion, this superficially convincing argument is actually off-track for two main reasons: first, only a worker who has a full understanding of the advantages and viability of self-managed firms can be said to accept capitalism and reject self-management in full awareness; second, Braybrooke never as much as mentions Marx's idea that fetishism is generated by markets. Braybrooke's line of reasoning seems to pass over the distinction that Marx drew between work done for the sake of the pleasure deriving from it (and, hence, free) and work done for purposes of subsistence (which is always alienated).

19 This recalls Engels's argument that only 'within those social forms in which commodities are not exchanged' can we speak of value (Engels 1890–1891: 460).

20 Closing his description of the central planning system that Marx had in mind, Bigo wrote: 'no alienation would arise under such circumstances, nor would we be faced with any such thing as an exchange value' (Bigo 1953: 113). A concordant reflection is found, *inter alia*, in Colletti (1977: 131–132).
21 Economists rate it as a sign of immaturity or poor intelligence to criticise markets and bureaucracy in one stroke (see, *inter alia*, Lindbeck 1972; Samuelson's introduction to Lindbeck's book (xiii, xiv)).
22 Proudhon, too, held that centrally planned socialist systems had not improved upon capitalistic systems, because they had stripped workers of every initiative, maintained hired labour and fixed wage levels (see Ansart 1967: 17–20).
23 In point of fact, the following excerpt from Marx would seem to validate Bigo's approach:

> Freedom, in this sphere, can consist only in this, that socialized man, the associated producers, govern the human metabolism with nature in a rational way, bringing it under their collective control instead of being dominated by it as a blind power.
>
> (Marx 1894a: 959)

This passage is also quoted by Roberts and Stephenson (1970: 196–197) in support of their contention that Marx held centralised planning to cancel alienation (though not the division of labour, as mentioned before) by purging markets of their impersonal and non-manageable mechanisms. Dissenting from this view, let me stress that the excerpt concerned is followed by the already quoted passage where Marx argued that as the realm of freedom would start as soon as labour was no longer determined by necessity or external expediency, it lay beyond the sphere of material production proper by its very nature. Consequently, it is possible to conclude that neither Bigo nor Roberts and Stephenson have laid sufficient emphasis on the plain fact that in Marx any work that is done for earning one's daily bread is classified as alienation and that the label 'free labour' is restricted to just such work as is freely done for the sake of the pleasure deriving from it. In point of fact, the one precondition for sweeping away alienation is doing away with hired labour and putting an end to scarcity, as mentioned above.
24 On the essence of man according to Marx, see Luporini (1963b), Baczko (1965), Schaff (1965), Schaff and Sève (1975) and Screpanti (2013: ch. 3).
25 On Marx's alienation theory, see also, Baczko (1965) and Vranicki (1965).

10 The democratic firm as a merit good

1 Introduction

The analysis of the plus points of a democratic firm system is in line with the assumption that democratic firms are merit goods, which satisfy both the needs of their partners and those of society at large. This finding is a suitable introduction to the ultimate aim of this book: providing the demonstration that a system of producer cooperatives gives rise both to a new mode of production and to a genuine form of socialism.

However, before the discussion of this specific point, it may be convenient to develop a number of additional reflections on the nature of democratic firms and the criticisms levelled against them by other authors.

2 Economic democracy and spontaneous growth

In part, the scant concern with democratic firms in the current mainstream literature can be traced to the belief of most economists that what is of benefit to society will inevitably assert itself in due time and that what fails to emerge spontaneously cannot be of advantage to the community as a whole. Although this is the typical approach of economic liberalists and supporters of 'social Darwinism' (see, for example, Nozick 1974: 314–317; Williamson 1985: 265–268), even academics who do not think of themselves as liberalists share a somewhat less radical version of this view. Among them, Putterman holds that given the absence of legal barriers preventing workers from founding firms entirely run by themselves, this kind of business enterprise will assert itself in market economies, as soon as workers realise that its advantages exceed the costs involved (see Putterman 1990: 161).[1]

In fact, the social benefits flowing from economic democracy would suggest furthering the establishment of democratic firms, even in situations where they are slow to emerge spontaneously. Greater worker participation in the firm's decisions, which is tantamount to increased economic democracy, can indeed be rated as a benefit that workers should pursue, even at the price of lesser efficiency. Be that as it may, there can be little doubt that worker management – like justice or education – is a 'merit good' working to the advantage of private individuals and the general public alike.

3 Democracy as a private good

The idea that economic democracy is a good in itself, irrespective of its results, is often termed a self-evident truth that does not need the support of detailed argumentation (see, for example, Dahl 1985: 153; Bowles and Gintis 1986: 3–4). It is a plain fact that decision-making and the resulting power to exercise sovereignty over a group are highly rewarding experiences, as is the decision-maker's freedom from the constraints stemming from other people's commands. Hayek is one of the authors who most forcefully identified freedom with the absence of subjection to other people's decisions (see, for example, Hayek 1960: ch. 1). As a result, a major advantage of economic democracy is to satisfy the fundamental human desire for freedom and self-determination.[2]

An additional major advantage of democracy within the firm is, quite naturally, its ability to satisfy the requirements of workers. One argument in support of this assumption runs as follows: although capitalistic firms often find it in their best interests to satisfy the preferences and requirements of their workers, they consider the needs of marginal – not average – workers. Suffice it to think of a resolution concerning the introduction of a given safety device. If marginal workers (i.e. those indifferent to the option of whether or not to accept the job) are young people wishing to earn an income as soon as possible and thus are willing to take risks for the sake of obtaining just any job, the firm concerned will not think it worthwhile to install the safety device (to which these workers can be assumed to attach little, if any, importance). On the contrary, in a worker-managed firm, the resolution would be put to the vote and the opinion of the majority would prevail (Hansmann 1996: 30–31).

In this vein, let us add that while democratically made choices reflect the preferences of the group's median partner, the most efficient solution would be the one endorsed by the average partner (provided always such a one can be defined); and the preferences of the median partner may widely diverge from those of the average partner (see Hansmann 1996: 40).

The exercise of discretionary power on the part of workers is both an invaluable good and one obtainable at low direct costs (for example, the cost of providing the premises needed for meetings). As mentioned above, this entails that the actual efficiency level of a democratic firm will never be correctly appraised if one fails to give proper consideration to the freedom associated with it. Moreover – and this is the crux of the matter – as economic democracy is in many respects a 'merit' or 'public' good (which will be discussed later in this chapter), the labour-managed firm will generate both greater satisfaction for its direct workforce and, simultaneously, appreciable external economies in terms of advantages for those not directly involved in the firm's production processes.

Denying that economic democracy can be obtained at no (or little) direct cost, some authors have argued that the cost of vesting decision-making powers entirely and exclusively in workers is depriving investors of this power. According to Hansmann, for instance, as shareholder-managed firms are no less democratic, the correct approach would be to acknowledge that capitalistic and democratic firms respectively confer power on one of the two main actors of production activity, workers versus investors, and emphasise that the 'fairer' – or, in any case, better – solution is to vest decision-making powers in all those who are directly related to the firm – i.e. in 'stakeholders' or, in Hansmann's words, 'patrons' (see Hansmann 1996: 43–44). However, as my conception of production cooperatives suggests that cooperatives should fund their investments with borrowed capital – and lenders funding a firm all know that their investments will not give them any decision-making powers – I dissent from this line of reasoning. Labour-managed firms adopt the truly democratic 'one person, one vote' principle, while advocates of investor power uphold the (plutocratic) 'one share, one vote' criterion, and these antithetical principles simply cannot be reconciled.

This approach is refuted by neoclassical theorists, who look upon employment contracts as the result of a bargain struck between employer (A) and the worker (B), from which either party draws equal benefits (since otherwise it would not be entered into) and which vests no power in A. As neoclassical theorists assume that there is always full employment, when A and B enter into a contract of employment, the utility accruing to B equals the utility he would have derived from the next-best alternative available to him. Failing this – i.e. where the contract should vest special benefits in B – a third individual (C) would take up the job on less advantageous terms and would eventually be hired in place of A. Hence, neoclassical theorists claim that A has no power over B, since B is in a position to quit and opt for the next-best alternative available to him.

Refuting the neoclassical theory of the employment contract, efficiency-wage theorists claim that the wage rate bargained for upon the execution of the contract is higher than the full employment wage, since A, upon hiring B on particularly advantageous terms, intends to pressure B into seeing to his tasks properly and with utmost commitment for fear of dismissal. As a result, A does wield power over B, since B is afraid that A might resolve to fire him.

The question is: can A's power over B account for the alleged superiority of the democratic firm over the capitalistic company? As mentioned above, both democratic and capitalistic firms have to elect managers entitled to dismiss workers in case of need. It is also known that in a system of democratic firms, the pay rates of qualified workers vary from firm to firm. From this, it follows that the managers of democratic firms – having the power to dismiss the workers of the most/more efficient firms – wield equal power over their workers.

In my estimation, however, the superiority of the democratic firm in this area can be traced to at least two major reasons. There can be little doubt that the greatest shortcoming of the capitalistic firm is the fact that power over the firm's workers is vested in masters. First, just as it is better to feel like a master within the firm than to experience dependence (as mentioned above), so it is evident that acting at the orders of a manager elected by the majority of the workers is preferable to obeying the commands of a master who does not hold his position by any election. Second, whereas the master of a capitalistic business may use his powers to make choices dictated by a race or gender bias, it is clear that no such bullying would be tolerated from an elected manager.[3]

4 Economic democracy deprives capital of all its power

In their analysis of economic democracy, Dahl and Wolff argue that one of its major benefits is to act as a vehicle for political democracy (see Dahl 1985: 94–98; Wolff 2012: 146–148; and, for a different view, Baglioni 1995: 95–99). From the perspective of this chapter, instead, economic democracy is not simply a 'vehicle' for, but a basic component of, political democracy.

According to Dahl (1989: 311), democracy is superior to any other form of government for at least three reasons. First, democracy tends to promote and further expand particular forms of freedom, including collective self-determination. Second, by promoting human growth it makes for the realisation of diverse human abilities. Third, it guarantees the protection of property and the interests of individuals.

Moreover, as equality is in many respects a necessary prerequisite of democracy, the close link between democracy and certain forms of equality leads to a powerful moral conclusion: if freedom, self-development and the advancement of shared interests are desirable goals, and if persons are intrinsically equal in their moral worth, then opportunities for attaining these ends should be equally distributed among the population. From this perspective, the democratic process is a basic requirement of distributive justice. And greater distributive justice is a means of magnifying economic growth (see Alesina and Rodrik 1994; but also Tavares and Wacziarg 2001).

As is well known, one central idea propounded in Marxian theory by militant Marxists and other theorists critical of capitalist society is that political democracy is just a façade and that all power is actually in the hands of capitalists; in short, that the power of capital holds everything under its sway. A quotation from *The German Ideology* runs as follows:

> In the history up to the present it is certainly an empirical fact that separate individuals have, with the broadening of their activity into world-historical activity, become more and more enslaved under a power alien to them…, a power which has become more and more enormous and, in the last instance, turns out to be the world-market.
>
> (Marx and Engels 1845–1846: 27)[4]

Although this quotation and similar concepts expressed in *Capital* (see, for example, Marx 1867: 799, 1027–1028, 1054, 1058; Marx 1894a: 298–299, 319, 343–344, 373) back up the claim that Marx thought of democratic firm management as dethroning capital from its dominant position, numerous Marxist authors reject this approach. In Sweezy's opinion, for instance, control of these firms from within, the selective action of the market and the use of material incentives are three factors that, taken together, generate a strong tendency towards the emergence of an economic order that will increasingly reproduce capitalist working modes irrespective of the name we give it. In other words, Sweezy' argues that when such firms are run by small groups striving to maximise their incomes by producing commodities for sale on markets, the resulting system will generate the basic production and class relations of a capitalist system (see Sweezy 1968). On this same subject, Adorno (1969: 25) wrote: 'Sway over men continues to be exercised through the economic process, faced with which not only the masses, but also those who own capital are reduced to mere objects'.

Our objection to these criticisms is that Sweezy and Adorno were not familiar with Ward and Vanek's theory of production cooperatives and have failed to consider the different role that competition plays in capitalism versus a self-managed firm system. As mentioned in Chapter 7, competition – the very 'heart of capitalism' – acts itself out mainly through the threat of bankruptcy proceedings; and inasmuch as this is true, the absence of labour costs in self-managed firms removes the danger of bankruptcy proceedings and makes competition much less oppressive than it is in a capitalist system. More precisely, although competition does survive in labour-managed firms, it ceases to be an 'external power' obliging individuals and firms to rush as hard as they can.

Coming to the heart of the matter, in firms run in accordance with the 'one person, one vote' principle, the power of capitalists is nil by definition. While there is no denying that such firms have to abide by the law of markets, capitalist power will draw to an end. Hence my reply to Sweezy and Adorno: although the rules of the market continue to apply in a system of labour-managed firms, it is no less true that in such a system capitalists are prevented from turning their superior financial standing into a position of power. In a system of labour-managed firms, all of the media, including the press and television, would consequently secure greater levels of freedom and the influence of economic lobbies on policy-making would lose much of its present grip.

Without pushing this argument too far, it is hardly to be doubted that even in a system of democratic firms, managers of large-sized firms will gain external power of some sort, but what can be ruled out is the danger that a firm may exercise control over others by acquiring majority holdings in them. Agreements between firms, though not altogether impossible, would become more difficult to contrive and could be kept under more effective check by a competition authority.

5 More about the power of capital

The shortcomings of representative democracy are well known. In a survey of the 'perverse effects' of democracy, the well-known Italian political theorist Norberto Bobbio pointed to unfulfilled promises and disillusionment with universal suffrage – i.e. the awareness that, 'due to the ability of mass media to condition the minds of electors', universal suffrage fails to attain the goal for which it is ultimately intended – 'keeping in check the power structure' (see Bobbio 1989; for an in-depth analysis of 'unfulfilled promises', see Bobbio 1991).

Another well-known author, Charles Wright Mills, laid stress on the tendency of the masses to cling to values that holders of vested interests had instilled into them by accident or on purpose (see Mills 1959: 194). Hence, it is hardly overstating the truth if I argue, with Raniero Panzieri, that obstacles to progress and risks of a downward spiral in democracy stem from the fact that political struggle has as yet not been waged in the workplace – the very seedbed of totalitarian Integralism.

> It is there that the power of the class of employers puts down roots before extending its range well beyond the factory and shaping the basics of economic and political action across the country, and it is there that the hostility of capitalists towards prospects of a positive evolution of society acts itself out in forms such as oppression and blackmail and ends up by breeding imbalance, unemployment and misery. The place where totalitarianism keeps society and its political institutions under constant check is the factory.
>
> (Panzieri 1975: 122–123)

It is there that workers will have to battle 'for a new, genuinely democratic power structure capable of overthrowing the dominance of large capitalists' (Panzieri 1975: 122–123; see also, Vanek 1985: 27–28).

Thanks to democratic firm management, workers would gain full freedom and grow into fully-fledged members of society. In Marx's view, these goals are at odds with the capitalist mode of production and will only be achieved at a stage where any step forward in the evolution of the material conditions and attributes of socialised production activity will prove to be incompatible with the social form of production prevailing in capitalism (see Kicillof and Starosta 2007: 26–27). The importance of depriving capital owners of all (or at least the greater part) of their power will be easily perceived by anyone who has earnestly considered the extent to which direct democracy is in contrast with the power of money. The media, press and television would no longer be subservient to the interests of their owners, nor would they be monopolised by anybody (at least, not by a single individual). As mentioned by Marramao, this idea is reflected in Max Adler's distinction between 'political democracy' and 'social democracy'. Although the former is usually described as democratic, he argues, it is nothing but a dictatorship of sorts, since the 'general will' it is said to express is, in fact, a compound of the specific interests of the class in power (and its underlying rationale is the liberalist principle of the atomisation of society into abstract individuals). As for the latter, Adler adds, it amounts to real democracy, but can only become reality in a class-less society (see Marramao 1980: 292). More recently, an advocate of industrial democracy, Noam Chomsky, has argued that 'of all the crises that afflict us, I believe this growing democratic deficit may be the most severe' (2009: 41).

Raising the question if capitalism really guarantees full freedom, Huberman has asked: 'Do we really tolerate all political and economic dissenting opinions?' And whereas he owns that in ordinary times, it is true, we do not clap liberals or radicals in jail, he wonders what happens in times of great tension. 'Isn't it also true' – he continues – 'that jobs, power and prestige almost always to go those who do not dissent, those who are sound and safe?' (see Huberman and Sweezy 1968: 74).

Capitalist society is typified by economic inequality, which is also at the root of political inequality. In our political lives, each of us casts a vote, but there is little denying that the wealthy are able to secure more political power, both because they control the media and because they can obtain favours by bribing politicians.

To some extent, the interest groups discussed in numerous treatises on democracy might work towards redressing these imbalances. However, although nothing prevents the poor from joining forces in an effort to combat the power of industrialists and bankers, even the best organised of these groups will have access to fewer resources than those of the wealthy and will consequently fail to root out political inequality for want of the required strength.

One aspect of the unequal distribution of political power is that most of the issues with which the more disadvantaged part of the population is most concerned will never enter the political agenda. The task of politics is problem-solving, but the power to draw up political agendas is in the hands of the powerful class. Suffice it to quote just one example – i.e. publicly run crèche facilities that less affluent families consider to be one of their priorities. An additional relevant example is the issue of democracy in the firm. Why has it never been put to the vote or at least earnestly discussed?

In abstract terms, stripping power from capitalists should be a major aim of the bourgeoisie, since decisions made in line with the 'one share, one vote' principle are incompatible with the principle of democracy to which this class is used to paying lip service. Concerning democracy, Lukàcs remarked that 'the fact that a scientifically acceptable solution does exist is of no avail', because 'to accept that solution, even in theory, would be tantamount to observing society from a class standpoint other than that of the bourgeoisie', and 'no class can do that – unless it is willing to abdicate its power freely' (Lukàcs 1923: 70). The class consciousness of the bourgeoisie – he also commented – is

> cursed by its very nature with the tragic fate of developing an insoluble contradiction at the zenith of its powers. As a result of this contradiction it must annihilate itself. This tragedy of the bourgeoisie is reflected historically in the fact that even before it had defeated its predecessor, feudalism, its new enemy, the proletariat, had appeared on the scene.
>
> (Lukàcs 1923: 80)

Politically – Lukàcs thought – its strategy was to fight against the organisation of society into layers in the name of a 'freedom' which at the very moment of victory could not but generate a new kind of repression that Lukàcs identified with capitalist exploitation, but which we prefer to identify with the exclusion of workers from the right to cast votes in their firms.

The failure of the bourgeoisie to realise that preventing workers from voting in firms runs counter its own principles can be explained if we bear in mind that

> when capitalism was in the ascendant, even the ideological exponents of the rising bourgeoisie acknowledged the class struggle as a basic fact of history and that in proportion as the theory and practice of the proletariat made society conscious of this unconscious revolutionary principle inherent in capitalism, the bourgeoisie was thrown back increasingly on to a conscious defensive.
>
> (Lukàcs 1923: 85)

The inability of the bourgeoisie to acknowledge the importance of power in economic relationships explains the publication of writings (e.g. Coase's well-known 1937 article and, even more so, those published by Alchian and Demsetz in 1972; see also, Cheung 1987, 1992) that come up with the entirely unwarranted idea that employers wield no power in the firm (see Braverman 1974; Marglin 1974; Gordon 1976; Edwards 1979; Jossa 2005b, 2009b).

From the perspective of Habermas, Offe and O'Connor, the crisis of liberalist democracy is the effect of a growing imbalance between the incessant demand for ever more welfare services from citizens and the dwindling ability of capitalist economies to meet such demands. And as they trace this inability to a growing aversion to state intervention on the part of firms operating in a globalised economy, these authors have stressed the need to strip power from capitalists. Now, then, inasmuch as it is true (as will be shown further on) that no such opposition would come from firms operating in a democratic firm system, this bare fact corroborates the need to deprive capitalists of their power.

Besides suppressing capitalist power, democracy in the firm both favours and enhances political democracy. In the opinion of Cole, a stout advocate of economic democracy, there are at least three reasons why democracy is largely un-influential in practice, so long as it is merely political. First, the only benefit – and a largely illusory one – that citizens derive from democracy is the right to elect their representatives. It is not by chance that many authors prefer to speak of the 'supremacy of parliament', instead of the 'sovereignty of the people'. Second, political democracy affects a restricted sphere and hardly stands in the way of the manoeuvres of non-democratic organisations in other areas of social action. Third, as the domain covered by political action expands, those termed the 'representatives of the people' gradually cease representing those who returned them to parliament and get ever more out of touch with their electors (Cole 1920: 13–14).

Analysing the differences between representative democracy and direct democracy, the already mentioned Italian political theorist Norberto Bobbio remarked that

> in contemporary society the domain of democracy is expanding not only thanks to a combination of representative democracy and direct democracy, but also, and even more so, due to growing democratisation, i.e. the

establishment and implementation of procedures enabling individuals to participate in the decision-making processes of collective bodies other than political organs.

(1985: 147)

As mentioned before, as the task of running business enterprises must lie with directors and managers, within this extended domain of democracy, it is not the major operating issues that workers will be called upon to make collective choices. The issues on which the partners will state their opinions are those that do not impair the efficiency of the firm. The partners will be free to call meetings to discuss issues related to their production activities and, above all, they will be free to make proposals designed to impress a given direction on the decisions that will subsequently be made by their managers and directors. Properly-weighted decisions made following in-depth discussion are advantageous in many respects. For one, the preferences of the individual partners will be revealed to those attending and will consequently receive the required attention. Second, debate stimulates reflection, since each participant will present points other than those the others had in mind and, as a result, each participant will draw benefit from what the others say. Let us add that group discussion offers scope for stating wishes and considering issues that the speakers have as yet not fully thought out and on which they would probably like to hear the opinions of others. Third, resolutions passed at the end of a debate acquire legitimacy and a moral authority that individual decisions necessarily lack and can therefore be implemented with more conviction (see Fearon 1998).

Inasmuch as it is true that capitalism is hardly ever praised in its own right, but only for its supposed potential for guaranteeing freedom and democracy (see Levine 1984–1988: 2), a system of democratic firms – i.e. socialism – is superior to capitalism in that it ensures greater democracy.

As Macpherson puts it, pre-Marxian forms of socialism and capitalist theories of democracy have elements in common. Neither of them is scientific, since it would barely be correct to describe as democratic a society where de-facto democracy is denied. In his celebrated *Development of Socialism from Utopia to Science*, Engels explained that utopian theories were those which, despite pursuing lofty aims, were unrealistic and ineffectual. These adjectives perfectly describe the theories of democracy framed by advocates of capitalism holding that no turn for the better is possible (Macpherson 1984: 141).

Dissenting from Lindblom's argument that no feasible options to democracy, though badly needed for the survival of polyarchy, have been developed so far or probably would be developed in the future (see Lindblom 1977: 365–366), I am confident that a system of democratic firms would effectively remedy these shortcomings.

Braudel and Arrighi have expatiated on the idea that a market economy where the capitalistic firms are not supported by the state cannot be described as a capitalist order real and proper (see Arrighi 2007). Most of the steps in the process of re-establishing a market economy in China, Arrighi has argued, are in keeping with Smith's idea of market development, rather than with Marx's idea that in mature capitalist systems, governments act as committees managing the common affairs of the whole bourgeoisie. In all probability, though, the idea of an economic system with firms in the hands of capitalists and the state working towards protecting general interests may apply to today's China, thanks to the legacy of its socialist past, but sounds hardly convincing in overall terms. In due course, if Chinese firms continue to be run by private individuals, the country will end up resigning the greater part of its state power to the hands of capitalists.

6 The costs of democracy in business firms

Although democracy is doubtless a valuable good, there are grounds for maintaining that it is not advantageous as a matter of course. Numerous academics and general practitioners (i.e. non-specialists) have argued that the main benefit of self-management – namely, a more democratic environment – is actually its main shortcoming (see, for example, Webb and Webb 1921, 1923: 133; Hodgson 1982–1983, 1987: 137–138; Benham and Keefer 1991; Klein 1991: 219–220). However, in this book, I will be discussing the disadvantages of democracy at large, rather than the inefficiencies that may arise in democratic firms.

One of the costs of democracy is difficult joint decision-making. Problems are likely to arise right from the start-up phase of a democratic firm. To set up a new firm, a group of individuals with equal decision-making powers must adopt a consensus-based resolution. As all participants are expected to concur on all of the main aspects of a project, agreement is far from easy to reach. The same does not apply to the capitalist firm: here, the founder has to negotiate bilateral agreements with individual stakeholders and therefore potentially conduct negotiations from which all of the other participants are excluded. In other words, whereas by definition the democratic firm originates from a multilateral contract entered into by unanimous agreement amongst a number of parties, the capitalist firm is based on a set of bilateral contracts, in which one party – always the same – invariably has access to a greater amount of information and is thus in a position to dictate the required stipulations. And as a multilateral contract is more difficult to negotiate than a bilateral one (McCain 1992: 214–215), this is doubtless a convincing explanation of why cooperative firms are rarely set up.

One additional cost of democracy is the risk that majority and minority groups may line up against each other. In a capitalist firm, workers lack decision-making powers, but they can 'vote with their feet'. Unable to make or influence decisions, they have no option but to accept the role assigned to each of them and 'get accustomed' to the fact that their needs are seldom, if ever, heeded. On the contrary, in a democratic firm, workers do have a say, and whenever they are in the minority, they may resent the scant respect given to their needs. If such a situation arises, a minority group may oppose majority resolutions and accuse those who refuse to listen to their opinions of abusing their positions of power. The resulting conflict between the partners of the cooperative may induce the minority group to stop cooperating or attempt to reverse the resolutions adopted.

The costs highlighted above may be even higher if the final solution reflects, not the stance of a numerical majority, but that of a particularly energetic or resourceful minority, which, as often happens, manages to impose its will on the majority, thanks to the indifference of many or a better knowledge of circumstances.

As a result, the partners of a democratic firm may even prove less cooperative than those of a capitalist firm.

A similar objection was raised by the economic liberalist Hayek. As is well known, this author prioritises market choices over policy decisions, because the latter, being passed by a majority vote, may enable a majority to abuse its position of power. In Hayek's words, economic freedom is 'the state in which a man is not subject to coercion by the arbitrary will of another or others' and 'describes one thing and one thing only, a state which is desirable for reasons different from those which make us desire other things also called "freedom"' (Hayek 1960: 11, 12). Faced with this argument, supporters of Alchian and Demsetz's approach may contend that democracy in the firm is anything but advancement. Indeed, whereas a worker entering into a contract with a capitalist firm can be assumed to freely accept its clauses and perform his tasks without feeling subject to other people's will, in a democratic firm, where resolutions are adopted by a majority vote, minority partners may experience the decisions made by other partners as a constraint and resent such a state of affairs.[5]

On closer analysis, however, these are reflections that highlight the costs of economic democracy, without undermining its quality as a public/merit good.[6]

A very general argument that clarifies the nature of such costs is that joint decisions take much time and effort to make. If the decision-maker sets out to reconcile the preferences of all the participants involved in the initiative, he/she must call a number of meetings, in order to provide an opportunity for exchanges of opinion and the taking of polls. As each participant can be assumed to have his/her distinct preferences, there will hardly be such a thing as a single option, and polling operations may prove all the more cyclic the more such preferences are found to diverge. In addition to this, the cyclical nature of joint resolution processes may result in attempts to manipulate the voting procedures themselves. Although the practice of delegating powers may give rise to principal-agent conflicts (see Weingast and Marshall 1988: 32), vesting delegated powers in committees and having them devise options or pass resolutions in place of the meeting is one way to reduce the impact of these drawbacks. This is the rationale behind the contention that the more that firms are owned and managed by individuals, the more efficiently they will be run (see Putterman *et al.* 1998: 884).

In point of fact, many cooperative firms, including smaller ones, are not run by a majority of their partners, but by a small group of senior partners or a sole manager, who is often a salaried employee of the firm. While this is not a cost of economic democracy proper, it is certainly an aspect that detracts from its value. Consequently, when appraising the real benefits of labour management, it is probably appropriate to stress that within a hierarchical organisation such as a firm, democracy must necessarily act itself out by delegation and that meetings may be confined to just a few – for example, those needed to elect the members of the managing body.[7]

This last point deserves particular emphasis. According to Hansmann (1996), the main cause that prevents labour-managed firms from making headway is the high costs of democracy.[8] Given the hierarchical structure of the firm and the difficulties attending the adoption of joint resolutions, those who advocate a greater role for democratic firms in society – because they look upon them as merit or even public goods (to be discussed later in this chapter) – have no option but to endorse the passing of legislation that will vest full autonomy in managers and confine the power of meetings to the casting of votes at elections for the managing board and the adoption of just a few, particularly important resolutions.[9]

But there is more to this. The rational behaviour ascribed to economic agents by current mainstream theory determines that the partners of a democratic firm, faced with the cost and inefficiencies of joint decision-making, will freely resolve to do without joint decisions every time this is feasible. The result would be a reduction in the powers vested in meetings, without the need for specific legislation to this effect.

7 Bobbio and Vacca on 'industrial democracy'

In the light of these reflections, one cannot but agree with those who argue that – by removing the primary causes and social roots of authoritarian modes of governance – self-management automatically averts any forms of top-down command from governments intending to regulate society and the living conditions of the working class. This quite naturally entails that any changes in production relations in the direction of labour management will pave the way for more democratic patterns of social life.

As a rule, political theorists hardly concern themselves with industrial democracy. According to Norberto Bobbio, political representation within a capitalist society is far from perfect, since the people's sovereign power is severely curtailed by the fact that weighty economic decisions are made, not by constitutional bodies proper, but in forums where few citizens have a say (see Bobbio 1975: 63). While this is doubtless true, Bobbio fails to take this one step further – i.e. to suggest that the introduction of 'industrial democracy' might help overcome the current limitations of political representation. He remarks that 'leftist criticisms of representative democracy are actually levelled at lack of direct democracy' and that 'direct democracy is the crucial, and perhaps the only founding principle behind the socialist theory of the state' (1975: 58). However, just a few pages further on, discussing the subject of self-governing producers and writings by Marx and Korsch, he misses the opportunity to highlight links between direct democracy and 'industrial democracy' and, above all, makes the same mistake he imputes to others: he confines himself to raising the query as to whether industrial democracy is at all possible, but does not enter upon the closely associated issue of its relations with representative democracy.

More precisely, Bobbio argues that 'theoreticians of industrial democracy hold on to the illusory belief that political democracy will melt into economic democracy and that self-governing citizens will grow into self-governing producers' (Bobbio 1975: 64). To this, theorists of producer cooperative systems organised in line with Ward and Vanek's theories can be expected to object that, far from suggesting that political democracy melts into industrial democracy, this author is only suggesting that political democracy should be supplemented with economic democracy.

Compared to Bobbio's, the arguments of Giuseppe Vacca – another well-known Italian political theorist – sound far more convincing. Vacca rightly notes that

> as novel institutions are set up in keeping with producer democracy and gain ground, political liberties are sure to receive more effective protection and to assert themselves. The proliferation of viable institutions of this kind will effectively inhibit those forms of authoritarianism, old and new, into which late capitalist societies tend to lapse as a result of their very structure.
>
> (Vacca 1976: 63)

However, as Vacca's idea of economic democracy does not fall in with the position taken in this book, he takes it for granted that salaried labour will survive for a long time to come and dwells on ways and means of doing away with market economies.

For my part, I feel that opposing the power of capital is one thing and opposing the power of markets – or market economies – is another. One reason why this idea is slow to assert itself within Marxist thought is that Marxian and non-Marxian political theorists do not concern themselves with Ward and Vanek's economic theory of cooperatives. In this connection, I am inclined to support Bobbio's argument that the somewhat blurred relationship between socialist thought and democracy is mainly due to serious theoretical shortcomings inherent in Marxist tradition (see Bobbio 1975: 54–56).

8 Economic democracy as a merit good

The foregoing reflections can help us decide whether, and in what ways, economic democracy is a 'merit good' (see Musgrave 1958, 1959, 1987) or even a public good. Economic democracy may come about in two ways: through the abolition of salaried labour by act of parliament or, as is both more convenient and more probable, thanks to piecemeal increases in the number of labour-managed firms. In the former case, those holding that the advantages of democratic firms outnumber their disadvantages will speak of the creation of a public good; in the latter case, each new democratic firm will rather be categorised as a merit good.

According to Musgrave (1987: 453), 'the setting in which the concept of merit or demerit goods is most clearly appropriate' is a situation where a good, besides benefiting its direct users, produces advantages that are consistent with the main values of the relevant community. This means that whenever a newly-found firm simultaneously generates benefits for its direct workforce and reduces capitalist power through the introduction of the 'one person, one vote' principle, slows down inflation or improves the characters of workers, it can be rightly cat-egorised as a merit good.

This categorisation explains why democratic firms are unlikely to emerge spontaneously in due time (as mentioned above). In a 'free competition' context, cooperatives are at risk of losing out to the capital-managed corporate, because they may prove to be less efficient than their capitalist competitors and because businessmen have little incentive to opt for the cooperative form either when reorganising existing firms or setting up new ones. If this is true, and if demo-cratic firms are actually merit goods, the task of furthering them cannot be left to private initiative. Deploring the narrow scope of so many economic policy deci-sions, Rawls commented that considerations of efficiency are but one factor of decision-making and often a relatively minor one. Indeed, he spoke out against the tendency of society 'to acquiesce without thinking in the moral and political conception implicit in the status quo or leave things to be settled by how con-tending social and economic forces happen to work themselves out' and expressed the hope that economic policy specialists would at long last broaden their horizons (see Rawls 1971).

On this point, though, Dow (2003: 75) has objected that nothing can prevent sceptics from arguing that the social benefits stemming from the proliferation of cooperatives are not such as to justify the (government) expenditure entailed in furthering the cooperative sector.

This train of thought begs the question: why does a public good such as the democratic firm not assert itself by democratic means?

Very often, democratic governments fail to promote the welfare of their citizens, because in an effort to alleviate the miserable conditions of the popula-tion, they strive to meet the demands of the general public, without realising that people are seldom able to decide exactly what it is that may increase, if not max-imise, their happiness.

Rejecting the overly optimistic assumption of democrats that each of us is the best judge of his/her own interests, Lane (2000: 283) argues that there are people who are unaware of the nature and origins of their feelings and, above all, that social institutions called upon to promote the interests of the general public often fail to make the right choices. Setting out from the failure of individuals to identify the causes of their feelings, Lane speaks of a 'hedonistic fallacy' – i.e. a mistaken belief that those aware of their feelings also know the origins from which they stem. In fact, research findings have suggested that people are in the dark about the causes of their happiness or unhappiness.

On closer analysis, irrespective of whether or not one shares Lane's argu-ments, there are other reasons why a system of self-managed firms fails to make headway democratically – i.e. through the enactment of parliamentary legisla-tion. A well-known subject that needs not be further addressed here is the role of vested interests. For my part, I wish to point out that in consequence of theoretical objections against a system of self-managed firms and uncertainties regarding the way it works, few people, including economists, are prepared to acknowledge the superiority of a system of labour-managed firms over a capitalist system; and this may explain why a move in this direction is not part of the agenda of any political party. The scant attention of economists and politicians on the subject of democracy in the firm is in part the result of the sheer unorthodoxy of such a proposal. Throughout the past century, political debate was the scene of endless confrontation between advocates of capitalism and Soviet socialism. Few, if any, concerned themselves with a democratic approach to socialism other than the intermediate solution, social democracy. A survey of mainstream economic theory shows that criticising capitalism is equated with combating markets.

The truth of this is borne out by the cultural experience of a critic of capitalism and socialism such as Oskar Lange. His original and theoretically valuable approach to market socialism has never received sufficient attention, despite the undeniable fact that the collapse of the Berlin Wall would have provided a clear opportunity for its practical implementation (see Jossa 1993).

9 Conclusion

From the classification of cooperatives as merit goods, it follows that any government, regardless of political-economic orientation, should make it its task to support the growth of the democratic firm system by enforcing tax or credit benefits in its favour.

Anyone prepared to subscribe to the reflections developed in this chapter is likely to attach little value to theoretical approaches in which self-management is exclusively appraised by reference to the efficiency criterion. This means that a comparative analysis of the efficiency of cooperatives versus their capitalist 'twins' is, in itself, not enough to provide conclusive evidence of the comparative superiority of a self-managed firm system over a capitalist system or vice-versa. Those who accept the distinction of Barry and Rawls between want-regarding principles and ideal-regarding principles argue that the moment some characteristic traits are encouraged to the detriment of others, the theory concerned becomes oriented towards ideals instead of wants (see Barry 1973: 46). And there is little denying that any theory that is not oriented towards wants – e.g. the theory of justice of Rawls (1971: 273–274) and Barry (1973: 42–56) and those discussed here – will hardly attach much importance to a comparison exclusively based on efficiency considerations.[10]

Notes

1 Evolutionary theory is often described as an appeal to the sacred altar of tradition and, at the same time, as a set of arguments endorsing the view that what is *must necessarily be* (see Hodgson 1995: 204). However, as pointed out by many authors, Darwinian approaches to economic theory are generally inspired by the faith in *laissez faire* policies, rather than by an attentive scrutiny of facts.

2 Many jurists and business operators within the cooperative movement also endorse the view that the most prominent social aspect of cooperation is economic democracy (see, for example, Galgano 1982: 81; Graziani *et al.* 1994: 241; as well as Passini 2000: 197).

3 Concerning the reflections developed in this section, see Bowles and Gintis (1996b).

4 In the words of Simone Weil (1959: 170), 'our social system is grounded on coercion. Workers do not accept it; they just suffer its consequences. Coercion is incompatible with democracy'.

5 Despite a different political background, Bobbio's line of reasoning on the important distinction between public and private action closely recalls both Alchian and Demsetz's and Hayek's:

> following the emergence of political economy and the resulting clear-cut distinction between economic and political relations – the former involving entities formally viewed as equals in the marketplace, but actually unequal in consequence of the division of labour the public-private dichotomy reappeared in the form of a distinction between the political community (made up of equals) and the economic community (made up of non-equals).
>
> (Bobbio 1985: 6–7)

On this point, however, it is probably convenient to mention that Bobbio has constantly emphasised both the distinction between formal and substantive democracy and the primacy of public over private action in all this theoretical work (see Bobbio 1985: 149–150, 10–15). Opinions close to Bobbio's are widely shared in political theory.

6 An antithetical opinion to Hayek's is owed to Gobetti, according to whom 'irrespective of whether liberalism is viewed as an economic, ethical or constitutional movement, its method entails the acknowledgement that political strife is crucial to the survival of modern society' (Gobetti 1923: 514). And it is against this background that one has to view his contention that 'both in the past and today, the real contrast is not between dictatorship and freedom, but between freedom and unanimity' (Gobetti 1948: 25).

7 A general argument to this regard is that 'evolution has given our species an inherent preference for hierarchically structured social and political systems' (cf. Somit and Peterson 1995: 27, cited in Lane 2000: 49). Lane writes, also, that the recognition of authority in historical evolution seems to be the prescription. But it is also true that the value of economic democracy is not necessarily curtailed by the firm's hierarchical structure, since the supervisor-blue collar relationship (in which the latter obeys the instructions of the former) will not strike us as an instance of repression provided that the parties involved are social equals (Heller 1980: 37–38).

8 According to John Stuart Mill (1871: 790–791), for example, the advantages of single-owner management over joint management in a firm are many. A single unit of command affords taking actions that would hardly prove feasible if they were made to depend on improbable consensus-carried decisions from board partners diverging in their views or on sudden policy changes. An able, private capitalist free from the control of a managing body is far better able to take balanced risks or adopt costly improvements than a group of people. It is therefore correct to say that self-management is not, and simply cannot, be equated with collective management proper, since any commission-type management is incompatible with the proper conduct of the business of any firm. No assembly will ever be in a position to meet such crucial requirements for the proper running of a firm as superior professional expertise, efficiency and prompt decision-making (Galgano 1982: 81).

9 The main reason why most Marxists ceased endorsing the cooperative movement from 1870 onwards was its inability to do away with the costs of democracy (see Bernstein 1899: 109–121).

10 On the argument of this chapter, see also, Jossa (1999: ch. 7).

11 The democratic road to socialism and Marxist thought

1 Introduction

In this chapter, reviewing the approach of Marx and Engels to the transition to democratic socialism, I will ask if this transition is at all workable and in what way it is to come about. The starting points are the definition of revolution as the turn to a different production mode – a notion that is not always correctly understood – and the awareness that Marx and Engels, far from theorising a sudden leap to communism, spelt out that the transition from one production mode to a different production mode was bound to be a long-term process.

Bhaskar has rightly remarked that 'transforming society towards socialism depends upon knowledge of these underlying structures' (Bhaskar 1989: 5) – i.e. on the knowledge of both capitalism and the socialist society towards which one intends to progress. Accordingly, as the theory of producer cooperatives has already been discussed at some length, it is possible to proceed to the issue of the transition.

2 The concept of revolution

In Marx's approach, a production mode is a combination of given productive forces and the relations of production existing between them. The more we go back into history, he wrote, the more clearly we will see man as part of a greater whole: the family first, the clan later on and, subsequently, the various forms of communal society. The standpoint of the isolated individual acquired relevance no earlier than the eighteenth century – the period in time when social relations reached an acme. This means that man is a gregarious animal and, as such, carries on gregarious – i.e. social – production activities, whose laws are summed up in the celebrated passage quoted below:

> In the real production of their existence men inevitably enter into definite relations, which are independent of their will, namely relations of production appropriate to a given stage in the development of their material forces of production. The totality of these relations of production constitutes the economic structure of society, the real foundation on which arises a legal

and political superstructure, and to which correspond definite forms of social consciousness.... At a certain stage of development, the material productive forces of society come in conflict with existing relations or production or – this merely expresses the same thing in legal terms – with the property relations within the framework of which they have operated hitherto. From forms of development of the productive forces these relations turn into their fetters. Then begins an era of social revolution.

(Marx 1859: 263)[1]

According to Althusser (1995), Marx's notion of production modes opened up the 'Continent of History' to scientific knowledge and thereby created the assumption of the further evolution of all human sciences, from sociology and psychology to any other scientific discipline concerned with investigating society and man (Althusser 1969, 1995: 23; Luporini 1954; Vygodskij 1967: 4–5).[2] Although Marx held each material societal structure to be primarily shaped by the dominant production mode, he also attached great importance to non-dominant production modes: the older production mode that has not yet been completely outgrown and the future one just arising within the existing social order. Accordingly, to argue that the production relations existing at a particular point in time are no longer consistent with the corresponding productive forces and, hence, to predict the emergence of a new production mode is tantamount to acknowledging that the existing social order is at a transitional stage – i.e. that the current production mode is becoming obsolete, due to changes under way in productive forces.

Based on these reflections, it is possible to say that the 'revolution = change in production mode' equation is a correct approach from the perspective of both economic science and political science (see, *inter alia*, Kühne 1972: 26–30).[3]

The productive forces constitute the material basis of a production mode, but as they can only act themselves out within the corresponding relations of production, it is the relations of production between the productive forces concerned that must be said to play a decisive role. According to Althusser, most Marxists had given insufficient attention to this point.[4]

Hence, it is possible to say that Marx's notion of revolution is a fairly simple one: it is the replacement of one mode of production with a different one. As a result, I do not agree with Struve, a Marxist who defined this notion as one of the ideas which, despite their importance in practical terms, 'are wholly groundless from the angle of theory' (Struve 1899: 136).

From the centrality of the 'revolution = change in production mode' equation in Marx's thought, it follows that Marxism must be looked upon as a 'theory of revolution' (Lukàcs 1923). This determines: (1) that the qualification of 'Marxists' should be restricted to those who think it feasible to realise a socialist order (consistent with Marx's thought) in practice and denied to all those who are inimical to the idea of revolution (see, for example, Panaccione 1974: 4; Bordiga 1976: 99; Sève 2004: 106–107; Wolff 2012: 115–116); and (2) only those thinking of the establishment of a (strictly Marxian) socialist system as a feasible project can qualify as Marxists (see, *inter alia*, Karsz 1974: 40; Panaccione 1974: 4; De Giovanni 1976: 8–9). The latter claim parallels Korsch's argument that no one denying the possibility of a feasible revolution can be termed a Marxist (Korsch 1923: 59).[5]

In conclusion, it is probably appropriate to specify that numerous Marxists think of revolution as a historical necessity in the main for ethical reasons (see, *inter alia*, Rubel 1965: 245).

3 The transition to socialism in Marx and Engels

It is now necessary to ask how Marx and Engels pictured the transition period.

To understand Marx and Engels's view of transition, one must distinguish between a dialectical approach to the transition from one social order to another and a 'nihilistic' approach, entailing the outright destruction of the older order. The latter is the stance of those who hold that the takeover by the working class would instantly give rise to a new social order, in which the characteristics of capitalism criticised by Marx and Engels would be utterly reversed. It is known that the aspects of capitalism that Marx and Engels most forcefully opposed were the anarchical nature of production and the division of society into two classes, with masters exploiting the working class. This may explain why the new social order to be set up promptly after the abolition of capitalism (in the nihilistic view) was assumed to be a society without classes, but with centralised planning – exactly the organisational structure that the Soviet Union established after Stalin's rise to power and that ultimately collapsed in 1989.

This view of transition is expressed in writings by Marx and Engels. Among these is the *Manifesto of the Communist Party*, where it is stated that after the takeover, the proletariat will have to centralise all instruments of production in the hands of the state (1848: 505). In *Antidühring*, Engels (1878: 270) argued: 'With the seizing of the means of production by society, production of commodities is done away with, and, simultaneously, the mastery of the product over the producer'; and a quote from the fourth edition of *Socialism: Utopian and Scientific*, dated 1891, runs as follows:

> The proletarian seizes the public power, and by means of this transforms the socialised means of production, slipping from the hands of the bourgeoisie, into public property. By this act, the proletariat … makes the existence of different classes of society thenceforth an anachronism. In proportion as anarchy in social production vanishes the political authority of the State dies out.
>
> (1891b: 325)

Without denying that Marx's view of transition occasionally acquires 'nihilistic' overtones, Marx's view is a dialectical approach, which entailed that the aspects of capitalism negated were dependent both on what is negated and on the goal to be achieved and that those in power are consequently required to transfer some aspects of the older society into the new social order. From this perspective, private property is a step or stage in the evolution of humankind, rather than a form of cancer that has to be eradicated if the healthy agents of the social organism are to assert themselves (Lawler 1994: 188). The goal of socialism is to negate capitalism for the purpose of outdoing it, not of turning back the clock of history; and with regard to the creation of material wealth, socialism is expected to magnify the level of growth attained within the capitalist system, instead of levelling down conditions to a state of generalised, though egalitarian, poverty. 'Superseding' – a Marxian notion based on Hegel's term 'Aufhebung' – implies negating and, simultaneously, preserving what is being superseded. In this dialectical view, transition cannot be a short-term process sparked off by the sudden reversal of major aspects of capitalist society; it will necessarily require a long-term process, during which the older social order is gradually turned into a new one through piecemeal adjustments.

The contradictoriness of the two notions of transition first surfaces in an early work, such as the *Economic and Philosophic Manuscripts of 1844* (1844a: 294), which describes a coarse and material form of communism aiming 'to destroy everything which is not capable of being possessed by all as private property'. This form of communism – Marx writes – is supported by those who would like to seize all private property in any form and turn it into public property on the very morrow of the takeover by the working class. In Marx's words, it requires, *inter alia*, 'a community of labor and equality of wages, paid out by communal capital – by the community as universal capitalist' and can consequently be defined as the generalisation of wage – or hired – labour, because in it 'both sides of the relationship are raised to an imagined universality – labour as the category in which every person is placed, and capital as the acknowledged universality and power of the community' (1844a: 295).

Since it negates the personality of man in every sphere, this view of the new social order is characterised by Marx as nothing but 'the logical expression of private property which is this negation', as something that is born of envy and greed, because 'the thought of every piece of private property as such is at least turned against wealthier private property in the form of envy and the urge to reduce things to a common level' (1844a: 295). In Marx's words, this coarse and material form of communism is

> the abstract negation of the entire world of culture and civilization, the regression to the unnatural simplicity of the poor and crude man who has few needs and who has not only failed to go beyond private property, but has not yet even reached it.
>
> (1844a: 295)

The reflections developed in the paragraph above lead us to assume that the form of communism upheld by the mature Marx did not substantially differ from the system he had in mind when he wrote the *Economic and Philosophic Manuscripts of 1844* – i.e. a system entailing 'the positive transcendence of private property as human self-estrangement and therefore as the real appropriation of the human essence by and for man' (1844a: 296), a kind of communism that enables 'the complete return of man to himself as a social (i.e. human) being' (1844a: 296) and calls for the retention of the major achievements of history up to the present day. This communism, 'as fully developed naturalism, equals humanism', Marx adds, (1844a: 297) concluding that: 'The entire movement of history, just as its [communism's] actual act of genesis – is the birth act of its empirical existence'.[6]

According to Vercelli, to seek to interpret a historical phenomenon from a correct Marxian perspective is an extremely risky undertaking. On the one hand, there is the risk of reducing economic categories to their general determinants only (the procedure of orthodox economists who hold that the capital–labour relation as we know it today is a natural, eternal and universal relation); on the other, there is the opposite risk that economic categories may be reduced to their historical determinants only (see Vercelli 1973: 31). In other words, there is both the danger of overstating the historical import of given phenomena and assuming capitalism to be eternal and the risk of underrating certain phenomena. The latter stance – let us add – is often taken by Marxist currents, which assumes that capitalism can be erased at one stroke.

The reason why a great many Marxists endorse the view of a long-term transition period is that business relations take time to sever, even in a socialist economy (see *inter alia*, Baran and Sweezy 1966: 337; Sweezy 1969; Bettelheim 1968: ch. 3; Bettelheim 1969).

4 Should the state provide support to cooperatives?

The fact that spontaneous evolution is a poor stimulant to the achievement of a system exclusively formed of cooperatives seems to be confirmed by historical experience. Such individual cooperatives or groups of cooperative firms as have spontaneously arisen so far have failed to free the masses from capitalist oppression, because of their inability to trounce competition from capitalist monopolies. This would suggest that state intervention is a must.

Although the seizure of state power by the enemies of capitalism is doubtless the prerequisite for the emergence of a nationwide state-supported cooperative movement, nothing in Marx's work rules out the hypothesis of a working-class majority taking power by peaceful means and supporting the proliferation of cooperatives on a national scale. In point of fact, a cursory analysis of his writings would seem to offer *prima facie* evidence against such a hypothesis, because in the *Critique of the Gotha Programme*, Marx rejected both Lassalle's theory of the state and the idea that the emancipation of labour should be brought about by state-subsidised producer cooperatives. However, the establishment of producers' cooperatives under the democratic control of the working people that was proposed in the *Gotha Programme* is opposed by Marx on grounds that 'the workers' desire to establish the conditions for cooperative production on a social scale, and first of all on a national scale, in their own country, only means that they are working to transform the present conditions of production, and it has nothing in common with the foundation of co-operative societies with state aid' (Marx 1875a: 93–94). Otherwise – he argues – socialism would come about through state action – in stark contrast to the central idea of scientific socialism that workers are to achieve emancipation through their own efforts. If workers were to demand state support for their revolutionary movement, they would only be providing evidence of their 'full consciousness that they neither rule nor are ripe for rule!' (Marx 1875a: 93).

Thus, Marx's conclusion is that 'as far as the present co-operative societies are concerned, they are of value only insofar as they are the independent creations of workers and not *protégés* either of the governments or of the bourgeois' (Marx 1875a: 94).

On closer analysis, though, the real meaning of these excerpts is that Marx conceived of a gradual growth of the cooperative movement 'fostered by national means' as possible only after the takeover by the working class; hence, even after a peaceful vote passed by a parliament formed of a majority of partners representing the interests of the working class. The truth of this is clearly borne out by the *Inaugural Address* of 1864 and, even more so, by the above-quoted passage from the *Critique of the Gotha Programme*, which continues with the remark that 'cooperative labour ought to be developed to national dimensions and, consequently, to be fostered by national means' (Marx 1875a: 94).

5 Solving the capital–labour conflict

All those who hold that parliamentary acts in support of producer cooperatives can set off a gradual and peaceful transition to socialism appear to attach paramount importance to the attainment of a working-class majority in parliament and, hence, to a positive solution regarding the conflict between the interests of the bourgeoisie and those of the working class. In the minds of most Marxists, therefore, the main contradiction of capitalism to be resolved during the transition to socialism is the conflict between capital and labour.

This contradiction – i.e. the struggle between two opposed classes – occupies centre stage within the historical process. As is well known, the idea that class struggle is the main issue in any capitalist economy is one of Marx's major contributions to the interpretation of the society in which we live. As this idea was first discussed in works from an early period when Marx had as yet little grounding in political economy, it was not borrowed from any of the writers on whom he drew for his later professional development. It made its first appearance in such an early work as the *Critique of Hegel's Philosophy of Right*, which Marx wrote in the autumn of 1843 and issued in the early months of 1844, and it was crucial to his later evolution as a theorist (see, *inter alia*, Brewer 2002: 364). As is well known, in Marx's approach, class struggle is a matter of great consequence, because it is assumed to be the main driving force behind history and fits within a dialectical view of social evolution.

Capitalist production has itself brought it about that the work of supervision is readily available and quite independent of the ownership of capital. It has therefore become superfluous for this work of supervision to be performed by the capitalist. A musical conductor need in no way be the owner of the instruments in his orchestra, nor does it form part of his function as a conductor that he should have any part in paying the 'wages' of other musicians. Cooperative factories provide the proof that the capitalist has become just as superfluous as a functionary in production as he himself, from his superior vantage-point, finds the large landlord.

(Marx 1894a: 511)

This single passage is sufficient evidence that Marx envisaged the possibility that capitalists should be stripped of their power within a market economy, but its full import will be perceived even more clearly in the light of Marx's view that capital is not tantamount to the bulk of production means, but a given social production relationship. As he put it:

The most essential factor of the labour process is the worker himself, and in the ancient production process this worker was a slave. It does not follow from this that the worker is by nature a slave (although Aristotle is not very far removed from holding this opinion) any more than it follows that spindles and cotton are by their nature capital because they are at present consumed in the labour process by wage labourers.

(Marx 1863–1866: 405)

In Marx's opinion, both Ricardo, who defined capital as that part of the wealth of a country that is employed in production, and other economists, who described capital as the bulk of capital goods, were the victims of an 'illusion'. This illusion, which caused them to mistake social relations established in the production environment for a natural ownership title to the assets used in production processes, was 'an absurdity', though one inherent in the very nature of the capitalist production process and 'a very convenient method of demonstrating the eternal character of the capitalist mode of production, or of showing that capital is a permanent natural element of human production in general' (Marx 1863–1866: 28).

An additional in-depth analysis of the fundamental contradiction in capitalism will be developed in Chapter 13.

6 The transition in producer cooperative theory

At this point, I will try to establish how those believing (like the older Lenin) that a system of producer cooperatives would help supersede capitalism figure the process leading up to socialism – i.e. the transition.

Three distinct high roads to the establishment of a system of producer cooperatives have been theorised so far.

One is endorsed by those who think of cooperatives as merit goods – i.e. as producing positive externalities. The greater benefits that the community may draw from self-managed, rather than capitalistic, firms have been mentioned above. Consequently, if the cooperative firm is a 'merit good', the first measures to be enforced, in order to foster the emergence of a new mode of production, are tax and credit facilities commensurate with the benefits that the community draws from these firms.

The second 'high road' is identifying businesses that capitalists prove unable to run efficiently and changing them into democratic firms. This method is applicable both on a case-by-case basis and via a general strike.[7] A process of this kind was about to materialise in Italy during the so-called 'red biennium' (1920–1912), when the labour unrest instigated by Gramsci's *Ordine Nuovo* movement made it so difficult for capitalists to run their firms that Giovanni Agnelli declared himself prepared to hand over the management of Fiat to the workers.[8] The idea of a general strike as the preferred springboard for the transition to socialism is the true leitmotif in the thought of Rosa Luxemburg, the most democratic of all Marxists (see Negt 1979a).

Several countries have a record of capitalistic firms which, at various points in time, were actually changed into cooperatives, instead of being wound up. In years nearer to us, numerous firms on the brink of bankruptcy were occupied by the workers and run as producer cooperatives in the aftermath of the economic crisis in Argentina. Most of the approximately 200 cooperatives conducting business in Argentina in 2005 were firms that had been set up following the crisis. In Italy – to mention another case – a great many firms in serious difficulties were taken over by their workforces in 1970–1971 and about 100 of these were formed into cooperatives between 1974 and 1978. Most of the cooperatives that were set up in the manufacturing industry in those days were originally defaulting capitalistic companies (see, *inter alia*, Zevi 1982). Some scholars have gone so far as to argue that rescuing defaulting business is one of the main functions of cooperative firms (Roelants 2000: 67).[9] Among them, Vanek (1977: 46) has written that the default of an existing business is, quite naturally, an excellent opportunity for setting up a self-managed firm.

An elementary truth to be emphasised here is that – contrary to a widely held opinion – firms that do not report any profits are not destroying resources. Provided that work is looked upon as a value instead of a burden, in situations marked by Keynesian unemployment, the firm that actually wastes resources is the firm that fails to produce added value. And a firm that does not report any profits may nevertheless produce considerable amounts of added value.[10]

This specific road from capitalism to socialism is endorsed, among others, by Tronti in a Marxist analysis of the evolution of capitalism. 'At the highest level of capitalistic development', Tronti argues,

> the social relation becomes a moment of the Relation of production, the whole of society becomes an articulation of production; in other words, the whole of society exists as a function of the factory and the factory extends

its exclusive domination over the whole of society. As a result, the State machinery itself tends to be ever more markedly identified with the figure of the collective capitalist. It is ever more thoroughly appropriated by the capitalistic mode of production and hence becomes a function of the capitalistic society.

(1962: 20)

From this, he draws the conclusion that it is a historical necessity to fight bourgeois society within the social relation of production – i.e. to challenge it from within the capitalistic production system (1962: 24). In other words, from Tronti's perspective,

there is a need to break the state within society, to dissolve society within the production process and to reverse the production relation within the factory and the social relationships existing there. In short, the goal is to destroy the bourgeois state machine right within the capitalistic factory.

(1962: 30)[11]

This policy goes to refute the reflections on class action developed by Olson (1965) and Buchanan (1979) in connection with the free-riding issue. Both of these authors start out from the idea that revolution is a public good and that the proletariat as a whole is fully aware of this. As revolution is a costly undertaking that exposes the revolutionaries to a violent backlash from the bourgeoisie, it is exactly its quality as a public good that will prevent it from being carried through. Each proletarian will find it convenient to shirk involvement on the assumption that he will, in any case, reap the benefits that flow from the efforts of his fellow citizens, where they should prove successful. In the words of Buchanan:

Even if revolution is in the best interest of the proletariat and even if every member of the proletariat realizes that this is so, so far as its members act rationally, this class will not achieve concerted revolutionary action. This shocking conclusion rests on the premise that concerted revolutionary action is for the proletariat a public good in the technical sense. Concerted revolutionary action is a public good for the proletariat as a group. Yet each proletarian, whether he seeks to maximise his own interests or those of his class, will refrain from revolutionary action.

(1979: 63)

In the opinion of Vahabi (2010), this line of reasoning entails that – contrary to Marxist theory – the masses fail to make history, because their rationality induces them to opt for political inaction.

The degree to which both of these authors are off-track will be clear if one considers that the benefits stemming from every action geared towards helping workers run firms on their own will be reaped by the workers themselves, in terms that they will turn from hired workers into their own masters.

The third high road to the new order is a parliamentary act providing for the conversion of the stocks of existing companies into bonds of equal value (by means of suitable regulations intended to solve the difficulties associated with such a transaction) and, at the same time, outlawing hired labour to the extent that will be deemed opportune. Such an act would automatically strip capitalists of all power and, simultaneously, change existing capitalistic businesses into self-managed firms.[12] The prerequisite for the passing of such an act is obviously a parliamentary majority of representatives of the workers or, at any rate, Members of Parliament favourable to such a solution.[13]

On the assertion that safety can only come from piecemeal social changes and improvements in the living conditions of individuals (see, *inter alia*, Sapelli 2006: 4), I would express a preference for the first two of the three policies outlined above.[14] The quote below is clear evidence that this was also the option advocated by Rosa Luxembourg:

> The conquest of power will not be effected with one blow. It will be a progression. We shall progressively occupy all the positions of the capitalist state and defend them tooth and nail.... It is a question of fighting step by step, hand-to-hand, in every province, in every city, in every village, in every municipality, in order to take and transfer all the power of the state bit by bit from the bourgeoisie to the workers.
>
> (1918: 629)

An additional reason why the first two transition processes are particularly opportune is that the simultaneous existence of socialist and capitalistic firms might destabilise the latter to the point of causing them to rethink part of their strategies in a manner that would ultimately expedite a democratic transition to socialism (see Wolff 2012: 158–161)

In 1982, Hayek argued that no real breakthrough in politics would ever be achieved through mass propaganda. The problem, he wrote (see Hayek 1983: 192), was persuading intellectuals that the positive externalities of a democratic firm system compared to capitalism would afford a significant leap forward and inducing them to press this idea on political parties and the electorate as a whole. At that point, he concluded, the hoped-for political change might be enforced by a parliamentary vote and would be tantamount to a fully democratic revolution.

From a liberalist perspective, the crux of the matter is that being at the orders of a majority is barely more reassuring than obeying the commands of one or a few individuals. As argued by Popper, 'we are democrats not because the majority is always right, but because democratic traditions are the least evil ones which we know' (cited in Zanone 2002: 131).

An additional point probably requires discussion in greater depth here. In the mind of a liberalist, there is no sense in racking one's brains over the issue of the transition to a new order. Provided it is found that cooperatives are more efficient than capitalistic companies, they will eventually prevail as a matter of course; in the opposite case, the transition will never come about. For my part,

I reject this idea, because I firmly believe that a transition might come about, even if the efficiency levels of cooperatives were found to fall short of those ensured by capitalistic companies. I think that the transition is desirable if the benefits it offers to the community are such as to vouchsafe superior social conditions. The transition under consideration is, indeed, not a spontaneous process, but one that is purposely pursued by a nation through the enforcement of suitable policies.

7 Conclusion

Today, it is widely argued that Marx's writings, especially those sketching the economic system of the future, contains fragmentary theoretical approaches, instead of offering fully developed theories (see Balibar 1993: 169; Tarrit 2006: 600). In point of fact, this is consistent with Lukacs' saying that, in Marx, methodology only is what really matters.

With specific regard to their approach to the transitional social order, Marxists fall into two broad divisions: those assuming that the correct Marxian view of a socialist economy is one that equates socialism with self-management and those identifying socialism with a command economy founded on planning. And there are reasons in support of the contention (to which either group would be prepared to subscribe) that little textual support is actually available for either assumption. In a 1914 book entitled *Marxismo e cooperativismo, Le due grandi vie della rivoluzione economica*, the renowned Italian theorist of cooperation Antonio Vergnanini identified two roads to a socialist revolution, which he described as mutually exclusive (one of them being cooperativism); and it is well known that Yugoslav and other theorists of self-management tend to endorse the view that a system of labour-managed firms (or producer cooperatives) has its roots in Marx's works (see, *inter alia*, Damjanovic 1962; Bourdet 1978a: 49ff.; Pelikan 1977: 143ff.; Jossa 2005a).

In this book, I have been arguing that a system of cooperative firms reversing the existing capital–labour relation (see, *inter alia*, Dubravcic 1970; Srinivasan and Phansalkar 2003) is tantamount to a revolution, since it results in the introduction of a new production mode. I have also asked if the idea of a revolution enacted by peaceful and democratic means and in successive steps – until worker-managed firms outnumber capitalist companies – is fully compatible with the letter of Marx and Engels's writings. From my perspective, the prerequisite for such a revolution is a certain amount of support from the public hand, in terms that the state would have to look upon democratic firms as 'merit goods' and make provision for tax and/or other benefits in their favour. An additional query that has been explored is whether a form of socialism established through state intervention would be consistent with the thought of Marx and Engels.

The next point addressed was if, and in what way, the two social orders that followers of Marx tend to class as antithetical can be reconciled in a truly Marxian perspective. This question has been answered in the affirmative, though with the major qualification that a social order with central planning can only be in line with a Marxian view of transition if it arises within a system of labour-managed firms.[15] A social system with self-managed firms is both conceivable in a centrally planned economy and in a society organised in line with market principles. The best proxy for Marxian thought is doubtless a society in which democratically managed firms operate within a centrally planned system, but I endorse the view that a social system with self-managed firms would be consistent with Marxian thought, even though it should fail to adopt central planning.

Notes

1 A highly appreciative comment by Meiksins Wood (2000b: 25) is that the mode of production is 'the most operative concept of historical materialism'.
2 This view is shared both by Labriola (1965: 87–96) and Wright Mills (1962), according to whom Marx formulated an all-embracing scientific discipline, whose underlying theoretical model covers the whole gamut of social phenomena. In the opinion of Aron, instead, Marx's theoretical approaches to production relations and social classes are 'not fully consistent' (see Aron 1969: 48).
3 In his younger years, Marx held the revolt against the world to be implicit in Hegelian philosophy (see Marx 1841).
4 Both Althusser (Therborn 1971: 104) and other commentators emphasising the revolutionary essence of Marxism are agreed that the production mode is a core notion of historical materialism and of Marx's entire theoretical approach. On the importance of the notion of the 'production mode' in Marx's thought, see also, Volpi (1989: 34–36).
5 In a 1902 work, Kautsky denied the assumption that reformism differed from revolutionism because of its rejection of violence, though elsewhere he expressed the opposite view (see, for instance, Kautsky 1892: part 2, ch. 1). According to Kautsky, the essence of revolution was the takeover of political power by a new class. Equating non-violence with passivity, other authors hold violence to be a necessary prerequisite for the success of a revolution (see, among others, Settembrini 1973: vii; Geary 1974: 92–93).
6 'Any negation aiming to supersede something must, at the same time, contain within itself the aspects it negates and show them true: this is why history is, simultaneously, unity and multiplicity' (see Mondolfo 1952: 112).
7 In 1909, Robert Michels remarked that producer cooperatives are often set up at the end of a prolonged strike as tangible proof that workers are able to run production activities independently of capitalists (see Michels 1909: 195).
8 A situation is termed 'revolutionary' when the ruling classes are no longer able to exercise power as they used to before and the working classes are no longer prepared to live as they had been doing until then (see Lukàcs 1972: 51).
9 At the other end of the spectrum are historians of the cooperative movement who strongly deny that bail-out operations fall within the mission of the cooperative movement (see, *inter alia*, Zamagni and Felice 2006: 112–113).
10 In the opinion of some, the reason why workers tend to take over enterprises in temporary distress is that sometimes the enterprises have difficulty obtaining new credit, due to asymmetrical information on capital markets (see De Bonis *et al.* 1994: 30).
11 The road to worker power under discussion can be purposely pursued by proclaiming a general strike with the aim of handing over to workers the management of all – or at least the most important – firms. In my estimation, the aim of a general strike should not necessarily be the disintegration of the state machinery recommended by Tronti. The democratic form of socialism endorsed in this book requires the maintenance of state power. This is why I do not share the opinion of Benjamin that a general strike

can be defined as 'non-violent violence', because its aim is not to found a new state, but to abolish the existing one; in other words, because its purpose is to give rise to a new system where work is neither 'imposed' by law nor by the need to survive (Benjamin 1995: 21).

12 The transitional process suggested by Dow (2003) is a combination of the first and third high roads just described. Specifically, Dow suggests putting the issue to a referendum among workers and, in the event of a democratic response for a self-managed firm system, enforcing subsidies in favour of those firms that are assumed to generate benefits for the community at large (see Dow 2003: ch. 12).

13 In this connection, Panzieri (quoted in Gattei 2007: 163) comments that as soon as the working class takes cognisance of its status as variable capital and forcefully rejects such a role, its demands will become ever more pressing and will ever more markedly be focused on the acquisition of worker power than on the labour issues typically featuring in trade union platforms (Panzieri 1976: 38).

14 The sixth chapter of Archer's 1995 book is entirely devoted to demonstrating that there is at least one feasible road to the acquisition of a democratic socialist order.

15 An interesting point to be discussed against the backdrop of Marxian theory is whether it is possible to speak of the 'death of the state' in such a situation. Quoting Engels (1891a: 321), when, at long last, the state 'becomes the real representative of the whole of society, it renders itself unnecessary', because

> as soon as there is no longer any social class to be held in subjection; as soon as class rule, and the individual struggle for existence based upon our present anarchy in production, with the collisions and excesses arising from these, are removed, nothing more remains to be repressed, and a special repressive force, a State, is no longer necessary.

Hence, there are reasons to argue that the state exists as long as 'a special repressive force' continues to exist and obliges one class to supply means of subsistence to another, and the state would consequently die out, even within a system without labour-managed firms. On closer analysis, though, Engels's argument is hardly convincing, since the protection of the interests of one class from the assaults of another is not the only aim of state repression.

12 Gramsci and the transition to socialism

1 Introduction

Antonio Gramsci's approach to the issue of the transition is also of absorbing interest. In his opinion, 'the fundamental event in the Russian revolution is the creation of a new type of State: a State of Councils. This is what historical research is called upon to address. The rest is contingent' (Gramsci 1919–1920: 374).[1] This unequivocal advocacy of workers' councils is contained in the articles that Antonio Gramsci, the best-known Marxist theorist of workers' councils,[2] wrote for the political weekly *Ordine Nuovo* in 1919–1920, and analysts of his work hold this to be a basic element of continuity in his thought.[3]

Although Gramsci's theory of workers' councils found no immediate followers and has little in common with the modern labour-management theories developed in the wake of Ward's and Vanek's writings, it is nevertheless highly interesting, since Gramsci claimed that democratic firm management was a means of paving the way for socialism. In the mind of Gramsci, a socialist revolution was 'a process whose roots lie at the heart of the productive forces and which gives rise to a new order as a direct emanation of the lives and power of the proletariat' (Cicerchia 1959: 30).

Before analysing Gramsci's revolutionary approach, it is worth emphasising that in orthodox economics, the prerequisite for the proper functioning of an economic system is the adoption of one of two possible resource allocation methods: private profit considerations or the commands of a planning organ. A third option is simply ruled out. In the 1930s, a well-known debate on planning confirmed the feasibility of different combinations of plan and market, but until the (improbable) appearance of a 'new man' entirely devoid of selfishness or self-interest, any orthodox economist will confirm that private profit motives or the commands of a planning organ are a necessity for the proper conduct of production.

As Gramsci (like most Marxists) rejected the idea of only two possible allocation methods, an additional aim of this chapter is to show that this is why he did not think of workers' councils as a means of remedying possible shortcomings of centralised planning. On the assumption that central planning was the essence of socialism, he failed to ask himself if the weaknesses of socialist systems highlighted in the already mentioned debate were to be traced to centralised planning without worker control. This was certainly a mistake, because as long as workers' councils are not allowed to run firms efficiently in line with the partners' personal utility calculations, what remains is the centralised planning model adopted by the USSR, which is a type of firm governance that historical experience has shown to be abortive.

The foregoing reflections highlight one major difference between Gramsci's council theory and modern theories of democratic firm governance in a system of producer cooperatives: whereas theorists of producer cooperatives equate socialism with democracy in the firm, Gramsci looked to a system of workers' councils, not as socialism proper, but as a step towards its establishment. Doubting the willingness of democratic parliaments or even workers' unions to further a transition to socialism, he looked upon councils as transitional tools paving the way for a new social order, but not necessarily as a means of running firms efficiently.

Neither will it do to describe Gramsci as a revolutionary and modern democratic firm governance theorists as reformists. As mentioned in the preceding chapter, the essence of revolution is the substitution of a new production mode for the existing one, and modern economic theory has provided ample proof that labour management triggers a revolution in the socialist direction by reversing the current capital–labour relationship.

Boiled down to its essentials, the main idea underlying this chapter is that modern producer cooperative theory and Gramsci's theory of workers' councils have in common the assumption that workers' councils are the instrument that will trigger the transition to socialism.[4]

2 Hegemony and workers' councils in Gramsci's approach

The core element in Gramsci's approach to firm governance in the transition period is a system of workers' councils, which prepares the ground for worker rule by providing an alternative to liberalism and fusing economic and political action into a consistent whole (see De Felice 1971: 275–279, 338–345; Nardone 1971: ch. 4). Yet in order for this to come about, hegemony must be attained first.

Although the notion of hegemony is derived from Lenin (see, *inter alia*, Vacca 1985: 64–65), Gramsci's theorisation of this subject is held to be his most important contribution to Marxist thought (see Gruppi 1969: 160; Gerratana 1977; Macciocchi 1974: 199). It is a recurring theme in the *Prison Notebooks* and is closely associated with workers' councils as the seedbed of a 'spontaneous self-education process' (see Salvadori 1976: 20; Badaloni 1977: 9).[5] Contrasting the spontaneity of this process with the voluntary character of the parallel process in trade unions and political parties, Gramsci makes it clear that economic crises or spur-of-the-moment revolts, while creating fertile ground for the emergence of certain ways of thinking and approaches to tackling problems, will not produce any far-reaching effects, unless they are kept under control (Gramsci 1975: 1586–1589).

On the one hand, hegemony is the ability to build consensus – i.e. to secure the assent of the majority of the working class to the options that lie ahead – on the other, it is the ability to understand the dynamics of events and identify those social forces that are prepared to support just those political choices that are likely to realise the potential for evolution inherent in the present.[6] Pizzorno describes it as the position gained by the dominant class in its efforts to secure the consensus of other social groups on a unifying ideology and contrasts it with the inability of the lower classes to frame an aggregating ideology of their own. Despite their wish to dismantle the dominant organic relationship, in periods of crisis the latter will only take action if they can rely on an organisational structure to represent and support their interests. Without the help of such an organisation, they will hardly be able to build an opposed historic bloc preparing the ground for the advent of a new state. In other words, in Gramsci's view, the basic assumption of worker hegemony is an organic crisis – a crisis in political representation, which subverts the harmonious relationships between social groups, their parties and social bases and the actors that they have traditionally represented (Pizzorno 1969: 119).

As argued by Bobbio, the dialectical relation between base and superstructure is manifest in all Gramsci's writings, but in Gramsci (unlike Marx), 'civil society' (i.e. the positive and pro-active agents behind historical growth) is part of the superstructure, not of the base (see Bobbio 1969: 85–86; Prestipino 1990: 36–59, 65),[7] and hegemony is the stage when the latter is influenced by the former. In Gramsci's approach, there are two major superstructural plains: 'civil society' (private entities) and 'the body politic or State', which is the expression of the dominant group's hegemonic position in society at large (Gramsci 1975: 1518, 1020, 1590).

Gramsci's notion of hegemony is part of a worldview that conceives of the rise of the working class to power as a process shaped in the main by friction between base and superstructure:[8] a bottom-up social process, which, according to Gramsci's critics, is connoted by a significant degree of subjectivism.[9]

The hegemony issue is also closely linked to the 'historical bloc', which should not be simply construed as an alliance of classes necessary to secure power. It is a fairly more complex phenomenon that is founded on the role of intellectuals as consensus-builders and the party as the 'modern Prince' (Portelli 1972). The resulting notion is a maze, whose constituent concepts are cross-linked and interconnected like the pieces of a jigsaw puzzle and which does not require further discussion here.[10]

Despite his theory of hegemony, Gramsci can hardly be termed a theorist of the democratic transition from capitalism to socialism. Spriano (1967: 32) has rightly argued that Gramsci's political writings of the so-called 'legal decade' do not support the assumption that his idea of democracy departed from that of the Third International or that he advocated political democracy and representation as a means of attaining socialism (see also, Macciocchi 1974: 211–217; Bobbio 1988; Cafagna 1988). It is a plain fact that nowhere in Gramsci's writings do we find an approach to economic democracy comparable to that of today's producer cooperative theorists.

Nonetheless, Gramsci's view of hegemony, his advocacy of a bottom-up revolutionary process and his emphasis on the role of intellectuals combine to suggest that he, of all Marxists, was the one that came closest to theorising the feasibility of a democratic transition. In his opinion, revolution comes about when the working classes 'manages to persuade the majority of the people, i.e. the amorphous middle classes, intellectuals and peasants, that their immediate and future interests fall in with those of such majority' (Gramsci 1919–1920: 144).

As shown by the passage quoted below, this was also the opinion of Engels:

> One can conceive that the old society may develop peacefully into the new one in countries where the representatives of the people concentrate all power in their hands, where, if one has the support of the majority of the people, one can do as one sees fit in a constitutional way: in democratic republics such as France and the U.S.A., in monarchies such as Britain.
>
> (Engels 1891a: 174)[11]

That this transition should come about by democratic means is what most modern theorists of producer cooperatives and many Marxists, both old and new, strongly recommend.[12] The need to address this point in association with the grand issue of hegemony can be explained as follows: in Gramsci's opinion, only if intellectuals, left-wing parties and the people at large come to conceive of self-management as a viable system can the revolt against the injustices inherent in capitalism give rise to worker management and pave the way for a democratic transition to socialism. Gramsci stoutly opposed subversion: 'a revolutionary minority seizing power through the use of violence' – he wrote (1919–1920: 307) – 'would certainly be overthrown by the rebound from the mercenary forces of capitalism'. However, he also knew that only those blinded by ideology could expect workers to shape historical processes autonomously or spark off and carry on revolutionary actions on their own initiative.

3 A workable transition

As pointed out in previous chapters, Marx encouraged the establishment of producer cooperatives at various stages of his theoretical approach. Far from nihilistic, his idea of transition was 'dialectical', because it postulated the evolution of one form of society into the other (dialectical view), instead of the abrupt replacement of the older order with a new one (nihilistic view). Is this true of Gramsci as well?

Gramsci held that the preparatory process leading up to a revolution would necessarily be a fairly long one. Thinking of history as an unstoppable process aiming to set mankind free through repeated adjustments, he simply could not 'share the myth of a proletarian revolution as a sudden leap from necessity to freedom to which the greater part of the European communist intelligentsia were holding on in those days' (Paggi 1970: 236). At the same time, he also conceived of revolution as the ultimate victory (Gramsci 1975: 802) entailing the overthrow of the older order with its institutions and the final defeat of the enemy (Gramsci 1975: 800). This is why Gramsci's view of the aftermath of the revolution appears as a rigid – not dialectical – sequence of historical phases ending with the advent of the reign of freedom (understood as the utter negation of the reign of necessity). In other words, while deferring revolution in time, Gramsci held that the older order would have to be rapidly replaced by the new order as soon as workers took charge.

As mentioned above, in Gramsci's approach, workers' councils are tools for the achievement of hegemony, and this necessarily entails a long-term process during which workers' councils and markets would have to coexist. But Gramsci's approach is marred by two shortcomings: first, his silence on the difficulties attending worker's councils in a capitalist economy; second, lack of indications concerning post-revolutionary firm management modes and the way in which worker management and centralised planning could or should be combined.

The fact that his *Prison Notebooks* make no mention of the conclusions reached during the debate in the 1930s is not surprising, since his imprisonment prevented him from following this debate. A different, though probably even more convincing, explanation of this silence has been suggested by Anderson, who describes Gramsci as a representative of 'Western Marxism' – a movement that (compared to classical Marxism) focuses mainly on philosophical and cultural issues, rather than economics or politics. In Anderson's opinion, this holds true, although Gramsci, of all 'Western Marxists', is probably the one that most penetratingly concerned himself with combinations of theory and practice typical of the Western tradition (Anderson 1976: 25).[13]

With reference to the issue of firm management modes in the new order, Gramsci wrote (1919–1920: 46–47):

> A worker will only begin to think of himself as a producer when, aware of his contribution to the specific manufacturing process under way in a given workshop (e.g. the automobile floorshop of a Turin factory) and his role as an indispensable agent within the social environment where cars are manufactured, he takes one step further and comes to view Turin and its automotive industry as a production system centred on automobiles and the greater part of the general activities carried on in Turin and its labour market as mainly associated with the automotive industry. His next step is an understanding of the workers assigned to that myriad general activities as part-creators of the automotive industry since it is they that created the necessary and sufficient assumptions for its very existence. From this cell, i.e. from the factory as the unit and agent of growth behind a given product, the worker moves on to an awareness of a range of ever vaster units and, finally, of the nation as a gigantic production apparatus [...]. He develops class consciousness and becomes a communist when he realises that private property is not a function of productivity; and he turns into a revolutionary when he comes to conceive of the capitalist, the private owner, as a deadbolt and obstacle to be dismantled. From this stage he will proceed to an apprehension

of the notion of the 'State' as a complex organisational structure which is the tangible expression of society, a huge production apparatus characterised by the same web of relations typical of life in an industrial floorshop, though magnified and enriched thanks to the new functions demanded by its sheer size.[14]

This single quotation (to which one might add many others – e.g. 1919–1920: 95) is clear evidence of Gramsci's advocacy of the central planning model. But did Gramsci also think that firms were to be autonomous? And, above all, on what grounds did he assume that firms would actually conform to the commands of a planning organ?

He certainly believed that 'a socialist state cannot do without the continuing active participation of comrades in the life of its institutions' (Gramsci 1919–1920: 381). 'Such a democratic workers' society', he wrote,

> would act as a magnificent educational tool in impressing discipline on the masses and providing political and administrative instruction; it would help men find their place in society as the soldiers of an army which is about to engage in warfare and needs cohesion to avoid being destroyed and reduced to slavery.
>
> (Gramsci 1919–1920: 12)

In his opinion, however, the discipline needed to set factories going would be a spontaneous offspring of the revolutionary process; upon seizing power, he argued, the proletariat would rapidly discard utopian ideologies founded on myth and permanently develop the typical mindset of a communist nourished by a measure of unswerving enthusiasm (Gramsci 1919–1920: 30) with the result – he concluded – that each worker would promptly exercise self-restraint (Gramsci 1919–1920: 81). Moreover, Gramsci thought that no incentives would be needed to inhibit free riding among workers, and workers would cash their shares of the net operating results of their firms in a system where firms were not fully autonomous and had no independent accounting systems. Discipline would be ensured without any authoritarian commands by the state bureaucracy, because in a post-revolutionary society, 'all social relationships will be shaped, not by organised power structures, but by the technical requirements of production and the organisational structure resulting therefrom' (see Gramsci 1919–1920: 183). Workers' councils – he wrote – will 'eradicate individualism and personalism in every form' (Gramsci 1919–1920: 48).

In all probability, Gramsci did change his mind in later years. In a well-known analysis of 'Americanism and Fordism' included in the *Prison Notebooks*, he described Fordism as a 'rational' method 'whose generalised adoption, though necessary, required a lengthy process of change both in social conditions and customs and in personal modes of conduct' and predicted its temporary adoption in the transition period – i.e. after the takeover of the proletariat. As Gramsci assumed that this production method called for a combination of coaction and the kind of persuasion that comes from high wages and the result-ing higher standards of life, one might ask if he looked upon persuasion and coaction as specific to the initial stage of a socialist order. Although Gramsci's definition of man as 'a being with insatiable appetites that only strict controls can keep in check' (cited in Gallino 1969: 106) seems to suggest exactly this, one might object that such a radical turnaround would have had to be clearly stated – i.e. that Gramsci should have expressly disavowed his initial idea (dealt with in detail further on) that the reign of necessity was to give way to the reign of freedom instantly after the revolution.

4   Timing the transition period

Gramsci shared Marx and Engels's view of the transition to socialism as a long-term process. The kind of revolution he had in mind (the ultimate victory and advent to power of the working class) was to be the climax of a long-term process designed to attain hegemony. This poses a need to put the subsequent steps of this transition process in their right time sequence.

Whereas the need for a long drawn-out preparatory process led Gramsci to defer revolution over time, he assumed that the 'reign of necessity' would instantly give way to the 'reign of freedom' after the revolution. 'A proletarian revolution', he wrote,

> is a long-term historical process during which certain forces engaged in pro-duction emerge and gain in influence.... What we term the 'revolutionary act', i.e. the violent overthrow of the economic and political apparatus and resulting subversion of the status quo, takes place at this particular step.
>
> (Gramsci 1919–1920: 123)

Gramsci's timing of events lies open to one strong objection. If the need to attain hegemony before the outbreak of revolution necessitates a lengthy trans-ition period, and pre-revolution hegemony is mainly achieved through the action of workers' councils, it is reasonable to assume that during such a long-term process, the government of a capitalist society would forcefully contrast the establishment of workers' councils in factories. A gradual but steady increase in the number of workers' councils amounts (as Gramsci rightly recognised) to a creeping revolution, which a non-socialist government is sure to oppose by all means. The same argument is set forth in Salvadori (1973: 127): if the Party uses workers' councils to secure freedom of action until the process 'enters the violent civil war stage' that leads up to the dictatorship of the proletariat, capital-ists would be able to strike back and inhibit the growth of the council movement.

A way out of this deadlock is to think of the transition period as part of the post-takeover stage, but this solution would contradict both Gramsci's explicit deferral of revolution over time and his belief that the older order would be instantly replaced by the new one.

One passage from Gramsci's work seems to come to our aid. Commenting on the worker control bill laid before the Chamber of Deputies by M.P. Giolitti, Gramsci wrote:

> Any laws enforced by a bourgeois power to regulate this subject tell us ultimately this and only this: that the terrain on which class struggle acts itself out in real – not just verbal – terms has changed thoroughly and that the resulting circumstances are such as to oblige the bourgeois class to make concessions in terms of creating new legal institutions. And this is a clear sign of an organic weakness of the dominant class.
>
> (1921–1922: 67–68)

The idea behind this statement – i.e. the assumption that the working class may press a parliament into setting up a system of workers' councils – is one point where Gramsci's approach overlaps with that of modern theorists of producer cooperatives. If workers' councils can be created by a bourgeois government and their generalised adoption does amount to a real and proper revolution, one can think of the transition to socialism as a process that comes about within a parliamentary democracy. But this is in contrast to the idea that the old order will instantly give way to the new one after the takeover of the proletariat.

5 A critique of Gramsci's workers' councils

As mentioned above, Gramsci rated workers' councils as a necessary tool to discipline the masses and create the necessary assumption of worker rule in periods of severe conflict. He expected the working class to check not only the disorders set off by the war and the Russian revolution during Italy's 'red biennium', but all of the turmoil that every revolution carries in its track.

It has also been mentioned that his concern was not with worker management as such, but with factory councils as the only organisational form capable of vouchsafing the transition to socialism – i.e. the handover of power to the proletariat. However, although he vested major tasks ('taking over the original functions of the capitalist entrepreneur, acting as the true "hero" of the industrial scenario' and 'demolishing any form of state'; see Gramsci 1919–1920: 105) in workers' councils and rated the plan as a *resumé* of the proposals and projects of single firms and even single workers (Gramsci 1919–1920: 184), he never as much as mentioned the workers' right to appropriate part of the surplus earned by their firms.[15] And this is where Gramsci's approach to workers' councils departs from that of modern theorists of producer cooperatives.[16]

For my part, the objectionable approach is Gramsci's, not that of modern theorists of producer cooperatives. Having regard to the criticisms levelled against the Soviet model during the debate in the 1930s, today it is possible to argue that the most feasible and widely accepted model of socialism is market socialism with labour-managed firms, which is not what Gramsci had in mind. The only alternative to allowing workers to run their firms autonomously in their own interests is centralised bureaucratic planning, which both the debate during the 1930s and the experiences of the Soviet Union and other Eastern European countries have shown to be abortive. A centrally-planned system without autonomous firms would be found wanting in incentives for proper functioning. The end result would be a pure 'command economy' allocating resources based on external instructions to firms, rather than by reference to individual preferences. During the debate of the 1930s, socialist economists got the better of their liberalist colleagues, because they provided evidence that centralised planning could be reconciled with pricing systems based on individual preferences. What they failed to address was the incentive issue (see, *inter alia*, Roemer and Silvestre 1993: 108), whilst today there is general agreement that no economic system will ever function properly without adequate incentives to underpin choices deemed in the interest of the economy.

One further point that needs to be stressed is the belief of modern democratic firm management theorists that a gradual transition to socialism can be started by a parliament with peaceable methods. Advocates of democratic firm management describe employee-managed firms as 'merit' goods for a number of reasons, as discussed in Chapter 10. From this perspective, fiscal or other public benefits in favour of employee-managed firms are not only reasonable, but may play an all but negligible role. Thanks to the enforcement of such benefits by a parliamentary majority, employee-managed firms might gradually but steadily increase in number, supplant capitalist firms altogether and, hence, bring about a gradual transition to socialism.

6 Gramsci and Fordism

The scant fortune of Gramsci's theory of workers' councils is sometimes traced to the spreading of Fordism and Taylorism. Skilled labour forces are a necessary prerequisite for the success of a system of cooperative firms. Gramsci himself believed that a worker-managed economy could only arise if workers inimical to the capitalist yoke gained a correct understanding of their potential role in production and trained themselves in the technical, financial and managerial functions that they intended to takeover in the future. According to Bonazzi (2002: 13), Gramsci looked upon the working class 'as a "political agent" striving to achieve its emancipation from capitalism while maturing a conscience as a "civil producer" and thereby preparing the ground for its hegemony in society', but the introduction of Fordism and Taylorism inhibited the evolution of the working class in this direction. In early post-war Germany, when assembly-line workers were the exception and trade unions were hardly influential, a movement for worker participation was launched by multi-skilled workers capable of vying with their managers in developing process innovations in advanced sectors of the engineering industry. However, from 1924 onwards, conditions changed thoroughly, and Fordist production and working models swept rapidly across the country.

Turning to Italy, there is general agreement that the factors responsible for the evolution of society in directions other than those predicted by Gramsci include difficult labour relations in large-sized northern factories and, later on, the emergence of an entrepreneurial class in the part of the country that we name 'Third Italy'. Moreover, when workers faced with growing workloads resolved to battle in the main for improved work conditions, the result was the spread of unskilled labour, due to the influx of migrants from Italy's south.

Suggesting a different interpretation of the course taken by Italian society, Bonazzi argues that the advancement of Taylorism (analysed in-depth by Braverman in 1974) was hardly perceived 'as a deterministic process entailing the debasement of labour in capitalist societies as a matter of course' (Bonazzi 2002: 12), because the level of conflict that industrial relations had reached by that time seemed to justify the assumption that workers would manage to fend off the evils of Taylorism that were being denounced.

This argument may shed light on the reasons behind the failure of Gramsci's council movement. In the presence of different cultural traditions, the radical changes recorded in Italy (and elsewhere) in the 1970s might well have led to the rise of workers' councils. As far as Fordism is concerned, he never suggested that it was in conflict with his council theory. As for Taylorism, which Gramsci termed 'the latest step in a long-term process whose inception dates back to the birth of industrialism' (Gramsci 1975: 2165), he thought that it had produced both corporatism and the so-called 'high wage' (see Gramsci 1975: 2156–2158, 2171–2177), but his rejection of determinism induced him to argue that just as Taylorism had generated a corporatist reaction such as Fascism, it might with equal probability have produced a response in the socialist direction (i.e. the establishment of a council system). From his perspective, the ability to exercise power in the factory need not necessarily precede the material establishment of factory councils, for it is these that are the educational tool that will 'radically change the minds of workers' and 'prepare them for the exercise of power' (Gramsci 1919–1920: 89–90).

Hence, the conclusion that both Taylorism and Fordism, far from conflicting with Gramsci's approach, have a place in his theory as factors capable of sparking off a socialist response to the degradation of labour in capitalist societies.

7 Conclusion

Although Gramsci's workers' councils have little in common with Ward, Vanek and Meade's employee-managed firms, a comparison of the different views of the transition to socialism reflected in them is interesting in many respects. From a theoretical (though not strictly interpretative) perspective, each of them may suggest cross-fertilising insights for use in reappraising and modernising the other.

The most obvious difference between Ward and Vanek's employee-managed firms and Gramsci's workers' councils is that the former are assumed to operate within a market economy, while the latter were evidently intended to prepare the ground for a planned command economy.

Gramsci never shifted from his firm belief that workers' councils were a necessity for a socialist revolution. In his opinion, the events that marked the climax of the revolutionary surge – i.e. the seizure of factories by workers in Italy and the march of the Red Army on Warsaw – had revealed that the revolutionary groups of the time were as yet unable to provide the leadership needed for the handover in favour of the masses (Gramsci 1923–1926: 165). However, he never suggested that workers' councils could be used to run firms efficiently and thus prevent a waste of resources within a planned economy.

Notes

1 Tamburrano (1959: 55) thinks that the theory of factory councils is the very core of Gramsci's approach to democracy.

2 On Gramsci's place in Marxist world literature, see Cicerchia (1959), Badaloni (1977: 1–2), Forgacs (1989), Cammett (1991) and Hobsbawm (1995). In Garin (1964: 136), one reads that his council theory, 'though appreciated in general terms, has increasingly been glossed over' (1963: 136) and that it was 'suffocated, branded as misleading and set aside just because his workers' councils were not turned into practice' (1963: 131). Guiducci (1977: 195) has gone so far as to argue that a major Marxist classic such as Gramsci and his works seem to have been 'embalmed'. Similarly, while admitting that his research was based on 'a Gramscian reading of Marx as its main reference point', Giuseppe Vacca thought it necessary to add that he was speaking of Gramsci's work of the seventies – i.e. the years when he produced his critical edition of the *Prison Notebooks* (see Vacca 1985: viii). For a completely different view, see Buey (1995: 33–34).

3 See Gramsci (1923–1926: 21; 1975: 330, 1137–1138; Garin 1958: 47–48; Ragionieri 1969; Paggi 1970: introduction; Spriano 1971; Gruppi 1972: 29, 42; Bonomi 1973: 7–9, 157–158; Salvadori 1973: 43–44, 388–394; Macciocchi 1974: 84–85; Badaloni 1975: 108; Gerratana 1977, 1997: 108; Vacca 1985: 62; Santucci 2001: 157–158).

4 As a rule, it may be misleading to read an author without considering the temper of the age during which he/she produced his/her writings. Obviously, to avert the risk of misinterpreting Gramsci's line of reasoning, it is advisable to also use caution with regards to his work. For a diverging view, see Gerratana (1997: xi–xviii).

5 The close link between Gramsci's approach to hegemony and the issue of workers' councils is confirmed by Gramsci himself (1923–1926: 137ff. and elsewhere), as well as by Gruppi (1972: 75) and Macciocchi (1974: 201). For a different view, see Spriano (1967) and Riechers (1970).

6 Behind Gramsci's concept of hegemony, Anderson (2002: 8, fn. 2) detects a myriad of different combinations of coercion and consensus-building; and in situations where coercion is deemed to be too hazardous, he even notes recourse to corruption and fraud – i.e. dealings aimed to enervate and paralyse the antagonist or adversary (see Gramsci 1975, vol. III: 1638).

7 Gramsci's 'civil society' is a complex compound of ideological-cultural, rather than material relationships (Bobbio 1969, vol. I: 85). For different definitions of 'civil society' in Gramsci, see Badaloni (1990: 16–18).

8 Bobbio's controversial statement that Gramsci considered 'civil society' part of the superstructure is likely to originate from Gramsci's description of 'civil society' as the arena where the struggle for hegemony acts itself out (see Texier 1990: 28; Prestipino 1990: 38).

9 The frictions that Gramsci theorised between base and superstructure were not only aimed at stressing the dialectical nature of Marxist thought, but also at downplaying the prevailingly mechanistic/positivistic view of Marxism held by the Italian Socialist Party in those days. Within a positivist interpretation of the base-superstructure relationship, the argument that the superstructure was mechanically created by the base

entailed, in practice, the cancellation of the second term of the relationship; and the resulting one-way relationship between the two terms deprived the superstructure of every autonomy, thereby negating the dialectical nature of the historical process (see Bonomi 1973: 25–31). Althusser (1965) maintained that Marxist theorists had failed to shed full light on the specific functions of superstructures and 'other circumstances'. In his opinion, Gramsci's notion of hegemony marked a considerable advance in this direction, although it was just the first step on the road towards a theory on the close-meshed relations between economics and politics.

10 The self-standing role of political action entailed in the notion of hegemony deprives the working class of its centrality and ends up by conferring greater weight on the issue of alliances (see Forgacs 1995: 66–67).

11 The argument that 'the adoption of Gramsci's theoretical model... might have averted the contradictions responsible for the self-destruction of Marxism in the Eastern world' (see Pellicani 1981: 1–2) can be subscribed to, although it is owed to a critic of Gramscism.

12 See, *inter alia*, Togliatti (1958b: 260–261).

13 In many countries, including Brazil, 'Western cultural Marxism' and 'political Marxism-Leninism' developed alongside each other for a long time (see Coutinho 1995: 126–128).

14 In his earlier writings, Gramsci described Turin as a city where class conflict was particularly tough (see Gramsci 1916a: 225; 1916b: 320).

15 'The charge of "productivism" that has been levelled against Gramsci (because of his approach to councils and the ideas on Americanism and Fordism expressed in the *Prison Notebooks*) is totally unwarranted' (Gerratana 1977: 108).

16 On the functions of workers' councils in Gramsci, see also, Grisoni and Maggioni (1973: 99–112).

13 The key contradiction of capitalist systems

1 Introduction

To develop the analysis of the issue of the transition it is now necessary to explore the issue of the key contradiction of capitalism in further depth. While opinions on this point tend to diverge, the central theme of this book – i.e. the idea that a system of producer cooperatives gives rise to a new mode of production – may come to our help.

2 The key contradiction of capitalist systems

Besides discussing the active function of thought as the faculty allowing man not only to contemplate nature and society, but to act upon them and work towards change, in his *Theses on Feuerbach* Marx made it clear that the precondition for changing and advancing society was solving its inherent contradictions. This may explain why it is deemed important to identify the most glaring contradiction of capitalism from a Marxist perspective.

The first idea to cross the minds of Marxists and non-Marxists alike is the capital–labour polarity. Quoting Godelier, for instance:

> the first contradiction we come up against in capitalism is the conflict between capital and labour, between capitalists as a class and workers as a class. The former own capital; the latter are bereft of it. The profits of the former amount to the value of the work for which the latter have not been remunerated.
>
> (1966: 29)

As Gramsci puts it:

> the control issue boils down to the question of industrial power, the question of deciding whether industrial production plans are to be framed in the interests of bankers and stockjobbers or, in contrast, in the interests of the masses; by the trustees of capitalists or those of the working class.
>
> (1921: 148–149)

The workers' state (i.e. a state where workers are in control of both businesses and government) is specific to the transitional stage from capitalism to communism, he added, and

> the workers' state is not an arbitrary choice, nor is it a vain hope. It is a historical necessity which grows out of the very circumstances created by class conflict. When, in response to the errors or ineptitude of the bourgeoisie, individual categories of working people gain a sense of their joint interests, then communists claim that the social assumptions for the rise of a workers' state are given.
>
> (1921: 149)

Accordingly, it is possible to argue that the true precondition for superseding capitalism is not the planning-market opposition, but the need to solve the conflict between a class yielding all power and a class expected to obey passively.[1] To look upon the plan-market option as the key problem – Bettelheim wrote – is a severe mistake, which diverts attention towards side issues and, hence, away from the real crux of the issue: the existence of a class – the 'bourgeoisie' – whose primary aim is to prevent workers from attaining power. This is why an occasional acceleration or stalemate in market relations at one stage or other is, in itself, not enough to make us assume that the world is progressing towards socialism or moving away from it (see Bettelheim 1969; also, among others, Poulantzas 1974; Marek 1982: 751).[2]

In contrast, Engels and orthodox Marxists did not think of the capital–labour opposition as the basic contradiction in capitalism. In orthodox Marxist terms, this contradiction originates from a mismatch between the socialised character of production in large-sized industrial concerns (where hundreds and even thousands of workers see to their jobs side by side) and the private character of appropriation (the very underpinning of privately owned production means).

According to Engels (and other Marxists), this contradiction sparks off an additional one, which is described as follows: 'The contradiction between socialised production and capitalist appropriation now presents itself as an antagonism between the organization of production in the individual workshop and the anarchy of production in the society as a whole' (Engels 1878: 260–261). At several points in his work, Engels explained that these contradictions were actually nothing but different ways of describing one and the same state of affairs. In *Anti-Dühring* (1878b: 260–261), he wrote: 'The contradiction between socialised production and capitalist appropriation now presents itself as an antagonism between the proletariat and the bourgeoisie'. Commenting on this passage, Sève (1970: 145) quite appropriately objected that each of these contradictions obeys a different logic and that, consequently, Engels could not be assumed to have described them as identical in purely abstract terms.[3]

But why is it important to distinguish between these two main contradictions of capitalism?

Lack of agreement on the basic contradiction of capitalism has a major bearing on the possibility to predict the kind of social order that will rise from the ruins of capitalism. Those looking on the capital–labour polarity as the main contradiction will argue that socialism – the social order of the transitional stage between capitalism and communism – arises when the capital–labour relation is reversed as a result of the replacement of a system controlled by capital owners with a system of worker-run firms. Conversely, those thinking that the key contradiction of capitalism is the contrast between socialised production and private appropriation will contend that the social order to rise from the ashes of capitalism will be a centrally planned system.[4]

The question, then, is: are these two contradictions really antithetical?

As I will show in greater detail further on, an interesting finding is that even those who look upon the capital–labour conflict as the most glaring contradiction and draw a clear-cut distinction between this contradiction and the socialised production/private appropriation contrast may contend that the latter helps ignite the former as it escalates and undergoes maturation.

This requires answering the question regarding whether an escalating capital–labour conflict is actually a condition precedent for its solution. But before I expatiate on this issue, it is probably expedient to examine a 'querelle' between Godelier and Sève, which may shed further light on the subject of this chapter.[5]

3 A 'querelle' between Godelier and Sève

Describing Marx's analysis of the contradictions of capitalism as a rigorous scientific approach founded on a sound distinction between economic science and ideology, the Structuralist Maurice Godelier claimed that the main contradiction is not the capital–labour opposition. This contradiction – he argued – is internal to capitalist production relations and specific to capitalism and, due to its specificity, it necessarily connotes the system right from the outset and reproduces itself incessantly, as long as capitalism exists.

In fact, Godelier (1970) argued, the most glaring contradiction within the capitalist mode of production is a mismatch between the social character of productive forces and the private nature of the means of production. This contradiction, he added, is not internal, but external to the mode of production. It originates from a structural discrepancy between growingly socialised productive forces and persistently private production relations, arises at a given stage in the evolution of productive forces (specifically upon the rise of industry) and is consequently not coeval with capitalism. Hence, Godelier concluded, Marx dealt with two different types of contradictions. One of these, Godelier claims, is a structural discrepancy that is internal to production relations and is the first to arise; and although it changes during the transition from free competition to monopoly, it persists over the whole course of capitalism. The other type of contradiction, he adds, arises at successive steps in-between the two structural elements of the mode of production, relations of production and productive forces. This explains Godelier's claim that the contrast between socialised production and private appropriation is the key contradiction of capitalism.

At this point, it is worth trying to establish if Godelier's line of reasoning is correct.

According to Sève (1967: 66), one point in Godelier's approach is consistent with Marx's thought, while the rest of his line of reasoning is objectionable. First of all, he argues, by downscaling the worker-capitalist polarity to a non-crucial contradiction, Godelier denies the role of class struggle as the main driving force behind revolutionary change. Marx – he continues – did not think that this crucial contradiction would automatically be superseded as a result of the pressure of the evolution of productive forces; he only emphasised the role that the revolutionary efforts of the working class and its allies – i.e. the dynamics underlying antithetical production relations – were bound to play (see Sève 1967: 67). And insomuch as it is true that class struggle is the solution, he asked himself, how can one claim, from a strictly Marxian perspective, that such intrinsically contradictory capitalist production relations should not self-breed the preconditions necessary for their solution? In Marx, he added, the dynamics behind the evolution of productive forces will clash and cause conflict with production relations from within, rather than from without, because they self-generate the external and internal prerequisites for superseding class antagonism.

An additional point of Godelier's approach to which Sève takes exception is the idea that the conflict between socialised production and private appropriation does not date back to the very origins of capitalism – i.e. his contention that productive forces were initially pressed into action by the capitalist production relations and that the opposite applies to a later stage only. If this should hold true, Séve objects, growth rates would have to slow down *pari passu* with the advancement of capitalism, which they do not. In fact, historical evidence has proven that they are usually slack in early capitalist phases and tend to accelerate at mature capitalist stages. Capitalist systems, Sève remarks, have always been characterised by contradictory relations between productive forces and production relations and, accordingly, by contradictory growth trends. Engels himself emphasised this point when he spoke of these two contradictions as coeval with capitalism and (as mentioned above) of the socialised production versus private appropriation contradiction as an antagonism between the proletariat and the bourgeoisie.

From Sève's perspective, Godelier's mistake is to have ignored such a crucial Marxian notion as the mode of production. In Marx, the phrase mode of production designates a blend of two elements, production forces and production relations. Far from being 'two distinct things' (as argued by Godelier), in Marx they are closely related to each other. Concluding, then, Sève's main objection is that the crucial contradiction of capitalism is internal to the mode of production, rather than an external opposition between two distinct structures.[6]

What should one say about this debate? In my opinion, the most significant objection raised in the debate about the key contradictions of capitalism is that the two main contradictions will both be superseded upon the reversal of the

capital–labour relation and that this applies even if one attaches equal importance to either of them, as both Godelier and Sève do. In addition to solving the
capital–labour contradiction, democratic management will turn privately-owned
production means into collective property and thereby cancel the discrepancy
between socialised production and private appropriation.

In point of fact, this chapter's train of reasoning so far is open to at least one
objection. Marx distinguished between an *a priori* and an *a posteriori* coordination mechanism; the former, he argued, is specific to the firm, where a global
process is devised by tailoring goals to available resources, whereas the latter,
which is typical of markets, is devised by reference to equilibrium points generated by the competitive mechanism from time to time (see Bidet 2005: 285). If
this holds true, there are reasons for arguing that while central planning helps
supersede this contradiction thanks to the adoption of *a priori* coordination in
both cases, a system of cooperative firms, which does not abolish markets, leaves
this contradiction unaltered.

To counter this objection, one may answer that, as maturation is a necessary
assumption for the solution of a contradiction, the question to be answered is
which of the two main contradictions – the capital–labour conflict or the plan-
market opposition – will reach maturity in due course.

4   A cursory historical review

The argument that there are two possible forms of 'Marxist socialism' is confirmed by examining the course of history.

Around 1870, when Marxism was gaining a stable foothold, the advocate of
firm self-management Pierre-Joseph Proudhon and the radical Anarchist Mikhail
Bakunin, who preached of the destruction of the state through violent means,
still enjoyed much prestige, whereas Marx and Engels conceived of them as their
adversaries and were forcefully opposing their teachings. This state of affairs
changed when syndicalism took the place of anarchism.

At the turn of the century, most German Marxists had embraced the ideas
propounded by Engels late in life – i.e. a statist version of Marxism envisaging a
peaceful parliamentary transition to socialism. In contrast, the successors of the
Anarchists, the Syndicalists, had made a radical break with Bakhunin (not a theoretician proper) and were propounding an anti-statist and anti-authoritarian
version of Marxism. In other words, instead of calling for a radical revolt against
capitalism and the state, the Syndicalists were upholding a form of socialism that
was not inimical to Marxism and were working towards helping workers gain
control of industry, without repudiating the state. It hardly comes as a surprise
that by 1889 the statist Social-Democrats and the anti-authoritarian Syndicalists
had permanently joined the Second International. Although the Anarchists did
not disappear from the political arena overnight, they became less and less influential. In place of the fierce clashes between Anarchists and Marxists that had
precipitated the failure of the First International, the age witnessed less radical
confrontations between Syndicalists and Marxists. The French Syndicalists,

including the orthodox Marxist Jules Guesde and Paul Brousse, kept alive the memory of the Paris Commune and forcefully propounded a labourist version of Socialism. The one thing to be emphasised – let this be repeated – is that Social-Democrats and Syndicalists worked side by side within the Second International and that their differences of opinion concerning 'revisionism' and 'Milleran-dism' (the option, for socialists, to join bourgeois governments) did not result in a split.

Although Marx did theorise the death of the state, the 'libertarian' strain of Marxism reflects, in the main, the anti-centralist and anti-statist stances of the Syndicalists. Consequently, although the idea of a form of socialism typified by publicly owned means of production and democratic firm management has its roots in Marxian writings, it is ultimately a child of the Anarcho-Syndicalists. The publication of the *Critique of the Gotha Programme* in 1875 made it clear that Marx had completed his turn to statism and that this entailed putting off the actualisation of his libertarian ideas to a remote future assumed to witness the emergence of a communistic system without markets. Similarly, when the German Social-Democrats embraced the gradual approach theorised by Engels in old age, they started professing statism openly and deferred the implementa-tion of the Marxian idea of the death of the state till doomsday. The political strategies framed by the German Marxists within the Second International had little in common with the ideas that Marx propounded during the time which he thought of himself as the heir of the French Revolution – e.g. his writings on the Paris Commune. Although the German Social-Democrats advocated statism, their political programme called for action to democratise the state and never as much as mentioned the principle of the dictatorship of the proletariat that the Bolsheviks took up after the 1917 revolution.

Today, it can be concluded, in retrospect, that the alliance between Social-Democrats and Syndicalists can in part be understood if we bear in mind that the *Economic-Philosophical Manuscripts* written by the younger Marx were the work of a humanist, rather than a statist.

At this time, however, the rival factions were the gradualist pro-statism German Marxists on the one hand and, on the other, the anti-authoritarian revo-lutionary French Marxists quarrelling over the comparative power positions of trade unions versus the Party – with the Social-Democrats advocating the subor-dination of trade unions to the Party and the Syndicalists supporting the opposite view. Moreover, whereas the former set themselves up as the guardians of orthodox Marxism, the latter, despite being much more fiery revolutionaries than the former, cared far less for orthodoxy. The minds of most Syndicalists were shaped both by Marxism and the memory of the Paris Commune and by the teachings of Pierre-Joseph Proudhon.

In short, for a long period of time (until after the Bolshevik Revolution), post-1890 Marxists showed themselves open to two different stances (and are becom-ing so again today): the 'German' social-democratic programme envisaging a gradual and peaceful road to power, the creation of a statist social order and the final establishment of socialism on the one hand; on the other hand, the

Syndicalist anti-statist stance of the French, who advocated a form of socialism characterised by self-managed firms, but who did not repudiate the idea of a violent revolution.

In the words of Sabine (1937: 588): while taking Hegel as a starting point, Marx dropped the idea that nations are the real agents of social history (a point which was hardly consistent with Hegel's overall system) and substituted the topos of warring social classes for warring nations. By so doing, he changed Hegelism from a distinctive political doctrine into a new and powerful form of social radicalism. This may help explain why Marx's statist ideas can be said to derive directly from Hegel, whereas the Syndicalist strain of Marxism is more closely associated with French syndicalism and turns around the idea that history is the chronicle of class struggle over time.

5 On the dynamics of the plan-market contradiction

As mentioned above, according to orthodox Marxists, the revolution sparked off by a mounting conflict between socialised production and private distribution is the adoption of central planning.

Lenin spelt this out in bold letters. In *The Impending Catastrophe and How to Combat It*, a pamphlet written on the eve of the October Revolution, he clearly stated that the material preconditions for the transition to socialism were created during the state-controlled monopoly capitalism phase, which he termed 'state capitalism' and described as the 'ante-chamber' of socialism or 'the rung on the ladder of history between which and the rung called socialism there are no inter-mediate rungs' (see Lenin 1917b: 341).

Capitalism differs from pre-capitalist systems – the first Lenin wrote – because it is characterised by close interconnections between its production branches and, hence, by an increasing interdependence between production activities. At the monopoly capitalism stage, he argued, these interdependencies reach levels at which control over production is taken over by the banking system. As pointed out by Hilferding, in Lenin's approach the banking system plays a major role in this process, and banks are the vital ganglia of modern cap-italist organisation. Thanks to the involvement of banks in trade and industry, Lenin argued, the banking system reaches a concentration level from which it appears as the trunk from which the bulk of business activities branch out and as a basic factor accelerating such interconnections and concentration.

In Lenin's approach, on the one hand, the capitalist state tends to exacerbate capitalist exploitation due to these interconnections, the resulting interdepend-ence of production activities and increasing concentration levels, specifically by steering and controlling production in the interests of business magnates and the propertied class; on the other, the banking system paves the way for the advent of socialism, since 'a large-scale capitalist economy, by its very technique, is socialised economy' (Lenin 1917b: 322). 'If a huge capitalist undertaking becomes a monopoly, it means that it serves the whole nation' (Lenin 1917b: 340), because it works for millions of people and, even more importantly, whether directly or indirectly, it 'unites by its operations thousands and tens of thousands families' (Lenin 1917b: 322). In Lenin's approach, therefore, socialism is 'merely state-capitalist monopoly which is made to serve the interests of the whole people and has to that extent ceased to be capitalist monopoly' (Lenin 1917b: 340); as a result, it will be established as soon as the state of capitalists and landowners is replaced with a state intending to abolish all privileges and introduce the fullest level of democracy.

In short, in Lenin's opinion, ever closer interconnections between industrial branches and central planning pave the way for the nationalisation of the production apparatus as a whole and set off a head-on clash with private appropriation. And at that stage, the first Lenin argued, the nationalisation of production means, while triggering the socialisation of production activities, turns distribution into a socialised activity (because decreed by the state), thereby sweeping away the most glaring contradiction of capitalism. Both production and distribution turn into state-controlled activities.

What should one say of this approach? A close look at the contemporary scene is enough to show that it is no reliable proxy for the situation prevailing in the present day, when the competitive pressure of a globalised economy is obliging businesses to opt for more flexible and cost-effective organisational structures and is thereby generating a proliferation of smaller-sized firms. Throughout the world, businesses are joining together to form 'network systems' founded on a key role of product-, transport- and telecommunications-related links. In Italy, for instance, from the mid-1960s onwards, vertically integrated 'column-fashion' business groups have been gradually replaced by 'network system groups', where each firm specialises in one or a few production process steps and links up to the remaining network businesses along an 'assembly line' of sorts. The effect of this process has been a marked increase in the number of comparatively small-sized firms. In Italy, this business downsizing process was sparked off both by the transfer of part of the manufacturing processes of large-sized concerns to smaller associated firms and by the creation of horizontally integrated chains of smaller firms, which started exchanging finished and semi-finished articles, as well as services. And thanks to the networking model, chains of smaller manufacturing firms have been able to thrive on world markets.

Moreover, in due course, the service sector tends to expand to the detriment of the industrial sector to become predominant; and service firms are usually fairly small in size.

In the light of this, it can be denied that the discrepancy between socialised production and private distribution is still on the increase.

6 Is planning the solution?

Inasmuch as one thinks that the crucial contradiction of capitalism is the socialised production-private appropriation opposition, to what extent – this chapter moves on to ask – can planning help supersede this contradiction?

If the train of reasoning adopted in the previous section is correct, this contradiction will not be further accelerating and, as a result, nothing suggests that it will be superseded as a matter of course. However, the idea that the fundamental contradiction of capitalism will be swept away upon the establishment of a centrally planned system is also contradicted by another reflection. Even though Marx rated the discrepancy between socialised production and private appropriation as the severest contradiction of capitalism, unlike Lenin and many other Marxists he did not assume it to be at the root of the mismatch between planned production and anarchical distribution. In actual fact, this second contradiction is not a corollary of the first, but was theorised by Engels and Lenin in connection with their approach to transition.

Marx's analysis of the contradictions in capitalism was mainly developed in the third volume of *Capital*, where one reads:

> We have seen how the growing accumulation of capital involves its growing concentration.... Capital shows itself more and more to be a social power – with the capitalist as its functionary – a power that no longer stands in any possible kind of relationship to what the work of one particular individual can create, but an alienated social power which has gained an autonomous position and confronts society as a thing, and as the power that the capitalist has through this thing. The contradiction between the general social power into which capital has developed and the private power of the individual capitalists over these social conditions of production develops ever more blatantly while this development also contains the solution to this situation.
>
> (1894a: 373)

An additional relevant quote is found in the first volume of *Capital* (1867: 826): 'The centralization of production means and the socialization of labour reach a level at which they become incompatible with their capitalist integument. This integument bursts asunder. The knell of capitalist private property sounds. The expropriators are expropriated'.

These passages from Marx clearly suggest an escalating contradiction between socialised production activity and privately-owned production, but not a contradiction between planned production activities and anarchical distribution – a subject that Marx never concerned himself with in any of his writings.

As a result, it is possible to conclude that while Marx rated nationalised means of production as an essential component of a socialist revolution, he did not establish a precise link between revolution and central planning.[7]

7 Is the capital–labour contradiction systematically escalating?

Conversely, the claim that an escalating capital–labour confrontation paves the way for reversing the capitalist capital–labour relation can hardly be called into question. Bourgeois individualism necessarily breeds a tendency towards proletarian collectivism. The association emerges as a counterpart to the capitalist, and the shopkeeper is matched by the cooperative – Gramsci wrote (1918a: 189), and then posed the question of the causes that might explain the increasing tendency of workers to be joined into cooperatives.

As is well known, technological evolution is currently moving in the opposite direction to Fordism. As a result, at this stage the argument that the advent of economic democracy is being expedited by the degradation of human labour caused by Fordism and Taylorism is unwarranted. Does this validate the opposite assumption that the higher educational and expertise levels required by modern technology are expediting the transition to democratic firm management and, hence, restoring momentum to labour management theory? According to Laibman (2006: 315–316), there is a stage, in the evolution of production processes, at which efficiency and productivity gains become strictly dependent on autonomy, creativity and critical discernment, as well as modes of behaviour supported by sound criteria. From this, he argues, it follows that when this threshold is reached and people interiorise the idea that quality and productivity are inextricably interconnected, the high road to socialism will be followed through as a matter of course.

This idea is widely shared. By general agreement (see, for instance, Ben Ner 1987, 1988: 295–296), the living standard of workers is a major determinant of both the advantages granted to labour-managed firms and the difficulties they come up with. There is evidence that workers become less averse to risk and develop greater entrepreneurial skills accordingly as their income levels increase. This is why I agree with Zamagni that 'as human and social capital acquire a greater strategic role than physical and financial capital, the overriding importance of democratic governance modes becomes more and more evident also on a strictly economic plane' (Zamagni 2006: 60). Indeed, the greater a worker's educational levels and qualifications, the less he will be prepared to work at the behest of another and the more he will tend to acquire the abilities necessary to run a firm first-hand. According to Bowles and Gintis (1996a: 82), higher-income workers find it more convenient to work for a firm that they run directly. Very often, workers in self-managed firms have the feeling that their incomes may be at risk and that they may prove unable to finance a decent standard of living for their families, but this feeling recedes in proportion to increases in income. In the words of Rosselli (1930: 453), 'the call for worker control … reflects the emergence of a new kind of average workman, whose dignity requires not only material improvements, but the assertion of an autonomous personality both within and outside the factory'.

Hayek (1960) described coercion as a social evil that turns a useful, thinking individual into a lifeless tool for the achievement of another's ends. That is why the abolition of hired labour in an employee-managed economy would result in the emergence of a fully democratic system where workers, freed from coercion from employers, would cease being alienated. As a result, anyone thinking, like Marx, that mankind will gradually gain more and more freedom (even though via the most tortuous of paths) can hardly doubt that democratic firm management is bound to become a reality at some point in time. In the words of Lukàcs (1968a: 34), 'Marx, much like German philosophers and chiefly Hegel, conceived of world history as a unitary process and the highroad towards liberation'.[8]

In short, it is reasonable to assume that labour management is bound to make headway in history accordingly as manual labour loses importance and workers acquire greater educational and professional qualifications (see, for example, Mandel 1973: 349).[9]

The widening contrast between capital and labour – let this be re-emphasised – is the offshoot of a contradiction between productive forces that change over time. On the one hand, the working class is acquiring ever greater entrepreneurial skills; on the other, production relations are still controlled by capitalists, because it is capitalists that run enterprises.[10]

According to Proudhon, revolution is inevitable, since the division of labour, while admittedly adding to the qualifications of workers, simultaneously worsens their condition through the parcelling out of jobs that it entails (see Ansart 1967: 39–40).

As pointed out by Harman:

> Gramsci often uses the bourgeois struggle for power against feudalism as a metaphor for the workers' struggle for power against capitalism. In point of fact, this comparison is highly misleading. As capitalist production relations are closely associated with commodity production, which may arise within feudal society, the bourgeoisie can use its growing economic dominance to build up its ideological position within the framework of feudalism before seizing power. Conversely, the only way for the working class to become economically dominant is by taking collective control of means of production – an aim which requires rallying to arms in order to seize political power.
>
> (1977: 107)

On this point, however, it is Gramsci, not his critic, who is right.

But there is more to this. Even abstracting from the class essence of the capital–labour contrast, it is possible to argue that today, 'at all of the institutional levels that make up the galaxy of our globalised world people are busily re-writing the existing catalogue of rights – providing different readings of long-established rights, adding new ones' and, simultaneously, 'putting in place manoeuvres designed to nullify them all' (Rodotà 2012: 4).

From my perspective, the reflections developed in this section lead up to the following conclusion. From the undeniable need to keep socialism apart from communism, it follows that democratic firm management, which solves the capital–labour conflict during its present escalation process, will breed socialism, whereas the escalation of the plan-market opposition will lead to communism.[11]

8 An analysis of social conflict

The above reflections can now be re-examined in the light of an interesting article on the evolution of Marx's thought published by Finelli in 2007.

In Marx, Finelli identified two different, even antithetical, theoretical approaches to social conflict. The first of these, though specific to his younger years, extends to later years and was variously blended with the theories that Marx enunciated after he had become a major expert and critic of political economy.[12]

In the *Economic and Philosophical Manuscripts of 1944*, alienation is the general category against which the younger Marx reads all of the topoi of modernity. From a Feuerbachian perspective, man is an organic being made for community life, but in capitalist systems he undergoes a process of ontological perversion and alienation whenever he lives in isolation and egotistically keeps apart from his fellow-beings. In other words, as a young man and an enthusiastic supporter of the French Revolution and Rousseau's claim that man, born free, is a creative being with a marked inclination for interpersonal relations, Marx contrasted these ideals with the situation in capitalist systems, where disrupted social relations combine with a mechanistic vision in expropriating and emptying individuals and determining an inversion between subject and predicate.

Discussing the *Manuscripts of 1844*, Finelli argued that Marx interpreted 'all modern economic notions as the categories of an irrational society founded on the distinction between individual and gender, between the egotistic interests of a single individual and the universalistic value of humankind' (2007: 128).

In his early years, Marx did not concern himself with the passage from 'class in itself' to 'class for itself', because the economic function of the proletariat originates from the awareness of its own alienation and tends to coincide ever more markedly with its revolutionary action. In other words, as the worker is alienated and dispossessed, he cannot look upon himself as a class, as a collective subject, which in due time will gain keener awareness of the necessity of revolution.

When Marx acquired a sound grounding in political economy, Finelli continues, his ontological outlook on society changed radically. In his maturity, he no longer thought of work as an essential category of human life. Rather, he came to think of labour power as a generic category of history that takes a step back, as it were, and suffers capitalists to set themselves up as the historical subject of modernity par excellence. However, the moment that workers come under the control of capital, concrete work turns into abstract work and stops being the unifying factor behind the construction of society: this role is taken over by an equally abstract kind of wealth, capital, which tends to change whatever it perceives as extraneous into something internal to itself and a tool for satisfying the need for ceaseless accumulation.

In Finelli's view, the theoretical distance between Marx's previous subject and his newly-theorised subject is wide indeed, because the specific function of this new subject is to strip work of its creative potential and of the fullness associated with its social nature: 'The poietic, feverishly creative potential of *homo faber*, a social being, turns into its opposite' (2007: 135). Capital – he argues – can no longer be defined by reference to the subject-object reversal module, because abstract labour, unlike alienated labour, can only be brought to bear on the relation between labour power and capital, not on the subject-object relationship.

Finelli's conclusion is that while the main focus points of Marx's earlier theoretical work were alienation and the resulting need to rise against something perceived as unnatural, in a later work such as *Capital* he had come to think of revolution as determined by changes in the balance of powers between classes.

The question now is: is this conclusion convincing and, above all, is it consistent with the reflections in the previous section? As far as I can see, it is acceptable for anyone thinking that higher educational and income levels are the prerequisite for the working class to develop firm management skills and, consequently, that revolution is the offshoot of changing power relations between classes and the determination of workers to abolish hired labour and substitute labour for capital in the management of firms.

9   The main contradiction of capitalism and the essence of dialectics

At this point, one comes to the core point of the entire issue. The idea that the post-capitalist mode of production can be predicted by reference to the key contradiction of capitalism suggests analysing Marx's dialectical method. The moment that one determines the real characteristics of the dialectical method that Marx took over from Hegel, then we will be in a position to demonstrate that the new mode of production to emerge from the ashes of capitalism is a democratic firm system.

From Cohen's interesting analysis of the Hegelian core of Marx's dialectical method, one learns that all living beings unfold their inner nature in outward forms throughout their growth, and that the moment they have fully realised their nature and attained full maturity, they die and change into successor forms. In other words, the idea of dialectics is the idea of self-fulfilment as part of a process of self-destruction capable of generating a fresh offshoot (Cohen 2000: 46). Within the framework of such a dialectical proposition, socialism stands for the full realisation of liberalism.[13] And inasmuch as it is true that the principles of liberalism are fully realised when all those involved in production, workers and managers are free to make business decisions in line with the 'one head, one vote' principle, the full realisation of the principles of liberalism will necessitate the self-destruction of capitalism and its transformation into a socialist economy.

As clarified by Cohen, the field to which Hegel mainly applied the dialectical method just explained is world history. In Hegel's approach, world history is the history of the *Weltgeist*, the spirit of the world, which is God as He makes Himself manifest on earth through the consciences of humans. In Hegel's view, God sees Himself reflected in humans, and His self-awareness is the self-awareness of humanity. Marx reversed Hegel's dialectics. Specifically, he equated world history with the history of human industry, which is magnified by the growth of productive forces within an economic base that ceases to exist when it has used up all its energy (Cohen 2000: 46–49). Accordingly, the claim that Marx and Engels held socialism to be a self-bred offshoot of capitalism purged of the capitalist class can hardly be rated as an overstatement (Cohen 2000: 48).

In other words, if a system ceases to exist when it has realised its nature to the full, it follows that capitalism will draw to an end upon the attainment of full economic freedom. However, economic freedom will only be fully attained when the freedom to decide what is to be produced is extended from capitalists to workers and all those involved in the production – all the partners of a firm – are allowed to make business decisions in line with democratic principles. As a result, the high-water mark of capitalism coincides with its transformation into a successor form, and it is the self-destruction of capitalism that brings forth a new offshoot – a system of democratic firms.[14]

10 Coase, Demsetz, the neoclassical model and the democratic firm

As discussed previously, orthodox Marxists equate the contrast between social-ised production and private appropriation with the plan-market contradiction and think of planning and markets as two alternative approaches to production. This calls to mind that the dual organisational approach to production – within firms or via the market – was also theorised by Coase in a celebrated 1937 essay and can hence be discussed in close association with the plan-market contradiction. In the opinion of Coase, firms differ from markets, because – unlike the latter – they plan production. But Demsetz (2011: 59) objected to Coase's dual organisa-tional approach on the grounds that it entailed the conclusion that 'the price system is an alternative producer of goods'. According to Demsetz, this was a weak point of Coase's critique of neoclassical economics, because the price system 'does not marshal resources for the production of goods' (2011: 59) – i.e. because the price system can by no means be an alternative producer of goods. In fact, Demsetz's objection is out of place, since Coase never explicitly described the price system as 'an alternative producer of goods'.

This clarification is a convenient starting point for a review of Demsetz's cri-tique of Coase, with specific regard paid to the case of labour-managed firms.

Demsetz starts out from the received neoclassical thesis that production is either carried on within firms or households. In the absence of specialisation advantages – neoclassical economists argue – production would still be entirely carried out within households. Production starts being conducted in firms as soon as it is recognised that this is advantageous.

From this starting assumption, Demsetz proceeds to remark that firms arise for two main reasons: (1) because specialisation makes it more advantageous for people to stop carrying on production at home and join firms; and (2) because the organisational scheme providing for managerial decisions – i.e. direct choices – is more rational than the one envisaging exchanges of inputs in markets. Neoclassical economics (albeit only implicitly) – he continues (Demsetz 2011: 58) – traces the existence of firms to the first of the above two reasons (in his own words, 'neoclassical economics does offer a definition of the firm and a rationalisation for its existence, but these must be "teased" out of theory'), while Coase and his followers only have regard to the second reason. From the standpoint of Demsetz, therefore, Coase's claim that neoclassical economics has no theory of the firm is unwarranted. Instead of offering an alternative approach, Coase's theory of the firm is complementary to the neoclassical approach.

Whereas neoclassical economists think of firms as an alternative to households, Coase holds them to be an alternative to markets rather than households. In the minds of neoclassical economists – Demsetz argues – managers are not indispensable for the existence of firms, while Coase obviously holds the opposite view. Neoclassical economists assume that thanks to the benefits flowing from specialisation, firms would continue to exist even under the zero transaction-cost hypothesis, whereas in Coase's approach they would altogether disappear. Demsetz's conclusion is that 'there is no place for firms in Coase's framework if the price system carries the full burden of guiding owners of resources' (2011: 59).

On closer scrutiny, however, provided that it is true that there are two rationalisations for the existence of firms, then markets are both an alternative to households and an alternative to firms – and both of these views are correct.

At this point, it is assumed that transaction costs in markets are on the increase. According to neoclassical economists, the effect of such a situation is to reduce corporate production volumes (because of the greater costs incurred by firms in purchasing their inputs) and boost household production, whereas according to Coase its effects are increasing corporate outputs and declining trade volumes in markets.

In a comparative analysis of capitalistic versus self-managed firms, the effects of this situation are even more complex. By way of example, let us assume that the numerous functions performed by managers are artificially reduced to just two: purchasing inputs and monitoring the work inputs of the labour force. Under the zero transaction-cost hypothesis, managers in capitalistic firms would end up by seeing to a single task – watching employees at work – whereas in democratic firms, they would become altogether redundant as a consequence of the already mentioned tendency of the members to exercise mutual control over the commitment to work of their peers (see Chapter 5 above). In the opinion of Coase, the effect of the hypothetical zero transaction-cost situation would be to impede the creation of new firms; in the opinion of neoclassical theorists, capitalistic firms would be set up for the specific purpose of taking advantage of the resulting specialisation benefits and would be run by managers, whereas self-managed firms (as studied in neoclassical theory) would also arise, but would have no managers.

At this point, it is important to remember that specialisation benefits increase in direct proportion to firm size and monitoring cost levels. In such a situation, democratic firms (whose workforce monitoring costs are nil) would record increases in number above those of capitalistic businesses. This means that the findings of neoclassical economists (a proliferation of capitalistic firms) and Coase (a stable number of capitalistic firms) would both be proved wrong (as far as Coase is concerned, because he disregards specialisation benefits). In point of fact, in this case, capitalistic firms might either increase in number, thanks to greater specialisation benefits, or, with equal likelihood, decline in number in consequence of the greater benefits generated by cooperatives.

11 Conclusion

What conclusions can be drawn from this analysis?

In economics – I repeat – the term 'revolution' (in the way that a society is organised) designates a change in the production mode. This was certainly the view of Marx – the great theoretician of modes of production and the ways they arise, grow and die (in this connection, see McQuarie and Amburgey 1978); it is also the opinion of anyone prepared to admit that different production modes are possible and that socialism is an alternative to the capitalist production mode.[15] Ever since the earliest formulation of the market socialism theory (following the so-called 'debate of the thirties'), the claim that socialism is a possible new social organisation mode has never been called into question, either by those who look upon it as an advancement or those who rate it as an evil.

As Marx and Engels defined socialism as the transitional society immediately before communism, nothing should prevent a Marxist from rating a system of democratically self-managed firms as a genuine form of socialism. One of the first theorists to draw attention to Marx's views on self-management has commented: 'anyone equating socialism with a system where the production and interchange apparatuses are managed by workers moves in unison with Marx's approach' (see Brachet 1975: 303; see also, Damjanovic 1962; Bourdet 1974: 49ff.; Pelikan 1977: 143ff.; Lawler 1994; Ollman 1998b: 113–118, and others); and as far as I can see, the approach in this book should have dispelled any doubts concerning this point.

However, revolution can be carried through in two different ways, both of which entail nationalising means of production: (1) by substituting the plan for the working of markets; or (2) by substituting labour for capital in the management of firms. The question is: which of these options is feasible today?

The conclusions that have been reached in this chapter are: (1) that the prerequisite for the implementation of one or the other type of revolution is an escalating conflict between productive forces and production relations; and (2) that the key contradiction of capitalism is the capital–labour conflict – the clash between a productive force connoted with rapidly increasing entrepreneurial skills and production relations that continue to be shaped by the power of capitalists to make all the decisions in the area of production. From these conclusions, it clearly follows that the only way to attain socialism is through exacerbating the conflict between productive forces and production relations, reversing the current capital–labour relation and establishing a system in keeping with the principles of market socialism.[16]

Notes

1 Vacca (1967a: 333; 1967b: 253) reports quotes from Marcuse, in which the key contradiction of capitalism is described as 'an oppressive relation opposing man to nature, subject to object, which is perceived at the root of our civilisation and which generates oppressive social relations', and industrial societies are said to be 'the outgrowth of a historical design aimed to establish control of man over man'.

2 The idea that the contrast between capitalists and workers is the main contradiction of capitalism runs counter to Peyrelavade's unwarranted claim that Marx died for lack of a clearly identifiable enemy (Peyrelavade 2005: 91).

3 According to Elster, the idea of modes of production as governed by inherent contradictions is closely associated with Marx's main contribution to social analysis methodology: the idea that intentional actions generate unplanned effects. As a result, Elster argues, it is ultimately inconsequential if one describes this method as dialectics or as a method for analysing social contradictions (1985: 48).

4 As stated by Lockwood (1964), Marx examined two categories of contradictions that, respectively, have to do with the social integration level resulting from the presence/absence of class conflict and the so-called system integration level – i.e. the degree to which the structural elements of the social order are, or are not, harmonised. In point of fact, the former category reflects conflicts between social classes and the latter reflects structural contradictions.

5 In the opinion of Marcuse (1968: 124), the internal contradictions of capitalism are not only those discussed in this section, but also a third – namely, the contradiction between the growing productivity rates of the system and its ever greater destructive potential.

6 Countering Sève's criticisms, Godelier remarked that the point he had intended to refute was the idea that contradictions internal to production relations should subsume within themselves the whole gamut of preconditions necessary for their solution; all these preconditions, he added, are both internal and external to production relations, but invariably internal to the production mode. Moreover, Godelier argued that the capital–labour opposition (which is internal to production relations) is in itself incapable of sparking off revolution, unless it combines with the pressure of the production forces/production relations opposition (which, by its very nature, is external to production relations). Lastly, he objected that: (1) his emphasis on the internal opposition between capital and labour was designed to direct attention to the role of class conflict; and that (2) he had never denied the relevance of the notion of production mode (see Godelier 1970). Among those who hold the antagonism opposing the class of capitalists to the class of workers as the main contradiction behind the capitalist production mode, one may also mention Balibar, who rates it a constitutive element of capitalism and, as such, a historical necessity, though he simultaneously stresses the need that it be dismantled (see Balibar 1993: ch. 3).

7 On this point, the Marx expert Roberto Fineschi has claimed that Marx 'provided vague indications on the society of the future and not even the rough draft of a theoretical approach' (Fineschi 2007: 189; see also, Fineschi 2006: 9).

8 In this connection, Engels wrote that 'history moves often in leaps and bounds and in a zigzag line' and never in a linear step-by step fashion (see Nordhal 1982: 515). The idea that history progresses towards the full emancipation of humankind has been called into question by many commentators, including Colletti, who has strongly criticised the finalist and teleological component of Marxism (see the 1979 interview reported in Colletti 1979).

9 The subsumed classes mentioned by Resnick and Wolff (1982: 4, 5) include merchants, money dealers and lenders (bankers), landlords and mine owners, supervisory managers and shareholders in joint stock companies, as well as state administrators. If this approach to class is accepted, hordes of people would be involved, and this is the reason why I assume that the establishment of socialism is feasible today. For my part – let me clarify – I fully agree with Simone Weil (1955: 156) that 'only when there are material prospects of success should the oppressed be encouraged to revolt'.

10 Anyone believing that the transition to socialism is heralded by declining friction between opposed classes should give their best attention to the younger Marx's saying (see Rapone 2011: 169–170) that the precondition for class conflict to become an element of progress is that the two opposed actors develop an awareness of their respective roles, as well as the determination to follow them through – and this happens during the phase termed industrial capitalism and not in the decadent phase termed financial capitalism.

11 As argued by Bronfenbrenner (1970: 135), predictions concerning the transition to socialism invariably fail to specify when or where this event is expected to come about. As a result, they cannot be refuted, but are ultimately irrelevant.

12 This means that I do not share Bernstein's claim that class interests ebb down accordingly as democracy gains strength (see Bernstein 1901: 335). I must, however, admit that 'with the disappearance of proletariat class misery in developed capitalist contries, the problem of class consciousness has become an ever more unrgent one' (Fetscher 1973: 227, fn. 17).

13 In the twentieth century (unlike the nineteenth), Marx stopped being looked upon as the heir of liberalism, and liberalism and socialism became strongly antithetical movements. This explains why marginalism was received with enthusiasm as a theory that would ultimately confer scientific dignity on economic individualism (Favilli 2001: 381).

14 In the estimation of Cohen, capitalism can only be swept away by creating socially oriented firms in which capitalist competition self-destroys itself and capitalists become unnecessary (Cohen 2000: 48). Moreover, Cohen has pointed out that the Hegelian dialectical method that Marx reversed highlights the pressing need to change the world into a home for mankind by solving the issue of scarcity, which is responsible for the disturbed relations between mankind and nature that is the cause of this division (Cohen 2000: 49). The division of labour is made necessary by scarcity, which requires splitting society into classes and assigning nasty jobs to some of them. However, both such nasty jobs and, hence, class divisions become unnecessary as a result of increases in production capacity recorded in capitalist systems. Cohen's analysis of Marx's attempt to identify the new production mode via the dialectical method is not entirely convincing. On the one hand, he makes no mention of Marx's clear distinction between socialism and communism (see the *Critique of the Gotha Programme*); on the other, his analysis of transition should have been backed up by an outline of the kind of system – socialism – that will rise from the ashes of capitalism in the earlier phase of the transition.

15 In contrast, Rowthorn (1974) has rightly argued that the notion of production mode was unknown to neoclassical and neo-Ricardian economists.

16 There is no need to adopt the dialectical speculative method in order to theorise contradictions in capitalism. According to Galvano della Volpe (1964: 184):

> The methodological dimension of dialectics as a science (i.e. the concrete-abstract-concrete chain, also termed matter-reason or induction-deduction model) is little less than revolutionary: it entails that any knowledge described as scientific is not mere knowledge or contemplation; it suggests that there is only one science because there is only one method, one logic: the materialistic logic behind modern experimental science.

14 A democratic firms' system as the true socialism

1 Introduction

In the introduction, it was specified that in Jaroslaw Vanek's theoretical approach, the Labour Managed Firm (LMF) is defined as a firm that funds its investments solely with loan capital and segregates capital incomes from worker incomes. From this, it follows that the LMF is the 'pure labour' firm in which labour is internal and capital is exclusively external.

One major consequence derives from this.

In contrast to the past, when economic theorists used to identify three factors of production – capital, labour and land – today, given the lesser role of farming at a mature capitalist stage, they preferably concern themselves simply with capital and labour only. Accordingly, it seems possible to argue that capitalism arises when owners of capital (or their representatives) hire labour power, pay workers a fixed income (wages), make all the decisions within the enterprise in line with the 'one share, one vote' principle and appropriate the profits earned. Conversely, if workers (or their representatives) borrow capital, pay capitalists a fixed income (interest), make every decision in line with the 'one head, one vote' principle and appropriate the residual, the firms that arise are run by workers and the resulting system is socialism (see Jossa 2012c).

In other words, there are but two antithetical options: capital goods are either owned or not owned by capitalists. In the former case, the system concerned is capitalism; in the latter case, when firms are run by workers (and are the LMF-type), the usual capital–labour relation is reversed and the system is non-capitalist by definition. The change in the mode of production entailed in this process triggers a revolution real and proper.

In a 1935 paper weighing up the benefits and shortcomings of Marxian political economy against those of mainstream economic theory, Oskar Lange (1935) argued that the former fell short of the latter in areas such as pricing and resource allocation, but offered other advantages. Specifically, besides bringing to the foreground economic organisation patterns, class divisions within society and different modes of production, Marxian political economy mainly aims to reveal the laws governing the evolution of human society through a long-term perspective. Similarly, Gramsci did not think that Marxism would help solve the problems traditionally explored by philosophers and economists and emphasised instead the philosophical and economic insights that had flown from notions such as 'social production relations' and 'mode of production'.

In other words, the strong points of Marxian theory can be summed up as follows: it highlights a sequence of different production modes throughout history (the mode of the ancients, feudalism, capitalism, etc.), suggesting that capitalism can hardly be the last link in this chain; and it makes clear that the mechanisms and evolution of each production mode obey specific rules and laws and that individual behaviour is greatly affected by the way in which production activities are organised.

Those rating Marx's 'history-as-totality' conception as the true core of his theory of society attach major importance to the concept of the 'mode of production'. As mentioned in the first chapter, in Marxian theory, production, distribution, exchange and consumption are different links of a single chain – i.e. different facets of one unit. Commenting on this point in a youthful work on historical evolution, Lukàcs (1968a: 34) remarked that Marx, much like the German philosophers and chiefly Hegel, conceived of world history as a unitary process and an everlasting revolutionary avenue towards liberation and that the uniqueness of his approach lay in the way that he consistently prioritised a comprehensive global approach.

In the light of these ideas, the point to be analysed in this chapter is whether or not an all-cooperatives system would give rise to a new production mode and whether or not this new production mode is a socialist order. This chapter is concerned with Marxism, but not with a correct interpretation of Marx's thought. It defines capital in orthodox terms as the production's means.

2 Early theorists on cooperatives as a new mode of production

When cooperatives arose and took hold in the latter half of the nineteenth century, there was widespread agreement that they did implement a new mode of production.

Robert Owen is widely held to be the true founding father of the cooperative movement. Based on first-hand knowledge of industrial life in Manchester, the ruthless conduct of industrialists and the race for wealth triggered by the ongoing Industrial Revolution in his day, Owen concluded that free competition and the factory system were bound to breed greed, inhumanity and moral decay. On this assumption, he planned new forms of social organisation designed to do away with competition-based profit.[1] First, he set up 'unity and cooperation villages', which provided jobs for the unemployed, but eventually he came to look upon these communities as universal regeneration tools and a springboard for freeing the world from competition-based profit systems. He soon found himself the leader of a large movement, but upon realising that more and more partners of newly-established cooperatives and most of the union representatives listening to his speeches had in mind a democratic organisation aimed to help workers throw off the capitalist yoke and see to their interests directly, he had to bring his propaganda into tune with their expectations (Cole 1953).

Another well-known theorist of cooperation was Charles Fourier (1772–1837). In *Theory of the Four Movements* (1808), he suggested organising social life along cooperative lines founded on principles of universal harmony. He imagined society to be divided into 'phalanges': communities of about 1,600 people each, which were to adopt modes of organisation founded on generally accepted rules: communal life, extensive use of jointly owned assets, competence-based distribution of tasks and so forth.

Pioneers of cooperation include William Thompson, a strong advocate of trade unionism as a tool for cutting the profits of capitalists and furthering the gradual rise of a system of cooperatives to replace existing capitalist firms. Convinced of the superiority of the cooperative production mode over the capitalist mode, he strongly advocated the establishment of a system of producer cooperatives aimed to oust capitalists from the production process (see Thompson 1827).

A major impetus to the growth of the cooperative movement in Italy came from Giuseppe Mazzini, a champion of the country's unification process, who encouraged workers to get rid of the 'wage yoke' and become 'self-standing producers appropriating the full value of production'.[2] To Mazzini, capital was the 'arbiter of a production system to which it is alien'. As a result, its role was to be taken over by associated labour: associations of workers called upon to see that 'all their partners were given equal voting rights in the election of pro-tempore (i.e. revocable) managers' and were paid profits commensurate with the quantity and quality of the work input contributed by each of them. This, he argued (1935: 109, 132), would be 'the ideal revolution', since its effect would be to make labour 'the economic basis of human society'.

All this is clear evidence that Owen, Fourier, Thompson and Mazzini looked upon the cooperative movement both as an option for capitalism and as a new mode of production (see Pesciarelli 1982: 9–11).[3] Their idea was shared by Proudhon, who was probably the most powerful voice speaking in favour of the cooperative ideal and whose 'theory of an anti-authoritarian non-statist type of socialism ... opens up a new course in the evolution of socialism' (Ansart 1978: 29). Proudhon described capitalism as a close-meshed web of contradictions, the most glaring of which was the oppositional relation between capital and labour. And as he held that these contradictions could not be wiped out within a capitalist system, he concluded that capitalism was beyond reform and had to be overthrown altogether. As a result, he called for a socialist order enabling workers to organise production activities autonomously in the workplace. A recurring slogan in his work, *destruam et aedificabo*, suggests that dismantling the private ownership regime and establishing a form of emancipatory libertarian socialism were, to him, the prime goals of any revolutionary movement. Discussing labour appropriation mechanisms, he argued that capitalism was grounded in the opposition between the haves and the have-nots and the 'struggle' between capital and labour, and that privately-owned production means were nothing but loot plundered from workers by rapacious capitalists. Capitalism could not be reformed, because the precondition for any reform was the straightforward abolition of hired labour and the exploitation it entailed. Proudhon strongly argued for 'industrial democracy' or 'mutualism' as desirable forms of social organisation, but rejected 'state capitalism' as a system in which means of production are entirely appropriated by the state, instead of being assigned to workers as their joint and indivisible property (see Proudhon 1851; Ansart 1978).

3 The Vanek-type LMF as a firm reversing the capital–labour relationship

To account for the claim that a producer cooperative system organised in accordance with the rules of economic science gives rise to a new mode of production, it is necessary to start from Jaroslav Vanek's distinction between two kinds of cooperatives.

And as the description of a firm as one where labour hires capital (by borrowing investment resources), runs production activities and cashes the surplus is only applicable to a cooperative separating labour incomes from capital incomes, the point I wish to make in this chapter is that the capital–labour relation is only reversed if the firms concerned are LMFs (see Dubravcic 1970; Jossa 1986; Srinivasan and Phansalkar 2003). In other words, as this description does not apply to WMFs, an anti-capitalist revolution can only be triggered by a system formed of LMFs, which are firms that reverse the capital–labour relation.

The anti-capitalist firm proper is thus the LMF, and the fact that existing cooperatives are mostly the WMF type can probably explain why those wishing to establish a new production mode are seldom attracted to the cooperative form.[4]

A short glance at the history of the cooperative movement will confirm the relevance of these reflections. The proceedings of the earliest meetings of the First International reached markedly pro-cooperation conclusions, and the 1868 Brussels Congress sustained a pro-cooperation motion, which had been put forward with specific reference to the longstanding 'machinery issue'. Concerning the question of the ownership of production means, several delegates argued that capital goods had always been used to exploit and enslave labour and that it was high time they were turned to the benefit of the working class and given to workers as their property.

However, whereas some saw producer cooperatives as the tool with which to attain this goal, some objected that the appropriation of production means by the working class was likely to breed a new form of capitalism. At the Brussels Congress, a committee in charge of analysing this point in greater depth denounced interest-bearing capital accumulation and dividend distribution as practices of cooperatives that would perpetuate capitalism to the exclusive advantage of a portion of the working class and give rise to a sort of 'fourth estate' with bourgeois characteristics (Cole 1954, vol. II).

4 Revolution as the reversal of the capital–labour relationship

In Marx, the subversion of the traditional capital–labour opposition triggers a real and proper revolution. Indeed, if one accepts Marx's claim that the severest contradiction in capitalism is the capital–labour antithesis, we will realise that revolution is a radical change in production relations (not only in legal forms, as argued by Sweezy). In a capitalist system, the rules governing production and the motive of maximising profits are outgrowths of capital. The moment that the capital–labour relation is capsized and capital starts being managed in accordance with rules set by labour, man will acquire control of the conditions of production and regain mastery over what he himself has created.

Regardless of whether one thinks of capital as a thing or a social relation, the 'capitalism as an upside-down world' view and the description of revolution as reversing the capitalist capital–labour relation will be recognised for what they are: truly scientific propositions. Indeed, the view of capitalism as a reversed world has the same scientific standing as the distinction between living individuals and inanimate objects. In terms of scientific standing, it is on par with Keynesian underconsumption, the separation of ownership and control, the scientific revolution and other notions that today are widely accepted in mainstream economics.

One of Marx's major teachings is that those who control production control men's lives, because they own the tools that men need to pursue whatever aim they have in mind (see, *inter alia*, Pellicani 1976: 62; Bahro 1977: 23). On closer analysis, the idea that revolution is nothing but the handover of means of production from capitalists to workers and the concomitant disempowerment of capital receives further confirmation from this notion.

A mistake made by Marx (and, generally, by classical economists) may help us understand why Marx did not think of revolution as reversing the capital–labour relation. Developing his analysis of classes, Marx wrote (1894a: 1025):

> The owners of mere labour-power, the owners of capital and the landowners, whose respective sources of income are wages, profit and ground-rent – in other words wage-labourers, capitalists and landowners – form the three great classes of modern society based on the capitalist mode of production.

Marx was wrong (and so were Smith and Ricardo), because he failed to recognise that the sources of income of the three classes concerned are not wages, profit and ground-rent, but wages, *interest* and ground-rent, and that profit is a *fourth* source of income that capitalists keep entirely to themselves, since it is they that manage production activity. As a result, if workers should make themselves masters of production, they would quite naturally retain the relevant profits. If wages, profit and ground-rent were actually the only sources of income, then upon the reversal of the capital–labour relation, capitalists would continue to cash profit – their assumed source of income – and there would be no change whatsoever.[5]

This conclusion is rejected by theorists who distinguish between revisionists and revolutionaries based on whether they think of the state as an even-handed institution or a power structure to be overthrown during the turn to socialism. However, in my opinion, it seems clear that when revolution is equated with a change in the production mode, a system of producer cooperatives reversing the capital–labour relation will spark off a revolution, even though it should prove unable to overthrow the state.[6]

5 Reflections on historical materialism

Against this background, I will now attempt an assessment of historical materialism in the light of the recognised keystone of Marxian theory: the mode of production as the underpinning of material life.

In the opinion of Strachey (1956: 159–160) and Habermas (1971: 349–350), historical materialism lies open to the major criticism that it is only applicable to a free competition economy. In consequence of growing concentration (a process that Marx himself theorised) and the resulting transformation of the economy into an oligopoly, ever more increased state intervention in the economy results in the emergence of new actors, especially in politics, who are barely in line with the idea of the supremacy of the economy over politics perceived behind the materialist conception of history.

A suitable objection to this criticism is that so long as the economy is the expression of the interests of big capitalists, the state acts in the best interests of the ruling class in full harmony with the rationale underlying historical materialism.

An additional criticism is the following.

A seldom quoted 1958 book by Corrigan *et al.* and a series of lectures by Sweezy suggest an unusual approach to Marx's analysis of modes of production. These authors do not deny that the notion of the mode of production was one of Marx's major achievements, but they strongly object to Althusser's claim that its importance lay in enunciating a general law to account for the way in which modes of production emerge, assert themselves and die out. In support of their argument, they quoted a passage from *The German Ideology* (Marx and Engels 1845–1846: 35): 'empirical observation must in each separate instance bring out empirically, and without any mystification and speculation, the connection of the social and political structure with production'. They interpret this passage as ruling out the existence of a single law governing a unitary historical path behind different modes of production, despite evidence to the contrary in the *Manifesto*.[7]

Sweezy's opinion has been mentioned because it offers an opportunity for arguing that free will would be given much more scope in a system of democratic firms than it has ever had in any other system to-date. In Sweezy's article (1981), the primacy of production and, hence, of 'being' over conscience in capitalist societies is traced to the fact that the mechanisms governing commodity production are necessarily regulated by the laws of capital. If this holds true, it follows that within a system of democratic firms historical materialism would either be less deterministic or not apply at all, because the reduced insolvency risks and less competitive climate fostered by the disempowerment of capital would enable workers to organise their society at will and 'being' would again be determined by conscience.[8]

Is this opinion true?

According to Marx and Engels (1845–1846: 438), in a capitalist society

> the domination of material relations over individuals and the suppression of individuality by fortuitous circumstances has assumed its sharpest and most universal form, thereby setting existing individuals a very definite task: ... replacing the domination of circumstances and of chance over individuals by the domination of individuals over chance and circumstances.

And the reversed capital–labour relation in economic democracy is a fair proxy for this type of replacement.

6 The potential of capital versus science

The last point to be discussed has probably the greatest bearing on my line of reasoning in this chapter. As society moves forward, technological progress is expedited by the growing role of such basic factors as knowledge, science and process innovation in production. Provided the well-known Saint-Simonion prediction that applied science was bound to acquire primacy (an idea that was later taken up by Marx in the *Grundrisse*) is proved true, the role of capital or labour as the primary driving force behind production – it is possible to think – will be taken over by knowledge. As a result, the question regarding whether the management of firms should be vested in capitalists or workers and the revolutionary reversal of the capital–labour relation would both become of little consequence.

In the *Grundrisse*, Marx wrote that:

> in the degree in which large scale industry develops the creation of real wealth becomes less dependent upon labour time and the quantity of labour employed than upon the power of agents set in motion during labour time. Another power – their powerful effectiveness ... depends, rather, upon the general level of development of science and the progress of technology, or on the application of the science and the progress of technology, or the application of the science to production.
>
> (1857–1858a, vol. II: 90)

Thanks to this transformation, he argued a few lines further on, 'no longer does the worker interpose a modified natural object as an intermediate element between the object and himself.... He stands beside the production process, rather than being its main agent' (1857–1858a, vol. II: 91–92).

Marx concluded that

> the development of fixed capital shows the degree to which society's general science, knowledge, has become an immediate productive force, and hence the degree to which the conditions of social life process itself have been brought under the control of the general intellect, and remoulded according to it.
>
> (1857–1858a, vol. II: 92)

Marx's approach in the *Grundrisse* has received major attention ever since the appearance of this work in 1941. Claudio Napoleoni (1985: 75–78) has described Marx's analysis of machinery in the *Grundrisse* as the only theoretical approach in which the collapse of capitalism is linked to the labour theory of value. Napoleoni also drew attention to Marx's description of pre-capitalist societies as those in which the tool functions as the intermediate term between labour and nature, with labour acting as the initial term and capitalist societies as those in which the introduction of machinery reverses this relation, making labour the intermediate term between machinery and nature and the machine the initial active term determining the workman's activities.

In Napoleoni's view, this raised the question of whether the reversal of the man-tool relation in capitalist production processes (as a result of which tools cease being tools) meant that machines had become neutral implements that can neither be put in the service of man (as happens in democratic firms) or used to enslave him.

Napoleoni answered this question in the negative, because for machinery to be neutral the capitalist man-tool relation would have to be reversed 'just metaphorically', whereas Marx had spoken of a material occurrence that 'cannot be assumed to affect neither of the terms of this reversed relation' (1985: 82).

If Napoleoni is correct, as I believe he is, it follows that the increasing role of science in production seems to have no bearing on the capital/labour option in the management of firms.

7 Domenico Settembrini and the advent of machines

In his analysis of the Marxian view that the advent of machines marks the point in time when science takes the place of labour as the active factor in production, Domenico Settembrini (1973) argues that socialism will evolve into social democracy as soon as science comes to occupy centre stage, and that upon such an occurrence, revolution will become unnecessary.

In Marx's thought, Settembrini identified two alternative approaches, one of which was a peaceful, democratic and evolutionary form of socialism. Although the individual constituents of Marx's approach are barely original in themselves, he argued, in combination they make up a 'highly original synthesis' blending elements of Saint-Simon's science-based socialism with a critical approach to capitalism, which Marx drew from the works of Sismondi and Buret and to which he added a revolutionary twist (Settembrini 1973: ix; see also Avineri 1968).

The form of socialism that Marx and Engels theorised – Settembrini argued – would align with Saint-Simon's if they 'had not vested an active role in the workers' party and the organisational forms devised by labour to conduct its struggle: trade unions, cooperatives, strikes' (Settembrini 1973: ix). In sum, Settembrini's claim was that Marx and Engels had theorised the first post-revolution phase – socialism – 'in strict accordance with a Saint-Simonian approach, that is to say as a democratic social process', and that their 'call for a re-birth of society and the integral abolition of markets, money and private property' boiled down to 'pure reformism' (Settembrini 1973: x).

Concluding, Settembrini raised the following question: if socialists are prepared to subscribe to the teachings of Sismondi and Saint-Simon to the point of subordinating politics to science in line with Enlightenment principles, what point is there in tracing the influence of the Enlightenment on Western culture to Marx, instead of emphasising this much more straightforward link? (see Settembrini 1973: xi).

Settembrini's approach is marred by manifest weaknesses. The process he categorises as social democracy is a peaceful, democratic and evolutionary view of socialism, which – far from reversing the capital–labour relationship – preserves the capitalist mode of production. In fact, Marxian socialism is a real and proper revolutionary movement marked by the advent of a new mode of production, which will result either in the piecemeal abolition of markets and private property or in the substitution of worker-run firms for enterprises that, up until then, were run by capitalists.

Concerning the subject of the real driving factor behind production, to underrate the role of science would be a mistake, but it must be emphasised that science can be put in the service of either capital or labour. As mentioned above, the main advantage of labour management is to strip capitalists of their decision-making powers and thereby translate political democracy into practice (see also, Jossa 2005b: ch. 11).

My argument, in this book, is that the main reason why capitalism is objectionable is that firms are run in the interests of capitalists. Evidence of this is provided both by the persistence of unemployment and the contrasting attitudes of capitalists as against democratic firms responding to looming crises: the former will not hesitate to fire workers for the sake of boosting profits; the latter will tend to cut work hours in an effort to avert de-staffing. In capitalist systems, capital is the tool whereby the bourgeois class exercises its power over the economy and over life as a whole; this is why labour will not be set free until capitalists are deprived of their power to manage firms.

The upshot of all this is that the growing role of science in production has no bearing on the capital/labour option in firm management.

8 Conclusion

The reason why worker management generates a new mode of production is that the reversed capital–labour relation marks the end of capitalism, the system which arose when wage labour became the rule and which is sure to last until wage labour is abolished.[9] Ever since the appearance of Ward and Vanek's pioneer works, labour management has been addressed in a vast body of literature that covers a variety of subjects, including the management modes of worker-run firms and differences with respect to capitalist management mechanisms. From a Marxian vantage point, the main contradiction of capitalism is a conflict between the opposed interests of capitalists and workers. The preceding discussion suggests that since self-management entails the collapse of capitalism as a matter of course, the market nature of a labour-managed system is not at odds with its classification as a new mode of production.

Notes

1 Even classical economists took over this approach from Owen (see Pesciarelli 1982, 2006).
2 Simone Weil also thought (1955: 162) that 'the status of a hired worker is just a different form of slavery'.
3 Max Adler (1919: 10) reports that Saint Simon, Fourier, Owen and other pioneers of modern socialism thought that political change alone was unable and inadequate to improve the conditions of the lives of the masses appreciably.
4 In a book published in 2012, Wolff argues that a system of self-managed firms gives rise to a new mode of production, but fails to draw a distinction between LMFs and WMFs.
5 On this point, see Tronti (2008b: 68–70) and Vercellone (2008), both of whom deny that Marx defined classes by reference to their respective sources of income.
6 The equation of a system of democratic firms with a new production mode is supported by Marx's contention that hired labour was specific to capitalism (see Bober 1950: 177; Screpanti 2001).
7 As argued by Sweezy (1981: 17), the laws put forth by Marx and Engels 'are only applicable to capitalism. In other production modes, there are no *a priori* reasons for assuming that change will originate from production or gain impetus from it'. Inasmuch as this is true, neither the well-known base superstructure relation nor historical materialism as such would necessarily be applicable to all modes of production. According to Wetter (1948: 51), in ancient times economic considerations carried even greater weight in human life, since means of production were much more rudimentary than they are today.
8 In Gramsci's view, the doctrine of materialism entails a critical review of our notions concerning the way that historical necessity acts itself out in the evolution of human society; it is not the search for a natural law, allegedly unrelated to the human spirit, which governs the course of history in absolute terms (Gramsci 1948: 519).
9 In Lenin's words (1917a: 105), when democracy is implemented to the fullest and most consistent extent conceivable, it turns from bourgeois democracy into proletarian democracy, from the state to something which is no longer the state proper. This statement of Lenin's, which has aroused much debate, reflects the view that revolution, the collapse of capitalism, implements democracy to the fullest degree and in the most consistent manner conceivable.

15 A system of self-managed firms as a new perspective on Marxism

1 Introduction

One of the key points made in this book is that two production systems are possible at a post-capitalist stage: a centrally planned economy with public firms or a market economy with labour-managed firms. In Chapter 8, discussing Marx's belief that the two main contradictions of capitalism are the capital–labour opposition and the contrast between planned production in firms and anarchical market distribution mechanisms, this chapter drew the conclusion that while the latter contradiction may induce the erroneous belief that capitalism can be superseded through the introduction of centralised planning, the former suggests equating revolution with the introduction of labour management.

To advocate a return to central planning against the adverse twentieth century record of experience would doubtless be unrealistic, but contrary to modern-day mainstream opinion, this is no reason for predicting the final eclipse of Marxism. For over fifty years now, economic analysts have been theorising a system of labour-managed firms as a possible alternative to capitalism, and the viability of this system backs up the claim that Marx has happily survived a spell of near-hibernation. Unlike what happened in the past century, his name will no longer be associated with an oppressive bureaucratic system (see Bensaïd 2002: xi).[1]

In the eyes of most Marxists, since the direction in which change will spur on a post-revolutionary world is not easy to predict, it is safer to look upon the post-revolution period as an open scenario where necessity has no place. In the words of Oskar Negt (1978: 116), for example, there is hardly any sense in speaking of tomorrow. At the other end of the spectrum, however, are theorists who do not rate scenario painting as an unproductive exercise. Among them, Hutchison (1978: 197) thinks it irresponsible to call for revolution without offering suggestions on the predictable organisational lines of the prospective new social order, while Miller (1989: 6) claims that Marx's refusal to provide a detailed picture of the hoped-for post-revolutionary order would now be reckoned as both intellectually objectionable and politically non-expedient.[2] At different points in this book, however, it has been shown that Marx thought of the end of capitalism as the starting point for a truly democratic economy where individual and consumer preferences would receive full attention, and this is evidence that he was in favour of a system of cooperative firms as the organisational form for the transitional social order.

In the opinion of most Marxists, a system with firms competing in markets is incompatible with Marx's revolutionary approach. Setting out from this assumed incompatibility, Brus and Laski (1989: 6) went so far as to contend that Lange's defence of market socialism in the plan versus market debate of the 1930s was argued, not so much from a Marxist perspective, as from the position of a neo-classicist (see 1989: 52). The argument that market socialism has nothing in common with Marxism has been set forth by many other authors, including Sweezy (1968), Ollman (1998b), Ticktin (1998) and Mészàros (1995: 981), who argued that 'capital is a metabolic system, a system of socio-economic metabolic control. You can overthrow the capitalist, but the factory system remains, the division of labour remains, nothing has changed in the metabolic function of society'. Capital 'either controls you or you do away with it'.

The best way to refute these criticisms is to re-emphasise that the subject of this book is not Marx's thought, but the identification of a new form of Marxism. After all, since Marx formulated his system 150 years ago, it is natural that some points of his approach require rethinking. Indirectly, this need was underscored by de Schweinitz Jr. back in 1962, when he argued that 'it is the tragedy of Marxism that the ideologues have been in the ascendancy for so long that the Marxian system as an analysis has been perverted by dogma' (see de Schweinitz Jr. 1962: 49).[3]

An additional major point that I wish to make is that, while the subject of a self-managed system as the possible future social order has occasionally been touched upon in Marxist writings, the 'grand themes' of Marxian thought have never been analysed by reference to such a system. In 1982, Hobsbawm (1982: 7) remarked that even those Marxist political platforms that were sharply out of tune with the Bolshevik model failed to substitute democratic firm management for central planning in their programmes for the future. Conversely, in this chapter, I will be arguing that the labour theory of value, dialectics, the subject-object inversion and other major points of Marxism can be seen from a different perspective when they are approached against the background of such a system.[4] In my approach to Marxism, I consequently support the view of Derrida, according to whom its heritage is to be kept alive at any cost, albeit by changing it radically.[5]

In sum, whereas orthodox Marxists do not look upon the economic theory of producer cooperatives as the theorisation of a new mode of production, the moment one accepts the idea that a system of producer cooperatives is the true underpinning of a socialist order, we will realise that the resulting different perspective on Marxism necessitates a fresh theorisation effort. Although my suggestions for a new approach to Marxism are consistent with the idea that the true foundation of socialism is worker management, rather than central planning, the aim of this chapter is not to develop an exhaustive critique of central planning, but to provide evidence that Marxism will appear in a new light if one accepts the idea that revolution boils down to establishing worker management of firms.

The following is a list of the points of Marxian theory that I will be addressing from the new perspective offered by self-management:

1. value theory, in order to show that economic labour management theory can be used to refute the labour theory of value as a price theory;
2. the idea that the world in which we live today is turned upside down, in order to show that labour management theory can help develop a method for putting the world back in its right position;
3. ideas about the transition to socialism, to decide if it can be carried through by peaceful means; and
4. dialectics, in order to refute the idea that it necessarily entails rejecting the non-contradiction principle.

Capital will continue to be defined in orthodox terms, as the bulk of existing production means (not as a social relation) and the labour theory of value will be discussed in line with mainstream approaches to Marxism. Moreover, whereas this chapter furthers the claim that human nature is historically conditioned, departing from Marx one assumes that a 'human nature' does exist, that a system where capital is controlled by labour conforms to the natural order of things and that capitalism, the system where man is dominated by things (capital), is against nature.

2　The labour theory of value and democracy in the firm

In the light of the foregoing, let me preliminarily touch upon the subject of how commodity prices are determined in a system of producer cooperatives that do not use hired labour and whose output is appropriated by workers. The question is: can the labour theory of value account for the pricing process in such a system? Before I answer this question, it is important to mention that Dréze's comparative studies of capitalist and labour-managed economies in perfectly competitive contexts have shown that equilibrium prices in both systems would be identical in the long run (Drèze 1976, 1985, 1989).

As mentioned before, in a labour-managed system labour power ceases to be a commodity thanks to organisational characteristics, such as the employment of capital by labour and the different remuneration levels in the short run of workers of equal capacity. Accordingly, the labour theory of value (which measures everything in labour power units) does not apply to a system of LMF-type firms for two main reasons. First, labour power is not treated as a commodity; second, the income assigned to certain categories of workers would not tend to level out at equilibrium points in individual firms, as taught by producer cooperative theory.

In other words, in Marx's approach, it is the employment contract (the assumption for the existence of hired labour) that triggers the transformation of the value advanced in the form of labour in an additional amount of value.[6] The absence of an employment contract explains why the labour theory of value fails to account for the way prices are formed in a labour-managed firm system.

As is well known, a great many Marxists hold that Sraffa's critique of the transformation of value in prices has not provided conclusive evidence of the inadequacy of the labour theory of value. However, as my approach is unrelated to Seton and Sraffa's demonstration that values defy conversion into prices, it should be acceptable even for those endorsing the labour theory of value on the assumption that neo-Ricardian theorists have failed to state the terms of the transformation problem convincingly.

The ability of the labour theory of value to account for pricing in a labour-managed firm system can also be denied for at least one additional reason: the different remuneration levels of equally skilled workers in individual firms in the short run rule out the possibility that concrete labour should be reduced to abstract labour.

In Marx, abstract labour is equated with hired labour. According to Kozo Uno, it is only in capitalist systems that abstract labour is turned into value-generating work (see Ishibashi 1995: 48). Sekine, a disciple of Uno's, holds that abstract labour falls in with hired labour (see Sekine 1995a, 1995b), and Fineschi has observed that, as in the *Grundrisse*, 'the living work of a hired worker is described as abstract labour "in the making", the foundation of abstract labour is the real subsumption of labour under capital' (Fineschi 2005b: 245, 147; Fineschi 2006: 99–103; also, see Marcuse 1954; Carandini 1971: 59; Eldred and Hanlon 1981: 40; De Vroey 1982: 44; De Angelis 1995: 108; Saad-Filho 1996, 1997; Bellofiore and Finelli 1998: 53–54; Arthur 2001; Wennerlind 2002: 4; Reitter 2011: 57).[7] This reinforces the claim that the labour theory of value, which is associated with abstract labour, does not apply in an employee-managed firm system where hired labour is a thing unknown.

The abstract labour notion is one of the most controversial points of Marxian theory. Paul Sweezy (1942) described it as not an easy concept to comprehend and as labour in general – i.e. as that kind of work that is common to any human production activity. Dissenting from Sweezy, Lucio Colletti argued that Marx's notion of abstract labour is not only a mental construct, but 'an abstraction which materialises in everyday exchange relations' (Colletti 1968: lii). For worker manufactured commodities to be exchanged in markets – he added – they must first be graded and matched in terms of value, and as exchanges are made without regard to the use values of commodities, one also abstracts from the degree of specificity of the work that went into the making of the commodities concerned.

Yet even Colletti's approach is objectionable in several respects. Initially, he links abstract labour to exchange and describes it as common to every mercantile society; however, when he adds that 'the process whereby work is abstracted from the individual worker and made independent of man as such reaches its high point in the modern hired worker' (Colletti 1968: liv, note), he clearly suggests that labour is abstract prevailingly, if not exclusively, in capitalism. Colletti associates abstract labour with alienation and expropriated human subjectivity (see Colletti 1968: liii–lviii), and as alienation is greatly attenuated in a system of democratic firms (as already argued in Chapter 9), it is possible to conclude that abstract labour, far from connoting commodity production as such, is specific to capitalism only.

The true meaning of the phrase 'abstract labour' became clear after the publication of the 1861–1863 manuscripts in MEGA2, where, as pointed out by Arthur (2009: 150), Marx argued that work is reduced to a certain amount of abstract labour when it is controlled by capital (see Marx 1861–1863, vol. 30: 71, 93).[8]

Concluding, the prerequisite for the validity of Marx's labour theory of value is its applicability to a market economy with self-managed firms – a system that Dréze analysed in perfectly competitive conditions, in order to show that prices in these conditions tend to be identical with those of capitalist systems in the long run.

At this point, it must be admitted that even my own approach in this chapter may come in for a number of objections. To start with, it remains to be established whether the labour theory of value is applicable to any market economy or to capitalist systems only.

In the *Supplementary Considerations* included in the preface to the Italian edition of the first book of *Capital*, Engels both maintained that the labour theory of value was applicable to any market economy (and to a simple mercantile system even more than to capitalism) and defined Marx's law of value as a correct, though somewhat approximate, reflection of the conditions prevailing between the time when products became marketable commodities (i.e. the rise of an early exchange economy) and the fifteenth century of our era (Engels 1894: 38, 39). This view conflicts with the opinion of several theorists, who have argued that a theory measuring value in terms of abstract labour hours is only applicable to capitalism – the only system in which the notion of abstract labour is relevant. Starting out from the fact that work in a labour-managed system has no exchange value, these theorists have also pointed to a contrast between Engels's analysis and Marx's claim that his most important theoretical finding was the notion of the dual nature of work – the true underpinning of his demonstration of the existence of surplus value. Lastly, since a 'somewhat approximate' conversion of values into prices is doubtless possible, they have also argued that Engels's approach to the labour theory of value strips the transformation issue of all its relevance.

The second possible objection is that where the theory of value should actually be applicable to capitalist systems only, the demonstration that it is not applicable to a system of labour-managed firms would become redundant.

This takes us back to the already mentioned demonstration by Dréze. Inasmuch as it is true that the price formation mechanism in perfectly competitive environments is the same in self-managed and capitalist systems, only a value theory that is either applicable to both these systems or to neither of them can be rated as valid. And while it is true that the perfect-competition model is abstract to the highest degree, it perfectly suits my purpose here, which is to provide evidence that the capitalism-self-management symmetry implicit in the reversal of the capital–labour relation requires that the labour theory of value be applicable in both of these systems or in neither of them.[9]

3 The 'upside-down world' and the reversed capital–labour relation

The theory of producer cooperatives may also offer clues for a better understanding of additional major points of Marxian theory.

A considerable part of Marx's approach turns around the appearance-reality contradiction. Marx's idea that the contrast between reality and appearance is a basic dialectical opposition has even suggested the conclusion that this distinction is the true underpinning of his dialectical method (see Sowell 1985: 16–21).

According to Marx, one major effect of this contradiction is the fact that the capitalist world is 'upside-down'. While those not familiar with Marxian theory will hardly think of the world as 'upside-down', self-management theory has provided evidence that there is much truth in this contention, although for reasons which (albeit consistent with Marx's approach) depart from Feuerbach's criticisms of Hegel's speculative philosophy that greatly influenced Marx's thought.[10]

The notion of capitalism as a 'reversed world' was first stated in the *Contribution to a Critique of Hegel's Philosophy of Right*. The passage concerned runs as follows: 'This state and this society produce religion, which is an inverted consciousness of the world, because they are an inverted world. Religion is the general theory of this world, its encyclopaedic compendium, its logic in popular form' (Marx 1843: 175). From this, Marx derived the conclusion that 'the criticism of religion ends with the teaching that man is the highest being for man – hence, with the categorical imperative to overthrow all relations in which man is a debased, enslaved, abandoned, despicable being' (Marx 1843: 182). Thus, in Volume 3 of *Capital*, he states:

> In competition, therefore, everything appears upside down. The finished configuration of economic relations, as these are visible on the surface, in their actual existence, and therefore also in the notions with which the bearers and agents of these relations seek to gain an understanding of them, is very different from the configuration of their inner core, which is essential but concealed, and the concept corresponding to it. It is in fact the very reverse and antithesis of this.

The *1861–1863 Manuscripts* published in MEGA2 include a passage where Marx clearly spells out that the 'inversion' produced by the subsumption of labour under capital turns the productive powers of social work into the productive powers of capital and arises from a specific cause: the objective conditions by which work is governed are not subsumed under the worker; on the contrary, it is the worker that appears to be subsumed under the conditions (Marx 1861–1863, vol. 34: 122).

In contrast with most orthodox approaches to Marx's work, which point to a close relation between the appearance-reality contradiction and the labour theory of value and dialectics, this book adopts a different approach suggested by producer cooperative theory.

Anyone thinking of revolution as the transition from capitalism to a self-managed firm system will be prepared to admit that the reversed capital–labour relation typical of a system of producer cooperatives would put production activities back into kilter. If capital is looked upon as a material thing instead of a social relation, it will become apparent that the capitalist world is 'upside down', since control is not exercised by people (workers) over things, as would be natural, but by things that dictate the laws that are to regulate labour. From this, it logically follows that the world would cease being 'upside-down' in a system of producer cooperatives, where labour switches roles with capital.[11]

In other words, in capitalist systems, both the subject-object inversion and the appearance-reality contradiction are caused by the fact that labour is controlled by capital, man is controlled by things and labour is driven by an inherent will, which is alien to workers: if the world is upside down without common people being aware of this, appearance and reality must indeed be in stark conflict.

Concluding, then, as soon as the appearance-reality contradiction is viewed against this background, it is found to be unrelated to either the labour theory of value or Hegelian dialectics.

4 A critique by Lucio Colletti

Lucio Colletti's critique may shed further light on this point.

In Colletti's opinion, on the lips of a theorist refuting the labour theory of value, the 'upside-down world argument' is stripped of any scientific underpinning. A theorist arguing the case for fairer capital–labour relations and revolution for the sake of justice – i.e. for ethical reasons – he explains, would simply be reviving utopian socialism, instead of working towards scientific socialism. To him, ' "reality" is bereft of any worth, and "facts" are irrelevant. For ideals to materialise, reality must be negated. Reason is Revolution' (Colletti 1970: 311). In the eyes of Colletti, a truly scientific approach requires testing ideas against facts, and when the reality to be put to the test is capitalism, the right approach is to deduce the relevant criterion from reality, not from ideal assumptions. The labour theory of value – he continues – may come to his assistance, because it teaches that capital is the product of labour – i.e. that labour is the whole and capital is just a part. In other words, when Colletti was still a Marxist, he strongly opposed the views of bourgeois economists on the assumption that capital was unproductive and that those endorsing the opposite view were mistaking appearance for reality. As Colletti (1970: 311–314) wrote:

> Capital is generated by labour and labour is the cause, capital is the effect; labour is the source, capital is the result. Nonetheless, both in corporate accounts and in the real context of an industrial concern the working class is just rated as 'variable capital' and reflected in the wages and salary entry only. The 'whole' is downsized to 'a part', and the part becomes 'the whole'. This is the true meaning of the phrase 'reversed' or 'upside down'

reality.... In that it distinguishes reality from appearance, the labour theory of value posits the existence of a dual reality:[12] the reality that Marx laid bare and the reality with which orthodox economists concern themselves.

Again, Colletti's analysis is barely convincing. If one thinks of capital as a thing and not as a social relation, the view of capitalism as a reversed world has the same scientific standing as the distinction between living individuals and inanimate objects. In terms of scientific standing, it is on a par with Keynesian underconsumption, the ownership-control separation, the scientific revolution and/or other notions that today are widely shared by mainstream economic schools.

It is worth repeating that in this approach, the appearance-reality contradiction is unrelated to the labour theory of value. It flows from the insight that in capitalist systems, where labour power is used by capital in exchange for wages, workers become the property of capitalists and man's subjection to things is recognised for what it actually is: a reversed relation where what should be up is turned downwards. Consequently, regardless of whether one accepts or rejects the labour theory of value, the acknowledgement of the scientific standing of the living individuals-inanimate things distinction entails the concomitant acknowledgement of the scientific basis of the notion of capitalism as an upside-down world.[13]

As such, the claim that reversing the capitalist capital–labour relation amounts to carrying through a socialist revolution real and proper has equal scientific standing. It has already been explained that what Marxists term 'revolution' is a change of the existing mode of production. Provided that one holds the 'production mode' notion to be scientifically grounded, the idea that the establishment of a system of producer cooperatives brings about a socialist order must be categorised as a scientific proposition.

An additional potential objection to the approach taken in this book is related to the fact that Marx denied the existence of a 'natural essence' of humankind. In Marx's view – the objection runs – man changes incessantly under the impact of the existing production mode; and if this holds true, it is inadmissible to speak of a reverse 'natural relation between man and things'. To refute this objection, one may simply emphasise the understanding that the existence of 'human nature' cannot be called into question. Marx argued that 'human nature' tends to change under the impact of the environment, and this is why his approach is often said to combine 'remnants' of a naturalistic vision with the acknowledgement of the concomitant existence of an ineliminable natural element in mankind.[14] It is indeed difficult to deny that circumstances under which man is subjected to the control of production means – instead of using them to his own benefit – are 'unnatural'.

5 Can revolution be carried through by peaceful means?

On several occasions, Marx and Engels made it clear that the revolution they had in mind could come about by democratic means and be enforced by a parliament. In 1847, for instance, Engels wrote: 'the proletarian revolution, which in all probability is impending, will transform existing society only gradually, and be able to abolish private property only when the necessary quantity of the means of production has been created' (Engels 1847a: 350; see also, Engels 1847b: 101). The point that interests us here is Marx and Engels's idea of revolution as a process that can come about by democratic means – i.e. by a vote passed in parliament. In *The Principles of Communism*, Engels emphasised that, once in power, the working class would enforce a democratic constitution, for 'democracy would be quite useless to the proletariat if it were not immediately used as a means of carrying through further measures' (Engels 1847a: 350). In more general terms, Engels's conclusion of the democratic transition to socialism runs as follows (1891a: 226):

> One can conceive that the old society may develop peacefully into the new one in countries where the representatives of the people concentrate all power in their hands, where, if one has the support of the majority of the people, one can do as one sees fit in a constitutional way: in democratic republics such as France and the U.S.A., in monarchies such as Britain.[15]

Like Engels, Marx also often recommended a peaceful transition to communism. With reference to his description of universal suffrage as one of the primary goals that the proletariat was to pursue, a commentator has argued that he equated the takeover of the proletariat with a successful battle for democracy even in such an early work as the *Manifesto of the Communist Party* (Avineri 1968). Moreover, in Engels's 'Introduction' to *The Class Struggles in France*, he states: 'The irony of world history turns everything upside down. We, the "revolutionaries", the "overthrowers", we are thriving far better on legal methods than on illegal methods and overthrow' (Engels 1895a: 552). Similarly, in *Capital*, Marx attached major importance to factory legislation and, generally, the role of assemblies returned in elections by universal suffrage, besides dwelling extensively (over hundreds of pages) on the fact that the interests of the working class had often taken precedence over those of employers in parliament (see Sidoti 1987: 280).

In works published during the last years of his life, Engels discussed specific events in the economic and political lives of individual nations and expatiated on changes in the political climate recorded over the years. As is known, the collapse of Bismarck's regime marked the eclipse of policies aimed at the outright suppression of socialist parties. Reviewing similar trends in other European nations, Engels remarked that on realising the changing scene, the socialist parties of the day found that legal methods served the interests of the working class much better than the violent methods associated with insurrections could have done:

> The attempt must be made to get along with the legal methods of struggle for the time being. Not only we are doing this, it is being done by all

workers' parties in all countries where the workers have a certain measure of legal freedom of action, and this for the simple reason that it is the most productive method for them.

(Engels 1890: 78)

In a polemical 1890–1891 paper written in stark opposition to Brentano, Engels argued that the power of factory legislation and trade unions to improve the conditions of the working class (which was Brentano's contention) had been underscored by Marx and himself in a wealth of writings, ranging from *The Condition of the Working Class in England* and *The Misery of Philosophy* through to *Capital* and several later texts. However, he also added that this statement was to be accepted with caution, since the positive effects of trade union action were confined to periods of thriving business and were bound to become erratic in times of stagnation and crisis. Moreover, he argued, neither labour legislation nor the opposition of trade unions could do away with the main obstacle to the freedom of workers: capitalist relations (Engels 1890–1891: 97–98).[16]

The most pregnant analysis of this subject is found in the 'Introduction' to *The Class Struggles in France* written by Engels in 1895. Both approaches, he admitted, had been greatly influenced by the teachings of earlier revolutions, especially those in France during 1789 and 1830, but later developments – he added – had proved those approaches wrong and, at any rate, the conditions under which the proletariat was expected to carry on its struggle had meanwhile undergone radical change. Each of the earlier revolutions had resulted in replacing one ruling class with another, but the ruling groups coming to power were all found to be small minorities compared to the mass of those who were ruled. Moreover, upon seizing power, each such minority group remodelled the state apparatus in accordance with its own needs and the majority of the governed just acquiesced or even supported that minority. In Engels's words: 'if we disregard the concrete content in each case, the common form of all these revolutions was that they were minority revolutions' (Engels 1895a: 510). After each such minority revolution – he continued – the feelings of the masses always, and often quickly so, changed from enthusiasm to utter disappointment and even despair.

These reflections taught Engels that the times were not ripe for a socialist revolution; in fact, as a result of post-1844 developments and the introduction of universal suffrage in Germany in 1866, he had come to believe that a revolution was to be enacted by parliamentary means, through a real and proper majority resolution. From Engels's perspective, therefore, universal suffrage had laid the foundations for a new method of proletarian struggle and from then on 'the bourgeoisie and the government came to be much more afraid of the legal than of the illegal action of the workers' party, of the results of elections than of those of rebellion' (1895a: 516).[17]

The prospect of a parliamentary road to socialism, however, far from eroded Engels's confidence in a final victory. The electoral successes of the proletariat and its new allies, he argued, were steady and irresistible and, though tranquil, as unavoidable as a natural process. For workers to win out in the end, they must 'simply refuse to let themselves be lured into street fighting' (1895a: 523).[18]

In sum, this chapter both subscribes to Sève's classification of Engels's 'Introduction' to *The Class Struggles in France* as a well-reasoned, unambiguous endorsement of a peaceful and democratic transition to socialism (Sève 2004: 144) and Sartori's claim that 'Marx not only thought of himself as a democrat, but actually was a one in the classical and, I dare say Aristotelian, meaning of this word' (Sartori 1969: 316–317).[19]

The question to be answered at this point is why the idea of socialism as the introduction of democracy in the firm can provide evidence that revolution can be carried through by non-violent means. The answer is, quite obviously, the finding that this system can be established piece by piece, by enacting parliamentary legislation designed to further self-management in manners that will encourage the creation of democratic firms, until these end up outnumbering capitalist firms.

In contrast, the measures that orthodox Marxists deem necessary to abolish markets or substitute centralised planning for the mechanisms of a market economy can neither be enforced by degrees, nor by peaceful means. And from this, it quite naturally follows that when Marx and Engels recommended a peaceful transition to socialism, they were not thinking of revolution as the instant introduction of a centrally planned system.

6 Dialectics and the democratic firm

As mentioned in Chapter 2, the risk of an insoluble contrast between Marxism and orthodox economic science can only be averted by reconciling dialectics with the non-contradiction principle; and Hegelian dialectics takes centre stage, especially in Marx's writings on the subject of the labour theory of value.

Accordingly, advocates of the labour theory of value tend to interpret Marx's dialectic method in Hegelian fashion, as a method that rules out the non-contradiction principle. As is well known, Marx's method makes use of determined abstractions, and in the opinion of these authors the most significant of these abstractions is the notion of abstract labour as a historical outgrowth of capitalism (which they rate as one of Marx's major contributions). According to them, the claim that commodities have both a use value and an exchange value is a dialectical contradiction. In Vinci's words (see Vinci 2008: 59): 'commodities have characteristics that set them apart (because they are things and, as such, differ from each other quite obviously), but they have in common one element that makes them all alike. And this element is value'. 'Speaking of commodities with focus on quantity, we abstract both from the material characteristics that satisfy given needs and from the nature of the work which went into their making'. In Vinci's opinion, this is why Marx and Marxists think that labour turns into its opposite (from concrete to abstract) in any exchange transactions with capital and define the logic underlying exchange (which Adam Smith saw as intrinsically associated with human nature) as a dialectical notion in which two opposites are concomitantly present.

According to many Marxists, in other words, in Marx's approach, commodities are all alike, because they share one and the same component – a certain amount of abstract labour – but they differ from each other, because of their different use values, and this is the foundation of dialectics.

Hence, Colletti's comment (1979: 124–125): 'One thing is certain. The analysis of commodities that Marx develops in the opening pages of *Capital* is a clear instance of the so-called "dialectical contradiction" method'.

At this point, it remains to be established what advocates of the realisation of socialism through the establishment of a democratic firm system think of the dialectical view subsumed in the notion of commodity – specifically, the notion of labour power as a commodity.

Based on my reflections so far, it is clear that the supposedly indissoluble link between the notion of commodity and Hegelian dialectics is severed when one provides the demonstration that a system of self-managed firms neither uses labour power in commodity fashion, nor, as a result, turns concrete labour into abstract labour. As mentioned above, work becomes abstract when it is done in exchange for wages, and as democratic firms use no hired workers, such work as is done in these firms will never be abstract. Accordingly, the idea that the labour power-commodity identity is a dialectical contradiction is ruled out as a matter of course.

To repeat: the close link between the capitalism-as-a-reversed-world assumption and the labour theory of value and a Hegelian use of dialectics in Marx is strongly contradicted by democratic firm management theorists on grounds that the reversed capital–labour relation in labour-managed firms highlights a link between the notion of the world as upside-down and the finding that it is natural for man to use things and hold sway over capital (and not vice versa). From this, it quite obviously follows that the view of the world as upside-down is no dialectical proposition.

Lastly, Sowell's claim that the principal aim of the dialectical method is to tell appearance from reality and that the appearance-reality opposition is the most important Hegelian distinction in Marx is refuted by the demonstration that in labour-managed systems the appearance-reality distinction is unrelated to the labour theory of value and, consequently, to dialectics.

7 Conclusion

It is widely held that the task of painting 'the inn of the future' – i.e. to predict the future organisation of society – was left by Marx with future 'chefs'. Faced with the generic, often fragmentary treatment of the future in Marx and Engels's works, some authors, including Hobsbawm (1978: 258), warned against the risks attending any attempt to provide a detailed outline of the future communistic order. In contrast, this criticism was forcefully refuted in Rosdolsky (1955), where Marx and Engels are said to have painted a picture of the future economic and social order and those denying it are described as mere opportunists. For my part, I rate it useful to clarify the organisational lines of the future social order and to use the resulting scenario for a new perspective on Marxist thought.

Anyone willing to accept the methodological reflections developed in this book will find that they offer both clues for a correct understanding of reality and a starting point for effective practical action. Advocates of central planning will look to the state – even today's capitalist state – as a major element of progress, while advocates of a violent revolution will attach little, if any, importance to parliamentary democracy. At the other end of the spectrum are those holding that the firms of the social order, in order to rise from the ashes of capitalism, will necessarily continue operating in markets. Advocates of democratic firm management will reject the labour theory of value, the idea that commodities analysis is an instance of the 'dialectical contradiction method' and the claim that the use-value/exchange-value contradiction sheds light on the capitalist appearance-reality conflict. Due to the importance that they attach to parliamentary democracy, they will not call for any violent revolution.

The idea that the post-capitalist social order will be a system of cooperative firms adds to our understanding of capitalism as a reversed world. If this approach is correct, a number of implications must arise.

First, the socialist revolution proposed by producer cooperative theorists is a major contribution to Marxism, since it suggests that revolution is still an option today.

Second, the theory of producer cooperatives makes a major contribution to Marxism in that it helps refute the labour theory of value as a price theory, suggests an appropriate use of dialectics and clarifies the notion of the capitalist world as upside-down.

Third, thanks to the demonstration that a new production mode is possible, Marxists are in a position to restate the claim that Marxism owes its primacy over orthodox theory to a distinctive method. Conceiving of the economic system as a totality, it closely combines economics, sociology and history and has a structurally dynamic view of the economic process. It focuses attention on ideas and notions such as dialectics, historical materialism, modes of production, social classes and the contradictions typical of all the social systems that emerged over the span of history and so forth.

Due to all of these reasons, a system of labour-managed firms is a suitable starting point for a new perspective on Marxism.

Concluding, then, it is important to remark that the rejection of Marx's value theory and Hegelian dialectics far from undermines the vitality of Marxism. Marx's class analysis, the notion of modes of production, the base-superstructure opposition, the alienation and fetishism theories, the contradictoriness of appearance and reality and other cornerstones of Marxian theory are fully acceptable, ground-breaking approaches that support the contention that Marxism is still viable today. I daresay that the description of a labour-managed system as a new production mode and the finding that even detractors of centralised planning can look upon revolution as feasible may even justify the claim that Marxism today is more topical than it used to be in the past.

In the light of these reflections so far, it is possible to conclude that an approach to Marxism that is unrelated to the labour theory of value or Hegelian dialectics may even prove acceptable to Keynesian or Walrasian economists. Modes of production, the idea of class conflict, the base-superstructure opposition, the alienation and fetishism theories, the idea that appearance is at odds with reality and the claim that revolution is not only possible but even desirable are notions that Keynesian and Walrasian anti-capitalist economists advocating a social revolution can subscribe to as their own.

Notes

1 There is widespread agreement that the collapse of Marxism was precipitated by the failure of the centrally planned Soviet system (see, *inter alia*, Fukuyama 1989). For dissenting views, see Stone (1998) and the forceful argument in Cohen (1978, 2000: 389) that the fall of the Soviet Union is, in fact, a triumph of Marxism.

2 In the present day, possible scenarios of the future can barely be expected to extol the advent of the social order that Marx termed 'communism' – i.e. an economic system without markets and without authoritarian commands – and it is difficult to deny that Marx's theorisations of 'communism' must now be considered as merely utopian and, hence, as the least viable part of his approach.

3 It is the excessively dogmatic attitude of Marxists (and, to a certain extent, his inadequate familiarity with Marx's actual writings) that induced Keynes to write (1925: 300): 'how can I accept a doctrine which sets up as its bible, above and beyond criticism, an obsolete economic textbook which I know to be not only scientifically erroneous but without interest or application for the modern world?'

4 While it is true that 'everything has long been said about Marx' (Salvati 1994: 69, fn. 1), the same is not applicable to Marxism. As I have been arguing over and over throughout this book, the new perspective on Marxism offered by the idea that socialism amounts to democratic firm management is grounded in the negation of the received ideas that socialism is to be identified with central planning.

5 Labriola described Marx and Engels's writings as 'fragments of a scientific and political approach which is still in the making and … which others can and must further develop' (Labriola 1965: 190). More recently, Bensaïd (2002: 2) made it clear that Marx's work offers no doctrine, but a practical approach allowing a variety of different interpretations.

6 In capital–labour exchanges, labour and labour power are to be kept apart. Marx himself rated this distinction as his main contribution to a correct interpretation of capitalism (see Marx 1867b: 111; 1867a: 132, 313, note; 1863–1866: 994), and many of his commentators and followers hold it to be a major point of Marxian theory (see, *inter alia*, Grossman 1940: 95; Dobb 1970: 14; Hodgson 1982: 235–236).

7 Colletti has often pressed the point that, as Marx's labour theory of value is founded on the notion of abstract labour, it strongly departs from Ricardo's value theory (see, *inter alia*, Colletti 1979: 69–76).

8 For a convincing analysis of abstract labour as a notion specific to capitalism, see Bonefeld (2010).

9 The failure of the labour theory of value does not undermine the validity of Marx's overall theoretical approach. As argued by Joan Robinson (1942: 20), the theory of value, looked upon as a theory of relative prices, is not the core of Marx's approach. As a result, no essential point of Marx's approach is made to descend from the labour theory of value.

10 Hegel, writes Tucker (1961: 85–86),

> represents man as God in his state of self-alienation and return to himself. This, says Feuerbach, expresses the truth about religion in a 'mystified' form. The true statement is just the reverse: God is man in his state of self-alienation, i.e. man in

his religious life is alienated from himself .... This is the constitutive formula of Feuerbach's philosophy of religion as elaborated in his *Essence of Christianity*. Thus it was not Marx, but Feuerbach, who originally turned Hegel 'upside down'. Marx was Feuerbach's follower in this pivotal operation.

11 The close link between Marx's notion of a reversed world and the capital–labour relation is mentioned by Colletti and emphasised by Fineschi (2005b: 111). These processes – Colletti writes (1979: 70) – 'are structured in the same way as is the subject-predicate inversion' and the reversal 'affects the realities of the capitalist world', which is turned upside down (see also, 1979: 82–92).

12 Colletti holds dialectics to be antithetical to the principle of noncontradiction by its very nature. In particular – he argues – the labour theory of value posits the existence of a dual reality and consequently negates the noncontradiction principle by showing that reality is but appearance. However, he warns, the claim that commodities are dialectical units between antithetical realities because they include one component that makes them all equal – value – (see, among others, Vinci 2008: 59) is a banality and, on closer analysis, even one that does not conflict with the noncontradiction principle, since it is obvious that two things may be equal in certain respects (for instance, the same colour) and different in others (for example, in shape). An equally banal claim – he continues – would be to describe sea waves as dialectical units between antithetical realities just because they differ in shape and size, but are equal in that they consist of water.

13 One major implication of the reversed capital–labour relation is the title of workers to appropriate what they produce, a fact which is fully in keeping with a 'natural' order. Several scholars, including Comte, Walras (1860: xlvi) and Ellerman (1992: 25), have strongly argued for vesting title in workers for the products that they manufacture.

14 The idea of the existence of an ineliminable natural element in mankind is in agreement with Timpanaro's reassertion of Marxist naturalism, according to which

> by materialism we understand above all the acknowledgement of the priority of nature over 'mind' or, if you like, of the physical level over the biological level, and of the biological level over the socio-economic and cultural level: both in the sense of chronological priority.
>
> (Timpanaro 1970: 34)

15 However, Engels forcefully opposed any interpretation of his thought that would make him appear a peaceful worshipper of legality at any price (see his letter of 1 April 1895). He also wrote: 'I know of nothing more authoritarian than a revolution.... If there had been a little more authority and centralization in the Paris Commune, it would have triumphed over the bourgeois' (Engels, letter to Terzaghi, 14 January 1872: 293).

16 For some time after the short-lived 1948 revolutions in Italy, Marx continued to believe that a new revolution was sure to break out before long, but that no new crisis was possible if not as 'a consequence of a new crisis', which would cause much 'panic' (Marx 1895: 135). In the January–February 1850 issue of the 'Review', however, he and Engels wrote that this new crisis, 'since it is bound to coincide with great collisions on the Continent, will bring forth results quite different from those of all previous crises', concluding that while previous crises had been 'the signal for a new advance, a new victory of the industrial bourgeoisie over landed property and the financial bourgeoisie', this new crisis would 'mark the beginning of the modern English revolution' – which is a clear sign that they both underrated the ability of the bourgeoisie to orchestrate 'passive revolutions'.

17 On the subject of the democratic road to socialism, see also, *inter alia*, Sidoti (1987) and Jossa (2005b).

18 In connection with Engels's approach to a parliamentary road to socialism, let us mention that in youthful writings and in *Der Weg zur Macht* (1909), Kautsky declared himself neither pro-revolution nor pro-legality at any price and traced this stance to a debt to Engels (see Kautsky 1909). In later years, he changed his mind and became, of all Marxists, the most avowed advocate of the democratic road to revolution.

19 See also, Merker (2010: ch. 3).

Conclusion

What conclusions may we draw from the foregoing?

A key idea of this book is that Marxism is a theory of revolution. As such, it will remain alive as long as revolution is perceived as possible and will die out only if it is found to be illusory or, at any rate, unfeasible. History and experience have taught that the loss or deficit in democracy entailed in central planning 'is worse than the disease it is supposed to cure' and 'stops up the very living source from which alone can come correction of all the innate shortcomings of social institutions' (Luxemburg 1905: 595). Specifically, the Soviet planning model was doomed to fail, due to its disregard of such a deeply rooted human drive as self-love. Hence, it is possible to argue, with Oskar Lange (1957: 169), that market socialism and the common control of enterprises are endorsed by socialists because they offer scope for economic incentives. And as cooperation fosters positive interpersonal relationships, the need that cooperatives meet is certainly far superior to the tendency for self-love that takes centre stage in capitalism.

In the opinion of Gramsci, on seeing workers seize factories in Italy, the masses considered this action a new Russian revolution carried through in a more advanced industrial system where the workforce was both better organised and trained and accustomed to holding together in the workplace (see Gramsci 1971: 346). Consequently, there can be little doubt that Gramsci looked upon democratic factory management as an improved version of the Bolshevik Revolution (see Mordenti 2007: 60).

My aim, in writing this book, was to stress that reliance on the ultimate advent of a socialist system founded on democratic firms is a must. Due to the antithesis between central planning and democracy, where this belief should be proved wrong, the very notion of 'socialism' would be emptied of its meaning. Although social democracy is often described as a form of democratic socialism, in point of fact it is nothing but a variant of capitalism. Hence, if capitalism were proved to have no alternatives, socialism itself would cease to exist and Marxism would die out in its wake. This is why I subscribe to the opinion of Rovatti (1973: 16) that analysts of Marxism, far from fully apprehending and spelling out the revolutionary gist of Marx's approach, have been engaging in a vain effort to concoct simplified versions or philosophical implications that Marx himself had proved wrong and rejected in his day.

In a recent book (*Missing Community*), Bauman has pointed to community feeling as a basic human need that capitalism has systematically left unsatisfied. If this is true, Marxism owes its lasting vitality to a potential for satisfying a deeply rooted exigency. According to Lelio Basso (2008: 166), the starting point for any reflection on Marxism is, quite evidently, individualism, a 'child of the capitalist mode of production', which Marx and Engels accused of drowning 'the most heavenly ecstasies of religious fervour, of chivalrous enthusiasm, of philistine sentimentalism, in the icy water of egotistical calculation', as well as of resolving 'personal worth into exchange value'. In *The Philosophy of Right*, Hegel described capitalism as a battlefield where everybody's individual private interest meets everyone else's and where human personality was prevented from developing harmoniously – a goal that socialism only can help achieve.

This conclusion is suggested by the belief that the most glaring defects of capitalism, including its adverse impact on human personality, stem from an appeal to self-love and excessive individualism – the main driving forces behind economic action. This poses a need to frame a different mode of production compatible with human frailty and capable of fostering meaningful interpersonal relationships. Even before Marx, Rousseau argued that Hobbes's definition of *homo* as *homini lupus* was not applicable to humankind as such, but only to people living in a capitalistic system. Unlike Rousseau, however, Marx realised that the assumption for the harmonious growth of an individual is active collaboration with his/her fellow-beings. And Marxists must envisage a social order formed of cooperative firms, because workers have to draw satisfaction from production activity not because it is the source of their personal incomes, but because it generates benefits for other people (see Fetscher 1965: 294).

Hence, the ultimate aim of this book was to provide evidence that such a system – which we name economic democracy – does exist and is viable.

Due to the belief in the feasibility of socialism even today, I are prepared to accept both the revisionist criticisms of Bernstein (see, for example, Fetscher 1979)[1] and some of the anti-Marx strictures of orthodox mainstream economists, though not their conclusion that Marxism is dead.

An additional major aim of this book was to analyse the place of Marxism in the modern-day, globalised world scene. The moment one equates socialism with a system of democratic firms run by workers in a market economy, a great many Marxian notions that used to be approached by reference to the assumed equation of socialism with planning will appear in a different light. The insight that socialism can be combined with a market economy and that socialists are not set on substituting planning for the market reveals that Marxism is not antithetical with bourgeois political economy and poses the need to compare and reconcile the basics of Marxism with the principles of orthodox mainstream economics.

Note

1 Fetscher (1979: 259) reports that Eduard Bernstein held socialism to be grounded on democracy and ethics, rather than on a historical process. Emphasising a contrast between political democracy and economic life, Bernstein argued that all adult males in Western democratic countries had, admittedly, been given equal political citizen rights, but that in economic terms the majority of the population remained one of utter dependence. The drawbacks impeding the hoped-for attainment of equal rights for all, he argued, were principally poor standards of living and uncertain prospects of employment, and only socialism was able to pave the way for full democracy. See also, Bernstein (1899: 185–194).

References

A.I.S.S.E.C. (Associazione Italiana per lo Studio dei Sistemi Economici Comparati), 1993, *IX Scientific Meeting*.

AA.VV., 1947, *Atti del Congresso internazionale di filosofia*, Castelli, Rome.

AA.VV., 1966, *Morale e società. Atti del Convegno promosso dall'Istituto Gramsci*, Roma, Editori Riuniti.

AA.VV., 1968, *Cent'anni dopo* Il Capitale, ital. transl., Samonà e Savelli, Rome, 1970.

AA.VV., 1969a, *Marx vivo*, Mondadori, Milan.

AA.VV., 1969b, *Gramsci e la cultura contemporanea*, Editori Riuniti, Rome.

AA.VV., 1969c, *Neocapitalismo e sinistra europea*, Laterza, Bari.

AA.VV., 1970, *Il controllo operaio*, Samonà e Savelli, Rome.

AA.VV., 1972, *I consigli operai*, Samonà e Savelli, Rome.

AA.VV., 1975a, *Storia d'Italia*, vol. IV, Einaudi, Turin.

AA.VV., 1975b, *L'autogestione in Italia; realtà e funzione della cooperazione*, De Donato, Bari.

AA.VV., 1977, *Stato e teorie marxista*, ed. by G. Carandini, Mazzotta, Milan.

AA.VV., 1978–1982, *Storia del marxismo*, Einaudi, Turin.

AA.VV., 1986, *Cooperare e competere*, Feltrinelli, Milan.

AA.VV., 1996, *Companion to the History of Science*, Routledge, London.

AA.VV., 2008, *Lessico marxiano*, manifestolibri, Rome.

Aage H., 1995, The Optimum Size of Brigades, in D.C. Jones and J. Svejnar (eds), 1992, *Advances in the Economic Analysis of Participatory and Labor-Managed Firms*, vol. 5, JAI Press, Greenwich, CT.

Abell P., 1983, The Viability of Industrial Producer Cooperation, in C. Crouch and F. Heller (eds), 1989, *International Yearbook of Organizational Democracy*, Wiley, Chichester.

Abendroth W., 1958, Il marxismo è 'superato'?, in W. Abendroth, 1967, *Socialismo e marxismo da Weimar alla Germania Federale*, ital. transl., La Nuova Italia, Florence, 1978.

Abendroth W., 1967, *Socialismo e marxismo da Weimar alla Germania Federale*, ital. transl., La Nuova Italia, Florence, 1978.

Adaman F. and Devine P., 1996, The Economic Calculation Debate: Lessons for Socialism, in *Cambridge Journal of Economics*, vol. 20, n. 5.

Adaman F. and Devine P., 2002, A Reconsideration of the Theory of Entrepreneurship: A Participatory Approach, in *Review of Political Economy*, vol. 14, n. 3.

Adams J.S., 1963, Towards an Understanding of Inequity, in *Journal of Abnormal and Social Psycology*, vol. 67, n. 5.

Adler M., 1919, *Democrazia e consigli operai*, ital. transl., De Donato, Bari, 1970.

Adorno T.W., 1969, È superato Marx?, in AA.VV., 1969a, *Marx vivo*, Mondadori, Milan.

Agazzi E., 1984, Introduction, in M. Eldred, M. Hanlon, L. Kleiber and V.B. Roth (eds), 1884, *La forma-valore. Progetto di ricostruzione e completamento del frammento di sistema di Marx*, Lacaita Editore, Manduria, 1984.

Akerlof G.A., 1982, Labor Contracts as a Partial Gift Exchange, in *Quarterly Journal of Economics*, vol. 96, November.

Akerlof G.A., 1984, Gift Exchange and Efficiency-Wage Theory: Four Views, in *The American Economic Review*, vol. 74, n. 2.

Akerlof G.A. and Yellen J.L., 1990, The Fair Wage-Effort Hypothesis and Un-Employment, in *Quarterly Journal of Economics*, vol. 105, n. 2, May.

Albanese M., 2003, Le difficoltà di finanziamento delle LMF ed il finanziamento del credito, in *Economia politica*, vol. 20, n. 3.

Albert M., 2003, *L'economia partecipativa*, Datanews, Roma.

Albert M. and Hahnel R., 1990, *Quiet Revolution in Welfare Economics*, Princeton University Press, Princeton.

Albert M. and Hahnel R., 1991, *Looking Forward*, South End, Boston, MA.

Albritton R. and Sekine T.T., 1995, *A Japanese Approach to Political Economy*, Palgrave, New York, NY.

Alchian A.A., 1984, Specificity, Specialization, and Coalitions, in *Journal of Economic Theory and Institutions*, vol. 140, n. 1, March.

Alchian A.A. and Allen W.R., 1983, *Exchange and Production*, 3rd edn, Wadsworth Publishing Company, Belmont, Boston, MA.

Alchian A.A. and Demsetz H., 1972, Production, Information Costs and Economic Organization, in *American Economic Review*, vol. 62, December.

Alesina A. and Rodrik, D., 1994, Distributive Politics and Economic Growth, in *Quarterly Journal of Economics*, vol. 109, n. 2.

Althusser L. and Balibar E., 1965, *Leggere il Capitale*, ital. transl., Feltrinelli, Milan, 1968.

Althusser L., 1965, *Per Marx*, ital. transl., Editori Riuniti, Rome, 1969.

Althusser L., 1969 and 1995, *Sur la reproduction*, Presses universitaires de France, Paris.

Altvater E., 1982, La teoria del capitalismo monopolistico di stato e le nuove forme di socializzazione capitalistica, in E.J. Hobsbawm, G. Haupt, F. Marek, E. Ragionieri, V. Strada and C. Vivanti (eds), 1978–1982, *Storia del marxismo*, vol. IV, Einaudi, Turin.

Amirante C., 2008, *Dalla forma stato alla forma mercato*, Giappichelli, Turin.

Anderson P., 1976, *Considerations on Western Marxism*, N.L.R. Books, Verso, London.

Anderson P., 2002, Force and Consent, in *New Left Review*, vol. 17, September–October.

Andreani T., 2008, Market Socialism: Problems and Models, in J. Bidet, S. Kouvelakis (eds), *Critical Companion to Contemporary Marxism*, Brill, Leiden.

Angel P., 1974, Stato e società borghese nel pensiero di Bernstein, in Istituto Giangiacomo Feltrinelli, *Storia del marxismo contemporaneo*, Feltrinelli, Milan.

Ansart P., 1967, *La sociologia di Proudhon*, trad. ital., Il Saggiatore, Milan, 1972.

Ansart P., 1978, *P.J. Proudhon*, La Pietra, Milan.

Anweiler O., 1958, *Storia dei soviet, 1905–1921*, ital. transl., Laterza, Bari, 1972.

Archer R., 1995, *Economic Democracy: The Politics of Feasible Socialism*, Oxford University Press, Oxford.

Arena R. and Salvadori N., eds, 2004, *Money, Credit and the Role of the State*, Ashgate, New York, NY.

Arienzo A. and Borrelli G., 2011, *Emergenze democratiche, ragion di Stato, governance, gouvernementalité*, Giannini editore, Naples.

Aron R., 1965, The Impact of Marxism in the Twentieth Century, in M.M. Drachkovitch (ed.), *Marxism in the Modern World*, Oxford University Press, London.

Aron R., 1969, Equivoco e inesauribile, in AA.VV., 1969b, *Gramsci e la cultura contemporanea*, Editori Riuniti, Rome.

Aron R., 1970, *Marxismi immaginari; da una sacra famiglia all'altra*, ital. transl., F. Angeli, Milan, 1977.

Arrighi G., 2007, *Adam Smith a Pechino*, Feltrinelli, Milan.

Arthur C.J., 1998, Engels, Logic and History, in R. Bellofiore (ed.), *Marxian Economics; A Reappraisal*, Palgrave, Macmillan, New York, NY.

Arthur C.J., 2001, Value, Labour and Negativity, in *Capital and Class*, vol. 73, Spring.

Arthur C.J., 2009, The Possessive Spirit of Capital: Subsumption/Inversion/Contradiction, in R. Bellofiore and R. Fineschi (eds), *Re-Reading Marx; New Perspectives after the Critical Edition*, Palgrave Macmillan, New York, NY.

Arthur J. and Shaw W.H., eds, 1978, *Justice and Economic Distribution*, Prentice-Hall, Englewood Cliff, N.J.

Ashenfelter O. and Card D., eds, 1999, *Handbook of Labour Economics*, Elsevier, Amsterdam.

Asor Rosa A., 1975, La cultura, in AA.VV., 1975a, *Storia d'Italia*, vol. IV, Einaudi, Turin.

Asor Rosa A., Colletti L., Salvadori M.L. and Spriano P., 1978, *Il socialismo diviso*, Laterza, Bari.

Aspromourgos T., 2000, Is an Employer-of-Last-Resort Policy Sustainable? A Review Article, in *Review of Political Economy*, vol. 12, n. 2.

Atkinson A.B., ed., 1993, *Alternatives to Capitalism: The Economics of Partnership*, Macmillan, London.

Avineri S., 1968, *The Social and Political Thought of Karl Marx*, Cambridge University Press, London.

Backhaus H.G., 1997, *Dialektik der Wertform. Untersuchungen zur marxschen Ökonomiekritik*, Ça ira, Freiburg i. B.

Baczko B., 1965, Marx e l'idea dell'universlità dell'uomo, in E. Fromm, *L'umanesimo marxista*, ital. transl., Dedalo libri, Bari, 1971.

Badaloni N., Gruppi L., Buci-Glucksmann C., Nardone G., Agazzi E., Natta A. and Antonielli S., 1977, *Attualità di Gramsci*, Il Saggiatore, Milan.

Badaloni N., 1962, *Marxismo come storicismo*, Feltrinelli, Milan.

Badaloni N., 1972, *Il Marxismo Italiano negli anni sessanta*, Editori Riuniti, Rome.

Badaloni N., 1975, *Il Marxismo di Gramsci*, Einaudi, Turin.

Badaloni N., 1977, Attualità di Gramsci, in N. Badaloni, L. Gruppi, C. Buci-Glucksmann, G. Nardone, E. Agazzi, A. Natta and S. Antonielli, *Attualità di Gramsci*, Il Saggiatore, Milan.

Badaloni N., 1981, Gramsci: la filosofia della prassi, in E.J. Hobsbawm, G. Haupt, F. Marek, E. Ragionieri, V. Strada and C. Vivanti (eds), 1978–1982, *Storia del marxismo*, 5 vols, Einaudi, Turin.

Badaloni N., 1990, Marxismo e teoria politica in Gramsci, in B. Moscatello, *Gramsci e il Marxismo contemporaneo*, Editori Riuniti, Rome.

Baglioni G., 1995, *Democrazia impossibile?*, Il Mulino, Bologna.

Bahro R., 1977, *Eine Dokumentation*, Europäische Verlagsanstalt, Frankfurt am Main.

Baker G.P., Jensen M.C. and Murphy K.J., 1988, Compensation and Incentives: Practice *vs.* Theory, in *Journal of Finance*, vol. 43, n. 3, July.

Baldassarri M., Paganetto L., Phelps E.S., eds, 1993, *Privatization Processes in Eastern Europe*, Macmillan, London.

Balibar E., 1974, *Cinq études du matérialisme historique*, Maspero, Paris.

Balibar E., 1993, *La filosofia di Marx*, ital. transl., manifestolibri, Rome, 1994.

Ball T. and Farr J., eds, 1984, *After Marx*, Cambridge University Press, Cambridge.

Baran P. and Sweezy P., 1966, *Monopoly Capital*, Monthly Review Press, New York, NY.

Baratta G., 1999, Hall, Said, Balibar, Gramsci tra noi, in G. Baratta and G. Liguori (eds), *Gramsci da un secolo all'altro*, Editori Riuniti, Rome.

Baratta G. and Liguori G., eds, 1999, *Gramsci da un secolo all'altro*, Editori Riuniti, Rome.

Bardhan P., 1993, On Tackling the Soft Budget Constraint in Market Socialism, in P. Bardhan and J.E. Roemer (eds), *Market Socialism: The Current Debate*, Oxford Economic Press, New York, NY.

Bardhan P. and Roemer J.E., 1992, Market Socialism: A Case for Rejuvenation, in *Journal of Economic Perspectives*, vol. 6, n. 3, Summer.

Bardhan P. and Roemer J.E., eds, 1993, *Market Socialism: The Current Debate*, Oxford Economic Press, New York, NY.

Barlett W., Cable J., Estrin S., Derek C. and Smith S., 1992, Labour-Managed versus Private Firms: An Empirical Comparison of Cooperatives and Private Firms in Central Italy, in *Industrial and Labour Relations Review*, vol. 46, n. 1.

Barone E., 1908, Il Ministro della produzione in uno stato collettivista, in *Giornale degli economisti*, vol. 34, n. 36, September–October.

Barro R.J., 1996, Democracy and Growth, in *Journal of Economic Growth*, vol. 1, n. 1, March.

Barry B., 1973, *La teoria liberale della giustizia*, ital. transl., Giuffrè, Milan, 1994.

Barsony J., 1982, Tibor Liska's Concept of Socialist Entreprenorship, in *Acta Oeconomica*, vol. 28, nn. 13–14.

Bartlett W., Cable E.J., Estrin S., Jones D.C. and Smith S.C., 1992, Labor-Managed Cooperatives and Private Firms in North Central Italy: An Empirical Comparison, in *Industrial and Labor Relations Review*, vol. 46, n. 1.

Basso L., 1969, Appunti sulla teoria rivoluzionaria in Marx ed Engels, in AA.VV., 1969c, *Neocapitalismo e sinistra europea*, Laterza, Bari.

Basso L., 1971, Introduction, in R. Luxemburg, *Lettere ai Kautsky*, Editori Riuniti, Rome.

Basso L., AA.VV., 1977, *Stato e teorie marxiste*, ed. by G. Carandini, Mazzotta, Milan.

Basso L., 2008, *Socialità e isolamento: la singolarità in Marx*, Carocci, Rome.

Basterretxea I. and Martinez R., 2012, Impact of Management and Innovation Capabilities on Performance: Are Cooperatives Different?, in *Annals of Public and Cooperative Economics*, vol. 83, n. 3, September.

Bataille G., 1976, *La limite de l'utile (fragments)*, Gallimard, Paris.

Bauer O., 1920, Bolscevismo o socialdemocrazia, in G. Marramao, 1977, *Austromarxismo e socialismo di sinistra tra le due guerre*, La Pietra, Milan.

Bauer R., 1963, Presente e futuro dell'impresa cooperativa, in W. Briganti, 1982, *Il movimento cooperativo in Italia. Scritti e documenti, dal 1854 al 1980*, vol. III, Editrice cooperativa, Rome.

Baumol W., 1953, Firms with Limited Money Capital, in *Kyklos*, vol. 6, n. 2.

Becattini G., 1989, Mercato e comunismo nel pensiero di A. Marshall, in B. Jossa (ed.), *Teoria dei sistemi economici*, UTET, Turin.

Beckerman W., 1986, *Wage Rigidity and Employment*, Duckworth, London.

Bedeschi G., 1972, *Alienazione e feticismo nel pensiero di Marx*, Laterza, Bari.

Bell D., 1962, The Debate on Alienation, in L. Labedz, *Revisionism. Essays in the History of Marxist Ideas*, Allen & Unwin, New York, NY.

Bell J.R., 1995, Dialectics and Economic Theory, in R. Albritton, T.T. Sekine, *A Japanese Approach to Political Economy*, Palgrave, New York, NY.

Bell J.R., 2009, *Capitalism and the Dialectic; The Uno-Sekine Approach to Marxian Political Economy*, Pluto Press, London.

Bellas C., 1972, *Industrial Democracy and Worker-Owned Firm: A Study of Twenty-One Plywood Companies in the Pacific Northwest*, Praeger, New York, NY.

Bellofiore R., ed., 1998, *Marxian Economics; A Reappraisal*, Palgrave, Macmillan, New York, NY.

Bellofiore R., 2007, *Da Marx a Marx; un bilancio dei marxismi italiani del Novecento*, manifestolibri, Rome.

Bellofiore R. and Finelli R., 1998, Capital, Labour and Time: The Marxian Monetary Labour Theory of Value as a Theory of Exploitation, in R. Bellofiore (ed.), *Marxian Economics; A Reappraisal*, Palgrave, Macmillan, New York, NY.

Bellofiore R. and Fineschi R., eds, 2009, *Re-Reading Marx; New Perspectives after the Critical Edition*, Palgrave Macmillan, New York, NY.

Ben Ner A., 1987, Producer Cooperatives: Why Do They Exist in Market Economies?, in W. Powel (ed.), *The Non Profit Sector: A Research Handbook*, Yale University, New Haven, CT.

Ben Ner A., 1988, The Life-Cycle of Worker-Owned Firms in Market Economies: A Theoretical Analysis, in *Journal of Economic Behavior and Organization*, vol. 10, n. 3.

Ben Ner A., Han T. and Jones D.C., 1996, The Productivity Effects of Employee Participation in Control and in Economic Returns: A Review of Empirical Evidence, in U. Pagano and R. Rowthorn (eds), *Democracy and Efficiency in the Economic Enterprise*, Routledge, London.

Ben Ner A., Montias J.M. and Neuberger E., 1993, 'Basic Issues' in Organizations: A Comparative Perspective, in *Journal of Comparative Economics*, vol. 17, n. 2, June.

Benham L. and Keefer P., 1991, Voting in Firms: The Role of Agenda Control, Size and Voter Homogeneity, in *Economic Inquiry*, vol. 29, n. 4, October.

Benjamin W., 1995, *Angelus Novus; saggi e frammenti*, Einaudi, Turin.

Bensaïd D., 2002, *Marx for Our Times*, Verso, London.

Berger S. and Dore P., eds, 1996, *Differenze nazionali e capitalismo globale*, Il Mulino, Bologna.

Berle A. and Means G., 1932, *The Modern Corporation and Private Property*, revised edn, Harcourt Brace & World, New York, NY, 1967.

Berlin I., 1963, *Marx*, ital. transl., La Nuova Italia, Florence, 1967.

Berman M.D., 1977, Short-Run Efficiency in the Labour-Managed Firm, in *Jounal of Comparative Economics*, vol. 1, n. 3.

Berman K.V. and Berman M.D., 1989, An Empirical Test of the Theory of the Labour-Managed Firm, in *Journal of Comparative Economics*, vol. 13, n. 2, June.

Bernstein E., 1899, *I presupposti del socialismo e i compiti della socialdemocrazia*, ital. transl., Laterza, Bari, 1969.

Bernstein E., 1901, *Zur geschichte und theorie des Sozialismus*, Edelheim, Berlin.

Bernstein E., 1918, *Völkerbund oder staatenbund*, P. Cassirer, Berlin.

Bettelheim C., 1968, *La transizione all'economia socialista*, ital. transl., Jaca Books, Milan, 1969.

238   *References*

Bettelheim C., 1969, On the Transition between Capitalism and Socialism, in *Monthly Review*, March–April.

Bettelheim C., 1971, More on the Transition to Socialism, in *Monthly Review*, March.

Bettelheim C., 1974, *Class Struggles in the USSR; 1917–1923*, engl. transl., The Harvester Press, Brighton, 1977.

Bhaskar R., 1989, *Reclaiming Reality: A Critical Introduction to Contemporary Philosophy*, Verso, London.

Bhaskar R., 1991, Dialectics, in T. Bottomore (ed.), *A Dictionary of Marxist Thought*, 2nd edn, Blackwell, Oxford.

Bhaskar R., 2008, *Dialectic: The Pulse of Freedom*, Verso, London.

Bidet J., 1998, *Que faire du Capital?*, Presses Universitaires de France, Paris.

Bidet J., 2005, La ricostruzione metastrutturale del *Capitale*, in M. Musto (ed.), *Sulle tracce di un fantasma*, manifestolibri, Rome.

Bidet J. and Kouvelakis S., eds, 2008, *Critical Companion to Contemporary Marxism*, Brill, Leiden.

Bigo P., 1953, *Marxismo e umanismo*, ital. transl., Bompiani, Milan, 1963.

Birchall J., 2000, Some Theoretical and Pratical Implications of the Attempted Takeover of a Consumer Cooperative Society, in *Annals of Public and Cooperatives Economics*, vol. 71, n. 1.

Birchall J., 2012, The Comparative Advantages of Member-Owned Businesses, in *Review of Social Economy*, vol. 70, n. 3, September.

Birchall J. and Ketilson H., 2009, *Resilience of the Cooperative Business Model in Times of Crisis*, Sustainable Enterprise Programme, ILO, Geneva.

Birchall J. and Simmons R., 2004a, The Involvment of Members in the Governance of Large-Scale Co-Operative and Mutual Businesses: A Formative Evaluation of the Co-Operative Group, in *Review of Social Economy*, vol. 42, n. 4.

Birchall J. and Simmons R., 2004b, What Motives Members to Participate in Cooperative and Mutual Businesses: A Theoretical Model and Some Findings, in *Annals of Public and Cooperative Economics*, vol. 75, n. 3.

Blackledge P., 2004, *Perry Anderson, Marxism and the New Left*, The Merlin Press, London.

Blanchard O.J. and Summers L.H., 1986, Hysteresis and European Unemployment Problem, in *NBER Macroeconomics Annual*, vol. 1.

Blanchard O.J. and Summers L.H., 1987, Hysteresis in Unemployment, in *European Economic Review*, vol. 31, February–March.

Blanchard O.J. and Summers L.H., 1988, Beyond the Natural Rate Hypothesis, in *American Economic Review*, vol. 78, May.

Blejer M.I. and Škreb M., 1997, *Macroeconomic Stabilization in Transition Economics*, Cambridge University Press, Cambridge.

Blinder A., ed., 1990, *Paying for Productivity*, Brookings Institution, Washington DC, WA.

Blinder A., ed., 1995, *Paying for Productivity: A Look at the Evidence*, Brookings Institution, Washington DC, WA.

Bloch E., 1938–1947, *Il principio speranza*, ital. transl., Garzanti, Milano, 2005.

Bloch E., 1968, *Karl Marx*, ital. transl., Il Mulino, Bologna, 1972.

Bloch E., 1990, Scelta politica e 'logiche' multiple del capitale, in M. Magatti (ed.), *Azione economica come azione sociale*, F. Angeli, Milan.

Bloom S.F., 1943, Man of His Century: A Reconsideration of the Historical Significance of Karl Marx, in J.C. Wood (ed.), 1988, *Karl Marx's Economics: Critical Assessments*, vol. 1, Croom Helm, New South Wales.

Blumberg P., 1968, *Industrial Democracy. The Sociology of Participation*, Constable, London.

Blumberg P., 1973, On the Relevance and Future of Workers' Management, in G. Hunnius, G.D. Garson, J. Case (eds), *Workers' Control*, Vintage Books, New York, NY.

Bobbio N., 1958, La dialettica in Marx, in *Rivista di filosofia*, vol. 49, n. 2.

Bobbio N., 1969, Gramsci e la concezione della società civile, in Istituto Gramsci, 1969 and 1970, *Gramsci e la cultura contemporanea*, vols I and II, Editori Riuniti, Rome.

Bobbio N., 1970, *Quale socialismo?*, Einaudi, Turin.

Bobbio N., 1975, Quali alternative alla democrazia rappresentativa?, reprinted in N. Bobbio, 1970, *Quale socialismo?*, Einaudi, Turin.

Bobbio N., ed., 1982, *La cultura filosofica italiana dal 1945 al 1980*, Guida editori, Naples.

Bobbio N., 1985, *Stato, governo, società; frammenti di un dizionario politico*, 2nd edn, Einaudi, Turin, 1995.

Bobbio N., 1988, Gramsci e la teoria politica, in F. Sbarberi (ed.), *Teoria politica e società industriale. Ripensare Gramsci*, Bollati Boringhieri, Turin.

Bobbio N., 1989, An Interview with Bobbio by A. Massarenti, in *Il Sole-24 ore*, 5 April 1989, partially reprinted in *Il Sole-24 ore*, 11 January 2004.

Bobbio N., 1991, *Il futuro della democrazia*, 2nd edn, Einaudi, Turin.

Bobbio N., Firpo L. and Mathieu V., eds, 1965, *Scritti politici e di filosofia della storia e del diritto di Immanuel Kant*, U.T.E.T., Turin.

Bober M.M., 1950, *Karl Marx's Interpretation of History*, Harvard University Press, Cambridge.

Boffa G. and Martinet G., 1976, *Dialogo sullo stalinismo*, Laterza, Bari.

Bolaffi A., 1978, Introduzione, ital. transl., in G. Lukàcs, 1954, *Il giovane Marx*, Editori Riuniti, Rome, 1978.

Bolaffi A., 2002, *Il crepuscolo della sovranità*, Donzelli, Rome.

Bonazzi G., 2002, Perché i sociologi italiani del lavoro e dell'organizzazione, pur essendo pro labour, non sono post-bravermaniani e meno ancora foucaultiani, in *Sociologia del lavoro*, vols 2 and 3, nn. 86–87.

Bonefeld W., 2010, Abstract Labour: Against its Nature and on its Time, in *Capital and Class*, vol. 34, n. 2.

Bonefeld W., Gunn R. and Psychopedis K., eds, 1992, *Open Marxism*, vol. II, Pluto Press, London.

Bonin J.P. and Putterman L., 1987, *Economics of Cooperation and the Labor-Managed Economy, Fundamentals of Pure and Applied Economics*, n. 4, Harvard Academic Pub, New York, NY.

Bonin J.P., Jones D.C. and Putterman L., 1993, Theoretical and Empirical Studies of Producer Cooperatives: Will the Twain Ever Meet?, in *Journal of Economic Literature*, vol. 31, n. 3.

Bonomi G., 1973, *Partito e rivoluzione in Gramsci*, Feltrinelli, Milan.

Bordiga A., 1976, *Economia Marxista ed economia controrivoluzionaria*, Iskra, Milano.

Bordiga A. and Gramsci A., 1971, *Dibattito sui consigli di fabbrica*, Samonà e Savelli, Rome.

Bornstein M., ed., 1973, *Plan and Market: Economic Reform in Eastern Europe*, Yale University Press, New Haven, CT.

Botta G. and Martinet G., 1976, *Dialogo sullo stalinismo*, Laterza, Bari.

Bottomore T., ed., 1991, *A Dictionary of Marxist Thought*, 2nd edn, Blackwell, Oxford.

Bouchon C., Michard B., Plasse A. and Paranque B., 2012, Coopératives et gouvernance: modernité ou archaïsme?, in *Annals of Public and Cooperative Economics*, vol. 83, n. 3.

Bourdet Y., 1974, *Pour l'Autogestion*, Anthropos, Paris.

Bourdet Y., 1978a, L'autogestion, programme peu commun de la gauche, in Y. Bourdet, 1978b, *Qui a peur de l'autogestion?*, Union générale d'éditions, Paris.

Bourdet Y., 1978b, *Qui a peur de l'autogestion?*, Union générale d'éditions, Paris.

Bowles S., 1985, The Production Process in a Competitive Economy: Walrasian, Neo-Hobbesian, and Marxist Models, in *American Economic Review*, vol. 75, n. 1, March.

Bowles S. and Gintis H., 1986, *Democracy and Capitalism*, Basic Books, New York, NY.

Bowles S. and Gintis H., 1993, The Democratic Firms: An Agency Theoretic Evaluation, in S. Bowles, H. Gintis and B. Gustafsson (eds), *Markets and Democracy: Participation, Accountability and Efficiency*, Cambridge University Press, Cambridge.

Bowles S. and Gintis H., 1994, Credit Market Imperfections and the Incidence of Worker-Owned Firms, in *Metroeconomica*, vol. 45, n. 3.

Bowles S. and Gintis H., 1996a, The Distribution of Wealth and the Viability of the Democratic Firm, in U. Pagano and R. Rowthorn (eds), *Democracy and Efficiency in the Economic Enterprise*, Routledge, London.

Bowles S. and Gintis H., 1996b, Is the Demand for Workplace Democracy Redundant in a Liberal Economy?, in U. Pagano and R. Rowthorn (eds), *Democracy and Efficiency in the Economic Enterprise*, Routledge, London.

Bowles S. and Gintis H., 2002, Social Capital and Community Governance, in *Economic Journal*, vol. 112, n. 483.

Bowles S., Gintis H. and Gustafsson B., eds, 1993, *Markets and Democracy: Participation, Accountability and Efficiency*, Cambridge University Press, Cambridge.

Brachet P., 1975, *Lo Stato padrone*, ital. transl., Liguori, Naples, 1976.

Bradley K. and Gelb A., 1983, *Cooperation at Work: The Mondragon Experience*, Heineman, London.

Branco M.C., Economics against Democracy, in *Review of Radical Political Economics*, vol. 44, n. 1.

Braverman H., 1974, *Labour and Monopoly Capital*, Monthly Review Press, New York, NY.

Braybrooke D., 1958, Diagnosis and Remedy in Marx's Doctrine of Alienation, reprinted in J.C. Wood (ed.), 1988, *Karl Marx's Economics: Critical Assessments*, vol. 1, Croom Helm, New South Wales.

Brenner R., 1986, The Social Basis of Economic Development, in J.E. Roemer (ed.), *Analytical Marxism*, Cambridge University Press, Cambridge.

Brewer A., 2002, The Marxist Tradition in the History of Economics, in E.R. Weintraub (ed.), *The Future of the History of Economics*, Duke University Press, Durham and London.

Brewer A.A. and Browning M.J., 1982, On the Employment Decision of a Labour-Managed Firm, in *Economica*, vol. 49, n. 194.

Breyer F., 1992, Labor Market, Employment, and Economic Policy in Illyria: A Static One Sector Model, in D.C. Jones and J. Svejnar (eds), 1992, *Advances in the Economic Analysis of Participatory and Labor-Managed Firms*, vol. 4, JAI Press, Greenwich, CT.

Briganti W., ed., 1982, *Il movimento cooperativo in Italia. Scritti e documenti, dal 1854 al 1980*, Editrice cooperativa, Rome.

Bronfenbrenner M., 1967, Marxian Influences in 'Bourgeois' Economics, in J.C. Wood (ed.), 1988, *Karl Marx's Economics: Critical Assessments*, vol. 3, Croom Helm, New South Wales.

Bronfenbrenner M., 1970, The Vicissitudes of Marxian Economics, in J.C. Wood (ed.), 1988, *Karl Marx's Economics: Critical Assessments*, vol. 3, Croom Helm, New South Wales.

Bronowskj J. and Mazlish B., 1960, *La tradizione intellettuale dell'Occidente*, ital. transl., Edizioni di Comunità, Milan, 1962.

Brosio G., 1995, *Introduzione all'economia dell'organizzazione*, La Nuova Italia Scientifica, Rome.

Bruni L., 2006, *Reciprocità*, B. Mondadori, Milan.

Bruni L. and Pelligra V., eds, 2002, *Economia come impegno civile*, Città Nuova, Rome.

Bruni L. and Zamagni S., 2004, *Economia civile*, Il Mulino, Bologna.

Brus W. and Laski K., 1989, *From Marx to Market*, Clarendon Press, Oxford.

Buber M., 1959, *Sentieri in Utopia*, ital. transl., Edizioni di Comunità, Milan, 1967.

Buchanan A., 1979, Revolution, Motivation and Rationality, in *Philosophy and Public Affairs*, vol. 9, n. 1.

Bucharin N., 1925a, Critica della piattaforma economica dell'opposizione, in N. Bucharin and E. Preobrazhensky, 1969, *L'accumulazione socialista*, ed. by L. Foa, Editori Riuniti, Rome.

Bucharin N., 1925b, La nuova politica economica e i nostri compiti, in N. Bucharin, E. Preobrazhensky, 1969, *L'accumulazione socialista*, ed. by L. Foa, Editori Riuniti, Rome.

Bucharin N., 1982, *Selected Writings on the State and the Transition to Socialism*, Spokesman, Nottingham.

Bucharin N. and Preobrazhensky E., 1969, *L'accumulazione socialista*, ed. by L. Foa, Editori Riuniti, Rome.

Buck T., 1982, *Comparative Industrial Systems*, St Martin's Press, New York, NY.

Buey F.F., 1995, Gramsci in Spagna, in E.J. Hobsbawm (ed.), *Gramsci in Europa e in America*, Laterza, Bari.

Bulgarelli M. and Viviani M., eds, 2006, *La promozione cooperativa; Copfond tra mercato e solidarietà*, Il Mulino, Bologna.

Buonocore V. and Jossa B., eds, 2003, *Organizzazioni economiche non capitalistiche*, Il Mulino, Bologna.

Burchardt A., Kalecki M. *et al.*, 1979, *L'economia della piena occupazione*, Rosenberg e Sellier, Turin.

Burdin G. and Dean A., 2009, New Evidence on Wages and Employment in Worker Cooperatives Compared with Capitalistic Firms, in *Journal of Comparative Economics*, vol. 37, n. 4.

Burgio A., 2007, *Dialettica; tradizioni, problemi sviluppi*, Quodlibet Studio, Macerata.

Burke J.P., 1981, The Necessity of Revolution, in J.P. Burke, L. Crocker and L.H. Legters (eds), *Marxism and the Good Society*, Cambridge University Press, Cambridge.

Burke J.P., Crocker L. and Legters L.H., eds, 1981, *Marxism and the Good Society*, Cambridge University Press, Cambridge.

Burow J.I. and Summers L.H., 1986, A Theory of Dual Labor Markets with Applications to Industrial Policy, Discrimination, and Keynesian Unemployment, in *Journal of Labor Economics*, vol. 4, July.

Butkievicz J.L., Koford K.T. and Miller J.B., eds, 1986, *Keynes' Economic Legacy*, Praeger, New York, NY.

Buttigieg J.A., 1995, Gramsci negli Stati Uniti, in E.J. Hobsbawm (ed.), *Gramsci in Europa e in America*, Laterza, Bari.

Cable J. and Fitzroy F., 1980, Productive Efficiency, Incentives and Employee Participation: Some Preliminary Results from West Germany, in *Kyklos*, vol. 33, n. 1.

Cacciatore G. and Lomonaco F., 1987, *Marx e i marxismi cent'anni dopo*, Guida Editori, Naples.

Cafagna L., 1988, Figlio di quei movimenti. Il giovane Gramsci e la critica della democrazia, in F. Sbarberi (ed.), *Teoria politica e società industriale. Ripensare Gramsci*, Bollati Boringhieri, Turin.

Caffè F., 1979, Prefazione, in A. Burchardt, M. Kalecki *et al.*, *L'economia della piena occupazione*, Rosenberg e Sellier, Turin.

Cammett, J., 1991, *Bibliografia gramsciana 1922–1988*, Editori Riuniti, Rome.

Campbell A., 2011, The Role of Workers in Management: The Case of Mondragòn, in *Review of Radical Political Economics*, vol. 43, n. 3.

Campbell M. and Reuten G., ed., 2002, *The Culmination of Capital; Essays on Volume III of Marx's Capital*, Palgrave, London.

Cangiani M., 2011, Karl Polanyi's Institutional Theory: Market Society and its 'Disembedded Economy', in *Journal of Economic Issues*, vol. XLV, n. 1, March.

Caracciolo A. and Scalia G., 1959, *La città futura*, edizione ridotta, Feltrinelli, Milan, 1976.

Carandini G., 1971, *Lavoro e capitale nella teoria di Marx*, Marsilio, Padua.

Carlin W. and Soskice D., 1990, *Macroeconomia*, ital. transl., CLUEB, Bologna, 1992.

Carr E.H., 1953, *La rivoluzione bolscevica, 1917–1923*, ital. transl., Einaudi, Turin, 1964.

Carver T., 1984, Marxism as Method, in T. Ball and J. Farr (eds), *After Marx*, Cambridge University Press, Cambridge.

Carver T., 2008, Marx's Conception of Alienation in the *Grundrisse*, in M. Musto (ed.), 2008b, *Karl Marx's Grundrisse*, Routledge, London.

Carver T. and Thomas P., eds, 1995, *Rational Choice Marxism*, Macmillan, London.

Cassano F., 1973, *Marxismo e filosofia in Italia*, De Donato, Bari.

Castoriadis C., 1975, *L'institution imaginaire de la société*, Parigi, Le Seuil.

Catephores G., 1972, Marxian Alienation: A Clarification, in J.C. Wood (ed.), 1988, *Karl Marx's Economics: Critical Assessments*, vol. 1, Croom Helm, New South Wales.

Centorrino M. and Barcellona P., eds, 1982, *Economia politica dell'inflazione*, De Donato, Bari.

Cerroni U., 1973, *Teoria politica e socialismo*, Editori Riuniti, Rome.

Cerroni U., 1994, L'alterazione del progetto rivoluzionario: marxismo, leninismo, stalinismo, in A. Colombo (ed.), *Crollo del comunismo sovietico e ripresa dell'utopia*, Edizioni Dedalo, Bari.

Chaddad F., 2012, Advancing the Theory of Cooperative Organization: The Cooperative as a True Hybrid, in *Annals of Public and Cooperative Economics*, vol. 83, n. 4.

Chalkley M. and Estrin S., 1972, Income, Saving and Growth in a Labor-Managed Economy, in D.C. Jones and J. Svejnar (eds), 1992, *Advances in the Economic Analysis of Participatory and Labor-Managed Firms*, vol. 5, JAI Press, Greenwich, CT.

Chandler H.D. and Daems H., 1980, *Managerial Hierarchies*, Harvard University Press, Cambridge.

Chang J., Lai C. and Lin C., 2003, Profit Sharing, Worker Effort, and Double-Sided Moral Hazard in the Efficiency Wage Models, in *Journal of Comparative Economics*, vol. 31, n. 1, March.

Chaves R. and Sajardo A., 2004, Social Economy Managers: Between Values and Entrenchment, in *Annals of Public and Coperative Economics*, vol. 83, n. 3.

Cheney G., 1999, *Values at Work*, Cornell University Press, Ithaca, NY.

Cheung S.N.S., 1987, Economic Organization and Transaction Costs, in J. Eatwell, M. Milgate and P. Newman (eds), *The New Palgrave. A Dictionary of Economics*, vol. 3, Macmillan, London.

Cheung S.N.S., 1992, On the New Institutional Economics, in L. Werin, H. Wijkander (eds), *Contract Economics*, Basil Blackwell, New York, NY.

Chevalier J.J., 1949, *Le grandi opere del pensiero politico*, ital. transl., Il Mulino, Bologna, 1970.

Chilosi A., ed., 1992a, *L'economia del periodo di transizione; dal modello di tipo sovietico all'economia di mercato*, Il Mulino, Bologna.

Chilosi A., 1992b, Il socialismo di mercato: modelli e problemi, in A. Chilosi, 1992a, *L'economia del periodo di transizione; dal modello di tipo sovietico all'economia di mercato*, Il Mulino, Bologna.

Chitarin A., 1973, *Lenin e il controllo operaio*, Samonà e Savelli, Rome.

Chomsky N., 2009, Un mondo ingiusto, in *Internazionale*, vol. 16, n. 816.

Cicerchia C., 1959, Il rapporto col leninismo e il problema della rivoluzione italiana, in A. Caracciolo, G. Scalia, *La città futura*, edizione ridotta, Feltrinelli, Milan, 1976.

Cingoli M., 2001, *Il primo Marx (1835–1841)*, Edizioni Unicopli, Milan.

Cingoli M., 2005, Marx e il materialismo, in M. Musto (ed.), *Sulle tracce di un fantasma*, manifestolibri, Rome.

Clayre A., ed., 1980, *The Political Economy of Cooperation and Participation: A Third Sector*, Oxford Economic Press, Oxford.

Coase R.H., 1937, The Nature of the Firm, in *Economica*, vol. 4, n. 16, November.

Coase R., 1960, The Problem of Social Cost, in *Journal of Law and Economics*, vol. 3, n. 1.

Cohen G.A., 1978 e 2000, *Karl Marx's Theory of History: A Defence*, Clarendon Press, Oxford.

Cohen G.A., 1978, Robert Nozick and Wilt Chamberlain: How Patterns Preserve Liberty, in J. Arthur and W.H. Shaw (eds), *Justice and Economic Distribution*, Prentice-Hall, Englewood Cliff, NJ.

Cohen J. and Rogers J., 1983, *On Democracy: Toward a Transformation of American Society*, Penguin, London.

Cohen S.H., 1973, *Bucharin e la rivoluzione bolscevica*, ital. transl., Feltrinelli, Milan, 1975.

Cole G.D.H., 1920, *Chaos and Order in Industry*, Gollanz, London.

Cole G.D.H., 1953, *Socialist Thought*, vol. I, *The Forerunners (1789–1850)*, Macmillan, London.

Cole G.D.H., 1954, *Socialist Thought*, vol. II, *Marxism and Anarchism (1850–1890)*, Macmillan, London.

Colletti L., 1968, Bernstein e il marxismo della seconda internazionale, in E. Bernstein, 1899, *I presupposti del socialismo e i compiti della socialdemocrazia*, ital. transl., Laterza, Bari, 1969.

Colletti L., 1969, *Il marxismo ed Hegel*, Laterza, Bari.

Colletti L., 1970, *Ideologia e società*, Laterza, Bari.

Colletti L., 1974, *Intervista politico-filosofica*, Laterza, Bari.

Colletti L., 1977, Punti controversi del marxismo, reprinted in L. Colletti, 1979, *Tra marxismo e no*, Laterza, Bari.

Colletti L., 1979, *Tra marxismo e no*, Laterza, Bari.

Colletti L., 1980, *Tramonto dell'ideologia*, Laterza, Bari.

Colombo A., ed., 1994, *Crollo del Comunismo sovietico e ripresa dell'utopia*, Edizioni Dedalo, Bari.

Connock M., 1982, Capital Maintenance and Investment in Yugoslavia: Two Observations, in *Economic Analysis and Workers' Management*, vol. 6, n. 3.

Conte M.A., 1982, Participation and Performance in U.S. Labour-Managed Firms, in D.C. Jones and J. Svejnar (eds), *Participatory and Self-Managed Firms: Evaluating Economic Performance*, Heath, Lexington.

Conte M.A. and Svejnar J., 1988, Productivity Effects of Worker Participation in Management, in *International Journal of Industrial Organization*, vol. 6, n. 1.

Conte M.A. and Svejnar J., 1990, The Performance Effect of Employee Ownership Plan, in A. Blinder (ed.), *Paying for Productivity*, Brookings Institution, Washington DC, WA.

Cook M.L., Chaddad F.R. and Iliopoulos C., 2003, Advances in Cooperative Theory since 1990: A Review of Agricultural Economics Literature, in G. Hendrikse (ed.), *Restructuring Agricultural Cooperatives*, Erasmus University Press, Haveka.

Cornu A., 1949, *Karl Marx et la pensée moderne*, Edition sociales, Paris.

Cornu A., 1955, *Marx ed Engels dal liberalismo al comunismo*, ital. transl., Feltrinelli, Milan, 1962.

Corrigan P., Ramsay H. and Sawyer D., 1978, *Socialist Construction and Marxist Theory*, Monthly Review Press, New York, NY.

Cortesi L., 2010, *Storia del comunismo*, manifestolibri, Rome.

Coutinho C.N., 1995, Gramsci in Brasile, in E.J. Hobsbawm (ed.), *Gramsci in Europa e in America*, Laterza, Bari.

Craig B. and Pencavel J., 1993, The Objectives of Worker Cooperatives, in *Journal of Comparative Economics*, vol. 17, n. 2, June.

Craig B. and Pencavel J., 1995, Participation and Productivity: A Comparison of Worker Cooperatives and Conventional Firms in the Plywood Industry, in *Brookings Papers, Microeconomics*, vol. 1.

Crivelli L., 2002, Quando l' *homo oeconomicus* diventa *reciprocans*, in L. Bruni and V. Pelligra (eds), *Economia come impegno civile*, Città Nuova, Rome.

Croce B., 1899, *Materialismo storico ed economia marxista*, Laterza, Bari, 1968.

Crouch C., 2003, *Postdemocracy*, Polity Press, Cambridge.

Crouch C. and Heller F., eds, 1989, *International Yearbook of Organizational Democracy*, Wiley, Chichester.

Cugno F. and Ferrero M., 1991, Il problema degli incentivi al lavoro nella produzione cooperativa, in S. Zamagni (ed.), *Imprese e mercati*, UTET, Turin.

Cugno F. and Ferrero M., 1992, L'efficienza delle cooperative nella produzione di servizi pubblici, in E. Gramaglia and L. Sacconi (eds), *Cooperazione, benessere e organizzazione economica*, F. Angeli, Milan.

Cuomo G., 1997, Sottoinvestimento, diritti di proprietà ed orizzonte temporale nelle imprese autogestite, in B. Jossa and U. Pagano (eds), *Economia di mercato ed efficienza dei diritti di proprietà*, Giappichelli, Turin.

Cuomo G., 2003, La cooperativa di produzione italiana e i modelli teorici di riferimento, in V. Buonocore and B. Jossa (eds), *Organizzazioni economiche non capitalistiche*, Il Mulino, Bologna.

Cuomo G., 2004, Il finanziamento esterno delle imprese gestite dai lavoratori, in B. Jossa (ed.), 2004a, *Il futuro del capitalismo*, Il Mulino, Bologna.

Cuomo G., 2006, Cooperative e diritti di proprietà: il contributo di Hansmann, in M.P. Salani, *Lezioni cooperative*, Il Mulino, Bologna.

Cuomo G., 2010, *Microeconomia dell'impresa cooperativa di produzione*, Giappichelli, Turin.

Daems H., 1980, The Rise of the Modern Industrial Enterprise: A New Perspective, in H.D. Chandler and H. Daems, *Managerial Hierarchies*, Harvard University Press, Cambridge.

Dahl R.A., 1985, *A Preface to Economic Democracy*, Polity Press, Cambridge.

Dahl R.A., 1989, *Democracy and its Critics*, Yale University Press, New Haven, CT.

Dahrendorf R., 1959, *Classi e conflitto di classe nella società industriale*, ital. transl., Laterza, Bari, 1963.

Dal Pra L., 1972, *La dialettica in Marx*, 2nd edn, Laterza, Bari.

Damjanovic P., 1962, Les conceptions de Marx sur l'autogestion sociale, in *Praxis*, vol. 1, n. 1.

De Angelis M., 1995, Beyond the Technological and Social Paradigms: A Political Reading of Abstract Labour as the Substance of Value, in *Capital and Class*, vol. 57, Autumn.

De Bonis R., Manzone B. and Trento S., 1994, La proprietà cooperativa: teoria, storia e il caso delle banche popolari, Banca d'Italia, *Temi di discussione*, n. 238, December.

De Felice F., 1971, *Serrati, Bordiga, Gramsci e il problema della rivoluzione in Italia*, De Donato, Bari.

De Giovanni B., 1976, *La teoria politica delle classi nel 'Capitale'*, De Donato, Bari.

De Giovanni B., 1977, Gramsci e l'elaborazione successiva del partito comunista, in B. De Giovanni, V. Gerratana and L. Paggi, *Egemonia, Stato, partito in Gramsci*, Editori Riuniti, Rome.

De Giovanni B., Gerratana V. and Paggi L., 1977, *Egemonia, Stato, partito in Gramsci*, Editori Riuniti, Rome.

De Masi G., Garavini S., Gerratana V., Salvadori M.L. and Trentin B., eds, 1972, *I consigli operai*, Samonà e Savelli, Rome.

De Schweinitz K. Jr., 1962, On the Determinism of the Marxian System, in *Social Research*, vol. 29, April.

De Vroey M., 1982, On the Obsolescence of Marxian Theory of Value, in *Capital and Class*, vol. 17, n. 2, Summer.

Defourny J., 1992, Comparative Measures of Technical Efficiency for 500 French Workers' Cooperatives, in D.C. Jones and J. Svejnar (eds), 1992, *Advances in the Economic Analysis of Participatory and Labor-Managed Firms*, vol. 4, JAI Press, Greenwich, CT.

Defourny J., Estrin S. and Jones D.C., 1985, The Effects of Workers' Participation on Enterprise Performance, in *International Journal of Industrial Organization*, vol. 3, n. 2.

Dell'Ombra D., 2008, Review of Franco Soldani, Relazioni Virtuose, in *Rivista di recensioni filosofiche*, vol. 10.

Della Volpe G., 1956, *Logica come scienza positiva*, 2nd edn, G. d'Anna, Messina.

Della Volpe G., 1964, *Rousseau e Marx*, 4th edn, Editori Riuniti, Rome.

Demsetz H., 1988a, *Ownership, Control and the Firm; The Organization of Economic Activity*, vol. I, Basil Blackwell, Oxford.

Demsetz H., 1988b, The Structure of Ownership and the Theory of the Firm, in H. Demsetz, 1988a, *Ownership, Control and the Firm; The Organization of Economic Activity*, vol. I, Basil Blackwell, Oxford.

Demsetz H., 1988c, The Theory of Firm Revisited, in H. Demsetz, 1988a, *Ownership, Control and the Firm; The Organization of Economic Activity*, vol. I, Basil Blackwell, Oxford.

246   *References*

Demsetz H., 2011, Coase and the Neoclassical Model of the Economic System, in *The Journal of Law and Economics*, vol. 54, n. 4.

Derrida J., 1993, *Spettri di Marx*, ital. transl., Raffaello Cortina, Milan, 1994.

Deutscher I., 1970, *Lenin; frammento di una vita e altri saggi*, ital. transl., Laterza, Bari, 1970.

Devine P., 1988, *Democracy and Economic Planning*, Polity Press, Boulder CO, Westview.

Dinerstein A.C., 2005, A Call for Emancipatory Reflection: Introduction to the Forum, in *Capital and Class*, vol. 85, Spring.

Di Quattro A., 2011, Market Socialism is not Market Capitalism. Remarks on Robin Hahnel's 'Theory of Justice', in *Review of Radical Political Economics*, vol. 43, n. 4.

Dobb M., 1933, Economic Theory and the Problems of a Socialist Economy, reprinted in M. Dobb, 1955a, *Teoria economica e socialismo*, ital. transl., Editori Riuniti, Rome, 1974.

Dobb M., 1939, Gli economisti e la teoria economica del socialismo, in M. Dobb, 1955a, *Teoria economica e socialismo*, ital. transl., Editori Riuniti, Rome, 1974.

Dobb M., 1955a, *Teoria economica e socialismo*, ital. transl., Editori Riuniti, Rome, 1974.

Dobb M., 1955b, *On Economic Theory and Socialism: Collected Papers*, Routledge & Kegan, London.

Dobb M., 1969, *Welfare Economics and the Economics of Socialism*, Cambridge University Press, Cambridge.

Dobb M., 1970, *Le ragioni del socialismo*, ital. transl., Editori Riuniti, Rome, 1973.

Domar E.D., 1966, The Soviet Collective Farm as a Producer Cooperative, in *American Economic Review*, vol. 56, n. 4.

Doucouliagos C., 1995, Worker Participation and Productivity in Labor-Managed and Participatory Capitalist Firms: A Meta-Analysis, in *Industrial and Labour Relations Review*, vol. 49, n. 1.

Dow G., 2001, Allocating Control over Firms: Stock Markets vs Membership Markets, in *Review of Industrial Organization*, vol. 18, n. 2.

Dow G., 2003, *Governing the Firm; Workers' Control in Theory and Practice*, Cambridge University Press, Cambridge.

Dow G. and Putterman L., 2000, Why Capital (usually) Hires Labour: A Review and Assessment of Some Proposed Explanations, in *Journal of Economic Behavior & Organization*, vol. 43, n. 3, November.

Drachkovitch M.M., ed., 1965, *Marxism in the Modern World*, Oxford University Press, London.

Dreyfus M., 2012, La cooperazione di produzione in Francia dalle origini alla Grande guerra, in *Il Ponte*, vol. 68, nn. 5–6.

Drèze J.H., 1976, Some Theory of Labour Management and Participation, in *Econometrica*, vol. 44, n. 6.

Drèze J.H., 1985, Labor Management and General Equilibrium, in D.C. Jones and J. Svejnar (eds), 1985, *Advances in the Economic Analysis of Participatory and Labor-Managed Firms*, JAI Press, Greenwich, CT.

Drèze J.H., 1989, *Labour-Management, Contracts and Capital Markets. A General Equilibrium Approach*, Basil Blackwell, Oxford.

Drèze J.H., 1993, Self-Management and Economic Theory: Efficiency, Funding and Employment, in P. Bardhan and J.E. Roemer (eds), *Market Socialism: The Current Debate*, Oxford Economic Press, New York, NY.

Dubravcic D., 1970, Labor as an Entrepreneurial Input; An Essay on the Theory of the Producer Cooperative Economy, in *Economica*, vol. 37, n. 147.

Duffield J., 1970, The Value Concept in Capital in Light of Recent Criticism, reprinted in J.C. Wood (ed.), 1988, *Karl Marx's Economics: Critical Assessments*, Croom Helm, New South Wales.

Dunayewskaya R., 1988, *Marxism and Freedom: From 1776 until Today*, Columbia University Press, New York, NY.

Durkheim E., 1928, *Socialism and Saint-Simon*, Routledge and Kegan Paul, London.

Dymski G.A., 1991, Analytical Marxism, in T. Bottomore (ed.), *A Dictionary of Marxist Thought*, 2nd edn, Blackwell, Oxford.

Easton L.D., 1970, Alienation and Empiricism in Marx's Thought, in *Social Research*, vol. 37, n. 3.

Easton L.D., 1994, Marx and Individual Freedom, in L. Patsouras (ed.) *Debating Marx*, EmText, New York, NY.

Eatwell J., Milgate M. and Newman P., eds, 1987, *The New Palgrave. A Dictionary of Economics*, vol. 3, Macmillan, London.

Edwards R.C., 1979, *Contested Terrain*, Basic Books, New York, NY.

Efferson C., 2012, Book Review Feature: Two Book Reviews of *A Cooperative Species: Human Reciprocity and its Evolution*, in *Economic Journal*, vol. 122, n. 362.

Einaudi L., 1920, Il significato del controllo operaio, in L. Einaudi, 1966, *Cronache economiche e politiche di un trentennio*, vol. V, 1919–1920, Einaudi, Turin.

Einaudi L., 1966, *Cronache economiche e politiche di un trentennio*, vol. V, 1919–1920, Einaudi, Turin.

Eldred M., Hanlon M., Kleiber L. and Roth V.B., 1884, *La forma-valore. Progetto di ricostruzione e completamento del frammento di sistema di Marx*, Lacaita Editore, Manduria.

Eldret M. and Hanlon M., 1981, Reconstructing the Value-Form Analysis, in *Capital & Class*, vol. 13, Summer.

Ellerman D.P., 1986, Horizon Problems and Property Rights in Labor-Managed Firms, in *Journal of Comparative Economics*, vol. 10, n. 1.

Ellerman D.P., 1992, *Property and Contract in Economics*, Basil Blackwell, Oxford.

Elliott J.E., 1975, Professor Robert's Marx: On Alienation and Economic Systems, in J.C. Wood (ed.), 1988, *Karl Marx's Economics: Critical Assessments*, vol. 1, Croom Helm, New South Wales.

Elliott J.E., 1979, Continuity and Change in the Evolution of Marx's Theory of Alienation: From the *Manuscripts* through the *Grundrisse* to *Capital*, in J.C. Wood (ed.), 1988, *Karl Marx's Economics: Critical Assessments*, vol. 1, Croom Helm, New South Wales.

Elson D., 1988, Market Socialism or Socialization of Market?, in *New Left Review*, n. 172, November–December.

Elster J., 1985, *Making Sense of Marx*, Cambridge University Press, Cambridge.

Elster J., 1989, Marxism and Individualism, in J.E. Roemer, 1994, *Foundations of Analytical Marxism*, E. Elgar, Aldershot.

Elster J., ed., 1998, *Deliberating Democracy*, Cambridge University Press, Cambridge.

Elster J. and Moene K.O., 1989a, *Alternatives to Capitalism*, Cambridge University Press, Cambridge.

Elster J. and Moene K.O., 1989b, Introduction, in J. Elster and K.O. Moene, 1989a, *Alternatives to Capitalism*, Cambridge University Press, Cambridge.

Engels F., 1844, *La sacra famiglia*, ital. transl., Editori Riuniti, Rome, 1969.

Engels F., 1847a, Principles of Communism, in K. Marx and F. Engels, 1975–2001, *Collected Works*, vol. 6, Lawrence and Wishart, London.

Engels F., 1847b, Draft of a Communist Confession of Faith, in K. Marx and F. Engels, 1975–2001, *Collected Works*, vol. 6, Lawrence and Wishart, London.

Engels F., 1859, Review of *Per la critica dell'economia politica*, in K. Marx, 1859, Outline of the Critique of Political Economy, in K. Marx and F. Engels, 1975–2001, *Collected Works*, vol. 29, Lawrence and Wishart, London.

Engels F., 1872, Letter to C. Terzaghi of Jan. 14, in K. Marx and F. Engels, 1975–2001, *Collected Works*, vol. 44, Lawrence and Wishart, London.

Engels F., 1878, Anti-Dühring, in K. Marx and F. Engels, 1975–2001, *Collected Works*, vol. 25, Lawrence and Wishart, London.

Engels F., 1880, *Socialism: Utopian and Scientific*, Progress Publisher, Moskow, 1970.

Engels F., 1882, Additions to the Text of *Antidühring*, in K. Marx and F. Engels, 1975–2001, *Collected Works*, vol. 25, Lawrence and Wishart, London.

Engels F., 1884, Preface, in K. Marx, 1847, *Miseria della filosofia*, Editori Riuniti, Rome, 1969.

Engels F., 1886, Letter to Bebel, 20–23 January, in K. Marx and F. Engels, 1975–2001, *Collected Works*, vol. 47, Lawrence and Wishart, London.

Engels F., 1890–1891, In the Case of Brentano versus Marx. Regarding Alleged Falsifications of Quotations, in K. Marx and F. Engels, 1975–2001, *Collected Works*, vol. 27, Lawrence and Wishart, London.

Engels F., 1890, Farewell Letter to the Readers of the *Sozialdemokrat*, in K. Marx and F. Engels, 1975–2001, *Collected Works*, vol. 27, Lawrence and Wishart, London.

Engels F., 1891a, A Critique of the Draft of Social-Democratic Programme of 1891, in K. Marx and F. Engels, 1975–2001, *Collected Works*, vol. 27, Lawrence and Wishart, London.

Engels F., 1891b, Socialism: Utopian and Scientific, in K. Marx and F. Engels, 1975–2001, *Collected Works*, vol. 6, Lawrence and Wishart, London.

Engels F., 1892, Lettera a Lafargue, 12/XI, in K. Marx and F. Engels, *Opere complete*, vol. 38, Editori Riuniti, Rome.

Engels F., 1894, Preface, in K. Marx, 1894b, *Il capitale*, vol. III, Editori Riuniti, Rome, 1965.

Engels F., 1895a, Introduction to Karl Marx's *The Class Struggle in France, 1848 to 1850*, in K. Marx, F. Engels, 1975–2001, *Collected Works*, vol. 27, Lawrence and Wishart, London.

Engels F., 1895b, Lettera a K. Kautsky del 1° aprile, in K. Marx and F. Engels, *Opere complete*, vol. l, Editori Riuniti, Rome.

Estrin S., 1991, Some Reflections on Self-Management, Social Choice and Reform in Eastern Europe, in *Journal of Comparative Economics*, vol. 15, n. 2, June.

Estrin S. and Jones D.C., 1992, The Viability of Employee-Owned Firms: Evidence from France, in *Industrial and Labor Relations Review*, vol. 45, n. 2.

Estrin S. and Jones D.C., 1995, Worker Participation, Employee Ownership and Productivity: Results from French Producer Cooperatives, in D.C. Jones and J. Svejnar (eds), 1995, *Advances in the Economic Analysis of Participatory and Self-Managed Firms*, vol. 5., JAI Press, Greenwich, CN.

Estrin S., Jones D.C. and Svejnar J., 1987, The Productivity Effects of Worker Participation: Producer Cooperatives in Western Europe, in *Journal of Comparative Economics*, vol. 11, n. 1.

Eswaran M. and Kotwal A., 1989, Why are Capitalists the Bosses?, in *Economic Journal*, vol. 99, n. 394, March.

Faccioli D. and Fiorentini G., 1998, Un'analisi di efficienza comparata tra imprese cooperative e for profit, in G. Fiorentini and C. Scarpa (eds), *Cooperative e mercato*, Carocci, Rome.

Faccioli D. and Scarpa C., 1998, Il vantaggio comparato delle imprese cooperative: aspetti teorici, in G. Fiorentini and C. Scarpa (eds), *Cooperative e mercato*, Carocci, Rome.

Falk A. and Kosfeld M., 2004, Distrust. The Hidden Cost of Control, in *Cepr*, n. 4512.

Fama E.F., 1980, Agency Problems and the Theory of the Firm, in *Journal of Political Economy*, vol. 88, n. 2.

Fama E.F. and Jensen M.C., 1983, Agency Problems and Residual Claims, in *Journal of Law and Economics*, vol. 26, June.

Farr J., 1984, Marx and Positivism, in T. Ball and J. Farr (eds), *After Marx*, Cambridge University Press, Cambridge.

Faucci R., 1979, *Marx interprete degli economisti classici; una lettura storica*, La Nuova Italia, Florence.

Faucci R., 2010, Croce and Gramsci as 'Economists', in *Studi economici*, vol. LXV, n. 100.

Fausto D., Jossa B. and Panico C., eds, 2002, *Teoria economica e riformismo politico*, F. Angeli, Milan.

Favilli P., 2000, *Storia del marxismo italiano*, 2nd edn, F. Angeli, Milan.

Favilli P., 2001, Socialismo e marginalismo. La 'battaglia delle idee': una lettura, in M.E.L. Guidi, L. Michelini, *Marginalismo e socialismo nell'Italia liberale, 1870–1925*, Feltrinelli, Milan.

Fay M., 1983, The Influence of Adam Smith on Marx's Theory of Alienation, in J.C. Wood (ed.), 1988, *Karl Marx's Economics: Critical Assessments*, vol. 1, Croom Helm, New South Wales.

Fearon J.D., 1998, Deliberation as Discussion, in J. Elster (ed.), *Deliberating Democracy*, Cambridge University Press, Cambridge.

Fehr E. and Schmidt K., 1999, A Theory of Fairness, Competition and Cooperation, in *Quarterly Journal of Economics*, vol. 114, n. 3.

Fetscher I., 1965, Concretizzazione del concetto di libertà in Marx, in E. Fromm, *L'umanesimo marxista*, ital. transl., Dedalo libri, Bari, 1971.

Fetscher I., 1973, Karl Marx and Human Nature, in J.C. Wood (ed.), 1988, *Karl Marx's Economics: Critical Assessments*, vol. 1, Croom Helm, New South Wales.

Fetscher I., 1979, Bernstein e la sfida all'ortodossia, in E.J. Hobsbawm, G. Haupt, F. Marek, E. Ragionieri, V. Strada and C. Vivanti (eds), 1978–1982, *Storia del marxismo*, 5 vols, Einaudi, Turin.

Fetscher I., 2008, Emancipated Individuals in an Emancipated Society; Marx's Sketch of Post-Capitalist Society in the 'Grundrisse', in M. Musto (ed.), 2008b, *Karl Marx's Grundrisse*, Routledge, London.

Filippini L. and Salanti A., eds, 1993, *Razionalità, impresa e informazione*, Giappichelli, Turin.

Fine R., 2001, The Marx-Hegel Relationship: Revisionist Interpretations, in *Capital & Class*, special issue, n. 75, Autumn.

Finelli R., 2007, Un marxismo senza *Capitale*, in R. Bellofiore, *Da Marx a Marx; un bilancio dei marxismi italiani del Novecento*, manifestolibri, Rome.

Fineschi R., ed., 2005a, *Karl Marx: Rivisitazioni e prospettive*, Mimesis, Milan.

Fineschi R., 2005b, Teoria della storia e alienazione in Marx, in R. Fineschi (ed.), 2005a, *Karl Marx: Rivisitazioni e prospettive*, Mimesis, Milan.

Fineschi R., 2006, *Marx e Hegel*, Carocci, Rome.

Fineschi R., 2007, Attualità e praticabilità di una teoria dialettica del *Capitale* (ovvero: Marx è un ferrovecchio?), in A. Burgio, *Dialettica; tradizioni, problemi sviluppi*, Quodlibet Studio, Macerata.

Fineschi R., 2008, *Un nuovo Marx; filologia ed interpretazione dopo la nuova edizione storico-critica (Mega2)*, Carocci, Rome.

Fineschi R., 2013, Questo speciale, in R. Fineschi, T. Redolfi Riva, G. Sgrò and Karl Marx 2013, in *Il Ponte*, vols 5–6, May–June.

Fineschi R., Redolfi Riva T. and Sgrò G., 2013, Karl Marx 2013, in *Il Ponte*, vols 5–6, May–June.

Finocchiaro M.A., 1988, *Gramsci and the History of Dialectical Thought*, Cambridge University Press, Cambridge.

Fiorentini G. and Scarpa C., eds, 1998, *Cooperative e mercato*, Carocci, Rome.

Fischer L., 1964, *Vita di Lenin*, ital. transl., Mondadori, Milan, 1973.

Fitzroy F.R. and Kraft K., 1986, Profitability and Profit Sharing, in *Journal of Industrial Economics*, vol. 35, n. 2, December.

Fitzroy F.R. and Kraft K., 1987, Cooperation, Productivity and Profit Sharing, in *Quarterly Journal of Economics*, vol. 102, n. 408.

Flakierski H., 1989, The Economic System and Income Distribution in Jugoslavia, in *Eastern European Economics*, vol. 27, n. 4.

Fleetwood S., 2006, Rethinking Labour Market: A Critical–Realist–Socioeconomic Perspective, in *Capital and Class*, vol. 89, Summer.

Foote W., 1991, *Making Mondragón*, IRL Press, London.

Forgacs D., 1989, Gramsci and Marxism in Britain, in *New Left Review*, n. 176.

Forgacs D., 1995, Gramsci in Gran Bretagna, in E.J. Hobsbawm (ed.), *Gramsci in Europa e in America*, Laterza, Bari.

Fourier C., 1808, *Theory of the Four Movements*, Cambridge University Press, Cambridge, 1996.

Frančevič V. and Uvalic M., eds, 2000, *Equality, Participation, Transition*, Macmillan, London.

Freeman A. and Carchedi G., 1996, *Marx and Non-Equilibrium Economics*, E. Elgar, Cheltenham.

Freeman R.B., 1980, The Exit-Voice Trade off in the Labour Market: Unionism, Job Tenure, Quits and Separations, in *Quarterly Journal of Economics*, vol. 94, n. 4.

Frölich P., 1967, *Rosa Luxemburg*, ital. transl., La Nuova Italia, Florence, 1969.

Fromm E., 1961, *Marx's Concept of Man*, Frederick Ungar, New York, NY.

Fromm E., 1965, *L'umanesimo marxista*, ital. transl., Dedalo libri, Bari, 1971.

Fukuyama F., 1989, The End of History?, in *The National Interest*, Summer.

Fukuyama F., 1992, *La fine della storia e l'ultimo uomo*, ital. transl., Rizzoli, Milan.

Furubotn E.G., 1971, Toward a Dynamic Model of the Yugoslav Firm, in *The Canadian Journal of Economics*, vol. 4, n. 2.

Furubotn E.G., 1976, The Long-Run Analysis of the Labor-Managed Firm: An Alternative Interpretation, in *American Economic Review*, vol. 66, n. 1.

Furubotn E.G., 1978, The Long-Run Analysis of the Labor-Managed Firm: Reply, in *American Economie Review*, vol. 68, n. 4.

Furubotn E.G., 1980, The Socialist Labor-Managed Firm and Bank-Financed Investment: Some Theoretical Issues, in *Journal of Comparative Economics*, vol. 4, n. 2.

Furubotn E.G., 1998, Review of B. Jossa, G. Cuomo, The Economic Theory of Socialism and the Labour-Managed Firm, in *Economic Systems*, vol. 3, n. 3.

Furubotn E.G. and Pejovich S., 1970a, Tax Policy and Investment Decision of the Yugoslav Firm, in *National Tax Journal*, vol. 23, n. 3.

Furubotn E.G. and Pejovich S., 1970b, Property Rights and the Behavior of the Firm in a Socialist State: The Example of Yugoslavia, in *Zeitschrift für Nationalökonomie*, vol. 30, n. 5.

Furubotn E.G. and Pejovich S., 1973, Property Rights, Economic Decentralization and the Evolution of the Yugoslav Firm, 1965–72, in *Journal of Law and Economics*, vol. 16, October.

Galgano P., 1982, L'autogestione cooperativa e il sistema organizzato di imprese, in Lega Nazionale Cooperative e Mutue, *L'impresa cooperativa degli anni '80*, De Donato, Bari.

Gall G., 2012, Richard Hyman: An Assessment of His *Industrial Relations: A Marxist Introduction*, in *Capital & Class*, vol. 36, n. 1.

Gallagher W.E. and Einhorn H.J., 1976, Motivation Theory and Job Design, in *Journal of Business*, vol. 49, n. 3.

Gallino L., 1969, Gramsci e le scienze sociali, in AA.VV., 1969b, *Gramsci e la cultura contemporanea*, Editori Riuniti, Rome.

Gallino L., 1987, Su alcuni fraintendimenti di Marx e intorno a Marx in tema di evoluzione delle società, in G. Cacciatore and F. Lomonaco, *Marx e i marxismi cent'anni dopo*, Guida Editori, Naples.

Garaudy R., 1969, Il concetto di struttura in Marx e le concezioni alienate della struttura, in AA.VV., 1969a, *Marx vivo*, Mondadori, Milan.

Garaudy R., n.d., *L'alternativa; cambiare il mondo e la vita*, ital. transl., Cittadella editrice, Assisi, 1972.

Garegnani P., 1981, *Marx e gli economisti classici*, Einaudi, Turin.

Garin E., 1958, Gramsci nella cultura italiana, reprinted in E. Garin, 1997, *Con Gramsci*, Editori Riuniti, Rome.

Garin E., 1964, Per una nuova lettura, reprinted in E. Garin, 1997, *Con Gramsci*, Editori Riuniti, Rome.

Garin E., 1969, Politica e cultura in Gramsci, in AA.VV., 1969b, *Gramsci e la cultura contemporanea*, Editori Riuniti, Rome.

Garin E., 1997, *Con Gramsci*, Editori Riuniti, Rome.

Garnett Jr. R.F., 2011, Pluralism, Academic Freedom, and Heterodox Economics, in *Review of Radical Political Economics*, vol. 43, n. 4.

Garson G.D., 1973, Beyond Collective Bargaining, in G. Hunnius, G.D. Garson and J. Case (eds), *Workers' Control*, Vintage Books, New York, NY.

Gattei G., 2007, La via crucis dei marxismi italiani, in R. Bellofiore, *Da Marx a Marx; un bilancio dei marxismi italiani del Novecento*, manifestolibri, Rome.

Geary R.J., 1974, Difesa e deformazione del marxismo in Kautsky, in Istituto Giangiacomo Feltrinelli, *Storia del marxismo contemporaneo*, Feltrinelli, Milan.

George D.A.R., 1997, Self-Management and Ideology, in *Review of Political Economy*, vol. 9, n. 1, January.

Gerratana V., 1970, Stato socialista e capitalismo di Stato, in V. Gerratana, 1972a, *Ricerche di storia del marxismo*, Editori Riuniti, Rome.

Gerratana V., 1972a, *Ricerche di storia del marxismo*, Editori Riuniti, Rome.

Gerratana V., 1972b, L'estinzione dello stato nella concezione Marxista e la tematica consiliare, in G. De Masi, S. Garavini, V. Gerratana, M.L. Salvadori and B. Trentin (eds), *I consigli operai*, Samonà e Savelli, Rome.

Gerratana V., 1977, Stato, partito, strumenti e istituti dell'egemonia nei 'Quaderni del carcere, in B. De Giovanni, V. Gerratana and L. Paggi, *Egemonia, Stato, partito in Gramsci*, Editori Riuniti, Rome.

Gerratana V., 1997, *Gramsci, problemi di metodo*, Editori Riuniti, Rome.

Gibbons R., 1998, Incentives in Organizations, in *Journal of Economic Perspectives*, vol. 12, n. 4.

Gibson-Graham J.K., 2003, Enabling Ethical Economies: Cooperativism and Class, in *Critical Sociology*, vol. 29, n. 2.

Giddens A., 1981, *A Contemporary Critique of Historical Materialism*, University of California Press, Berkeley, CA.

Ginsborg P., 2006, *La democrazia che non c'è*, Einaudi, Turin.

Gintis H., 1989, Financial Markets and the Political Structure of the Enterprise, in *Journal of Economic Behavior and Organization*, vol. 11, n. 2.

Giolitti A., 1977, L'autogestione, in G. La Ganga (ed.), *Socialismo e democrazia economica*, F. Angeli, Milan.

Gobetti P., 1923, Revisione liberale, reprinted in P. Gobetti, 1969, *Scritti politici*, Einaudi, Turin.

Gobetti P., 1929, Rassegna di questioni politiche, reprinted in Gobetti, 1969, *Scritti politici*, Einaudi, Turin.

Gobetti P., 1948, *La rivoluzione liberale*, Einaudi, Turin.

Gobetti P., 1969, *Scritti politici*, Einaudi, Turin.

Godelier M., 1964, *L'economia politica e le società primitive*, ital. transl., in M. Godelier, 1970, *Antropologia, storia, marxismo*, ed. by M. de Stefanis and A. Casiccia (eds), Guanda, Parma.

Godelier M., 1966, Sistema, struttura e contraddizione nel *Capitale*, ital. transl., in M. Godelier and L. Sève, 1970, *Marxismo e strutturalismo*, Einaudi, Turin.

Godelier M., 1970, *Antropologia, storia, marxismo*, ed. by M. de Stefanis and A. Casiccia, Guanda, Parma.

Godelier M., 1982, Il marxismo e le scienze dell'uomo, in E.J. Hobsbawm, G. Haupt, F. Marek, E. Ragionieri, V. Strada and C. Vivanti (eds), 1978–1982, *Storia del marxismo*, vol. IV, Einaudi, Turin.

Godelier M. and Sève L., 1970, *Marxismo e strutturalismo*, Einaudi, Turin.

Goldstein W.S., ed., 2006, *Marx, Critical Theory and Religion*, Brill, Leiden.

Goodman P.S., 1974, An Examination of Referents Used in the Evaluation of Pay, in *Organizational Behavior and Human Performance*, vol. 12.

Gordon D.M., 1976, Capitalistic Efficiency and Socialist Efficiency, in *Monthly Review*, vol. 24.

Gorz A., 1970, Workers' Control is More than Just That, reprinted in K. Kipnis and D.T. Meyers, 1985, *Economic Justice; Private Rights and Public Responsibilities*, Rowman & Allanheld, Totowa.

Gould C.C., 1985, Economic Justice, Self Management and the Principle of Reciprocity, in K. Kipnis and D.T. Meyers, 1985, *Economic Justice; Private Rights and Public Responsibilities*, Rowman & Allanheld, Totowa.

Gramaglia E. and Sacconi L., eds, 1992, *Cooperazione, benessere e organizzazione economica*, F. Angeli, Milan.

Gramsci A., 1916a, Cristianismi, in A. Gramsci, 1980, *Cronache torinesi, 1913–1917*, ed. by S. Caprioglio, Einaudi, Turin.

Gramsci A., 1916b, Preludio, in A. Gramsci, 1958, *Scritti giovanili (1914–18)*, Einaudi, Turin.

Gramsci A., 1918a, Individualismo e collettivismo, in A. Gramsci, 1958, *Scritti giovanili (1914–18)*, Einaudi, Turin.

Gramsci A., 1918b, Stato e sovranità, in A. Gramsci, 1984, *Il nostro Marx, 1918–1919*, Einaudi, Turin.

Gramsci A., 1919–1920, *L'ordine nuovo*, Einaudi, Turin, 1954.

Gramsci A., 1921–1922, *Socialismo e fascismo; l'Ordine Nuovo*, Einaudi, Turin, 1955.

Gramsci A., 1921, Inganni, in A. Gramsci, 1971, *Socialismo e fascismo; l'Ordine Nuovo, 1921–1922*, Einaudi, Turin.

Gramsci A., 1923–1926, *La costruzione del partito comunista*, Einaudi, Turin, 1971.

Gramsci A., 1958, *Scritti giovanili (1914–18)*, Einaudi, Turin.

Gramsci A., 1967, *Scritti politici*, Editori Riuniti, Rome.

Gramsci A., 1971, *Socialismo e fascismo; l'Ordine Nuovo, 1921–1922*, Einaudi, Turin.

Gramsci A., 1975, *Quaderni dal carcere*, ed. by V. Gerratana, 4 vols, Einaudi, Turin.

Gramsci A., 1980, *Cronache torinesi, 1913–1917*, ed. by S. Caprioglio, Einaudi, Turin.

Gramsci A., 1984, *Il nostro Marx, 1918–1919*, Einaudi, Turin.

Graziani A., Minervini G. and Belviso U., 1994, *Manuale di diritto commerciale*, Marano, Naples.

Greenberg E.S., 1986, *Workplace Democracy: The Political Effects of Participation*, Cornell University Press, Ithaca, NY.

Grisoni D. and Maggioni R., 1973, *Guida a Gramsci*, Rizzoli, Milan.

Grossberg L. *et al.*, eds, 1992, *Cultural Studies*, Routledge, New York, NY.

Grossman H., 1940, *Marx, l'economia politica classica e il problema della dinamica*, ital. transl., Laterza, Bari, 1971.

Grossman H., 1983, Marx without the Labor Theory of Value?, in J.C. Wood (ed.), 1988, *Karl Marx's Economics: Critical Assessments*, vol. 3, Croom Helm, New South Wales.

Grossman S.J. and Hart O.D., 1986, The Costs and Benefits of Ownership: A Theory of Vertical and Lateral Integration, in *Journal of Political Economy*, vol. 94, n. 4, August.

Gruppi L., 1962, Contro l'impoverimento della dialettica marxista, reprinted in F. Cassano, 1973, *Marxismo e filosofia in Italia*, De Donato, Bari.

Gruppi L., 1972, *Il concetto di egemonia in Gramsci*, Editori Riuniti, Rome.

Gui B., 1981, Investment Decisions in a Worker-Managed Firm, in *Economie Analysis and Workers' Management*, vol. 15, n. 1.

Gui B., 1982, Imprese gestite dal lavoro e diritti patrimoniali dei membri: una trattazione economica, in *Ricerche economiche*, vol. 36, n. 3.

Gui B., 1985, Limits to External Financing: A Model and an Application to Labor-Managed Firms, in D.C. Jones and J. Svejnar (eds), 1985, *Advances in the Economic Analysis of Participatory and Labor-Managed Firms*, JAI Press, Greenwich, CT.

Gui B., 1993, The Chances for Success of Worker Managed Form Organization: An Overview, in AISSEC, *IX Scientific Meeting*.

Gui B., 1996, Is there a Chance for the Worker-Managed Form of Organization?, in U. Pagano and R. Rowthorn (eds), *Democracy and Efficiency in the Economic Enterprise*, Routledge, London.

Guicciardini F., 1512–1530, *Maxims and Reflections (Ricordi)*, University of Pennsylvania Press, Philadelphia, PA, 1972.

Guidi M.E.L. and Michelini L., 2001, *Marginalismo e socialismo nell'Italia liberale, 1870–1925*, Feltrinelli, Milan.

Guiducci R., 1977, Gramsci e la via consigliare al socialismo, in AA.VV., *Classe, consigli, partito*, Alfani edtore, Rome.

Gunn C.E., 1984, *Workers' Self-Management in the US*, Cornell University Press, Ithaca, NY.

Gunn C.E., 2006, Cooperative and Market Failure: Workers' Cooperatives and System Mismatch, in *Review of Radical Political Economics*, vol. 38, n. 3, Summer.

Gunn C.E., 2011, Workers' Participation in Management, Workers' Control of Production: Worlds Apart, in *Review of Radical Political Economics*, vol. 43, n. 3, Summer.

Gunn C.E., 2012, Introduction to the Special Issue on Economic Democracy, in *Review of Radical Political Economics*, vol. 44, n. 1.

Habermas J., 1963, *Teoria e prassi nella società tecnologica*, ital. transl., Laterza, Bari, 1969.

Habermas J., 1971, *Prassi politica e teoria critica della società*, ital. transl., Il Mulino, Bologna, 1973.

Hahn F.H., 1993, Il futuro del capitalismo: segni premonitori, in *Rivista Milanese di economia*, n. 46, April–June.

Hall S., 1975, The Rigidity of Wages and the Persistence of Unemployment, in *Brookings Papers in Economic Activity*, n. 2.

Hall S., 1992, Cultural Studies and their Theoretical Legacies, in L. Grossberg *et al.* (eds), *Cultural Studies*, Routledge, New York, NY.

Hansmann H., 1996, *The Ownership of Enterprise*, Belknap Press of the Harvard University Press, Cambridge, MA.

Harman C., 1977, Gramsci versus Eurocommunism, Part 2, in *International Socialism*, vol. 1, n. 99. Available online at www.marxists.anu.edu.au (accessed 28 October 2013).

Hart O., 1989, An Economist's Perspective on the Theory of the Firm, in *Columbia Law Review*, vol. 89, n. 7.

Hart O., 1995, Corporate Governance: Some Theory and Implications, in *Economic Journal*, vol. 105, n. 430, May.

Hart O. and Moore J., 1990, Property Right and the Nature of the Firm, in *Journal of Political Economy*, vol. 98, n. 6.

Hart O. and Moore J., 1996, The Governance of Exchanges: Members' Cooperatives versus Outside Ownership, *Working Paper*. Available online at http//ssrn.com/abstract=60039 (accessed 28 October 2013).

Harvey D., 2010, *L'enigma del capitale e il prezzo della sua sopravvivenza*, ital. transl., Feltrinelli, Milan, 2011.

Haupt G., 1978a, Marx e il marxismo, in E.J. Hobsbawm, G. Haupt, F. Marek, E. Ragionieri, V. Strada and C. Vivanti (eds), 1978–1982, *Storia del marxismo*, vol. 1, Einaudi, Turin.

Haupt G., 1978b, *L'internazionale socialista dalla Comune a Lenin*, Einaudi, Turin.

Haycock J.W., 1992, The Crises of Marxism in Post-Positivist Perspective, in *Review of Radical Political Economics*, vol. 24, nn. 3–4.

Hayek F.A., 1983, The Rediscovery of Liberty; Personal Recollections, in F.A. Hayek, 1992, *The Fortunes and the Ideal of Freedom*, Routledge & Kegan, London.

Hayek F.A., 1992, *The Fortunes and the Ideal of Freedom*, Routledge & Kegan, London.

Hayek F.A., 1960, *The Constitution of Liberty*, Routledge, London.

Hegedüs A., 1980, La costruzione del socialismo in Russia: il ruolo dei sindacati, la questione contadina, la nuova politica economica, in E.J. Hobsbawm, G. Haupt, F. Marek, E. Ragionieri, V. Strada and C. Vivanti (eds), 1978–1982, *Storia del marxismo*, vol. 3, Einaudi, Turin.

Hegel G.W.F., 1830, *Enciclopedia delle scienze filosofiche in compendio*, ital. transl., Laterza, Rome, 2009.

Hegel G.W.F., 1831, *Scienza della logica*, II ediz., ital. transl., Laterza, Bari, 1974.

Heller A., 1980, *Per cambiare la vita*; intervista di Ferdinando Adornato, Editori Riuniti, Rome.

Hendrikse G., ed., 2003, *Restructuring Agricultural Cooperatives*, Erasmus University Press, Haveka.

Hicks J.R., 1969, *A Theory of Economic History*, Oxford University Press, Oxford.

Hilferding R., 1923, *Il capitale finanziario*, ital. transl., Feltrinelli, Milan, 1961.

Hinden R., ed., 1964, *The Radical Tradition*, Pantheon Books, New York, NY.

Hirsch F., 1976, *The Social Limits to Growth*, Harvard University Press, Cambridge, MA.

Hirschmam A.O., 1982, Rival Interpretations of Market Society: Civilizing, Destructive or Feeble?, in *Journal of Economic Literature*, vol. 20, n. 4.

Hobsbawm E.J., 1978, Gli aspetti politici della transizione dal capitalismo al socialismo, in E.J. Hobsbawm, G. Haupt, F. Marek, E. Ragionieri, V. Strada and C. Vivanti (eds), 1978–1982, *Storia del marxismo*, 5 vols, Einaudi, Turin.

Hobsbawm E.J., 1979, La cultura europea e il marxismo fra Otto e Novecento, in E.J. Hobsbawm, G. Haupt, F. Marek, E. Ragionieri, V. Strada and C. Vivanti (eds), 1978–1982, *Storia del marxismo*, vol. 2, Einaudi, Turin.

Hobsbawm E.J., 1982, Il marxismo, oggi: un bilancio aperto, in E.J. Hobsbawm, G. Haupt, F. Marek, E. Ragionieri, V. Strada and C. Vivanti (eds), 1978–1982, *Storia del marxismo*, 5 vols, Einaudi, Turin.

Hobsbawm E.J., ed., 1995, *Gramsci in Europa e in America*, Laterza, Bari.

Hobsbawm E.J., Haupt G., Marek F., Ragionieri E., Strada V. and Vivanti C., eds, 1978–1982, *Storia del marxismo*, 5 vols, Einaudi, Turin.

Hobson J.A., 1902, *Imperialism: A Study*, 3rd edn, Allen & Unvin, London, 1938.

Hochschild A.R., 1983, *The Managed Heart: Commercialization of Human Feeling*, University of California Press, Berkeley, CA.

Hodges D.C., 1967, The Method of *Capital*, in J.C. Wood (ed.), 1988, *Karl Marx's Economics: Critical Assessments*, vol. 2, Croom Helm, New South Wales.

Hodgson G.M., 1982–1983, Worker Participation and Macroeconomic Efficiency, in *Journal of PostKeynesian Economics*, vol. 5, n. 2.

Hodgson G.M., 1982, Marx without the Labor Theory of Value, reprinted in J.C. Wood (ed.), 1988, *Karl Marx's Economics: Critical Assessments*, vol. 2, Croom Helm, New South Wales.

Hodgson G.M., 1987, Economic Pluralism and Self-Management, in D.C. Jones and J. Svejnar (eds), 1987, *Advances in the Economic Analysis of Participatory and Labor-Managed Firms*, JAI Press, Greenwich, CT.

Hodgson G.M., 1995, The Political Economy of Utopia, in *Review of Social Economy*, vol. 53, n. 2.

Hoff T.J.B., 1938, *Economic Calculation in the Socialist Society*, engl. transl., Liberty Press, Indianapolis, 1981.

Hollas D. and Stansell S., 1988, An Examination of the Effect of Ownership Form on Price Efficiency: Proprietary, Cooperative, and Municipal Electric Utilities, in *Southern Economic Journal*, vol. 55, October.

Holloway J., 1992, Crisis, Fetishism, Class Composition, in W. Bonefeld, R. Gunn and K. Psychopedis (eds), *Open Marxism*, vol. II, Pluto Press, London.

Holloway J., 2001, Why Read Capital?, in *Capital & Class*, special issue, n. 75, Autumn.

Holloway J., 2002, *Change the World Without Taking Power: The Meaning of Revolution Today*, Pluto Press, London.

Holmstrom B., 1982, Moral Hazard in Teams, in *Bell Journal of Economics*, vol. 13, n. 2.

Horowitz D., ed., 1968, *Marx, Keynes e i neomarxisti*, Boringhieri, Turin, 1971.

Horvat B., 1969, *An Essay on Yugoslav Society*, International Arts and Science Press, New York, NY.

Horvat B., 1974, Appunti critici sulla teoria dell'impresa autogestita e alcune considerazioni di ordine macroeconomico, in *Est-Ovest*, n. 1.

Horvat B., 1975, On the Theory of the Labor-Managed Firm, reprinted in D.L. Prychitko and J. Vanek (eds), 1996, *Producer Cooperatives and Labor-Managed Systems*, Cheltenham, E. Elgar.

Horvat B., 1982, Social Ownership, Report to the 10th *IAFEP Conference*, Trent, 6–8 July.

Horvat B., Markovic M. and Supek R., eds, 1975, *Self-Governing Socialism: A Reader*, International Arts and Science Press, New York, NY.

Houston D.B., 1983, Capitalism without Capitalists: A Comment on 'Classes in Marxian Theory', in *Review of Radical Political Economics*, vol. 15, n. 1, Spring.

Howard M.C. and King J.E., 1989, *A History of Marxian Economics*, vol. I, 1883–1929, Macmillan, London.

Howard M.C. and King J.E., 2001, Where Marx Was Wright: Toward a More Secure Foundation for Heterodox Economics, in *Cambridge Journal of Economics*, vol. 25, n. 6, November.

Huberman L. and Sweezy P.M., 1968, *Introduzione al socialismo*, ital. transl., Savelli, Rome, 1978.

Hudis P., 2000, The Dialectial Structure of Marx's Concept of 'Revolution in Permanence', in *Capital and Class*, n. 70, Spring.

Hunnius G., Garson G.D. and Case J., eds, 1973, *Workers' Control*, Vintage Books, New York, NY.

Hutchison T.W., 1978, Friedrich Engels and Marxist Economic Theory, in J.C. Wood (ed.), 1988, *Karl Marx's Economics: Critical Assessments*, Croom Helm, New South Wales.

Hyman R., 1975, *Industrial Relations: A Marxist Introduction*, Macmillan, Basingstoke.

Hyppolite J., 1969, Lo 'scientifico' e l''ideologico' in una prospettiva marxista, in AA.VV., 1969a, *Marx vivo*, Mondadori, Milan.

Ireland N.J. and Law P.J., 1981, Efficiency, Incentives and Individual Labor Supply in Labor-Managed Firms, in *Journal of Comparative Economics*, vol. 5, n. 1.

Ireland N.J. and Law P.J., 1982, *The Economics of Labour-Managed Enterprises*, Croom Helm, London.

Ishibashi S., 1995, The Demonstration of the Law of Value and the Uno-Sekine Approach, in R. Albritton and T.T. Sekine, *A Japanese Approach to Political Economy*, Palgrave, New York, NY.

Israelsen L.D., 1980, Collectives, Communes and Incentives, in *Journal of Comparative Economics*, vol. 4, June.

Istituto Giangiacomo Feltrinelli, 1974 e 1975, *Storia del marxismo contemporaneo*, Feltrinelli, Milan.

Istituto Gramsci, 1969 and 1970, *Gramsci e la cultura contemporanea*, vols I and II, Editori Riuniti, Rome.

Jacobsson F., Johannesson M. and Borgquist L., 2007, Is Altruism Paternalistic?, in *Economic Journal*, vol. 117, n. 520.

Jacoby R., 1987, *The Last Intellectuals*, Basic Books, New York, NY.

Jay P., 1980, The Workers' Cooperative Economy, in A. Clayre (ed.), *The Political Economy of Cooperation and Participation: A Third Sector*, Oxford Economic Press, Oxford.

Jensen M. C. and Meckling W.H., 1976, Theory of the Firm: Managerial Behavior, Agency Costs and Ownership Structure, in *Journal of Financial Economics*, vol. 3, n. 4, October.

Jensen M.C. and Meckling W.H., 1979, Rights and Production Functions: An Application to Labor-Managed Firms and Codetermination, in *Journal of Business*, vol. 52, n. 4.

Jocteau G.C., 1977, *Leggere Gramsci; guida alle interpretazioni*, 2nd edn, Feltrinelli, Milan.

Johnstone M., 1980, Lenin e la rivoluzione, in AA.VV., 1978–1982, *Storia del marxismo*, vol. III, Einaudi, Turin.

Jones D.C. and Backus D.K., 1977, British Producer Cooperatives in the Footwear Industry: An Empirical Evaluation of the Theory of Financing, in *Economic Journal*, vol. 87, September.

Jones D.C. and Pliskin J., 1991, The Effects of Worker Participation, Employee Ownership and Profit Sharing on Economic Performance: A Partial Review, in R. Russel and V. Rus (eds), *International Handbook of Participation in Organizations*, Oxford University Press, Oxford.

Jones D.C. and Svejnar J., eds, 1982, *Participatory and Self-Managed Firms: Evaluating Economic Performance*, Heath, Lexington.

Jones D.C. and Svejnar J., eds, 1985, *Advances in the Economic Analysis of Participatory and Labor-Managed Firms*, JAI Press, Greenwich, CT.

Jones D.C. and Svejnar J., eds, 1987, *Advances in the Economic Analysis of Participatory and Labor-Managed Firms*, JAI Press, Greenwich, CT.

Jones D.C. and Svejnar J., eds, 1992, *Advances in the Economic Analysis of Participatory and Labor-Managed Firms*, vol. 4, JAI Press, Greenwich, CT.

Jones D.C. and Svejnar J., eds, 1995, *Advances in the Economic Analysis of Participatory and Labor-Managed Firms*, vol. 5, JAI Press, Greenwich, CT.

Jossa B., 1978, *Socialismo e mercato; contributi alla teoria economica del socialismo*, Etas Libri, Milan.

Jossa B., 1983, Sulla teoria economica dell'impresa autogestita, *Rivista Internazionale di Scienze Sociali*, January–March.

Jossa B., 1986, Considerazioni su di un tipo ideale di cooperative di produzione, in *Studi economici*, vol. 41, n. 28.

Jossa B., 1988, Sul problema del sottoinvestimento delle imprese gestite dai lavoratori, in *AISSEC*, V Annual Scientific Convention, Pavia, 14–16 December 1988.

Jossa B., ed., 1989, *Teoria dei sistemi economici*, UTET, Turin.

Jossa B., 1992, Socialismo di mercato e distribuzione del reddito, in A. Chilosi, 1992a, *L'economia del periodo di transizione; dal modello di tipo sovietico all'economia di mercato*, Il Mulino, Bologna.

Jossa B., 1993, Is there an Option to the Denationalization of Eastern European Enterprises?, in M. Baldassarri, L. Paganetto and E.S. Phelps (eds), *Privatization Processes in Eastern Europe*, Macmillan, London.

Jossa B., 1997, *The Economic Theory of Socialism and the Labour-Managed Firm* (in collaboration with G. Cuomo), E. Elgar, Cheltenham.

Jossa B., 1998, *Mercato, socialismo e autogestione*, Carocci, Rome.

Jossa B., 1999, *La democrazia nell'impresa*, Editoriale Scientifica, Naples.

Jossa B., 2001, L'impresa gestita dai lavoratori e la disoccupazione classica e keynesiana, in *Rivista italiana degli economisti*, vol. VI, n. 1, April.

Jossa B., 2002, Il marxismo e le imprese gestite dai lavoratori, in *Economia Politica*, vol. XIX, n. 3.

Jossa B., 2003, Cooperativismo e teoria economica, in V. Buonocore and B. Jossa (eds), *Organizzazioni economiche non capitalistiche*, Il Mulino, Bologna.

Jossa B., ed., 2004a, *Il futuro del capitalismo*, Il Mulino, Bologna.

Jossa B., 2004b, L'impresa gestita dai lavoratori e la disoccupazione, in E. Screpanti and E. Tortia (eds), *Democrazia economica; tra Stato e mercato*, Pettirosso, Naples.

Jossa B., 2004c, The Democratic Firm as a Public Good, in R. Arena and N. Salvadori (eds), *Money, Credit and the Role of the State*, Ashgate, New York, NY.

Jossa B., 2004d, Schweickart and the Public Control of Investment, in *Review of Radical Political Economics*, vol. 36, n. 4, Autumn.

Jossa B., 2005a, Marx, Marxism and the Cooperative Movement, in *Cambridge Journal of Economics*, vol. 36, n. 1, January.

Jossa B., 2005b, *La teoria economica delle cooperative di produzione e la possibile fine del capitalismo*, Giappichelli, Turin.

Jossa B., 2006, Attualità delle cooperative, in M.P. Salani, *Lezioni cooperative*, Il Mulino, Bologna.

Jossa B., 2007a, Le cooperative di produzione come nuovo modo di produzione, in *Studi economici*, vol. LXII, n. 93.

Jossa B., 2007b, Qualche considerazione sul perché le imprese cooperative non si affermano, in *Economia politica*, vol. 24, August.

Jossa B., 2008a, How Cooperative Firms should be Organised from the Perspective of Today's Economic Theory, in *Politica Economica*, vol. 24, n. 3.

Jossa B., 2008b, Il lavoro come fonte del valore e l'attualità del marxismo, in *Rivista italiana degli economisti*, vol. XIII, n. 1.

Jossa B., 2009a, Alchian and Demsetz's Critique of the Cooperative Firm, Thirty-Seven Years After, in *Metroeconomica*, vol. 60, n. 4.

Jossa B., 2009b, Gramsci and the Economic Theory of the Labour-Managed Firm, in *Review of Radical Political Economics*, vol. 41, n. 1, March 2009.

Jossa B., 2009c, Gramsci, the Economic Theory of Cooperatives and the Transition to a Socialist Economy, in *Solidarity Economy Net*, April 2009, vol. IV.

Jossa B., 2009d, Unemployment in a System of Labour-Managed Firms, in N. Salvadori and A. Opocher, *Long-Run Growth, Social Institution and Living Standard*, Edward Elgar, Cheltenham.

Jossa B., 2010a, *Esiste un'alternativa al capitalismo?* manifestolibri, Rome.

Jossa B., 2010b, The Democratic Road to Socialism, in *Rivista Internazionale di Scienze Sociali*, n. 3, July–September 2010.

Jossa B., 2010c, Investment Funding: The Main Problem Facing Labor-Managed Firms?, in *Economia e Politica Industriale*, vol. 37, n. 2.

Jossa B., 2011, Le contraddizioni del capitalismo e il loro possibile superamento, in *Studi e note di economia*, n. 1.

Jossa B., 2012a (forthcoming), Alienation and the Self-Managed Firm System, in *The Review of Radical Political Economics*.

Jossa B., 2012b, A System of Self-Managed Firms as a New Perspective on Marxism, in *Cambridge Journal of Economics*, vol. 36, n. 4.

Jossa B., 2012c, Cooperative Firms as a New Production Mode, in *Review of Political Economy*, vol. 24, n. 3.

Jossa B., 2012d *Per un marxismo nell'epoca della globalizzazione*, manifestolibri, Rome.

Jossa B., 2012e, Sulla definizione del socialismo, in *Rivista di Politica Economica*, vols I–III, January–March 2012.

Jossa B., 2013 (forthcoming), Marx, Lenin and the Cooperative Movement, in *Review of Political Economy*.

Jossa B., 2013 (forthcoming), The Key Contradiction in Capitalism, in *Review of Radical Political Economics*.

Jossa B. and Casavola P., 1993, The Problem of Under-Investment in Firms Managed by Workers, in A.B. Atkinson (ed.), *Alternatives to Capitalism: The Economics of Partnership*, Macmillan, London.

Jossa B. and Lunghini, G., eds, 2006, *Marxismo oggi*, Il Ponte Editore, Florence.

Jossa B. and Pagano U., eds, 1997, *Economia di mercato ed efficienza dei diritti di proprietà*, Giappichelli, Turin.

Kahana N. and Paroush J., 1995, The Size of the Executive Board of Labour Managed Firms, in D.C. Jones and J. Svejnar (eds), 1995, *Advances in the Economic Analysis of Participatory and Labor-Managed Firms*, vol. 5, JAI Press, Greenwich, CT.

Kalecki M., 1937, The Principle of Increasing Risk, in *Economica*, vol. 3, November.

Kalecki M., 1943, Gli aspetti politici della piena occupazione, in M. Kalecki, 1975, *Sulla dinamica dell'economia capitalistica; saggi scelti, 1933–1970*, Einaudi, Turin.

Kalecky M., 1975, *Sulla dinamica dell'economia capitalistica; saggi scelti, 1933–1970*, Einaudi, Turin.

Kalmi P., 2000, Employment Share Trade under Employee Share Ownership: An Application to Transition Economies, in *Economic Analysis*, vol. 3, n. 1.

Kandel E. and Lazear E.P., 1992, Peer Pressure and Partnership, in *Journal of Political Economy*, vol. 100, n. 4, August.

Kander E., 1968, The Intellectual Sources of Karl Marx, reprinted in J.C. Wood (ed.), 1988, *Karl Marx's Economics: Critical Assessments*, Croom Helm, New South Wales.

Kant I., 1784, *Idea per una storia universale dal punto di vista cosmopolitico*, in N. Bobbio, L. Firpo and V. Mathieu (eds), 1965, *Scritti politici e di filosofia della storia e del diritto di Immanuel Kant*, U.T.E.T., Turin.

Kant I., 1797, *Fondazione della metafisica dei costumi*, La Nuova Italia, Florence, 1931.

Karsz S., 1974, *Teoria e politica: Louis Althusser*, ital. transl., Dedalo libri, Bari, 1976.

Kasmir S., 1996, *The Mith of Mondragon: Cooperatives, Politics and Working Class Life in a Basque Town*, State University of New York Press, Albany, NY.

Kauder E., 1968, The Intellectual Sources of Karl Marx, in *Kyklos*, vol. 21, n. 2.

Kautsky K., 1892, *Il Programma di Erfurt*, ital. transl., Samonà and Savelli, Rome, 1971.

Kautsky K., 1907, *Ethics and the Materialist Conception of History*, C.H. Kerr, Chicago, IL.

Kautsky K., 1909, *The Road to Power*, Bloch, Chicago, IL.

Kautsky K., 1960, *Erinnerungen und Erörterungen*, Gravenhage, Berlin.

Keynes J.M., 1925, A Short View of Russia, reprinted in J.M. Keynes, 1972, *The Collected Writings of John Maynard Keynes*, vol. IX, Macmillan, London.

Keynes J.M., 1933, The Distinction between a Cooperative Economy and an Entrepreneur Economy, reprinted in J.M. Keynes, 1979, *The Collected Writings of John Maynard Keynes, vol. XXIX; The General Theory and After: A Supplement*, Macmillan, London.

Keynes J.M., 1936, *The General Theory of Employment, Interest and Money*, Macmillan, London.

Keynes J.M., 1972, *The Collected Writings of John Maynard Keynes*, vol. IX, Macmillan, London.

Keynes J.M., 1979, *The Collected Writings of John Maynard Keynes, vol. XXIX; The General Theory and After: A Supplement*, Macmillan, London.

Kicillof A. and Starosta G., 2007, Value Form and Class Struggle: A Critique of the Autonomist Theory of Value, in *Capital and Class*, n. 92, Summer.

Kihlstrom R. and Laffont J.J., 1979, A General Equilibrium Entrepreneurial Theory of Firm Formation Based on Risk Aversion, in *Journal of Political Economy*, vol. 87, n. 4, August.

Kipnis K. and Meyers D.T., 1985, *Economic Justice; Private Rights and Public Responsibilities*, Rowman & Allanheld, Totowa.

Kirman V.G., 1991, Revolution, in T. Bottomore (ed.), *A Dictionary of Marxist Thought*, 2nd edn, Blackwell, Oxford.

Klein B., 1991, Vertical Integration as Organizational Ownership: The Fisher Body-General Motors Relationship Revisited, in O.E. Williamson and S. Winter, *The Nature of the Firm: Origins, Evolution and Development*, Oxford University Press, New York, NY.

Kliman A.J., 1998, Value, Exchange Value and the Internal Consistency of Volume III of Capital: A Refutation of Refutations, in R. Bellofiore (ed.), *Marxian Economics; A Reappraisal*, Palgrave Macmillan, New York, NY.

Kliman A.J., 2010, The Disintegration of the Marxian School, in *Capital & Class*, vol. 34, n. 1.

Knight F.H., 1921, *Risk, Uncertainty and Profit*, London School of Economics and Political Science, Boston, MA.

Kornai J., 1971, *Anti-Equilibrium*, North Holland, Amsterdam.

Korsch K., 1891, *Il programma di Erfurt*, ital. transl., Samonà e Savelli, Rome, 1971.

Korsch K., 1922, *Consigli di fabbrica e socializzazione*, ital. transl., Laterza, Bari, 1970.

Korsch K., 1923, *Marxismo e filosofia*, ital. transl., Sugar editore, Milan, 1966.

Korsch K., 1931, Crisi del marxismo, in K. Korsch, 1974, *Dialettica e scienza nel marxismo*, Laterza, Bari.

Korsch K., 1967, *Karl Marx*, trad. ital., Laterza, Bari, 1969.

Korsch K., 1974, *Dialettica e scienza nel marxismo*, Laterza, Bari.

Krugman P., 2007, *La coscienza di un liberal*, ital. transl., Bari, Laterza, 2008.

Kühne K., 1972, *Economics and Marxism*, engl. transl., Macmillan, London, 1979.

La Ganga G., ed., 1977, *Socialismo e democrazia economica*, F. Angeli, Milan.

Labedz L., 1962, *Revisionism. Essays in the History of Marxist Ideas*, Allen & Unwin, New York, NY.

Labriola A., 1902, *Discorrendo di socialismo e di filosofia*, Edizioni Millennium, Bologna, 2006.

Labriola A., 1965, *La concezione materialistica della storia*, ed. by E. Garin, Laterza, Bari.

Laibman D., 2006, The Future within the Present: Seven Theses for a Robust Twenty-First-Century Socialism, in *Review of Radical Political Economics*, vol. 18, n. 3, Summer.

Laibman D., 2007, *Deep History*, State of New York Press, New York, NY.

Landauer C., 1959, *European Socialism: A History of Ideas and Movements*, University of California Press, Berkeley, CA.

Landsberger H.A., 1958, *Hawthorne Revisited*, Cornell University Press, Ithaca, NY.

Lane R.E., 2000, *The Loss of Happiness in Market Democracies*, Yale University Press, New Haven, CT.

Lange O., 1935, Marxian Economics and Modern Economic Theory, in *The Review of Economic Studies*, vol. 2, n. 3, June.

Lange O., 1936–1937, On the Economic Theory of Socialism, in *The Review of Economic Studies*, vol. 4, nn. 1 and 2, reprinted with changes in B.E. Lippincott (ed.), 1938, *On the Economic Theory of Socialism*, University of Minnesota Press, Philadelphia, PA.

Lange O., 1957, Alcuni problemi riguardanti la via polacca al socialismo, in O. Lange, 1966, *Socialismo ed economia socialista*, ital. transl., La Nuova Italia, Florence, 1975.

Lange O., 1966, *Socialismo ed economia socialista*, ital. transl., La Nuova Italia, Florence, 1975.

Lavoie D., 1985, *Rivalry and Central Planning: The Socialist Calculation Debate Reconsidered*, Cambridge University Press, Cambridge.

Lawler J., 1994, Marx's Theory of Socialism: Nihilistic and Dialectical, in L. Patsouras (ed.) *Debating Marx*, EmText, New York, NY.

Layard R. and Nickell S., 1999, Labour Market Institutions and Economic Performance, in O. Ashenfelter, D. Card (eds), 1999, *Handbook of Labour Economics*, Elsevier, Amsterdam.

Lee F.S., 2011a, Pluralism Debate in Heterodox Economics, in *Review of Radical Political Economics*, vol. 43, n. 4.

Lee F.S., 2011b, Heterodox Economics, Tolerance, and Pluralism: A Reply to Garnett and Mearman, in *Review of Radical Political Economics*, vol. 43, n. 4.

Leete-Guy F., 1991, Federal Structure and the Viability of Labour-Managed Firms in Mixed Economies, in R. Russel and V. Rus (eds), *International Handbook of Participation in Organizations*, Oxford University Press, Oxford.

Lefebvre H., 1968, Bilancio di un secolo e di due mezzi secoli (1867–1917–1967), in AA.VV., 1968, *Cent'anni dopo* Il Capitale, ital. transl., Samonà e Savelli, Rome, 1970.

Lega Nazionale Cooperative e Mutue, 1982, *L'impresa cooperativa degli anni '80*, De Donato, Bari.

Lenin V.I., 1902, Che fare?, in V.I. Lenin, 1965, *Opere scelte*, Editori Riuniti, Rome.

Lenin V.I., 1917a, *L'imperialismo, fase suprema del capitalismo*, ital. transl., Editori Riuniti, Rome, 1969.

Lenin V.I., 1917b, *Stato e rivoluzione*, Editori Riuniti, Rome, 1974.

Lenin V.I., 1917c, Come organizzare l'emulazione?, in V.I. Lenin, 1957–1970, *Opere complete*, vol. XXVI, Editori Riuniti, Rome.

Lenin V.I., 1917d, I bolscevichi conserveranno il potere statale?, in V.I. Lenin, 1965, *Opere scelte*, Editori Riuniti, Rome.

Lenin V.I., 1917e, La catastrofe imminente e come lottare contro di essa, in V.I. Lenin, 1965, *Opere scelte*, Editori Riuniti, Rome.

Lenin V.I., 1918a, Speech in the Moscow Soviet of Workers', Peasants' and Red Army Deputies, 12 March 1918. Available online at www.marxists. org/archive/lenin/by-date.htm (accessed 28 October 2013).

Lenin V.I., 1918b, Six Theses on the Immediate Tasks of the Soviet Government, written between 30 April and 3 May 1918. Available online at www.marxists.org/archive/lenin/by-date.htm (accessed 28 October 2013).

Lenin V.I., 1918c, Speech at the *First Congress of Economic Councils*, 26 May 1918. Available online at www.marxists.org/archive/lenin/by-date.htm (accessed 28 October 2013).

Lenin V.I., 1918d, Speech at a Joint Session of the *All-Russia Central Executive Committee, the Moscow Soviet, Factory Committees and Trade Unions of Moscow*, 29 July 1918. Available online at www.marxists.org/archive/lenin/by-date.htm (accessed 28 October 2013).

Lenin V.I., 1918e, Speech to the *Third Workers' Co-Operative Congress*, 9 December

1918. Available online at www.marxists.org/archive/lenin/works/1918/dec/09.htm (accessed 28 October 2013).

Lenin V.I., 1920a, L'estremismo malattia infantile del comunismo, in V.I. Lenin, 1965, *Opere scelte*, Editori Riuniti, Rome.

Lenin V.I., 1920b, Report on The Work of the All-Russia Central Executive Committee and the Council of People's Commissars Delivered at the First Session of the *All-Russia Central Executive Committee*, Seventh Convocation, 2 February 1920. Available online at www.marxists. org/archive/lenin/by-date.htm (accessed 28 October 2013).

Lenin V.I., 1921a, La nuova politica economica, in V.I. Lenin, 1972, *La costruzione del socialismo*, Editori Riuniti, Rome.

Lenin V.I., 1921b, La tattica del partito comunista russo, in V.I. Lenin, 1972, *La costruzione del socialismo*, Editori Riuniti, Rome.

Lenin V.I., 1921c, Rapporto sulla sostituzione dei prelevamenti alle eccedenze con l'imposta in natura, in V.I. Lenin, 1957–1970, *Opere complete*, vol. XXXII, Editori Riuniti, Rome.

Lenin V.I., 1921d, Ancora sull'imposta in natura, reprinted in V.I. Lenin, 1972, *La costruzione del socialismo*, Editori Riuniti, Rome.

Lenin V.I., 1921e, Consumers' and Producers' Co-Operative Societies. Available online at www.marxists.org/archive/lenin/by-date.htm (accessed 28 October 2013).

Lenin V.I., 1921f, Recorded Speeches. Available online at www.marxists.org/archive/lenin/works/1921/apr/25.htm (accessed 28 October 2013).

Lenin V.I., 1922a, Discorso di chiusura, in V.I. Lenin, 1965, *Opere scelte*, Editori Riuniti, Rome.

Lenin V.I., 1922b, La funzione e i compiti dei sindacati nelle condizioni della Nuova politica economica, in V.I. Lenin, 1965, *Opere scelte*, Editori Riuniti, Rome.

Lenin V.I., 1922c, Lettera al Congresso e appunti 1922–1923, in V.I. Lenin, 1965, *Opere scelte*, Editori Riuniti, Rome.

Lenin V.I., 1922d, Cinque anni di rivoluzione russa e le prospettive della rivoluzione mondiale, in V.I. Lenin, 1965, *Opere scelte*, Editori Riuniti, Rome.

Lenin V.I., 1923a, Sulla cooperazione, in V.I. Lenin, 1965, *Opere scelte*, Editori Riuniti, Rome.

Lenin V.I., 1923b, Meglio meno, ma meglio, in V.I. Lenin, 1972, *La costruzione del socialismo*, Editori Riuniti, Rome.

Lenin V.I., 1957–1970, *Opere complete*, Editori Riuniti, Rome.

Lenin V.I., 1965, *Opere scelte*, Editori Riuniti, Rome.

Lenin V.I., 1972, *La costruzione del socialismo*, Editori Riuniti, Rome.

Leone E., 1902, Sul principio di cooperazione nei suoi rapporti con il socialismo, in *Critica sociale*, vol. XII, n. 18.

Leonetti A., 1971, Introduzione, in A. Bordiga, A. Gramsci, *Dibattito sui consigli di fabbrica*, Samonà e Savelli, Rome.

Leontief W., 1937, Il significato dell'economia marxiana per la teoria economica contemporanea, in D. Horowitz (ed.), 1968, *Marx, Keynes e i neomarxisti*, Boringhieri, Turin, 1971.

Leopardi G., 1920, *Dallo Zibaldone*, Utet, Turin.

Lepage H., 1978, *Autogestion et capitalisme*, Masson, Paris.

Lepre A., 1978, *Gramsci secondo Gramsci*, Liguori, Naples.

Levine A., 1984–1988, *Arguing for Socialism*, Verso, London.

Levine D.P., 1998, The Structure of Marx's Argument in *Capital*, in R. Bellofiore (ed.), *Marxian Economics; A Reappraisal*, Palgrave Macmillan, New York, NY.

Levine D.J., 1995, *Reinventing the Workplace. How Business and Employees Can Both Win*, Brookings Institution, Washington DC, WA.

Levine D.J. and Tyson L., 1990, Participation, Productivity and the Firm's Environment, in A. Blinder (ed.), *Paying for Productivity*, Brookings Institution, Washington DC, WA.

Lewin M., 1969, *L'ultima battaglia di Lenin*, Laterza, Bari.

Libertini L. and Panzieri R., 1958, Sette tesi sulla questione del controllo operaio, in *Mondo operaio*, febbraio.

Lichtheim G., 1965, *Marxism; An Historical and Critical Study*, F.A. Praeger, New York, NY.

Liguori G., 1996, *Gramsci conteso; storia di un dibattito, 1923–1996*, Editori Riuniti, Rome.

Lindbeck A., 1972, *The Political Economy of the New Left: An Outsider's View*, Joanna Cotler Books, New York, NY.

Lindbeck A., 1993, Unemployment and Macroeconomics, MIT Press, Cambridge, MA.

Lindbeck A. and Snower D.J., 1982, Involuntary Unemployment as an Insider–Outsider Dilemma, reprinted as Wage Rigidity, Union Activity, and Unemployment, in W. Beckerman, 1986, *Wage Rigidity and Employment*, Duckworth, London.

Lindbeck A. and Snower D.J., 1985, Explanations of Unemployment, in *Oxford Review of Economic Policy*, vol. 1, n. 2.

Lindbeck A. and Snower D.J., 1986a, Efficiency Wages versus Insiders–Outsiders, in *European Economic Review*, vol. 30.

Lindbeck A. and Snower D.J., 1986b, Wage Setting, Unemployment, and Insider–Outsider Relations, in *American Economic Review*, vol. 76.

Lindbeck A. and Snower D.J., 1988a, Cooperation, Harassment, and Involuntary Unemployment: An Insider–Outsider Approach, in *American Economic Review*, vol. 78, March.

Lindbeck A. and Snower D.J., 1988b, *The Insider–Outsider Theory of Employment and Unemployment*, MIT Press, Cambridge, MA.

Lindblom C., 1977, *Politica e mercato*, ital. transl., Etas Libri, Milan, 1979.

Lindsey J.K., 1983, Classes in Marxist Theory, in *Review of Radical Political Economics*, vol. 15, n. 1, Spring.

Lippincott B.E., ed., 1938, *On the Economic Theory of Socialism*, University of Minnesota Press, Philadelphia, PA.

Lipsey R.G. and Lancaster K., 1956, The General Theory of the Second Best, in *Review of Economic Studies*, vol. 24, n. 1.

Liss S.B., 1984, *Marxist Thought in Latin America*, University of California Press, Berkeley, CA.

Lissa G., 1982, Il marxismo italiano tra scienza e filosofia, in N. Bobbio (ed.), *La cultura filosofica italiana dal 1945 al 1980*, Guida editori, Naples.

Lockwood D., 1964, Social Integration and System Integration, in G.K. Zollshan and W. Hirsch (eds), *Explorations in Social Change*, Houghton Mifflin, Boston, MA.

Longo G.O., 2005, Cosa intendiamo quando parliamo di 'cultura', in C.P. Snow, 1959–1963, *The Two Cultures*, Cambridge University Press, Cambridge, 1993.

Lorenz R., 1974, La costruzione del socialismo in Lenin, in Istituto Giangiacomo Feltrinelli, *Storia del marxismo contemporaneo*, Feltrinelli, Milan.

Lowit T., 1962, Marx et le mouvement cooperatif, in *Cahiers de l'institut de science èconomique appliquée*, n. 129, September.

Löwy M., 2005, To Change the World We Need Revolutionary Democracy, in *Capital and Class*, vol. 85, Spring.

Lukàcs G., 1923, *Storia e coscienza di classe*, ital. transl., Sugarco Edizioni, Milan, 1974.

Lukàcs G., 1924, *Lenin*, ital. transl., Einaudi, Turin, 1970.

Lukàcs G., 1948, *Il giovane Hegel*, ital. transl., Einaudi, Turin, 1960.

Lukàcs G., 1954, *Il giovane Marx*, ital. transl., Editori Riuniti, Rome, 1978.

Lukàcs G., 1956, La lotta tra progresso e reazione nella cultura d'oggi, in G. Lukàcs, 1968b, *Marxismo e politica culturale*, Einaudi, Turin.

Lukàcs G., 1968a, *Scritti politici giovanili*, 1919–1928, Laterza, Bari.

Lukàcs G., 1968b, *Marxismo e politica culturale*, Einaudi, Turin.

Lukàcs G., 1970, *Cultura e potere*, ital. transl., Editori Riuniti, Rome, 1970.

Lukàcs G., 1971, Vecchia kultur e nuova kultur, in *Quaderni Piacentini*, vol. 43, April.

Lukàcs G., 1972, *L'uomo e la rivoluzione*, ital. transl., Editori Riuniti, Rome, 1973.

Luporini C., 1954, Marxismo e sociologia: il concetto di formazione economico sociale, in C. Luporini, 1974, *Dialettica e materialismo*, Editori Riuniti, Rome.

Luporini C., 1955, La consapevolezza storica del marxismo, in C. Luporini, 1974, *Dialettica e materialismo*, Editori Riuniti, Rome.

Luporini C., 1963a, Rovesciamento e metodo nella dialettica marxista, in C. Luporini, 1974, *Dialettica e materialismo*, Editori Riuniti, Rome.

Luporini C., 1963b, Le 'radici' della vita morale, in AA.VV., 1966, *Morale e società. Atti del Convegno promosso dall'Istituto Gramsci*, Editori Riuniti, Rome.

Luporini C., 1966, Realtà e storicità: economia e dialettica nel marxismo, in C. Luporini, 1974, *Dialettica e materialismo*, Editori Riuniti, Rome.

Luporini C., 1969, Introduction, in K. Marx and F. Engels, 1845–1846, The German Ideology, in K. Marx, F. Engels, 1975–2001, *Collected Works*, vol. 5, Lawrence and Wishart, London.

Luporini C., 1974, *Dialettica e materialismo*, Editori Riuniti, Rome.

Lutz M.A., 1997, The Mondragon Cooperative Complex: An Application of Kantian Ethics to Social Economies, in *Journal of Social Economics*, vol. 24, n. 1.

Luxemburg R., 1905, La rivoluzione russa, in R. Luxemburg, 1967, *Scritti politici*, ed. by L. Basso, Editori Riuniti, Rome.

Luxemburg R., 1908, *Riforma sociale o rivoluzione?*, in R. Luxemburg, 1963, *Scritti scelti*, Edizioni Avanti!, Milan.

Luxemburg R., 1918, Discorso sul programma, in R. Luxemburg, 1967, *Scritti politici*, ed. by L. Basso, Editori Riuniti, Rome.

Luxemburg R., 1963, *Scritti scelti*, Edizioni Avanti!, Milan.

Luxemburg R., 1967, *Scritti politici*, ed. by L. Basso, Editori Riuniti, Rome.

Luxemburg R., 1971, *Lettere ai Kautsky*, Editori Riuniti, Rome.

Macciocchi M.A., 1974, *Per Gramsci*, Il Mulino, Bologna.

MacGregor D., 1984, *The Communist Ideal in Hegel and Marx*, University of Toronto Press, Toronto.

MacLeod G., 1997, *From Mondragon to America: Experiments in Community Economic Development*, University College of Cape Breton Press, Sydney.

MacPherson C.B., 1984, Democracy: Utopian and Scientific, in T. Ball and J. Farr (eds), *After Marx*, Cambridge University Press, Cambridge.

MacPherson I., 2008, The Cooperative Movement and the Social Economy Traditions: Reflections on the Mingling of Broad Visions, in *Annals of Public and Cooperative Economics*, vol. 79, nn. 3/4.

Magatti M., ed., 1990, *Azione economica come azione sociale*, F. Angeli, Milan.

Magri L., 1977, 'Via italiana' e strategia consiliare, in AA.VV., 1977, *Classe, consigli, partito*, Alfani edtore, Rome.

Maietta O.W. and Sena V., 2010, Financial Constraint and Technical Efficiency: Some Empirical Evidence for Italian Producers' Cooperatives, in *Annals of Public and Cooperative Economics*, vol. 81, n. 1.

Major G., 1996, Solving the Underinvestment and Degeneration Problem of Workers' Cooperatives: Non-Voting and Vote-Weighted Value-Added Residual Shares, in *Annals of Public and Cooperative Economy*, vol. 67, n. 4.

Malcomson J.M., 1981, Unemployment and the Efficiency Wage Hypothesis, in *Economic Journal*, vol. 91, December.

Mallet S., 1963, *La nuova classe operaia*, ital. transl., Einaudi, Turin, 1967.

Mandel E., 1967, *La formation de la pensée économique de Karl Marx*, Maspero, Paris.

Mandel E., 1973, The Debate on Workers' Control, in G. Hunnius, G.D. Garson and J. Case (eds), *Workers' Control*, Vintage Books, New York, NY.

Marcuse H., 1954, *Ragione e rivoluzione*, ital. transl., Il Mulino, Bologna, 1966.

Marcuse H., 1958, *Soviet Marxism: le sorti del marxismo in URSS*, ital. transl., Guanda, Parma, 1968.

Marcuse H., 1964, *One-Dimensional Man*, Beacon Press, Boston, MA.

Marcuse H., 1968, *Critica della società repressiva*, antologia a cura di G. Camporesi, Feltrinelli, Milan.

Marcuse H., 1969a, Un riesame del concetto di rivoluzione, in AA.VV., 1969a, *Marx vivo*, Mondadori, Milan.

Marcuse H., 1969b, *Cultura e società*, Einaudi, Turin.

Marek F., 1982, Teorie della rivoluzione e fasi della transizione, in E.J. Hobsbawm, G. Haupt, F. Marek, E. Ragionieri, V. Strada and C. Vivanti (eds), 1978–1982, *Storia del marxismo*, 5 vols, Einaudi, Turin.

Marglin S., 1974, What Do Bosses Do?, in *Review of Radical Political Economics*, vol. VI, n. 2, Summer.

Markovic M., 1969, Marx e il pensiero critico-scientifico, in AA.VV., 1969a, *Marx vivo*, Mondadori, Milan.

Markovic M., 1991, Self-Management, in T. Bottomore (ed.), *A Dictionary of Marxist Thought*, 2nd edn, Blackwell, Oxford.

Marramao G., 1977, *Austromarxismo e socialismo di sinistra tra le due guerre*, La Pietra, Milan.

Marramao G., 1980, Tra bolscevismo e socialdemocrazia: Otto Bauer e la cultura politica dell'austromarxismo, in AA.VV., 1978–1982, *Storia del marxismo*, Einaudi, Turin.

Marshall A. and Marshall M., 1881, *The Economics of Industry*, 2nd edn, Macmillan, London.

Marshall A., 1873, The Future of the Working Classes, in A. Marshall, 1925, *Memorials of Alfred Marshall*, ed. by A.C. Pigou, Macmillan, London.

Marshall A., 1889, Cooperation, reprinted in A. Marshall, 1925, *Memorials of Alfred Marshall*, ed. by A.C. Pigou, Macmillan, London.

Marshall A., 1890, *Principles of Economics*, Macmillan, London.

Marshall A., 1897, The Old Generation of Economists and the New, in A. Marshall, 1925, *Memorials of Alfred Marshall*, ed. by A.C. Pigou, Macmillan, London.

Marshall A., 1925, *Memorials of Alfred Marshall*, ed. by A.C. Pigou, Macmillan, London.

Marshall R.C., 2003, The Culture of Cooperation in Three Japanese Worker Cooperatives, in *Economic and Industrial Democracy*, vol. 24, n. 4, November.

Marx K., 1841, On the Difference between Democritean and Epicurean Philosophies of Nature, in K. Marx and F. Engels, 1975–2001, *Collected Works*, vol. 1, Lawrence and Wishart, London.

Marx K., 1843, Contribution to the Critique of Hegel's Philosophy of Right, in K. Marx and F. Engels, 1975–2001, *Collected Works*, vol. 3, Lawrence and Wishart, London.

Marx K., 1844a, Economic and Philosophical Manuscripts of 1844, in K. Marx and F. Engels, 1975–2001, *Collected Works*, vol. 3, Lawrence and Wishart, London.

Marx K., 1844b, On the Jewish Question, in K. Marx and F. Engels, 1975–2001, *Collected Works*, vol. 3, Lawrence and Wishart, London.

Marx K., 1845, Theses on Feuerbach, in K. Marx and F. Engels, 1975–2001, *Collected Works*, vol. 5, Lawrence and Wishart, London.

Marx K., 1847, *Miseria della filosofia*, Editori Riuniti, Rome, 1969.

Marx K., 1849, *Lavoro salariato e capitale*, Editori Riuniti, Rome, 1960.

Marx K., 1857–1858a, Economic Manuscripts of 1857–1858, in K. Marx and F. Engels, 1975–2001, *Collected Works*, vols 28 and 29, Lawrence and Wishart, London.

Marx K., 1858, Lettera a Engels datata 14 gennaio, in K. Marx and F. Engels, 1972, *Carteggio Marx-Engels*, vols I–VI, Editori Riuniti, Rome.

Marx K., 1859, Outline of the Critique of Political Economy, in K. Marx and F. Engels, 1975–2001, *Collected Works*, vol. 29, Lawrence and Wishart, London.

Marx K., 1861–1863, Economic Manuscripts of 1861–1863, in K. Marx and F. Engels, 1975–2001, *Collected Works*, vols 30–34, Lawrence and Wishart, London.

Marx K., 1863–1866, *Il capitale: libro I, capitolo VI inedito*, La Nuova Italia, Florence, 1969.

Marx K., 1864, Inaugural Address of the Working Men's International Association, in K. Marx, F. Engels, 1975–2001, *Collected Works*, vol. 20, Lawrence and Wishart, London.

Marx K., 1867a, *Capital*, vol. I, Penguin Books, Harmondsword, 1986.

Marx K., 1867b, *Il Capitale*, vol. I, ital. transl., Editori Riuniti, Rome, 1964.

Marx K., 1868, Letter to Kugelmann of 6 March, in K. Marx and F. Engels, 1975–2001, *Collected Works*, vol. 42, Lawrence and Wishart, London.

Marx K., 1871, The Civil War in France, in K. Marx and F. Engels, 1975–2001, *Collected Works*, vol. 22, Lawrence and Wishart, London.

Marx K., 1875a, Critique of the Gotha Programme, in K. Marx and F. Engels, 1975–2001, *Collected Works*, vol. 24, Lawrence and Wishart, London.

Marx K., 1875b, Notes on Bakunin's 'Statehood and Anarchy', in K. Marx and F. Engels, 1975–2001, *Collected Works*, vol. 24, Lawrence and Wishart, London.

Marx K., 1894a, *Capital*, vol. III, Penguin Books, Harmondsworth, 1981.

Marx K., 1894b, *Il capitale*, vol. III, Editori Riuniti, Rome, 1965.

Marx K., 1895, *The Class Struggles in France, 1848–50*, in K. Marx and F. Engels, 1975–2001, *Collected Works*, vol. 10, Lawrence and Wishart, London.

Marx K. and Engels F., 1845–1846, The German Ideology, in K. Marx and F. Engels, 1975–2001, *Collected Works*, vol. 5, Lawrence and Wishart, London.

Marx K. and Engels F., 1845, *The Holy Family*, in K. Marx and F. Engels, 1975–2001, *Collected Works*, vol. 5, Lawrence and Wishart, London.

Marx K. and Engels F., 1848, *Manifesto of the Communist Party*, in K. Marx and F. Engels, 1975–2001, *Collected Works*, vol. 6, Lawrence and Wishart, London.

Marx K. and Engels F., 1850, Rassegna, in K. Marx and F. Engels, *Opere complete*, vol. 10, Editori Riuniti, Rome.

Marx K. and Engels F., 1972, *Carteggio Marx-Engels*, voll. I–VI, Editori Riuniti, Rome.

Marx K. and Engels F., 1975–2001, *Collected Works*, vols 1–49, Lawrence and Wishart, London.

Marx K. and Engels F., *Opere complete*, Editori Riuniti, Rome.

Massari R., 1974, *Le teorie dell'autogestione*, Jaca Book, Milan.

Massari R., 1994, L'inizio autentico: i 'Soviet', i comitati di fabbrica, in A. Colombo (ed.), *Crollo del Comunismo sovietico e ripresa dell'utopia*, Edizioni Dedalo, Bari.

Mazzini G., 1935, *Scritti editi ed inediti*, Galeati, Imola.

Mazzoli E. and Zamagni S., eds, 2005, *Verso una nuova teoria economica della cooperazione*, Il Mulino, Bologna.

Mazzoli M., 1998, Vantaggi e svantaggi comparati delle imprese cooperative nell'accesso ai mercati finanziari, in G. Fiorentini and C. Scarpa (eds), *Cooperative e mercato*, Carocci, Rome.

McCain R.A, 1977, On the Optimum Financial Environment for Worker Cooperatives, in *Zeitschrift für Nationalökonomie*, vol. 37, n. 3–4.

McCain R.A., 1992, Transaction Costs, Labor Management and Codetermination, in D.C. Jones and J. Svejnar (eds), 1992, *Advances in the Economic Analysis of Participatory and Labor-Managed Firms*, vol. 4, JAI Press, Greenwich, CT.

McConnell J.W., 1949, Discussion, in *American Economic Review*, vol. XXXIX, May, Papers and Proceedings.

McGlone T. and Kliman A., 1996, One System or Two? The Transformation of Values into Prices of Production versus the Transformation Problem, in A. Freeman and G. Carchedi, *Marx and Non-Equilibrium Economics*, E. Elgar, Cheltenham.

McLellan D., 1978, La concezione materialistica della storia, in E.J. Hobsbawm, G. Haupt, F. Marek, E. Ragionieri, V. Strada and C. Vivanti (eds), 1978–1982, *Storia del marxismo*, 5 vols, Einaudi, Turin.

McQuarie D. and Amburgey T., 1978, Marx and Modern System Theory, in J.C. Wood (ed.), 1988, *Karl Marx's Economics: Critical Assessments*, vol. IV, Croom Helm, New South Wales.

Meade J.E., 1972, The Theory of Labour-Managed Firms and of Profit Sharing, in *Economic Journal*, vol. 82, March, Supplement.

Meade J.E., 1979, The Adjustment Processes of Labor Cooperatives with Constant Returns to Scale and Perfect Competition, in *Economic Journal*, vol. 89, December.

Meade J.E., 1989, *Agathotopia: The Economics of Partnership*, Allen & Unwin, London.

Mearman A., 2011, Pluralism, Heterodoxy, and the Rhetoric of Distinction, in *Review of Radical Political Economics*, vol. 43, n. 4.

Medvedev R.A., 1980, Il socialismo in un solo paese, in E.J. Hobsbawm, G. Haupt, F. Marek, E. Ragionieri, V. Strada and C. Vivanti (eds), 1978–1982, *Storia del marxismo*, vol. III, Einaudi, Turin.

Meek C.B. and Woodworth W.P., 1990, Technical Training and Enterprise: Mondragon's Educational System and its Implications for Other Cooperatives, in *Economcs and Industrial Democracy*, vol. 11, n. 4.

Meek R.L., 1972, Marginalism and Marxism, in R.L. Meek, 1977, *Smith, Marx and After*, Chapman and Hall, London.

Meek R.L., 1977, *Smith, Marx and After*, Chapman and Hall, London.

Meiksins Wood E., 2000a, *Democracy against Capitalism: Renewing Historical Materialism*, Cambridge University Press, Cambridge.

Meiksins Wood E., 2000b, The Separation of the Economic and the Political in Capitalism, in E. Meiksins Wood, 2000a, *Democracy against Capitalism: Renewing Historical Materialism*, Cambridge University Press, Cambridge.

Melgarejo Z., Arcelus F.J. and Simon K., 2010, Differences in Financial Performance amongst Spanish SMEs according to their Capital-Ownership Structure: A Descriprtive Analysis, in *Annals of Public and Cooperative Economics*, vol. 81, n. 1.

Menard C., 2004, The Economics of Hybrid Organizations?, in *Journal of Institutional and Theoretical Economics*, vol. 160, n. 3.

Merker N., 2010, *Karl Marx; vita e opere*, Laterza, Bari.

Mészàros I., 1970, *Marx's Theory of Alienation*, The Merlin Press, London.

Mészàros I., 1978, Marx 'filosofo', in E.J. Hobsbawm, G. Haupt, F. Marek, E. Ragionieri, V. Strada and C. Vivanti (eds), 1978–1982, *Storia del marxismo*, 5 vols, Einaudi, Turin.

Mészàros I., 1995, *Behond Capital*, Merlin Press, London.

Meyer A.G., 1957, *Il leninismo*, ital. transl., Edizioni di Comunità, Milan, 1965.

Meyer T., 1994, *Analytical Marxism*, vol. I, Sage Publications, London.

Michels, R., 1909, L'uomo economico e la cooperazione, in *La Riforma sociale*, vol. XX, n. XVI.

Mill J.S., 1871, *Principles of Political Economy*, ed. by W.J. Ashley, Longmans, Green & Co., London, 1909.

Miller D., 1989, *Market, States and Community*, Clarendon Press, Oxford.

Miller D., 1993, Equality and Market Socialism, in P. Bardhan and J.E. Roemer (eds), *Market Socialism: The Current Debate*, Oxford Economic Press, New York, NY.

Mills C.W., 1948, *The New Man of Power*, Harcourt Brace, New York, NY.

Mills C.W., 1959, *The Sociological Imagination*, Oxford University Press, New York, NY.

Mills C.W., 1962, *I marxisti*, ital. transl., Feltrinelli, Milan, 1969.

Mises L. von, 1951, *Socialism, an Economic and Sociological Analysis*, Clarendon Press, Oxford.

Miyazaki H. and Neary H.N., 1983, The Illyrian Firm Revisited, in *Bell Journal of Economics*, vol. 14, n. 1.

Mondolfo R., 1952, *Il materialismo storico in Federico Engels*, La Nuova Italia, Florence.

Montesquieu C.L., 1748, *Esprit des lois*, a cura di La Brethe de la Grassaye, 4 vol., Les Belles Lettres, Paris, 1950–1961.

Montias J.M., 1976, *The Structure of Economics Systems*, Yale University Press, New Haven, CT.

Mordenti R., 2007, *Gramsci e la rivoluzione necessaria*, Editori Riuniti, Rome, 2011.

Morishima M., 2001, Teoria economica e democrazia, in *Studi e note di Economia*, n. 1.

Morley-Fletcher E., 1986, Certezze per rischiare, competere, per cooperare: una introduzione, in AA.VV., 1986, *Cooperare e competere*, Feltrinelli, Milan.

Morris D., 1992, *The Mondragon System Cooperation at Work*, Institute for Local Self-Reliance, Washington DC, WA.

Morse L.B., 2000, A Case for Water Utilities and Cooperatives, and the UK Experience, in *Annals of Public and Cooperative Economics*, vol. 71, n. 3.

Moscatello B., 1990, *Gramsci e il Marxismo contemporaneo*, Editori Riuniti, Rome.

Musgrave R.A., 1958, On Merit Goods, in R.A. Musgrave, 1986, *Public Finance in a Democratic Society*; Collected Papers of Richard A. Musgrave, vol. 1, Wheatsheaf Books, Brighton.

Musgrave R.A., 1959, *The Theory of Public Finance*, McGraw-Hill, New York, NY.

Musgrave R.A., 1986, *Public Finance in a Democratic Society*; Collected Papers of Richard A. Musgrave, vol. I, Wheatsheaf Books, Brighton.

Musgrave R.A., 1987, Merit Goods, in J. Eatwell, M. Milgate and P. Newman (eds), *The New Palgrave. A Dictionary of Economics*, vol. 3, Macmillan, London.

Musto M., ed., 2005, *Sulle tracce di un fantasma*, manifestolibri, Rome.

Musto M., 2008a, Dissemination and Reception of the *Grundrisse* in the World, in M. Musto (ed.), 2008b, *Karl Marx's Grundrisse*, Routledge, London.

Musto M., ed., 2008b, *Karl Marx's Grundrisse*, Routledge, London.

Musto M., 2010, Rivisitando la concezione dell'alienazione in Marx, in M. Musto, 2011, *Ripensare Marx e i marxismi*, Carocci, Rome.

Musto M., 2011, *Ripensare Marx e i marxismi*, Carocci, Rome.

Mygind N., 1997, Employee Ownership in Baltic Countries, in M. Uvalic and D. Vaughan-Whitehead (eds), *Privatization Surprises in Transition Economies: Employee Ownership in Central and Eastern Europe*, Cheltenham, E. Elgar.

Napoleoni C., 1985, Dalla scienza all'utopia, in C. Napoleoni, 1992, *Dalla scienza all'utopia, Saggi scelti, 1961–1988*, edited by G.L. Vaccarino, Bollati Boringhieri, Turin.

Napoleoni C., 1992, *Dalla scienza all'utopia, Saggi scelti, 1961–1988*, edited by G.L. Vaccarino, Bollati Boringhieri, Turin.

Nardone G., 1971, *Il pensiero di Gramsci*, De Donato, Bari.

Nassisi A.M., ed., 1987, *Marx e il mondo contemporaneo*, Editori Riuniti, Rome.

Negri A., 1974, *Crisi dello Stato-piano; comunismo e organizzazione rivoluzionaria*, Clusf, Florence.

Negri A., 1979, *Marx oltre Marx, Quaderno di lavoro sui 'Grundrisse'*, Feltrinelli, Milan.

Negt O., 1978, L'ultimo Engels, in E.J. Hobsbawm, G. Haupt, F. Marek, E. Ragionieri, V. Strada and C. Vivanti (eds), 1978–1982, *Storia del marxismo*, 5 vols, Einaudi, Turin.

Negt O., 1979a, Rosa Luxemburg e il rinnovamento del marxismo, in E.J. Hobsbawm, G. Haupt, F. Marek, E. Ragionieri, V. Strada and C. Vivanti (eds), 1978–1982, *Storia del marxismo*, 5 vols, Einaudi, Turin.

Negt O., 1979b, Il marxismo e la teoria della rivoluzione nell'ultimo Engels, in E.J. Hobsbawm, G. Haupt, F. Marek, E. Ragionieri, V. Strada and C. Vivanti (eds), 1978–1982, *Storia del marxismo*, vol. 2, Einaudi, Turin.

Neuberger H. and James E., 1973, The Yugoslav Self-Managed Enterprise: A Systemic Approach, in M. Bornstein (ed.), 1973, *Plan and Market: Economic Reform in Eastern Europe*, Yale University Press, New Haven, CT.

Nickell S., 1997, Unemployment and Labour Market Rigidities: Europe vs. North America, in *Journal of Economic Perspectives*, vol. 11, n. 3.

Nielsen P., 2002, Reflections on Critical Realism in Political Economy, in *Cambridge Journal of Economics*, vol. 26, n. 6.

Nordhal R.A., 1982, Marx on the Use of History in the Analysis of Capitalism, in J.C. Wood (ed.), 1988, *Karl Marx's Economics: Critical Assessments*, vol. 1, Croom Helm, New South Wales.

Nove A., 1980, Economia sovietica e marxismo: quale modello socialista?, in E.J. Hobsbawm, G. Haupt, F. Marek, E. Ragionieri, V. Strada and C. Vivanti (eds), 1978–1982, *Storia del marxismo*, 5 vols, Einaudi, Turin.

Nove A., 1986, *The Economics of Feasible Socialism*, Allen and Unwin, London.

Nozick R., 1974, *Anarchy, State and Utopia*, Basil Blackwell, Oxford.

Nuti D.M., 1992, Il socialismo di mercato. Il modello che avrebbe potuto esserci, ma che non c'è mai stato, in A. Chilosi, 1992a, *L'economia del periodo di transizione; dal modello di tipo sovietico all'economia di mercato*, Il Mulino, Bologna.

Nuti D.M., 1996, Efficiency, Equality and Enterprise Democracy, in U. Pagano and R. Rowthorn (eds), *Democracy and Efficiency in the Economic Enterprise*, Routledge, London.

Nuti D.M., 1997, Employeism: Corporate Governance and Employee Share Ownership in Transitional Economies, in M.I. Blejer and M. Škreb, *Macroeconomic Stabilization in Transition Economics*, Cambridge University Press, Cambridge.

Nuti D.M., 2000, Employee Participation in Enterprise Control and Returns: Patterns, Gaps and Discontinuities, in V. Frančevič and M. Uvalic (eds), *Equality, Participation, Transition*, Macmillan, London.

Nutzinger H.G., 1975, Investment and Financing in a Labour-Managed Firm and its Social Implications, in *Economic Analysis and Workers' Management*, vol. 9, nn. 3–4.

O'Brien J.C., 1981, Karl Marx, the Social Scientist, in J.C. Wood (ed.), 1988, *Karl Marx's Economics: Critical Assessments*, vol. 1, Croom Helm, New South Wales.

Oakeshott R., 1978, *The Case for Workers' Coops*, Routledge and Kegan Paul, London.

Offe C., 1972a, *Strukturprobleme des kapitalistischen Staates*, Suhrkamp Verlag, Frankfurt am Main.

Offe C., 1972b, Il capitalismo maturo. Un tentativo di definizione, in C. Offe, 1977, *Lo Stato nel capitalismo maturo*, ital. transl. of eight articles from German, Etas Libri, Milan.

Offe C., 1977, *Lo Stato nel capitalismo maturo*, ital. transl. of eight articles from German, Etas Libri, Milan.

Ollman B., 1976, *Alienation: Marx's Conception of Man in a Capitalistic Society*, Cambridge University Press, New York, NY.

Ollman B., ed., 1998a, *Market Socialism: The Debate among Socialists*, Routledge, London.

Ollman B., 1998b, Market Mystification in Capitalist and Market Socialist Societies, in B. Ollman (ed.), 1998a, *Market Socialism: The Debate among Socialists*, Routledge, London.

Ollman B., 2003. *Dance of the Dialectic; Steps in Marx's Method*, University of Illinois Press, Chicago, IL.

Olson M., 1965, *The Logic of Collective Action*, Harvard University Press, Cambridge, MA.

Oppenheimer P. and Putnam H., 1958, Unity of Science as a Working Hypothesis, in *Minnesota Studies in the Philosophy of Science*, vol. 2.

Orfei R., 1970, *Marxismo e umanesimo*, Coines Edizioni, Rome.

Owen R., 1891, *A New View of Society and Report of County of Lanark*, AMS Press, New York, NY, 1970.

Paci E., 1962, Sulla realtà oggettiva della contraddizione, reprinted in F. Cassano, 1973, *Marxismo e filosofia in Italia*, De Donato, Bari.

Pagano U., 2006, Marx fra autoritarismo e democrazia economica, in B. Jossa and G. Lunghini (eds), *Marxismo oggi*, Il Ponte Editore, Florence.

Pagano U., 2007, Karl Marx after New Institutional Economics, in *Evolutionary and Institutional Economic Review*, vol. 4, n. 1.

Pagano U. and Rowthorn R., eds, 1996, *Democracy and Efficiency in the Economic Enterprise*, Routledge, London.

Paggi L., 1970, *Antonio Gramsci e il moderno Principe*, Editori Riuniti, Rome.

Paggi L., 1974, La teoria generale del marxismo in Gramsci, in Istituto Giangiacomo Feltrinelli, *Storia del marxismo contemporaneo*, Feltrinelli, Milan.

Paggi L., 1977, Gramsci e l'egemonia dall' 'Ordine nuovo' alla 'Questione meridionale', in B. De Giovanni, V. Gerratana and L. Paggi, *Egemonia, Stato, partito in Gramsci*, Editori Riuniti, Rome.

Panaccione A., 1974, L'analisi del capitalismo in Kautsky, in Istituto Giangiacomo Feltrinelli, *Storia del marxismo contemporaneo*, Feltrinelli, Milan.

Panayotakis C., 2009, Individual Differences and the Potential Tradeoffs between the Value of a Participatory Economy, in *Review of Radical Political Economics*, vol. 41, n. 1.

Panebianco A., 2004, *Il potere, lo Stato, la libertà*, Il Mulino, Bologna.

Panizza R. and Vicarelli S., eds, 1981, *Valori e prezzi nella teoria di Marx*, Einaudi, Turin.

Pannekoek A., 1938, *Lenin filosofo*, ital. transl., Feltrinelli, Milan, 1972.

Pantaleoni M., 1898, Esame critico dei principi teorici della cooperazione, reprinted in M. Pantaleoni, 1925, *Erotemi di Economia politica*, Bari, Cacucci.

Pantaleoni M., 1925, *Erotemi di Economia politica*, Bari, Cacucci.

Panzieri R., 1958, Sul controllo operaio, in R. Panzieri, 1975, *La ripresa del marxismo leninismo in Italia*, Sapere Edizioni, Milan.

Panzieri R., 1964, Plusvalore e pianificazione (appunti di lettura del capitale), in R. Panzieri, 1975, *La ripresa del marxismo leninismo in Italia*, Sapere Edizioni, Milan.

Panzieri R., 1975, *La ripresa del marxismo leninismo in Italia*, Sapere Edizioni, Milan.

Panzieri R., 1976, *Lotte operaie nello sviluppo capitalistico*, Einaudi, Turin.

Pareto V., 1893, Introduction à Marx, in V. Pareto, 1966, *Marxisme et économie pure*, Librairie Droz, Genève.

Pareto V., 1926, *I sistemi socialisti*, UTET, Turin, 1963.

Pareto V., 1966, *Marxisme et économie pure*, Librairie Droz, Genève.

Park R., Kruse D. and Sesil J., 2004, Does Employee Ownership Enhance Firm Survival?, in *Advances in the Economic Analysis of Participatory and Labour-Managed Firms*, vol. 8.

Pasinetti L.L., 1984, *Dinamica strutturale e sviluppo economico*, UTET, Turin.

Passini R., 2000, La cooperazione nell'ordinamento costituzionale italiano e comunitario, in *Il Ponte*, vol. LVI, nn. 11–12, November–December.

Patsouras L., 1994, *Debating Marx*, Lewiston, New York, NY.

Pejovich S., 1975, The Firm, Monetary Policy and Property Rights in a Planned Economy, in B. Horvat, M. Markovic and R. Supek (eds), *Self-Governing Socialism: A Reader*, International Arts and Science Press, New York, NY.

Pelikan J., 1977, Il socialismo e l'Europa orientale, in ARA, *Quale socialismo; quale Europa*, Feltrinelli, Milan.

Pellicani L., 1976, Socialismo ed economia di mercato, in *Mondoperaio*, June.

Pellicani L., 1981, *Gramsci: an Alternative Communism?*, Hoover Institution, Stanford, CA.

Pencavel J., Pistaferri L. and Schivardi F., 2006, Wages, Employment, and Capital in Capitalistic and Worker-Owned Firms, in *Industrial and Labor Relations Review*, vol. 60, n. 1.

Perotin V., 2006, Entry, Exit, and the Business Cycle: Are Cooperatives Different?, in *Journal of Comparative Economics*, vol. 34, n. 2.

Perrotta C., 2006, Valori e interessi nella cooperazione. Una nota, in M.P. Salani, *Lezioni cooperative*, Il Mulino, Bologna.

Pesciarelli E., 1982, *Un nuovo modo di produrre; la cooperazione nel pensiero degli economisti classici da Smith a Cairnes*, Editrice CLUA, Ancona.

Pesciarelli E., 2006, Continuità ed asimmetrie nell'approccio degli economisti classici al tema degli incentivi personali e della cooperazione, in M.P. Salani, *Lezioni cooperative*, Il Mulino, Bologna.

Petrovich G., 1991a, Reification, in T. Bottomore (ed.), *A Dictionary of Marxist Thought*, 2nd edn, Blackwell, Oxford.

Petrovich G., 1991b, Alienation, in T. Bottomore (ed.), *A Dictionary of Marxist Thought*, 2nd edn, Blackwell, Oxford.

Peyrelavade J., 2005, *Le capitalisme total*, Seuil-La République des idées, Paris.

Pfeffer L., 1986, Il capitale come costo, in L. Sintini, A. Canosani, J. Zabaleta, P. Szarvas, F. Buzzi, D.C. Jones, P. Bianchi, S. Zan, T. Savi, G. Pasquini, I. Santoro, M. Zigarella and O. Prandini (eds), *Cooperare e competere*, Feltrinelli, Milan.

Pittatore S. and Turati G., 2000, A Map of Property Rights in Italy and the Case of Cooperatives: An Empirical Analysis of Hansmann's Theory, in *Economic Analysis*, vol. 3, n. 1.

Pizzorno A., 1969, Sul metodo di Gramsci: dalla storiografia alla scienza politica, in AA.VV., 1969b, *Gramsci e la cultura contemporanea*, Editori Riuniti, Rome.

Pizzorno A., 1970, 'Intervento' su *Gramsci e la teoria marxista*, in Istituto Gramsci, 1969 and 1970, *Gramsci e la cultura contemporanea*, vols I and II, Editori Riuniti, Rome.

Pizzorno A., 1980, *I soggetti del pluralismo*, Il Mulino, Bologna.

Polanyi K., 1934, Fascismo e marxismo, reprinted in K. Polanyi, 1987, *La libertà in una società complessa*, ital. transl., Bollati Boringhieri, Turin, 1987.

Polanyi K., 1987, *La libertà in una società complessa*, ital. transl., Bollati Boringhieri, Turin, 1987.

Poletti L., 1905, Un cimitero di cooperative, in *Giornale degli economisti*, series 11, vol. 31, September.

Portelli H., 1972, Gramsci e il blocco storico, ital. transl., Laterza, Bari, 1973.

Potter B., 1893, *The Cooperative Movement in Great Britain*, Swan Sonnershein, London.

Poulantzas N., 1974, *Classi sociali e capitalismo oggi*, ital. transl., Etas Libri, Milan, 1975.

Powel W., ed., 1987, *The Non Profit Sector: A Research Handbook*, Yale University, New Haven, CT.

Prandergast C., 1999, The Provisions of Incentives on Firms, in *Journal of Economic Literature*, vol. 37.

Prasnikar J. and Prasnikar V., 1986, The Yugoslav Self-Managed Firm in Historical Perspective, in *Economic and Industrial Democracy*, vol. 7, n. 1.

Preobrazhensky E.A., 1925, Ancora sull'accumulazione socialista. Note economiche, in N. Bucharin, E. Preobrazhensky, 1969, *L'accumulazione socialista*, ed. by L. Foa, Editori Riuniti, Rome.

Preobrazhensky E.A., 1926, *La nuova economia*, ital. transl., Jaca Book, Milan, 1970.

Prestipino G., 1990, Presenza di Gramsci filosofo della politica, in B. Moscatello, *Gramsci e il Marxismo contemporaneo*, Editori Riuniti, Rome.

Proudhon P.J., 1851, *Idea generale della rivoluzione nel XIX secolo*, partial transl. printed in P. Ansart, 1978, *P.J. Proudhon*, La Pietra, Milan.

Prucha M., 1965, Il marxismo e i problemi esistenziali dell'uono, in E. Fromm, *L'umanesimo marxista*, ital. transl., Dedalo libri, Bari, 1971.

Prychitko D.L. and Vanek J., eds, 1996, *Producer Cooperatives and Labor-Managed Systems*, Cheltenham, E. Elgar.

Przeworsky A., 1995, Class, Production and Politics: A Reply to Burawoy, in T. Carver and P. Thomas (eds), *Rational Choice Marxism*, Macmillan, London.

Przeworsky A., 1998, Deliberation and Ideological Domination, in J. Elster (ed.), 1998, *Deliberating Democracy*, Cambridge University Press, Cambridge.

Putterman L., 1982, Some Behavioural Perspectives on the Dominance of Hierarchical over Democratic Forms of Enterprise, in *Journal of Economic Behaviour and Organization*, vol. 3, nn. 2–3.

Putterman L., 1984, On Some Recent Explanations of Why Capital Hires Labor, in *Economic Inquiry*, vol. 22, April.

Putterman L., 1990, *Division of Labor and Welfare; An Introduction to Economic Systems*, Oxford University Press, Oxford.

Putterman L., 1993, After the Employment Relation: Problem on the Road to Industrial Democracy, in S. Bowles, H. Gintis and B. Gustafsson (eds), *Markets and Democracy: Participation, Accountability and Efficiency*, Cambridge University Press, Cambridge.

Putterman L., Roemer J.E. and Silvestre J., 1998, Does Egalitarianism Have a Future?, in *Journal of Economic Literature*, vol. 36, n. 2.

Quaderni di Mondoperaio, 1977, *Egemonia e democrazia. Gramsci e la questione comunista nel dibattito di Mondoperaio*, Edizioni Avanti!, Rome.

Raffaelli T., 2000, Sul movimento cooperativo nel pensiero di John Stuart Mill e Alfred Marshall, in *Il Ponte*, vol. LVI, nn. 11–12, November–December.

Ragionieri E., 1965, Il marxismo e la Prima Internazionale, in E. Ragionieri, 1968, *Il marxismo e l'Internazionale*, Editori Riuniti, Rome.

Ragionieri E., 1968, *Il marxismo e l'Internazionale*, Editori Riuniti, Rome.

Ragionieri E., 1969, Gramsci e il dibattito teorico nel movimento operaio internazionale, inIstituto Gramsci, 1969 and 1970, *Gramsci e la cultura contemporanea*, vols I and II, Editori Riuniti, Rome.

Rancière J., 1973, *Ideologia e politica in Althusser*, ital. transl., Feltrinelli, Milan, 1974.

Rapone L., 2011, *Cinque anni che paiono secoli; Antonio Gramsci dal socialismo al comunismo (1914–1919)*, Carocci Editore, Rome.

Rawls J., 1971, *A Theory of Justice*, Harvard Economic Press, Cambridge, MA.

Reich M. and Devine J., 1981, The Microeconomics of Conflict and Hierarchy in Capitalist Production, in *Review of Radical Political Economics*, vol. 12, January.

Reito F., 2008, Moral Hazard and Labour-Managed Firms in Italy after the Law 142/2001, in *Annals of Public and Cooperative Economics*, vol. 79, n. 2.

Reitter K., 2011, *Prozesse der Befreiung. Marx, Spinoza und die Bedingungen des freien Gemeinwesens*, Verl. Westfäl. Dampfboot, Münster.

Resnick S. and Wolff R.D., 1982, Classes in Marxian Theory, in *Review of Radical Political Economics*, vol. 13, n. 4, Winter.

Reuten G., 2002, Marx's *Capital III*, the Culmination of Capital, in M. Campbell and G. Reuten (eds), *The Culmination of Capital; Essays on Volume III of Marx's Capital*, Palgrave, London.

Reuten G., 2009, Il difficile lavoro di una teoria dl valore sociale: metafore e dialettica sistematica all'inizio del *Capitale* di Marx, in R. Bellofiore and R. Fineschi (eds), *Re-Reading Marx; New Perspectives after the Critical Edition*, Palgrave Macmillan, New York, NY.

Riechers C., 1970, *Antonio Gramsci e il marxismo in Italia*, Thelèma, Naples, 1975.

Riguzzi B. and Porcari R., 1925, *La cooperazione operaia*, Turin.

Roberts P.C. and Stephenson M.A., 1970, A Note on Marxian Alienation, reprinted in J.C. Wood (ed.), 1988, *Karl Marx's Economics: Critical Assessments*, vol. 1, Croom Helm, New South Wales.

Roberts P.C. and Stephenson M.A., 1975, On the Commodity Mode of Production: One More Time, in J.C. Wood (ed.), 1988, *Karl Marx's Economics: Critical Assessments*, vol. 1, Croom Helm, New South Wales.

Roberts W.C., 2006, The Origin of Political Economy and the Descent of Marx, in W.S. Goldstein (ed.), 2006, *Marx, Critical Theory and Religion*, Brill, Leiden.

Robertson D.H. and Dennison S.R., 1924, *The Control of Industry*, Cambridge University Press, Cambridge.

Robinson J., 1941, Marx on Unemployment, in *Economic Journal*, vol. 51, June–September.

Robinson J., 1942, *Marx e la scienza economica*, ital. transl., La Nuova Italia, Florence, 1951.

Robinson J., 1967, The Soviet Collective Farm as a Producer Cooperative: Comment, in *American Economic Review*, vol. 57, n. 1.

Rodinson M., 1969, Sociologia marxista e ideologia marxista, in M. Spinella (ed.), *Marx Vivo*, Mondadori, Milan.

Rodotà S., 2012, *Il diritto di avere diritti*, Laterza, Bari.

Roelants B., 2000, Worker Cooperatives and Socio-Economic Development: The Role of Mesolevel Institutions, in *Economic Analysis*, vol. 3, n. 1.

Roemer J.E., 1982, *A General Theory of Exploitation and Class*, Harvard University Press, Cambridge.

Roemer J.E., ed., 1986, *Analytical Marxism*, Cambridge University Press, Cambridge.

Roemer J.E., 1988, *Free To Lose: An Introduction To Marxist Economic Philosophy*, Harvard University Press, Cambridge, MA.

Roemer J.E., 1993, Can there be Socialism after Communism?, in P. Bardhan and J.E. Roemer (eds), *Market Socialism: The Current Debate*, Oxford Economic Press, New York, NY.

Roemer J.E., 1994, *Foundations of Analytical Marxism*, E. Elgar, Aldershot.

Roemer J.E. and Silvestre J., 1993, Investment Policy and Market Socialism, in P. Bardhan and J.E. Roemer (eds), *Market Socialism: The Current Debate*, Oxford Economic Press, New York, NY.

Romano S.F., 1969, Intervento alla prima seduta di lavoro, in Istituto Gramsci, 1969 and 1970, *Gramsci e la cultura contemporanea*, vols i and ii, Editori Riuniti, Rome.

Rosanvallon P., 1976, *L'age de l'autogestion*, Seuil/Politique, Paris.

Rosdolsky R., 1955, *Genesi e struttura del 'Capitale' di Marx*, ital. transl., Laterza, Bari, 1971.

Rosengarten F., 1995, Gramsci negli Stati Uniti, in E.J. Hobsbawm (ed.), *Gramsci in Europa e in America*, Laterza, Bari.

Rosenthal J., 1998, *The Myth of Dialectics: Reinterpreting the Marx-Hegel Relation*, Macmillan, London.

Rosselli C., 1930, *Socialismo liberale*, Einaudi, Turin, 1973.

Rothshild J. and Whitt J., 1986, *The Cooperative Workplace*, Routledge, London.

Rousseau J.J., 1755, *Discours sur l'origine et le fondements de l'inégalité parmi les hommes*, Garnier-Flammarion, Paris, 1971.

Rovatti P.A., 1973, *Critica e scientificità in Marx*, Feltrinelli, Milan.

Rowthorn R., 1974, Neo-classicism, Neo-Ricardianism and Marxism, in *New Left Review*, n. 86.

Rowthorn B., 1977, Conflitto, inflazione e moneta, ital. transl. in M. Centorrino and P. Barcellona (eds), 1982, *Economia politica dell'inflazione*, De Donato, Bari.

Rubel M., 1965, Riflessioni sull'utopia e la rivoluzione, in E. Fromm, *L'umanesimo marxista*, ital. transl., Dedalo libri, Bari, 1971.

Rubel M., 1974a, La légende de Marx ou Engels fondateur, in M. Rubel, 1974b, *Marx critique du marxisme. Essais*, Payot, Paris.

Rubel M., 1974b, *Marx critique du marxisme. Essais*, Payot, Paris.

Rubin I.I., 1928, *Saggi sulla teoria del valore di Marx*, ital. transl., Feltrinelli, Milan, 1976.

Rusconi G.E., 1968, *La teoria critica della società*, Il Mulino, Bologna.

Russel R. and Rus V., eds, 1991, *International Handbook of Participation in Organizations*, Oxford University Press, Oxford.

Saad-Fihlo A., 1996, The Value of Money, the Value of Labour Power and the Net Product: An Appraisal of the 'New Approach' to the Transformation Problem, in A. Freeman and G. Carchedi, *Marx and Non-Equilibrium Economics*, E. Elgar, Cheltenham.

Saad-Fihlo A., 1997, Concrete and Abstract Labour in Marx's Theory of Value, in *Review of Political Economy*, vol. 9, n. 4.

Sabattini G., 2009, *Welfare State; nascita, evoluzione e crisi. Le prospettive di riforma*, F. Angeli, Milan.

Sabine G.H., 1937, *Storia delle dottrine politiche*, ital. transl., Edizioni di Comunità, quarta edizione, Milan, 1962.

Sacco P.L. and Zamagni S., 2002, *Complessità relazionale e comportamento economico*, Il Mulino, Bologna.

Sacconi L., 1992, I costi di governo e i benefici della proprietà dei lavoratori, in E. Gramaglia and L. Sacconi (eds), *Cooperazione, benessere e organizzazione economica*, F. Angeli, Milan.

Salani M.P., 2006, *Lezioni cooperative*, Il Mulino, Bologna.

Salop S.C., 1979, Strategic Entry Deterrence, in *American Economic Review*, vol. 69, May.

Salvadori M.L., 1972, Lenin e i soviet, in AA.VV., *I consigli operai*, Samonà e Savelli, Rome.

Salvadori M.L., 1973, *Gramsci e il problema storico della democrazia*, 2nd edn, Einaudi, Turin.

Salvadori M.L., 1975, Non imbalsamiamo anche Gramsci, reprinted in M.L. Salvadori, 1978a, *Eurocomunismo e socialismo sovietico*, Einaudi, Turin.

Salvadori M.L., 1976, Gramsci e il PCI: due concezioni dell'egemonia, reprinted in M.L. Salvadori, 1978a, *Eurocomunismo e socialismo sovietico*, Einaudi, Turin.

Salvadori M.L., 1978a, *Eurocomunismo e socialismo sovietico*, Einaudi, Turin.

Salvadori M.L., 1978b, *Gramsci e l'eurocomunismo*, Einaudi, Turin, 1978a.

Salvadori N. and Opocher A., 2009, *Long-Run Growth, Social Institution and Living Standard*, Edward Elgar, Cheltenham.

Salvati M., 1981, Ciclo politico e onde lunghe. Note su Kalecki e Philips Brown, in *Stato e mercato*, n. 1, April.

Salvati M., 1994, Realismo e utopia, in P. Sylos Labini, *Carlo Marx: è tempo di un bilancio*, Laterza, Rome-Bari.

Salvemini G., 1928, *La dittatura fascista in Italia*, in G. Salvemini, 1961, *Scritti sul fascismo*, vol. I, Feltrinelli, Milan.

Salvemini G., 1961, *Scritti sul fascismo*, vol. I, Feltrinelli, Milan.

Santucci A., 2001, *Senza comunismo*, Editori Riuniti, Rome.

Sapelli G., 1982, Necessità di una teoria dell'impresa cooperativa, in Lega Nazionale Cooperative e Mutue, *L'impresa cooperativa degli anni '80*, De Donato, Bari.

Sapelli G., 2006, *Coop: il futuro dell'impresa cooperativa*, Einaudi, Turin.

Sartori G., 1969, *Democrazia e definizioni*, 3rd edn, Il Mulino, Bologna.

Sartori G., 1995, *Elementi di teoria politica*, 3rd edn, Il Mulino, Bologna.

Sbarberi F., ed., 1988, *Teoria politica e società industriale. Ripensare Gramsci*, Bollati Boringhieri, Turin.

Schacht R., 1970, *Alienation*, Doubleday, Garden City, New York, NY.

Schaff A., 1965, *Il marxismo e la persona umana*, ital. transl., Feltrinelli, Milan, 1966.

Schaff A., 1974, *Marxismo, strutturalismo e il metodo della scienza*, ital. transl., Feltrinelli, Milan, 1976.

Schaff A., 1977, *L'alienazione come fenomeno sociale*, ital. transl., Editori Riuniti, Rome 1979.

Schaff A. and Seve L., 1975, *Marxismo e umanesimo*, Dedalo libri, Bari.

Schlesinger R., 1965, The Continuity of Marx's Thought, in *Sciences and Society*, vol. 29, n. 1.

Schlicht E., 1978, Labour Turnover, Wage Structure and Natural Unemployment, in *Zeitschrift für die Gesamte Staatwissenschaft*, June.

Schlicht E. and von Weizsäcker C.C., 1977, Risk Financing in Labour Managed Economies: The Commitment Problem, in *Zeitschrift für die gesamte Staatswissenschaft*, Special Issue.

Schumpeter J.A., 1942, *Capitalismo, socialismo e democrazia*, ital. transl., Edizioni di Comunità, Milan, 1964.

Schumpeter J.A., 1954, *Storia dell'analisi economica*, ital. transl., Einaudi, Turin, 1959.

Schweickart D., 1993, *Against Capitalism*, Chicago University Press, Chicago, IL.

Schweickart D., 2002, *After Capitalism*, Rowman & Littlefield Publishers, Inc., Lanham.

Schweickart D., 2005, Marx's Democratic Critique of Capitalism, and its Implications for China's Development Strategy, in *Teaching and Research*, n. 10.

Schweickart D., 2011, *After Capitalism*, 2nd edn, Rowman & Littlefield Publishers, Inc., Lanham.

Screpanti E., 2001, *The Fundamental Institutions of Capitalism*, Routledge, London.

Screpanti E., 2002, Contratto di lavoro, regimi di proprietà e governo dell'accumulazione: verso una teoria generale del capitalismo, in D. Fausto, B. Jossa and C. Panico (eds), 2002, *Teoria economica e riformismo politico*, F. Angeli, Milan.

Screpanti E., 2004, *Il capitalismo. Ieri, oggi, domani*, Siena, *mimeo*.

Screpanti E., 2005, *Libertarian Communism: Marx Engels and the Political Economy of Freedom*, Palgrave Macmillan, London, 2007.

Screpanti E., 2007, *Comunismo libertario*, manifestolibri, Rome.

Screpanti E., 2013, *Marx dalla totalità alla moltitudine (1841–1843)*, II edizione, editrice petite plaisance, Pistoia.

Screpanti E. and Tortia E., eds, 2004, *Democrazia economica; tra Stato e mercato*, Pettirosso, Naples.

Sekine T.T., 1995a, A Uno School Seminar on the Theory of Value, in R. Albritton and T.T. Sekine, *A Japanese Approach to Political Economy*, Palgrave, New York, NY.

Sekine T.T., 1995b, The Necessity of the Law of Value, its Demonstration and Significance, in R. Albritton and T.T. Sekine, *A Japanese Approach to Political Economy*, Palgrave, New York, NY.

Sen A.K., 1966, Labour Allocation in a Cooperative Enterprise, in *Review of Economic Studies*, vol. 33, October.

Sen A.K., 1994, *Economic Wealth and Moral Sentiments*, Zürich Conference, April.

Sertel M.R., 1982, *Workers and Incentives*, North-Holland, Amsterdam.

Sesil J.C., 2006, Sharing Decision-Making and Group Incentives: The Impact on Performance, in *Economic and Industrial Democracy*, vol. 27, n. 4.

Settembrini D., 1973, *Due ipotesi per il socialismo in Marx ed Engels*, Laterza, Bari.

Sève L., 1967, Metodo strutturale e metodo dialettico, in M. Godelier, 1970, *Antropologia, storia, marxismo*, ed. by M. de Stefanis and A. Casiccia, Guanda, Parma.

Sève L., 1970, Lucien Sève a Giulio Einaudi, in M. Godelier, 1970, *Antropologia, storia, marxismo*, ed. by M. de Stefanis and A. Casiccia, Guanda, Parma.

Sève L., 1996, Le communisme, in Texier *et al.*, *Congrès Marx International. Cent ans de marxisme*, PUF, Paris.

Sève L., 2004, *Penser avec Marx aujourd'hui*, Tome I, Marx et nous, La Dispute, Paris.

Sève L., 2009, *Penser avec Marx aujourd'hui*; Tome II, L'Homme, La Dispute, Paris.

Shearmur J., 1996, *Hayek and After*, Routledge, London.

Sherman H., 1995, *Reinventing Marxism*, Johns Hopkins University Press, London.

Sichirollo L., 1973, *Dialettica*, ISEDI, Milan.

Sidoti F., 1987, Parlamento e governo in Marx. Alcune 'verità sociologiche' di un centenario, in A.M. Nassisi, *Marx e il mondo contemporaneo*, Editori Riuniti, Rome.

Siebert H., 1997, Labour Market Rigidities: At the Root of Unemployment in Europe, in *Journal of Economic Perspectives*, vol. 11, n. 3.

Simon H.A., 1951, A Formal Theory of the Employment Relationship, in *Econometrica*, vol. 19, July.

Sintini L., Canosani A., Zabaleta J., Szarvas P., Buzzi F., Jones D.C., Bianchi P., Zan S., Savi T., Pasquini G., Santoro I., Zigarella M. and Prandini O. (eds), 1986, *Cooperare e competere*, Feltrinelli, Milan.

Skillman G.L. and Dow G.K., 2007, Collective Choice and Control Rights in Firm, in *Journal of Public Economic Theory*, vol. 9, n. 1.

Smith S.C. and Ye M.H., 1987, The Behavior of Labor-Managed Firms under Uncertainty, in *Annals of Public and Cooperative Economics*, vol. 57, March.

Snow C.P., 1959–1963, *The Two Cultures*, Cambridge University Press, Cambridge, 1993.

Sobel R., 2008, Travail et justice dans la société communiste chez Marx. Un commentaire à propos de quelques ambiguïtés naturalistes de 'l'etage du bas' de la 'phase supérieure' du communisme, in *Économies et Sociétés*, vol. 40, n. 5.

Soldani F., 2001, Marx e la scienza; come il pensiero scientifico ha dato forma alla teoria della società di Marx, in *Actuel Marx*, vol. 3, nn. 31/1.

Soldani F., 2007, *Le relazioni virtuose. L'epistemologia scientifica contemporanea e la logica del capitale*, Editrice UNI Service, Trento.

Solow R., 1990, *The Labor Market as a Social Institution*, Basil Blackwell, Oxford.

Sombart W., 1894, Zur Kritik des oekonomischen Systems von Karl Marx, in *Archiv für Soziale Gesetzgebung und Statistik*, vol. VII, n. 4.

Sowell T., 1967, Marx's *Capital* after One Hundred Years, reprinted in J.C. Wood (ed.), 1988, *Karl Marx's Economics: Critical Assessments*, vol. 2, Croom Helm, New South Wales.

Sowell T., 1985, *Marxism; Philosophy and Economics*, Quill William Morris, New York, NY.

Spear R., 2004, Governance in Democratic Member-Based Organizations, in *Annals of Public and Cooperative Economics*, vol. 75, n. 1.

Spinella M., ed., 1969, *Marx Vivo*, Mondadori, Milan.

Spriano P., 1967, Introduzione a Gramsci, in A. Gramsci, *Scritti politici*, Editori Riuniti, Rome.

Spriano P., 1971, *L' 'Ordine nuovo' e i consigli di fabbrica*, Einaudi, Turin.

Spriano P., 1981, Marxismo e storicismo in Togliatti, in E.J. Hobsbawm, G. Haupt, F. Marek, E. Ragionieri, V. Strada and C. Vivanti (eds), 1978–1982, *Storia del marxismo*, 5 vols, Einaudi, Turin.

Srinivasan R. and Phansalkar S.J., 2003, Residual Claims in Cooperatives: Design Issues, in *Annals of Public and Cooperative Economics*, vol. 74, n. 3, September.

Stalin J., 1940, *Questioni del leninismo*, Edizioni in lingue straniere, Moscow.

Stauber L.G., 1989, Age-Dependence and Historical Effects on the Failure Rates of Worker Cooperatives. An Event-History Analysis, in *Economic and Industrial Democracy*, vol. 10, n. 1.

Stawar A., 1961, *Liberi saggi marxisti*, transl. from Polish, La Nuova Italia, Florence, 1973.

Stefanelli R., 1975, Un'interpretazione, in AA.VV., 1975b, *L'autogestione in Italia; realtà e funzione della cooperazione*, De Donato, Bari.

Steinherr A., 1975, Profit-Maximizing vs. Labor-Managed Firms: A Comparison of Market Structure and Firm Behavior, in *Journal of Industrial Economics*, vol. 24, n. 2.

Steinherr A. and Thiesse J.F., 1979a, Are Labour-Managers Really Perverse?, in *Economic Letters*, vol. 2, n. 2.

Steinherr A. and Thiesse J.F., 1979b, Is there a Negatively-Sloped Supply Curve in the Labour-Managed Firm?, in *Economic Analysis and Workers' Management*, vol. 13, n. 35.

Stephen F.H., 1978, Bank Credit and Investment by the Jugoslav Firm, in *Economic Analysis and Workers' Management*, vol. 12, n. 34.

Stephen F.H., 1980, Bank Credit and the Labor-Managed Firm: Comment, in *American Economic Review*, vol. 70, n. 4.

Stephen F.H., 1984, *The Economic Analysis of Producers' Cooperatives*, Macmillan, London.

Sterner T., 1990, Ownership, Technology and Efficiency: An Empirical Study of Cooperatives, Multinationals, and Domestic Enterprises in Mexican Cement Industry, in *Journal of Comparative Economics*, vol. 14, n. 2.

Stiglitz J.E., 1969, A Re-Examination of the Modigliani–Miller Theorem, in *American Economic Review*, vol. 59, December.

Stiglitz J.E., 1985, Credit Markets and the Control of Capital, in *Journal of Money, Credit and Banking*, vol. 17, May.

Stiglitz J.E., 1993, Market Socialism and Neoclassical Economic, in P. Bardhan and J.E. Roemer (eds), *Market Socialism: The Current Debate*, Oxford Economic Press, New York, NY.

Stiglitz J.E., 1994, *Whither Socialism?*, MIT Press, Cambridge, MA.

Stiglitz J.E. and Weiss, A., 1981, Credit Rationing in Markets with Imperfect Competition, in *American Economic Review*, vol. 71, June.

Stiglitz J.E., 1986, Theories of Wage Rigidity, in J.L. Butkievicz, K.T. Koford and J.B. Miller (eds), *Keynes' Economic Legacy*, Praeger, New York, NY.

Stone B., 1998, *Why Marxism Isn't Dead: The Case for Cooperative Socialism*, 20th World Congress of Philosophy, Paideia Archiv, Social Philosophy, Boston, MA.

Strachey L., 1956, *Il capitalismo contemporaneo*, ital. transl., Feltrinelli, Milan, 1957.

Strada V., 1980, Lenin e Trockij, in E.J. Hobsbawm, G. Haupt, F. Marek, E. Ragionieri, V. Strada and C. Vivanti (eds), 1978–1982, *Storia del marxismo*, vol. 3, Einaudi, Turin.

Streeten P., 1996, Free and Managed Trade, in S. Berger and P. Dore (eds), *Differenze nazionali e capitalismo globale*, Il Mulino, Bologna.

Struve P., 1899, La théorie marxienne de l'évolution sociale, reprinted in *Cahiers de l'Institut de science économique appliquée*, n. 129, September, 1962.

Sweezy P.M., 1942, *The Theory of Capitalist Development: Principles of Marxian Political Economy*, Oxford University Press, New York, NY.

Sweezy P.M., 1963, Communism as an Ideal, in *Monthly Review*, October.

Sweezy P.M., 1968, Cecoslovacchia, capitalismo e socialismo, *Monthly Review*, November.

Sweezy P.M., 1969, A Reply to Bettelheim, *Monthly Review*, March–April.

Sweezy P.M., 1971, Sulla teoria del capitalismo monopolistico, in P.M. Sweezy, 1972, *Il capitalismo moderno*, ital. transl., Liguori, Naples, 1975.

Sweezy P.M., 1972, *Il capitalismo moderno*, ital. transl., Liguori, Naples, 1975.

Sweezy P.M., 1981, *Il marxismo e il futuro: quattro lezioni*, Einaudi, Turin, 1983.

Sylos Labini P., 1994, *Carlo Marx: è tempo di un bilancio*, Laterza, Rome-Bari.

Sylos Labini P., 2004, *Torniamo ai classici*, Laterza, Bari.

Sylos Labini P., 2006, Perché gli economisti devono fare i conti con Marx, in B. Jossa and G. Lunghini (eds), *Marxismo oggi*, Il Ponte Editore, Florence.

Tamburrano G., 1959, Fasi di sviluppo nel pensiero politico di Gramsci, in A. Caracciolo and G. Scalia, *La città futura*, edizione ridotta, Feltrinelli, Milan, 1976.

Tarrit F., 2006, A Brief History, Scope and Peculiarities of 'Analytical Marxism', in *Review of Radical Political Economics*, vol. 38, n. 4.

Tavares J. and Wacziarg R., 2001, How Democracy Affects Growth, in *European Economic Review*, vol. 45, n. 8, August.

Tawney R.H., 1918, *The Conditions of Economic Liberty*, in R. Hinden (ed.), 1964, *The Radical Tradition*, Pantheon Books, New York, NY.

Texier B., 1990, Il concetto gramsciano di 'società civile', in B. Moscatello, *Gramsci e il Marxismo contemporaneo*, Editori Riuniti, Rome.

Therborn G., 1971, *Critica e rivoluzione; la Scuola di Francoforte*, ital. transl., Laterza, Bari, 1972.

Thomas A., 1990, Financing Worker Cooperatives in EC Countries, in *Annals of Public and Cooperative Economics*, vol. 61, June.

Thomas H. and Defourny J., 1990, Financing Workers' Cooperatives and Self-Managed Enterprises, in *Annals of Public and Cooperative Economics*, vol. 61, June.

Thomas H. and Logan C., 1982, *Mondragon, an Economic Analysis*, Allen and Unwin, London.

Thompson W., 1827, *Labour Rewarded: the Claims of Labour and Capital Conciliated by One of the Idle Classes, or, how to Secure to Labour the Whole Products of its Exertions*, reprint, August McKelley, New York, NY, 1969.

Ticktin H., 1998, The Problem is Market Socialism, in B. Ollman, 1998a, *Market Socialism: The Debate among Socialists*, Routledge, London.

Timpanaro S., 1970, *Sul materialismo*, Nistri-Lischi, Pisa.

Tobin J., 1972, Inflation and Unemployment, in *Economic Journal*, vol. 82, March.

Togliatti P., 1958a, *Scritti su Gramsci*, ed. by G. Liguori, Editori Riuniti, Rome.

Togliatti P., 1958b, Gramsci e il leninismo, in P. Togliatti, 1958a, *Scritti su Gramsci*, ed. by G. Liguori, Editori Riuniti, Rome.

Tonini V., 1967, *Che cosa ha veramente detto Lenin*, Astrolabio, Ubaldini.

Tortia E., 2005, The Accumulation of Capital in Labour-Managed Firms: Divisible Reserves and Bonds, University of Bologna, Sede di Forlì, *Working Paper*, n. 23, November.

Tortia E., 2007, Self-Financing in LMFs: Individual Capital Accounts and Bonds, in *Advances in the Economic Analysis of Participatory and Labour-Managed Firms*, vol. 10.

Tortia E., 2008a, *Le determinanti dello sforzo lavorativo nelle imprese sociali*, University of Trent, Trent.

Tortia E., 2008b, Dal contratto di lavoro al contratto di associazione nelle cooperative di lavoro, in *Il Ponte*, vol. 64, n. 10, October.

Tristan F., 1844, *L'Union ouvrière*, Lyon, Paris.

Tronti M., 1962, La fabbrica e la società, in *Quaderni Rossi*, II, reprint, Sapere, Milan and Rome, 1974.

Tronti M., 2008a, Dissemination and Reception of the *Grundrisse* in the World: Italy, in M. Musto (ed.), 2008b, *Karl Marx's Grundrisse*, Routledge, London.

Tronti M., 2008b, Classe, in AA.VV., *Lessico marxiano*, manifestolibri, Rome.

Trower C., 1973, Collective Bargaining and Industrial Democracy, in G. Hunnius, G.D. Garson, J. Case (eds), *Workers' Control*, Vintage Books, New York, NY.

Tseo G.K.Y., Hou Gui Sheng, Zhang Peng-Zhu and Zang Libain, 2004, Employee Ownership and Profit Sharing as Positive Factors in the Reform of Chinese State-Owned Enterprises, in *Economic and Industrial Democracy*, vol. 25, n. 1.

Tucker R.C., 1961, *Philosophy and Myth in Karl Marx*, Cambridge University Press, Cambridge.

Uvalic M., 1986a, Il comportamento dell'impresa autogestita nei confronti degli. investimenti: alcune osservazioni critiche sulle teorie esistenti, in AISSEC, *III Convegno scientifico annuale*, Università di Siena.

Uvalic M., 1986b, Theory of the Investment Behavior of a LMF, in *Annals of Cooperative and Public Economy*, vol. 57, n. 1.

Uvalic M. and Vaughan-Whitehead D., eds, 1997, *Privatization Surprises in Transition Economies: Employee Ownership in Central and Eastern Europe*, Cheltenham, E. Elgar.

Vacca G., 1967a, Lettura di *L'uomo a una dimensione*, in G. Vacca, 1969, *Lukàcs o Korsch?* De Donato, Bari.

Vacca G., 1967b, Tecnologia e rapporti sociali: Dahrendolf, Marcuse, Mallet, in G. Vacca, 1969, *Lukàcs o Korsch?* De Donato, Bari.

Vacca G., 1969, *Lukàcs o Korsch?* De Donato, Bari.

Vacca G., 1976, La democrazia del socialismo. Questioni di metodo, ristampato, in G. Vacca, 1977, *Quale democrazia?*, De Donato, Bari.

Vacca G., 1977, *Quale democrazia?*, De Donato, Bari.

Vacca G., 1985, *Il Marxismo e gli intellettuali*, Editori Riuniti, Rome.

Vahabi M., 2010, Integrating Social Conflict into Economic Theory, in *Cambridge Journal of Economics*, vol. 34, n. 4, July.

Valentinov V. and Fritzsch J., 2007, Are Cooperatives Hybrid Organizations? An Alternative Viewpoint, in *Journal of Rural Cooperation*, vol. 35, n. 2.

Valiani L., 1957, *Questioni di storia del socialismo*, Einaudi, Turin.

Vanek J., 1969, Decentralization under Workers' Management: A Theoretical Appraisal, in *American Economic Review*, vol. 59.

Vanek J., 1970, *The General Theory of Labour-Managed Market Economies*, Cornell University Press, Ithaca, NY.

Vanek J., 1971a, Some Fundamental Considerations on Financing and the Form of Ownership under Labour Management, reprinted in J. Vanek, 1977, *The Labor Managed Economy: Essays by J. Vanek*, Cornell University Press, Ithaca, NY.

Vanek J., 1971b, The Basic Theory of Financing of Participatory Firms, reprinted in J. Vanek, 1977, *The Labor Managed Economy: Essays by J. Vanek*, Cornell University Press, Ithaca, NY.

Vanek J., 1971c, *The Participatory Economy: An Evolutionary Hypothesis on a Strategy for Development*, Cornell University Press, Ithaca, NY.

Vanek J., 1975, *Self-Management: Economic Liberation of Man*, Penguin, Harmondsworth.

Vanek J., 1977, *The Labor Managed Economy: Essays by J. Vanek*, Cornell University Press, Ithaca, NY.

Vanek J., 1985, *Imprese senza padrone nelle economie di mercato*, Edizioni Lavoro, Rome.

Vanek J., 1993, From Partnership with Paper to Partnership among Human Beings, in A.B. Atkinson (ed.), *Alternatives to Capitalism: The Economics of Partnership*, Macmillan, London.

Vanek J., 2006, The Future, Dynamics and Fundamental Principles of Growth of Economic Democracy. Available online at www.eteo.mondragon (accessed 21 December 2007).

Vanek Jan., 1972, *The Economics of Workers' Management: A Yugoslav Case Study*, Allen & Unwin, London.

Vaughan-Whitehead D., 1999, Employee Ownership on the Policy Agenda: Lessons from Central and Eastern Europe, in *Economic Analysis*, vol. 2, February.

Veblen T., 1906, The Socialist Economics of Karl Marx and His Followers, reprinted in J.C. Wood (ed.), 1988, *Karl Marx's Economics: Critical Assessments*, vol. 1, Croom Helm, New South Wales.

Veblen T.B., 1923, *Absentee Ownership and Business Enterprise in Recent Times*, A.M. Kelly, New York, NY, 1964.

Vercelli A., 1973, *Teoria della struttura economica capitalistica*, Einaudi, Turin.

Vercellone C., 2008, Trinità del capitale, in AA.VV., *Lessico marxiano*, manifestolibri, Rome.

Vergnanini A., 1914, *Marxismo e cooperativistmo. Le due grandi vie della rivoluzione economica*, Biblioteca della cooperazione e della previdenza, Milan.

Vilar P., 1978, Marx e la storia, in E.J. Hobsbawm, G. Haupt, F. Marek, E. Ragionieri, V. Strada and C. Vivanti (eds), 1978–1982, *Storia del marxismo*, 5 vols, Einaudi, Turin.

Villari L., 1978, *Lotte sociali e sisterma democratico nella Germania degli anni venti*, Il Mulino, Bologna.

Vinci P., 2008, Astrazione determinata, in AA.VV., *Lessico marxiano*, manifestolibri, Rome.

Virno P., 2008, Forza lavoro, in AA.VV., *Lessico marxiano*, manifestolibri, Rome.

Vogt W., 1996, Capitalist versus Liberal Firm and Economy: Outline of a Theory, in U. Pagano and R. Rowthorn (eds), *Democracy and Efficiency in the Economic Enterprise*, Routledge, London.

Volpi F., 1989, Sistema economico e modo di produzione, in B. Jossa (ed.), *Teoria dei sistemi economici*, UTET, Turin.

Von Siemens F.A., 2011, Heterogeneous Social Preferences, Screening, and Employment Contracts, in *Oxford Economic Papers*, vol. 63, n. 3.

Vranicki P., 1965, Il socialismo e il problema dell'alienazione, in E. Fromm, *L'umanesimo marxista*, ital. transl., Dedalo libri, Bari, 1971.

Vroom K., 1964, *Work and Motivations*, John Wiley & Sons, New York, NY.

Vygodskij V.S., 1967, *Introduzione ai 'Grundrisse' di Marx*, ital. transl., La Nuova Italia, Florence, 1974.

Waldmann R.J. and Smith S.C., 1999, Investment and Supply Effects of Industry-Indexed Bonds: The Labor Managed Firm, in *Economic Systems*, vol. 23, n. 3.

Wallerstein I., 2006, *Comprendere il mondo*, Asterios editore, Trieste.

Walras L., 1860, *L'économie politique et la justice; examen critique et réfutation des doctrines économiques de M. P.J. Proudhon*, Guillaumin, Paris.

Walras L., 1865, *Les associations populaires*, Dentu, Paris.

Ward B.N., 1958, The Firm In Illyria; Market Syndicalism, in *American Economic Review*, vol. 48, n. 4, September.

Webb B., 1891, *The Cooperative Movement in Great Britain*, Swan Sonnenschein and Co., London.

Webb S. and Webb B., 1921, *A Constitution For The Socialist Commonwealth Of Great Britain*, Longman, London.

Webb S. and Webb B., 1923, *The Decay of Capitalistic Civilization*, Allen & Unwin, London.

Weber M., 1919, *Il lavoro intellettuale come professione*, ital. transl., Einaudi, Turin, 1958.

Weil S., 1934, *Riflessioni sulle cause della libertà e dell'oppressione sociale*, ital. transl., Adelphi, Milan.

Weil S., 1959, *Lezioni di filosofia*, ital. transl., Adelphi, Milan, 2012.

Weingast B.R. and Marshall W.J., 1988, The Industrial Organization of Congress; Or, Why Legislatures, Like Firms, Are Not Organized as Markets, in *Journal of Political Economy*, vol. 96, February.

Weintraub E.R., ed., 2002, *The Future of the History of Economics*, Duke University Press, Durham and London.

Weiss A., 1980, Job Queues and Layoffs in Labor Markets with Flexible Wages, in *Journal of Political Economy*, June.

Weiss A., 1990, *Efficiency Wages: Models of Unemployment, Layoffs and Wage Dispersion*, Princeton University Press, Princeton, NJ.

Weisskopf T.E., 1992, Toward a Socialism for the Future, in the Wake of the Demise of the Socialism of the Past, in *Review of Radical Political Economics*, vol. 24, nn. 3–4.

Weisskopf T.E., 1993, A Democratic Enterprise-Based Market Socialism, in P. Bardhan, J.E. Roemer (eds), *Market Socialism: The Current Debate*, Oxford Economic Press, New York, NY.

Weitzman M. and Kruse D., 1990, Profit Sharing and Productivity, in A. Blinder (ed.), *Paying for Productivity*, Brookings Institution, Washington DC, WA.

Wennerlind C. 2002, The Labor Theory of Value and the Strategic Role of Alienation, in *Capital and Class*, n. 77, Spring.

Werin L. and Wijkander H., eds, 1992, *Contract Economics*, Basil Blackwell, New York, NY.

West E.G., 1969, The Political Economy of Alienation: Karl Marx and Adam Smith, reprinted in J.C. Wood (ed.), 1988, *Karl Marx's Economics: Critical Assessments*, vol. 1, Croom Helm, New South Wales.

Wetter G.A., 1948, *Il materialismo dialettico sovietico*, Einaudi, Turin.

White W.F. and White K.K., 1988, *Cooperative Complex*, Cornell University Press, Ithaca, NY.

Wiles P., 1962, *The Political Economy of Communism*, Harvard University Press, Cambridge, MA.

Williamson O.E., 1975, *Markets and Hierarchies: Analysis and Anti-Trusts Implications*, Macmillan, New York, NY.

Williamson O.E., 1980, The Organization of Work: A Comparative Institutional Assessment, in *Journal of Economic Behavior and Organization*, vol. I.

Williamson O.E., 1985, *The Economic Institutions of Capitalism: Firm, Markets, Relational Contracting*, Free Press, New York, NY.

Williamson O.E., 1986, *Economic Organizations: Firm, Market and Policy Control*, Harvester Wheatsheaf, New York, NY.

Williamson O.E. and Winter S., 1991, *The Nature of the Firm: Origins, Evolution and Development*, Oxford University Press, New York, NY.

Wolff R., 2012, *Democracy at Work: a Cure for Capitalism*, Haymarket Books, Chicago, IL.

Wolff R. and Resnick S., 1983, Reply to Houston and Lindsey, in *Review of Radical Political Economics*, vol. 15, n. 1, Spring.

Wolfstetter E., Brown M. and Meran G., 1984, Optimal Employment and Risk Sharing in Illyria: The Labour Managed Firm Reconsidered, in *Journal of Institutional and Theoretical Economics*, vol. 140.

Wood J.C., ed., 1988, *Karl Marx's Economics: Critical Assessments*, Croom Helm, New South Wales.

Wren Dan A. and Bedeian A.G., 2004, The Taylorization of Lenin: Rethoric or Reality?, in *International Journal of Social Economics*, vol. 31, n. 3.

Wright E.O., 1995, What is Analytical Marxism?, in T. Carver and P. Thomas (eds), *Rational Choice Marxism*, Macmillan, London.

Yellen J.J., 1984, Efficiency Wage Models of Unemployment, in *American Economic Review*, vol. 74, March.

Young R., 1996, Marxism and the History of Science, in AA.VV., 1996, *Companion to the History of Science*, Routledge, London.

Zabaleta M.J., 1986, *Mondragon: un'esperienza integrata*, in AA.VV., *Cooperare e competere*, Feltrinelli, Milan.

Zafiris N., 1982, Appropriability Rules, Capital Maintenance and the Efficiency of Cooperative Investment, in *Journal of Comparative Economics*, vol. 6, n. 1.

Zafiris N., 1986, The Sharing of the Firm's Risks between Capital and Labour, in *Annals of Public and Cooperative Economics*, vol. 57, January–March.

Zamagni S., ed., 1991, *Imprese e mercati*, UTET, Turin.

Zamagni S., 2002, L'economia delle relazionni umane: verso il superamento dell'individualismo assiologico, in P.L. Sacco and S. Zamagni, *Complessità relazionale e comportamento economico*, Il Mulino, Bologna.

Zamagni S., 2005, Per una teoria economico-civile dell'impresa cooperativa, in E. Mazzoli and S. Zamagni (eds), *Verso una nuova teoria economica della cooperazione*, Il Mulino, Bologna.

Zamagni S., 2006, Promozione cooperativa e civilizzazione del mercato, in M. Bulgarelli and M. Viviani (eds), *La promozione cooperativa; Copfond tra mercato e solidarietà*, Il Mulino, Bologna.

Zamagni V. and Felice E., 2006, *Oltre il secolo: le trasformazioni del sistema cooperativo Legacoop alla fine del secondo millennio*, Il Mulino, Bologna.

Zangheri R., Galasso G. and Castronovo V., 1987, *Storia del movimento cooperativo in Italia*, Einaudi, Turin.

Zanone V., 2002, Il liberalismo di Franco Romani, in *Biblioteca della libertà*, vols 164–165, May–August.

Zevi A., 1982, *The Performance of Italian Producer Cooperatives*, in D.C. Jones and J. Svejnar (eds), *Participatory and Self-Managed Firms: Evaluating Economic Performance*, Heath, Lexington.

Zevi A., 2003, Il fenomeno cooperativo e le modifiche in corso nell'ordinamento italiano, in V. Buonocore and B. Jossa (eds), *Organizzazioni economiche non capitalistiche*, Il Mulino, Bologna.

Zollshan G.K. and Hirsch W., eds, 1964, *Explorations in Social Change*, Houghton Mifflin, Boston, MA.

Zolo D., 1974, *La teoria comunista dell'estinzione dello Stato*, De Donato, Bari.

Zolo D., 1977a, Introduzione, in C. Offe, 1977, *Lo Stato nel capitalismo maturo*, ital. transl. of eight articles from German, Etas Libri, Milan.

Zolo D., 1977b, Epistemologia e teoria politica nelle interpretazioni del pensiero politico di Marx, in AA.VV., 1977, *Stato e teorie marxiste*, ed. by G. Carandini, Mazzotta, Milan.

Index

288 *Index*

Jensen, M.C. 60, 72, 74, 76, 80–1, 91,
91n8, 93, 98100, 102, 104
Jossa, B. 6, 14n22, 55, 65, 66n13, 72, 76,
91, 123, 137, 152, 159, 171, 204, 207,
212, 228n17

Kalecki, M. 56, 125–7
Kant, I. 143n7, 143n14
Karsz, S. 44, 163
Kasmir, S. 1011, 94
Kautsky, K. 6, 33, 39n25, 53, 54n7, 130,
172n5, 229n18
Keynes, J.M. 63, 88–9, 123, 129n1, 227n3
Keynesian unemployment 109, 120, 123,
128–9, 168
Kihlstrom, R. 5, 91n4
Kliman, A.J. 40, 131
Knight, F.H. 5, 80, 91n5
Korsch, K. 35, 41, 46, 114–15, 131, 142n1,
156, 163
Kühne, K. 52, 142n1, 162

labour 132, 198, 217; abstract 218, 224–5,
227n7–8; division of 81, 143n8–9,
144n23, 160n5, 196, 203n14, 215; hired
17–18, 20, 29–30, 44, 123, 135, 137–9,
144n22–3, 170, 195, 207, 213n6, 216
labour-managed firms (LMF) 9–10, 35,
55–6, 58, 60–2, 65, 66n5, 67, 71–2, 88,
97, 100–2, 111, 123, 128–9, 147, 156–7,
159, 173n15, 181, 195, 199, 204, 213n4;
capitallabour relation 225; democratic
141; issuing bonds 57; liabilities 96;
property rights 98; self-financing 94;
system of 99, 115, 130, 149, 171–2,
214, 216, 218, 226; under-investment
73, 77; Vanek's 16, 32, 34, 93–4, 207;
see also cooperative firms
labour theory of value 41, 48, 52–3, 131,
211, 215–21, 224–6, 227n7, 227n9,
228n12
Labriola, A. 44, 172n1, 227n5
Laibman, D. 44, 195
Lane, R.E. 158, 160n7
Lange, O. 1112, 159, 204, 215, 230
Lawler, J. 20, 164, 201
Lenin, V.I. 5–7, 11, 16–17, 20–32, 36–7,
37n5, 37n8, 38n9, 38n12–14, 38n17–19,
39n21–4, 43, 167, 175, 192–4
Leninism 37n6, 38n32; Marxism-Leninism
185n14
Lepage, H. 95, 105n10, 119n9
Levine, A. 53, 153
Lichtheim, G. 15n26, 37n2

Lindbeck, A. 121–2, 144n21, 184n4
Lukàcs, G. 14n17, 25, 37, 37n6, 42–4, 46,
48, 130–1, 142n3, 151–2, 162, 171,
172n8, 196, 205
Luporini, C. 43, 46, 49, 131, 144n24, 162
Luxemburg, R. 4, 25, 50, 168, 230

McCain, R.A. 57, 76, 154
Macciocchi, M.A. 175–6, 184n6
Major, G. 57–8, 66n7
Marcuse, H. 13n9, 202n1, 202n5, 217
Marglin, S. 81, 152
Marshall, A. 2–3, 106–10, 139–40
Marx, K. 5–7, 11, 14n17, 15n28, 16–20,
32–3, 35–6, 37n2–3, 40–3, 45–53, 54n3,
54n5, 54n9, 81, 117, 123, 129n1, 131–9,
142n1–2, 142n5–6, 143n11, 143n14,
143n18, 144n20, 144n23–4, 148, 154,
156, 161–7, 171, 172n2–4, 176–7, 180,
184n2, 186, 188–92, 194–9, 201,
202n2–4, 202n7, 203n13–14, 205,
208–12, 213n5, 213n6–7, 214–19,
221–6, 227n2, 227n4–6, 228n10–11,
228n16, 2301; abstract labour 217;
alienation 130, 142n2; communism 227,
227n2; dialectic method 46, 198,
203n14; economic system 142n1;
fetishism 143n17; method 44–5, 50;
statist ideas 192
Marxism 11–12, 14n18, 36, 40, 43, 48–9,
51–3, 54n2, 54n9, 202n8, 204–5,
214–16, 224, 226, 227n4, 231;
alienation 135, 138, 141, 142n1, 143;
anti-statist 190–1; collapse of 227n1;
imperialism 38n12; positivistic vision
130, 185n10; pre-Marxian socialism
153; theory of revolution 50, 162,
172n4, 230
Massari, R. 28, 37n3
Mazzini, G. 206
Meade, J.E. 5, 40, 55, 57, 66n4, 98, 101,
111, 140, 183
merit goods 84, 91, 145, 155, 157–9, 168,
171, 182; demerit goods 157
Mészàros, I. 54n5, 131, 143n12–13, 215
Meyer, A.T. 28, 37n6, 44
Mill, J.S. 2, 18, 94, 106–8, 139–40, 160n8
Miller, D. 5, 82, 118n6, 214
Mills, C.W. 140, 150, 172n2
Mises, L. von 22, 104n4
mode of production 117, 139, 162, 172n1,
189, 204–5, 209; capitalist 18, 46, 49,
150, 167, 169, 188, 208, 212, 231; new
5–6, 10–12, 16–18, 37n4, 49, 53, 55,

upside-down world 208, 219–21
Uvalic, M. 73, 78n6

Vacca, G. 156–7, 175, 184n1, 202n1
Vanek, J. 5, 9, 16, 34, 40, 55–7, 65, 69, 71,
    73, 77n2, 78n6–7, 78n10, 93–4, 96–8,
    103, 116, 122, 124, 149–50, 157, 168,
    174, 183, 204, 213; Vanek-type LMF
    32, 207
Veblen, T. 41, 48, 84–5
Vilar, P. 54n5
Vinci, P. 224, 228n12
Vogt, W. 13n3, 96
Volpi, F. 44, 172n4

Waldmann, R.J. 57–8
Walras, L. 34–5, 228n13; Walrasian
    economists 227
Ward, B.N. 5, 8, 34–5, 40, 55, 65, 66n1,
    101, 120, 122, 128, 129n2, 149, 157,
    174, 183, 213
Webb, B. 6, 14n18, 34, 154
Weber, M. 117, 141
Weil, S. 13n8, 14n16, 160n4, 203n9,
    213n2
Weiss, A. 120–1
Weisskopf, T.E. 92n13

Weitzman, M. 84, 112
Williamson, O.E. 81, 91n1, 92n9, 101,
    111, 145
Wolff, R. 105n8, 118n4, 129n3, 148, 162,
    170, 203n9, 213n4
worker control 14n13, 26–9, 38n18,
    38n20, 54n8, 57, 128, 175, 181, 195
worker-managed firm (WMF) 14n23,
    34–5, 55, 62, 67, 78n7, 141, 146, 171,
    207, 213n4; capital incomes 10;
    investment choices 72; investment
    resources 9; partners 68, 71; self-
    financing 100–1; under-investment 69,
    73, 77, 94, 100
workers' councils 3, 16, 25, 28, 38n20,
    129n2, 174–5; Gramsci's 178–84,
    184n2, 184n6, 185n17
workers' democracy 4, 13n7
workers' movement 7, 42, 54n8
working week 125; length 87, 89–90;
    shorter 124, 137

Zafiris, N. 66n9, 78n6, 78n10
Zamagni, S. 84, 86, 92n12, 96, 195
Zevi, A. 94, 168
Zolo, D. 42, 47

For Product Safety Concerns and Information please contact our
EU representative GPSR@taylorandfrancis.com Taylor & Francis
Verlag GmbH, Kaufingerstraße 24, 80331 München, Germany